Forgotten
New York
Views of a Lost Metropolis

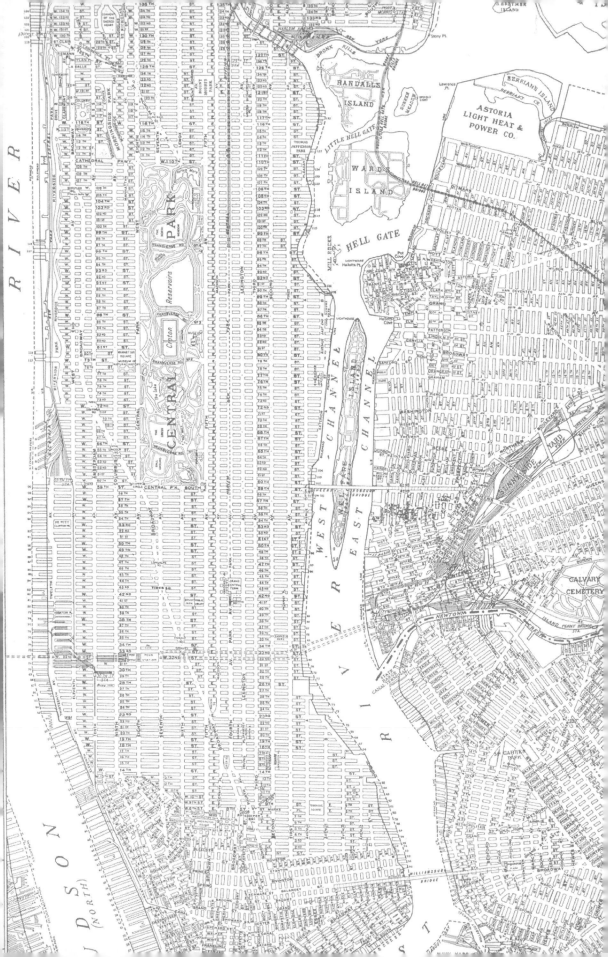

Forgotten New York

Views of a Lost Metropolis

Kevin Walsh

Collins

An Imprint of HarperCollinsPublishers

HarperCollins books may be purchased for educational, business, or sales promotional use. For information please write: Special Markets Department, HarperCollins Publishers, 10 East 53rd Street, New York, NY 10022.

FIRST EDITION

Designed by Emily Cavett Taff.
Maps designed by Patricia Keelin.

Photos © Kevin Walsh except where otherwise credited.

Photos on pages 5 (right column), 11, and 283 (bottom) courtesy Gary Fonville; photo on page 47 courtesy Jim Crowley; photo on page 104 courtesy Kevin W. Walsh; photos on page 163 (right column), 189 (left column), 197 (top) courtesy Emily Taff; photo on page 169 courtesy Mike Epstein; photo on page 176 (left column) courtesy of Mike Olshan; photo on page 211 courtesy Matthew Benjamin.

Library of Congress Cataloging-in-Publication Data:

Walsh, Kevin, 1957–
    Forgotten New York : views of a lost
        metropolis / by Kevin Walsh. — 1st ed.
      p. cm.
    Includes bibliographical references and index.

    ISBN-13: 978-0-06-114502-5
    ISBN-10: 0-06-114502-5

    ISBN-13: 978-0-06-075400-6 (pbk.)
    ISBN-10: 0-06-075400-1 (pbk.)

    1. New York (N.Y.)—Pictorial works. 2. Historic buildings—New York (State)—New York—Pictorial works. 3. Historic sites—New York (State)—New York—Pictorial works. 4. New York (N.Y.)—Buildings, structures, etc.—Pictorial works. 5. New York (N.Y.)—Description and travel. I. Title.

    F128.37.W35   2006
    974.7'10440222—dc22
                            2006041221

06 07 08 09 10 ❖/RRD 10 9 8 7 6 5 4 3 2 1

*To my mother, Elizabeth (1916–1974)
and father, Kevin (1918–2003).*

Contents

Introduction   ix

❧ **Bronx**   2

❧ **Brooklyn**   52

❧ **Manhattan**   136

❧ **Queens**   214

❧ **Staten Island**   284

Sources   339
Acknowledgments   355
Index   357
Map Index   372

Introduction

You're not supposed to notice. If you're a native New Yorker, you're not supposed to look up at the buildings or look down at the sidewalk, or even stop to appreciate the magnitude of the glorious, incredible city you live in. No, you're supposed to be way too busy—or afraid of looking like a tourist.

If you're from out of town, you're not supposed to see that there are other boroughs besides Manhattan. Bookshelves are full of New York City guides; all of them have about five pages on the outer boroughs, four of which focus on Brooklyn Heights, or, if it's been published in the past couple of years, there may be a page or two on hipster hangouts in Williamsburg or on the restaurants of Cobble Hill. You're not supposed to want to visit the Bronx or Staten Island and see what marvelous secrets and obscure delights all five boroughs are hiding.

In contrast to cities like Boston or Philadelphia, New York has always been a city that has allowed much of its past life to be razed to make way for new development. Most New Yorkers know about the destruction of the old Penn Station and Metropolitan Opera House, and maybe even the burying of Freedomland Amusement Park under Co-op City, but what about the loss of entire neighborhoods to public housing and highways? And how often do we pause to think about the miles of elevated track that have been torn down or the delicately wrought cast-iron lampposts replaced by less fancy public lighting?

Despite New York's insistence on renewing and reinventing itself every few years, thankfully there are many examples of things left behind, or perhaps clandestinely left in place, that provide clues as to what was there before. Maybe it's a street sign that the MTA has neglected to replace; a rusty cast-iron lamppost on a side street; an advertisement painted on a building for an obsolete product; or a sign in a subway station directing you to a street that has been renamed.

Beyond these non sequitur flashes of the past, the outer boroughs provide a treasure trove of neighborhoods lost in plain sight: colonial houses and centuries-old cemeteries; curiosities and oddities, such as the World's first Hall of Fame, and what may be the only statue commemorating a gynecologist.

This book is an extension of my website www.forgotten-ny.com. I have been compiling this material for many years, ever since my mother, father, grandmother and I used to take bus rides and walks through the streets of Bay Ridge and Borough Park, Brooklyn. Even before I went to school, I noticed the different styles of lampposts and street signs. I watched the Verrazano-Narrows Bridge being built, and I would file away in my head which streets were eliminated and which houses were torn down to create the ramps and expressways that funneled cars to the magnificent structure. My family was on the very first bus to cross the great bridge in November 1964, when I was seven. I began to note the cost-effective homogenization taking over public works, such as the replacing of wicker and rattan seating in subways with plastic benches.

In 1998, I sketched out a layout for my website on a piece of scrap paper. Then I grabbed a camera and a notepad, and walked, bussed, and rode the subway all over town, assembling a critical mass of photographs and information about remnants of a New York City of decades past that city planners, transportation departments, landowners and other agencies have somehow left intact. As I pressed on, I began to develop an insatiable curiosity about New York's infrastructure and history. Gradually, I had to purchase more and more bookshelves to handle the sheer number of New York City–related books. *Forgotten NY*, the website, was launched in March 1999, and the amount of positive feedback has amazed me. To my surprise, I wasn't the only forgottenphile out there. It's been fun meeting others that have the same concerns about NYC's vanishing legacy.

Forgotten New York, the book, is your passport to the New York City that has existed for more than 300 years but is now obscured by modern glass façades.

Just about all of the sites discussed in this book can be reached easily by public transportation. I do not own a car and have gotten to most of the locales featured here on foot or on my bicycle. The book is designed to be used as a walking tour guide with sections set up as mini-tours, complete with maps and subway and bus information.

Each borough opens with a map outlining the neighborhoods covered in the pages that follow.

The neighborhoods feature mini-maps, regions that are keyed to the borough maps and also to a map index at the back of the book.

These icons have been placed next to entries of special interest:

Quiet Places

Truly Forgotten

History Happened Here

What Is This Thing?

Forgotten People

An additional street atlas, and MTA subway and bus maps would be helpful, but you should be fine with just a Metro-Card and a good pair of walking shoes.

So stop a minute . . . look around . . . and maybe you'll see a New York that's been forgotten.

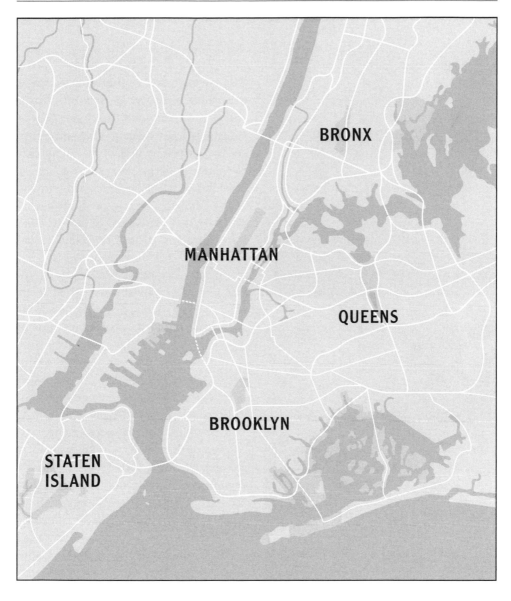

The Bronx,

as a borough and county, is a relatively new political entity. As New York City's only mainland outpost (except for Marble Hill, still a part of Manhattan), the Bronx has been a part of Westchester County and then New York County (Manhattan) for much of its history. In 1874, the western portion of the Bronx, consisting of the towns of Kingsbridge, West Farms, and Morrisania, was annexed by New York County, making them part of New York City proper. In 1895, the rest of the present-day Bronx east of the Bronx River joined. The following year, City Island voted to secede from Westchester County and join the Bronx. Finally, in 1914, the Bronx became its own county, separate from Manhattan. Traces of this former Bronx-Manhattan marriage can be seen in the street numbering system, which stretches across the Harlem River.

Much of the borough's persona over the years, unfortunately, has been shaped by the presence of crime and urban decay. Presidents Jimmy Carter and Ronald Reagan visited then-empty and desolate Charlotte Street, near Crotona Park, in the late 1970s and early 1980s, respectively, with promises of federal aid. During a World Series game in 1977, the camera panned over to an out-of-control conflagration and Howard Cosell intoned, "The Bronx is burning."

Though drugs and crime remain, as they always will in any urban area, much

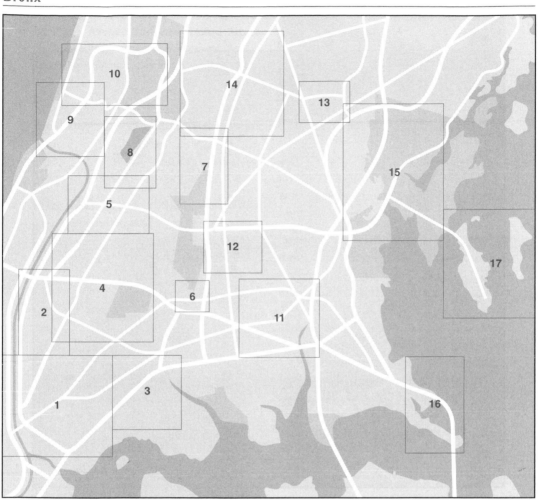

of the Bronx has been transformed by the construction of new housing and a diminution of crime beginning in the early 90s. Charlotte Street is now a pleasant, tree-lined stretch with detached homes, as is much of the surrounding area; disparate regions like Longwood and Wakefield have also enjoyed comebacks since their nadirs.

There's plenty to interest the urban explorer in the Bronx: the Grand Concourse, with its miles of magnificent apartment buildings and a revitalized Loew's Paradise Theatre; the hills of Morris Heights hold secrets like High Bridge and a lighthouse-shaped tower; Riverdale doesn't resemble the rest of the Bronx, but is a riverside village on the Hudson; and Westchester Square is also a small-town village, complete with a pair of colonial cemeteries. City Island is a fishing village, seemingly airlifted onto Long Island Sound from New England; and Pelham Bay and Van Cortlandt Parks offer hundreds of acres of wild and uncultivated woods, with the occasional abandoned rail line or colonial mansion tossed in.

such as St. Jerome's Church and attendant school, constructed in 1898 between East 137th and 138th Streets, the row between East 138th and 139th Streets, and the neo-Renaissance Mott Haven branch of the New York Public Library, built in 1905 by Babb, Cook & Willard.

4 St. Ann's Episcopal Church

St. Ann's Avenue, between East 139th and East 141st Streets

St. Ann's Episcopal Church is the Bronx's oldest church, having been built in 1841 and dedicated to Gouverneur Morris's mother Ann. Several of the Bronx's most noted families of the colonial era and beyond are buried in the church's graveyard, including Gouverneur and Lewis Morris. The church is surrounded by foliage and locked gates, so it's difficult to get a good look at it in the summertime. The best view is in winter, when there is no obscuring foliage, from East 139th Street.

5 Major Deegan Monument

Grand Concourse and East 138th Street

At East 138th Street and the southern end of the Grand Concourse, on the west side of the traffic overpass, you'll find a small marble monument that at least partially answers a question that more than a few Bronxites have posed over the years: Who is Major Deegan? The plaque indicates that he was a "patriot, civic leader and public officer," who "lived in the service of his fellow-man," and "died in the service of his city."

Major William Deegan (1882–1932) constructed army bases in and around New York during World War I. He was a State Commander of the American Legion, a Commissioner of Public Housing, and a close friend of Mayor Jimmy Walker, who appointed him Commissioner of Tenement Housing in 1928. He died from complications after an appendectomy at the young age of forty-nine.

6 Bronx Terminal Market ◄

East 149th Street and Major Deegan Expressway

The Bronx Terminal Market, a great example of the Art Moderne architectural design popular in the 1930s, opened during the John Hylan administration in the 20s. Since then, it's been a receiving point for the city's fruits and vegetables (though much of that has moved to Hunts Point in recent decades). It stretches along the Major Deegan Expressway between East 149th Street and the Macombs Dam Bridge near Yankee Stadium. The Related Companies purchased the buildings in 2005 in hopes of developing a retail complex and garage.

7 145th Street Bridge

East 149th Street at Harlem River

As late as the mid-1990s, the pedestrian walkway of the 145th Street Bridge, which connects West 145th Street in Harlem with East 149th Street in the Bronx, was illuminated by incandescent bulbs with old-fashioned "crinkled" radial-wave diffusers,

suspended from ornate cast-iron shafts. A testimony, perhaps, to the lack of use the walkway got in the overnights. The old lamps have since been updated. However, another set of cast-iron masts still holds signs reading "All persons must leave the draw when gong sounds."

The 145th Street Bridge, as well as its sister swing bridges over the Harlem River, the Willis Avenue, the Third Avenue, the Madison Avenue, the Macombs Dam, and the University Heights Bridge, were all constructed in the same era, between 1895 and 1910, with the 145th Street Bridge opening in 1905. They can all swing perpendicularly to allow ship traffic in the Harlem River to pass safely below, with hydraulic machinery controlled from an operator's house.

8 Mott Avenue Sign

East 149th Street IRT subway station at Grand Concourse

The platform serving the 2 train at 149th Street was the very first subway station built in the Bronx, opening in July 1905. The station boasts high, vaulted ceilings and mosaics with antique circle and diamond designs. Most of the mosaic nameplates have been covered by new signage, except for one between staircases on the Manhattan-bound side that still says "Mott Avenue." The Grand Concourse took over Mott Avenue's path when it was extended south in 1927.

9 Bronx Borough Courthouse

Third Avenue and East 161st Street

This massive Beaux Arts building at Third Avenue and East 161st Street was built in 1905 when the Bronx was a borough, but not yet a county. The courthouse features two statues representing Justice, one of which looked into the Third Avenue elevated cars as they rattled past decades ago.

The Bronx Borough Courthouse, designed by architect and artist Oscar Bluemner, should not be confused with the Bronx County Courthouse (the Mario Merola Building), the present home of the Bronx Supreme Court and Bronx Borough President. That building is located on the Grand Concourse between East 158th and East 161st Streets, and was built in 1933 by architects Max Hausel and Joseph Freedlander.

10 Eagle Avenue Bridge

East 161st Street, east of Third Avenue

Near the courthouse, walk east on 161st Street and check out the ornate, blue-painted iron bridge that carries Eagle Avenue over East 161st Street. The Bronx's steep valleys necessitate bridges and stepped streets that can be found all over the borough and are often missed by cartographers.

Decorative Deco

The Grand Boulevard and Concourse marches north from the Major Deegan Expressway to Mosholu Parkway through Mott Haven, Concourse Village, Mount Eden, Mount Hope (the Concourse is constructed on a hill), Fordham, and Bedford Park, a lengthy stretch. French engineer Louis Risse designed and built the Concourse between 1902 and 1909, inspired in part by the grand boulevards of Paris built in the 1860s by Baron Haussmann.

In 1927, the Grand Concourse absorbed Mott Avenue, which ran north from 138th to 161st Streets, and the older street was widened. The Grand Concourse became the Bronx's showpiece as the Bronx County Courthouse, Yankee Stadium, and an array of elegant apartment buildings were constructed along its length. The Concourse and surrounding streets are a wonderland of magnificent prewar architecture.

The Grand Concourse is dominated by two separate architectural trends: Art Deco, characterized by highly stylized and colored ornamentation, ironworked doors, colorful terra-cotta and mosaics, and Art Moderne, noted for its striped block patterns, and stylized letterforms.

11 Yankee Greats

East 161st Street and the Grand Concourse

At East 161st Street, between Walton Avenue and the Grand Concourse, you'll find tributes to two of the greatest New York Yankees of all time: George Herman "Babe" Ruth and Yorkville native Lou Gehrig. The city honored the sluggers with pedestrian mall plazas featuring handsome cast-iron signs after Babe's death in 1948.

In December 1979, a section of East 156th Street in the Concourse Village Houses near the Ruth and Gehrig plazas was renamed Thurman Munson Way, in honor of the all-star Yankee catcher who perished in a plane crash in Ohio on August 2 of that year.

12 Lorelei Fountain

Grand Concourse and East 161st Street

Ernst Herter's 1893 fountain statue in honor of Heinrich Heine, author of "Die Lorelei," was originally rejected by Düsseldorf, the German city of Heine's birth. A coterie of affluent German-Americans purchased the work and offered to place it at Grand Army Plaza in Manhattan. That site, too, was rejected, and the fountain was ultimately placed in Joyce Kilmer Park at the Grand Concourse near East 164th Street around the turn of the twentieth century. In 1999, the fountain was fully restored to a brilliant white, given a new iron railing, and moved to East 161st Street across from the Bronx County Courthouse.

13 Ruppert Place

Along the western edge of Yankee Stadium

Brewery magnate Colonel Jacob Ruppert (1867–1939) purchased the Yankees in 1914 with partner Tillinghast Huston, a successful engineer. Ruppert bought Huston out three years later and became sole owner. Ruppert oversaw the beginnings of a five-decade Yankee dynasty that saw them win more World Series titles by far than any other Major League team. Doughty Street, on the western edge of Yankee Stadium between East 157th and 161st Streets, was renamed for Ruppert in 1933.

BRONX

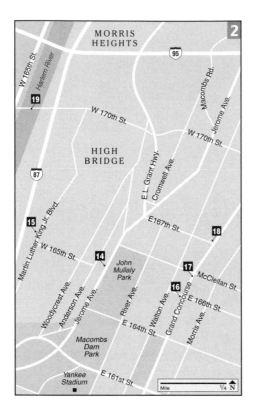

14 1005 Jerome Avenue

North of West 165th Street

The Park Plaza Apartments, built in 1928 at 1005 Jerome Avenue near the West 165th Street steps, is an exemplary Art Deco building with a gorgeous, multicolored terra-cotta façade. Look for High Bridge among the represented scenes. Just south of it, a winding stepped street ascends one of the Bronx's sheerest cliffs.

Some of New York City's hilliest terrain can be found clustered along the Harlem River in the southwestern Bronx. Some streets curve to make their way up the cliffs, while others give up completely and become steps; one of the most spectacular stepped streets in the city is at Jerome Avenue and West 165th Street—it zigs and zags in three different directions to reach the cliff's apex. The region was owned and farmed by the Morris family during the colonial era; the Morrises raised prize cattle on their estate here in the eighteenth century.

SUBWAY: ④ to 161st Street–Yankee Stadium, 167th Street, or Mount Eden Avenue; Ⓓ to 161st Street–Yankee Stadium, 167th Street, or 170th Street

BUS: Bx13 on Ogden Avenue; **Bx1** to Grand Concourse; **Bx18** on Macombs Road, Sedgwick, and Undercliff Avenues; **Bx3** on University Avenue

15 H.W. Wilson Lighthouse

950 University Avenue at Sedgwick Avenue

A look skyward at a building at Sedgwick Avenue and University Avenue (aka Martin Luther King, Jr. Boulevard) reveals a thirty-foot-tall copper lighthouse. The building is the home office of the H.W. Wilson Company, a bibliography and periodical index publisher for more than 100 years.

The firm built its eight-story building with the lighthouse here in 1929. The light-

house, shown perched on a book, is meant to symbolize their mission: "to give guidance to those seeking their way through the maze of books and periodicals, without which they would be lost." At night, the structure is bottom-lit; in 1998—the company's centennial—the lighthouse was relit after being out of commission for several years.

16 Andrew Freedman Home

Grand Concourse and East 166th Street

The Andrew Freedman Home for Older Adults, at Grand Concourse and East 166th Street, was built in 1924 with an endowment from the will of Freedman (1860–1915), an early owner of the New York Giants baseball team. But Freedman's stipulations were specific: It was not to be the usual retirement home, but one for indigent adults who had previously been rich and lost their fortunes! Freedman had nearly lost his own fortune in a 1907 stock market panic, and a fear of destitution apparently haunted him.

Residents lived in the accustomed luxury that their reversals of fortune had denied them: a kitchen with a restaurant-quality menu, spacious quarters, club rooms, and a staff of fifty-nine. By the 1970s, when there were apparently very few former millionaires left in the Bronx, the home changed its policy, and by the early 1990s, it became a regular home for the elderly and took applications from anyone over the age of fifty-five.

17 Admiral Farragut Bas-relief

Grand Concourse, north of East 166th Street

Admiral David Farragut, the Civil War naval hero ("Damn the torpedoes! Full-speed ahead!") is memorialized by a frieze on an apartment house just north of the Andrew Freedman home. Farragut is buried in Woodlawn Cemetery, a few miles north of here.

18 Fish Building λ

1150 Grand Concourse at East 167th Street

Of all the Grand Concourse's magnificent Art Deco apartment buildings, the one at 1150, at McClellan Place, may be the most attractive, with a huge mosaic depicting undersea life surrounding its front entrance. A look inside the lobby will reveal wall paintings, brushed aluminum surfaces, and brightly painted elevator doors with intricate designs.

BRONX

Unfortunately, the Fish Building has been compromised in later years by the addition of businesses, including a barbershop and tax preparer's office on the ground floor, but its entrance and lobby remain undiminished.

19 High Bridge

Best seen from Depot Place, spanning the Major Deegan Expressway from Sedgwick Avenue

High Bridge, which connects High Bridge Park near West 174th Street in Manhattan and West 170th Street in the Bronx, is the oldest remaining bridge connecting two boroughs. When the bridge was built between 1837 and 1848 by architect John Jervis, it actually connected two separate towns, since that area of the mainland would not become a part of New York County until 1874.

The High Bridge Water Tower in High Bridge Park (on the Manhattan side) was built by Jervis at the same time as the bridge and was used as a 47,000-gallon storage tank and as a water pressure equalizing structure. It has a winding spiral staircase inside whose climb rewards you with spectacular views of the surrounding Washington Heights, Harlem, and Morrisania neighborhoods.

High Bridge is best viewed from High Bridge Park at Amsterdam Avenue and West 174th Street in Manhattan, from University Avenue and West 170th Street, and from Exterior Street on the Harlem River, attainable from Depot Place crossing the Deegan Expressway.

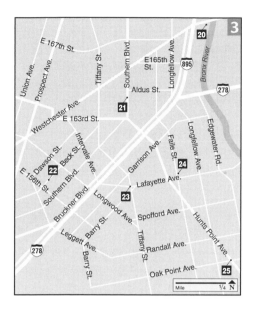

Longwood and Hunts Point, now heavily residential though still somewhat industrial toward the East River, are remnants of country estates: Longwood was an 1870s property owned by an S. B. White, and Hunts Point was formerly a collection of country estates owned by the Casanovas, Barrettos, Spoffords, Failes, and other wealthy families, many of whose names now grace local street signs. The area had been first settled by Thomas Hunt in 1670. Hunts Point (not to be confused with Hunters Point in Queens) has been home to the New York City Terminal Market since 1965. Much of the city's fresh produce is purchased by merchants here. The former Fulton Street Fish Market has been relocated to Hunts Point from its long-standing facility on South and Fulton Streets in lower Manhattan.

SUBWAY: ⑥ to Longwood, Hunts Point, or Whitlock Avenues

BUS: Bx17 on Prospect Avenue; **Bx19** on Southern Boulevard; **Bx6** on Hunts Point Avenue, Spofford Avenue, or Halleck Street; **Bx4** on Westchester Avenue

20 New York, New Haven, and Hartford Railroad Stations

Hunts Point Avenue and Bruckner Boulevard

Four former grand railroad stations on the rebuilt portion of the New York, New Haven, and Hartford Railroad, designed by renowned architect Cass Gilbert, still preside over ghost customers in the Bronx: two of them are in Hunts Point, one is in Morris Park, and the other is in Pelham Bay Park. A walk in Hunts Point will reveal the remains of two of the stations.

Hunts Point station

The southernmost station of the New York, New Haven, and Hartford Railroad was the Hunts Point station on Hunts Point Avenue near the Bruckner Expressway. Many of its peculiar architectural features, such as its dormer windows, remain, though the roof crenellation (decorative ironwork) is long gone. Like the other Gilbert railroad stations along the NY, NH, & H, it features a diamond terra-cotta motif, but at Hunts Point the diamonds are flanked by stylized fish.

A few blocks to the north is Westchester Avenue at the Sheridan Expressway (from the old Hunts Point station, walk along Hunts Point Avenue, then Bruckner Boulevard, follow Whitlock Avenue to Westchester Avenue, and then cross over the Sheridan).

BRONX

Westchester Avenue station

This station is truly in ruins: It has been collapsing since passenger service ended in the 1930s. The Italian palazzo-style station, however, still has its old Beaux Arts touches, like stylized foliage, torches, wheels, and a mysterious target-like device. The torches bear the initials NYH. The station is still marked clearly in metallic letters over the front entrance, and a short stretch of crenellation is still on the roof. Construction of the Sheridan Expressway in 1958

sheared off the station's front canopy, but its ghostly outline is still there.

21 Southern Boulevard Cinemas
Southern Boulevard, between West 163rd and 167th Streets

A pair of venerable theaters can still be found on Southern Boulevard between East 163rd and East 167th Streets. The Thomas Lamb–designed Boulevard Theater at 1024-1032 Southern Boulevard opened in 1913 and seated over 2,000. It's immediately recognizable by its magnificent arch.

A nearby arched theater, the Spooner

at 961 Southern Boulevard, also opened in 1913; both the Boulevard and the Spooner showed films into the 1970s.

Above Westchester Avenue, under the El, you can find the small 600-seat Art Theater at 1077 Southern Boulevard. Note the figures on the façade: the "tragic" sculpture in the center, two figures kissing, goddesses and gargoyles.

22 Longwood Historic District
Between Longwood and Leggett Avenues, Prospect Avenue and Beck Street

This is a section of gorgeous brownstone buildings developed by architect Warren C. Dickerson for landowner George Johnson between 1897 and 1901, consisting of parts of Beck, Kelly, and Dawson Streets, and Hewitt Place between East 156th Street and Longwood Avenue. Designated an NYC landmark district, its buildings are marked by their eclectic peaks and roof embellishments. The district is within easy walking distance of the Longwood Avenue subway station at Southern Boulevard.

23 American Bank Note Factory
Lafayette Avenue and Tiffany Street

This fortress-like building at Lafayette Avenue and Tiffany Street has produced stock certificates and traveler's checks, as well as paper money. The company later to become American Bank Note was founded in the 1790s by engraver Joseph Perkins, a Massachusetts native from Newburyport; the company was incorporated in 1858. American Bank Note produced U.S. currency from 1858 to 1879, and for a short time in 1861, it produced Confederate money. The company also entered into printing stock and bond certificates in association with the New York Stock Exchange in the later nineteenth century. This Bronx factory was built in 1911.

Today, the American Bank Note building is home to artists' studios and Wildcat High School, established for troubled students in 1972.

25 Drake Cemetery
Hunts Point and Oak Point Avenue

Drake Cemetery, also known as Drake Park, is one of the Bronx's smallest cemeteries.

Poet Joseph Rodman Drake rose to fame in the early 1800s with his most famous poem "The Culprit Fay." Drake was born in lower Manhattan, but discovered the then-bucolic fields of Hunts Point as a young man; in fact he would often brave the currents and row himself across the East River.

Drake died of tuberculosis at age twenty-five. Before his death, he requested to be laid to rest near the Bronx River, and so a burial ground was created at what is now Hunts Point and Oak Point Avenues. Since then, members of the Bronx's prominent families of the era, the Hunts, Leggetts, and others, have been buried here. At one time, all of Hunts Point was owned by the Leggetts; as one Leggett family member wrote in a letter in 1892, "One might roam all day through the woods and fields without going off the property. The nearest village was three miles away."

24 Sunnyslope Mansion
Faile Street, near Lafayette Avenue

While most of the grand Hunts Point estates disappeared in the early twentieth century, Peter Hoe's magnificent Sunnyslope at 812 Faile Street at Lafayette Avenue, a Gothic Revival extravaganza built in 1860, is still standing. The Hoe family business was printing; Peter's brother, Colonel Richard Hoe, invented the rotary printing press.

Sunnyslope was originally built on land belonging to William Gilbert. Its asymmetrical gray-stone construction is said to be derivative of some of the houses and cottages Calvert Vaux, co-architect of Central and Prospect Parks, was producing at the time it was built. It became a synagogue in 1919, and most recently has been the home of the African Methodist Episcopal Bright Temple.

BRONX

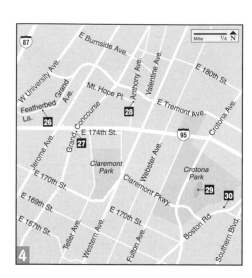

Mount Eden and Mount Hope are two communities in western Bronx that are built on a natural ridge along the Grand Concourse. Mount Eden is an old name deriving from Rachel Eden, a landowner living here in the 1820s. The reason for Mount Hope's name is unclear. According to the late Bronx historian John McNamara, it was originally named, much less poetically, the "Western Reserve" of Upper Morrisania, prior to the Civil War. Crotona Park was named for a colony in ancient Greece famed for Olympic athletes.

SUBWAY: IND ⒟ to 167th, 170th, 174–175th Street, or Tremont Avenue; IRT ② to 174th Street

BUS: Bx1 on Grand Concourse; **Bx11** on East 170th Street, Clay Avenue, or Claremont Parkway; **Bx32** on Morris Avenue; **Bx41** on Webster Avenue; **Bx15** or **Bx55** on Third Avenue; or **Bx17** on Crotona Avenue

26 Featherbed Lane
Between Jerome and University Avenues, north of the Cross Bronx Expressway

Hilly Featherbed Lane runs in two sections: from Jerome Avenue west to Ma-combs Road, and a little farther north, from Macombs Road west to University Avenue. Surprisingly, Featherbed Lane was not officially named until after 1890, when it began appearing on maps.

The late Bronx historian John McNamara's preferred explanation for the street name is that in the 1840s, while the Croton Aqueduct was being built, this was the red-light district and prostitutes entertained their customers on feather beds; in that era, the area had a Wild West atmosphere with gambling dens and illegal saloons.

27 Grand Concourse Overpass
East 174th Street

The Grand Concourse passes over a deep valley at East 174th and East 175th Streets—so deep that engineers led by Louis Risse who were building the Concourse in 1909 simply decided to bridge the roadway over it in a magnificent stone arch. Four stone monuments to the bridge's builders can be seen along the pedestrian walkways on each side of the bridge commemorating Bronx Borough President Louis Haffen, and highway engineers Josiah A. Briggs and Samuel C. Thompson. Looking west on the overpass, a wide panorama of the southern Bronx is visible, including the distant Hudson River. The Cross Bronx Expressway was threaded below the Concourse in the 1950s.

28 Shuttleworth House

Anthony Avenue and Mount Hope Place,
East 176th Street

Just a couple of blocks away from the Concourse in the heart of Mount Hope, you'll find a genuine suburban mansion at Anthony Avenue and East 176th Street. In 1896, Edwin Shuttleworth was a stone dealer who approached the Neville & Bagge architectural firm with the idea of creating a house using one of the varieties of stone he sold. The architects embellished the plan by bringing in stone-carvers who created ornate male and female forms, marine elements, and picturesque busts.

29 Indian Lake

In Crotona Park, north of Claremont
Parkway

After the city took title to the Andrew Bathgate Estate in 1888, it converted some of the manor grounds to parkland. There was a small pond, named Indian Lake by neighborhood children generations ago, complete with a brook that trailed off to the south, eventually entering the East River. The park, which became known as

Crotona Park, eventually encompassed more than 127 acres, and became known for its excellent views: the New Jersey palisades and the Brooklyn Bridge are visible from its heights in winter.

30 Herman Ridder Junior High School

Boston Road and East 173rd Street

Intermediate School 98, Herman Ridder Junior High, at 1619 Boston Road is a massive, stone fortress for learning built from 1929 to 1931 by architect Walter C. Martin in the Art Deco style, which he melded into the Beaux Arts stylings of the previous decades. Look for sculptures of books and lamps of knowledge; when riding north on the 2 train, gaze at it with awe as you pass it by.

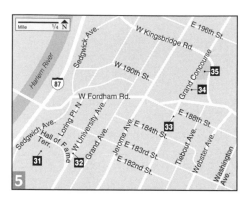

We're in the swiftly beating heart of the Bronx: here is Fordham Road—the greatest shopping street in the borough, Fordham University, the Bronx Zoo, New York Botanical Garden, and the very first Hall of Fame. University Heights is named for New York University, which built a grand uptown campus here in 1901 that later became Bronx Community College. Tremont was named by Bronx's first postmaster for three major hills in mid-Bronx: Mount Eden, Mount Hope, and Fairmount; and Fordham was named for a small settlement along the Harlem River that began in 1669 but was devastated by the Revolutionary War.

31 Hall of Fame for Great Americans

Hall of Fame Terrace and Loring Place North

The Bronx's very own Hall of Fame was the brainchild of Henry Mitchell MacCracken, President of New York University in 1901. He placed a classical arcade topped by a 630-foot semicircular colonnade at one of the highest points in the Bronx. This honored great Americans in the fields of government, science, and the arts. It was designed by architect Stanford White and was the first institution to be called a Hall of Fame.

MacCracken built the hall, along with the rest of the NYU campus, beginning in 1894 on a bluff overlooking the Harlem River, after purchasing an estate in what was then open country. The complex includes the domed Gould Memorial Library, Baker Hall of Philosophy, and the Hall of Languages, all NYC landmarks.

Walking around the Hall of Fame, you will find busts of ninety-eight of the country's greatest politicians, scholars, teachers, and authors, created by some of

the country's most noted sculptors. The nameplates under the busts were made by Tiffany Studios. Most of the names familiar from American history books can be found here, including Abraham Lincoln, Alexander Graham Bell, Samuel Morse, and Robert Fulton.

The busts, which have been cited by the National Society of Sculptors as "the most significant collection of bronzes in the country," suffered from the effects of acid rain, and the colonnade supports were crumbling in the 1970s. Fortunately, funds were found to rehabilitate and restore the hall between 1980 and 1985. However, four inductees are on hold until funding can be secured for the $25,000 each bust will require.

The Hall of Fame is open seven days a week from 10:00 AM to 5:00 PM. Enter the Bronx Community College campus at the gate on Hall of Fame Terrace just past Loring Place North. For more information, call (718) 289-5145, or visit www.bcc.cuny. edu/halloffame.

32 Aqueduct Walk
Along University Avenue, north of Tremont Avenue

Many of the Old Croton Aqueduct's New York City remnants are visible in the Bronx and upper Manhattan, as are some reminders of the New Croton Aqueduct, built in 1890.

At various points along the aqueduct, aboveground structures known as gatehouses were constructed. Under the gatehouses could be found machinery that assisted in routing and directing the flow of water. In Manhattan, there are gatehouses remaining at West 113th Street and Amsterdam Avenue—built in 1876, it is now a day-care center for the elderly; West 119th Street and Amsterdam Avenue, designated a city landmark in 2000; and the largest Manhattan gatehouse is at Convent

Avenue and West 135th Street, which is now being refurbished for use as a theater by City College.

In the Bronx, the Old Croton Aqueduct's length has been carefully marked and designated. Much of the Old Croton's path is now a walking trail in Van Cortlandt Park, continuing into Westchester County north of the park for twenty-six miles to Old Croton Aqueduct State Historic Park. Three Old Croton gatehouses can be seen along the Jerome Park Reservoir at Goulden and Reservoir Avenues, Goulden Avenue and West 205th Street, and at Goulden and Sedgwick Avenues.

The New Croton Aqueduct, completed in 1890 to replace the Old, runs much deeper than its predecessor; a New Croton gatehouse can be seen at West Burnside Avenue and Phelan Place.

33 Loew's Paradise Theatre
Grand Concourse and East 187th Street

Of the dozens of movie theaters in twentieth-century Bronx, the Loew's Paradise at Grand Concourse and East 187th Street was the Taj Mahal. John Eberson's grand movie and stage-show palace opened in 1929 and seated more than 4,000 patrons. The lobby was as much a spectacle as the shows presented therein. Ornamented like an Italian palazzo, it featured marble pillars, a goldfish pool, carpeted staircases, tapestries, and the best technology for sound and projection. In 2005, after years of rehabilitation, the Loew's was reopened as a concert hall.

34 Dollar Savings Bank

Grand Concourse, north of East Fordham Road

This Bronx landmark was built between 1932 and 1934 by Halsey, McCormack and Helmer, who also built Brooklyn's Williamsburg Savings Bank. Like that building, the Dollar (now an Emigrant Savings Bank branch) is best known for its towering four-faced clock.

Chiseled on the bank's exterior are some epigrams devoted to the importance of saving, such as "Teach economy: it is one of the first virtues—it begins with saving money" and "Without economy none can be rich; with it, few will be poor." The Dollar's exterior features bronze doors depicting classical feminine figures holding large keys. Inside, Angelo Magnanti's murals depict early Bronx history: original European settler Jonas Bronck negotiating with a group of Native Americans and two horsemen crossing King's Bridge. The clock was a later addition; the red-brick ten-story tower was constructed in 1950 to house the Dollar's offices.

35 Poe Park

Grand Concourse and Kingsbridge Road

When Edgar Allan Poe lived in this small farmhouse with his wife, Virginia, and her mother between 1846 and 1849, there was no Grand Concourse—the house stood far out in the country. Poe hoped the clear country air would invigorate his ailing young wife, who had tuberculosis. Tragically, it did not work and Virginia died; one of his best-known poems, "Annabel Lee," is thought to memorialize her.

Poe and his family were destitute while living in the little farmhouse. He was a literary success but had lost his savings in a failed magazine venture. The author and his mother-in-law had to forage in nearby fields for the family's sustenance. The cottage itself was built in 1812 by farmer John Wheeler, and stood on Kingsbridge Road until it was moved to its present location in 1913.

The house is one of four Poe museums in the U.S. It is thought that the bed, gold-framed mirror, and rocking chair belonged to Poe himself. Tours of Poe Cottage can be arranged with the Bronx Historical Society at www.bronxhistoricalsociety.org.

Poe Park, in which the cottage is situated, contains a distinctive circular bandstand built in 1925.

University Heights, Tremont, and Fordham

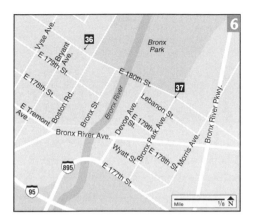

The New York Zoological Park, now known as the Bronx Zoo, was opened in 1899; its grounds and original buildings were designed by George Heins and Christopher LaFarge, who designed most of the city's original subway stations as well as the Cathedral Church of St. John the Divine in Manhattan. Zoologist Dr. William Hornaday had selected the site on 252 acres of the old Lorillard estate.

In its early days, the Bronx Zoo was instrumental in the preservation of the American bison. By 1907, the Bronx herd outstripped the Zoo's resources, so a few bulls and cows were transferred to Van Cortlandt Park. Later that year, they were sent to Oklahoma; some of the bison there today are descended from the Bronx specimens.

More recently, the zoo has pioneered the practice of presenting animals in their natural habitats, notably with the African Plains and Congo Gorilla Forest exhibits. For more information, go to www.bronxzoo.com.

Immediately south and west of the zoo, you will find the neighborhoods of Belmont, Bronx Park South, and West Farms. Visit the Rose Hill campus of Fordham University along East Fordham Road between Webster Avenue and Southern Boulevard, and take in views of imposing

Collegiate Gothic–style Keating Hall, as well as some of the older buildings, such as St. John's Residence Hall and the administration building. St. John's College, which became Fordham University, was founded here in 1841.

Belmont, the Bronx's chief Italian enclave, was named for the mansion of Jacob Lorillard. The Lorillard family, of tobacco fame, owned nearly all of what would become the Bronx Zoo, the New York Botanical Garden, and the neighborhoods of Belmont, Bronx Park South, and Norwood. It's famed for its Little Italy centered along Arthur Avenue, with its many delicatessens and intimate restaurants.

West Farms took its name from the farms west of the Bronx River, which served as the Bronx's main geographical dividing line from the colonial era up to the later 1800s. West Farms Road, which runs from Gladstone Square at Southern Boulevard and Westchester Avenue in Longwood north to West Farms Square at Boston Road and East Tremont Avenue, is among the oldest roads in the Bronx; it overlays an Indian trail along the river. It is referred to in documents from the 1720s and was known as the Lower Road and the Queen's Road in the Colonial era.

SUBWAY: ② or ⑤ to 180th Street

BUS: Bx19 on Southern Boulevard; **Bx36** on East 180th Street, Boston Road, or East 174th Street; **Bx40** or **Bx42** on East Tremont Avenue; **Bx15** or **Bx55** on Third Avenue; or **Bx9**, **Bx12**, or **Bx17**, or **Bx22** on East Fordham Road

36 West Farms Soldiers' Cemetery
East 180th Street, near Boston Road

West Farms Cemetery, an official New York City landmark since 1967 on Bryant

Avenue and East 180th Street has occupied this space since it was founded by John Butler as a family burial ground in 1815. There are just forty soldiers buried here in a plot that can accommodate more interments. Most of the soldiers buried here are Civil War veterans, some originally buried at Potter's Field on Hart Island, but reinterred here.

37 New York, Westchester, and Boston Railroad

East 180th Street and Bronx Park Avenue

This twin-towered Italian villa–style building at East 180th Street and Morris Park Avenue complete with a bust of Mercury on the second floor sits at an important transfer area for Bronx Els. This was the administration building of the New York, Westchester, and Boston Railroad, which never traveled to Boston and went out of business more than seventy-five years ago. The former route is now part of the NYC subway system. This station house now does double-duty as a police precinct and the entranceway of the IRT 180th Street Station.

A walk on East 180th Street, west of the old NYW&B administration building, will reveal another venerable neighborhood building from a lost era: an FDNY fire alarm and telegraph station.

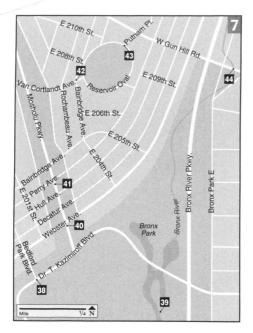

A model version of the Haupt Conservatory.

Bedford Park and Norwood are two quiet neighborhoods nestled to the west of the New York Botanical Garden (in Brooklyn, we have "Botanic" Gardens, but in the Bronx, Queens, and Staten Island, they get an extra "al").

Bedford, England, inspired the name of the Bedford Park neighborhood when it was conceived and laid out in the 1880s. The British town also influenced the neighborhood's use of Queen Anne architecture, and some of these grand old homes can still be seen crouching amid the area's now-predominant multifamily apartment buildings. Norwood was originally part of the Varian family's dairy farm. The Varians, who produced a New York City mayor, owned the oldest house in the area, which is still standing.

SUBWAY: Ⓓ to 206th Street; ② or ⑤ to Gun Hill Road

BUS: Bx41 or **Bx55** on Webster Avenue; **Bx34** on Bainbridge Avenue; **Bx28** on Mosholu Parkway or Bainbridge Avenue; **Bx10** on Jerome Avenue, East Gun Hill Road, or Bainbridge Avenue

38 New York Botanical Garden
Kazimiroff and Bedford Park Boulevards

The New York Botanical Garden and the Bronx Zoo are the two main divisions of Bronx Park, which was acquired by the city in late 1888 and early 1889, respectively. By 1891, the city had allocated 250 acres of Bronx Park to be used as a botanical garden, which has developed into one of the world's best, with many acres of groves and gardens. The Bronx River, generally a grimy, industrial flow of sludge south of the park, is magically transformed here back into the pristine freshwater brook it was before the Bronx was settled—it even enjoys some swiftly rushing waterfalls. A hemlock forest deep in the Botanical Garden is left over from the pre-Colonial era. The Garden's architectural marvels include the Enid A. Haupt Conservatory, built in 1902 and named for the woman who helped save it from demolition.

Every Christmas, there's an incredible model-train show that incorporates dozens of famous (and not as famous) NYC architectural highlights constructed from natural materials.

BRONX

39 Lorillard Snuff Mill

Along Bronx River within the Bronx Park

The Lorillard Snuff Mill was built in 1840 along the Bronx River. The Lorillard family was, and still is, prominent in the tobacco business, owning vast acreage in the mid-Bronx in the 1800s. Roses that grew naturally in the area added aroma to Lorillard's tobacco products. The mill's secluded, peaceful area made it a natural setting for weddings after the Botanical Garden acquired it. Two picturesque stone bridges can be seen spanning the Bronx River immediately north and south of the snuff mill, as well as swiftly running waterfalls and peaceful forestland. The mill has been designated a national historic landmark.

40 Clock Tower, 52nd Precinct Station House

Webster Avenue and Mosholu Parkway

One of the city's great brick clock towers, ranking with Woodhaven, Queens', Lalance and Grosjean kitchenware factory, can be found at this police station house at Webster Avenue and Mosholu Parkway. The clock is surrounded by colorful terra-cotta; the tower's design is based on Tuscan villas.

Nearby is Frisch Field, named for baseball's Frankie Frisch, the "Fordham Flash" who starred with the New York Giants from 1919 to 1926 and the St. Louis Cardinals from 1927 to 1937.

41 Mosholu Parkway

Between Van Cortlandt and Bronx Parks

Mosholu Parkway is among the many Native American place names that have been woven into the city's fabric. *Mo-sho-lu,* or "smooth stones," was the Algonquin name for a rural brook running through the heart of what became the Bronx's Spuyten Duyvil and Riverdale neighborhoods.

In 1888, when Mosholu Parkway was laid out, it ran only between Bronx and Van Cortlandt Parks. The general concept of the parkway system, devised by master urban architect Frederick Law Olmsted in the 1860s, was to extend large parks by making

Bedford Park and Norwood

the roads that connected them into parks themselves. The parkway's original stretch is still beautifully intact.

42 Valentine-Varian House

Bainbridge Avenue and Van Cortlandt Avenue East

Though the Bronx seems to have few pre–Revolutionary War houses, there is one in Norwood that qualifies, albeit just barely. In 1758, blacksmith Isaac Valentine purchased property from the Dutch Reformed Church at what today is Bainbridge Avenue and Van Cortlandt Avenue East, and, depending on which account you read, built this fieldstone cottage either in the 1750s or as a successor to a previous home in 1775.

By 1777, the home was occupied by British and Hessians but was recaptured by General William Heath after a brief but fierce battle that left the house surprisingly intact. After changing hands several times, the house became home to the Bronx County Historical Society in 1965 and was moved across the street. It is open to the public, featuring historic and archeological exhibitions. Call (718) 881-8900 or visit www.bronxhistoricalsociety.org for details.

 43 Reservoir Oval and Keeper's House

Reservoir Oval and Putnam Place

The Bronx and Byram Rivers water system was built between 1880 and 1889 to sup-

ply those sections of the Bronx not served by the Old Croton Aqueduct via pipeline from the two rivers and Kensico Reservoir. Water was stored in the Williamsbridge Receiving Reservoir in Norwood northeast of Bainbridge Avenue and East 207th Street. By 1925, it had been drained and filled in. In 1937, NYC Parks Commissioner Robert Moses constructed a new playground and park in the space vacated by the reservoir.

At Reservoir Oval and Putnam Place you will find the old reservoir keeper's stone house, built in 1889. It is now under the protection of the Mosholu Preservationist Corporation.

44 BRPR and the East Gun Hill Road Bridge

Gun Hill Road bridge spanning the Bronx River

East Gun Hill Road, a couple of blocks east of the reservoir, crosses the Bronx River on a stone bridge marked with the letters "BRPR" and the date 1918. According to Bronx historian Bill Twomey, the letters stand for "Bronx River Parkway Reservation." It's a 15.5-mile swath of parkland designed in the early years of the twentieth century by the Bronx Parkway Commission; architect Charles Stoughton designed many of the bridges and other architectural elements, including this one, and the bridge also has his name on it, under the BRPR inscription.

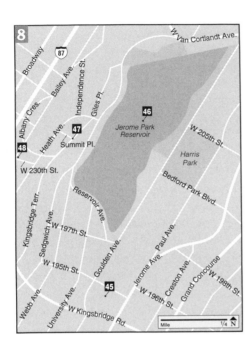

There are four streets in the Bronx, a section in Van Cortlandt Park, and two neighborhoods in the Bronx named "Kingsbridge." The history of the King's Bridge, for which the area is named, can be found on a grime-encrusted plaque on one of the Marble Hill Houses on Broadway just south of West 230th Street. The plaque is hard to read, since it's out of range of sight from the street; you have to climb the short fence or walk around it.

Frederick Philipse built the first King's Bridge, a tolled span over Spuyten Duyvil Creek, in 1693. Benjamin Palmer and Jacob Dyckman built a second bridge in 1759 to avoid paying the high tolls charged by Philipse. During his retreat from the Battle of Harlem Heights in 1776, General George Washington used both the King's Bridge and Palmer and Dyckman's free bridge to escape north to White Plains. The span survived till the excavations for the Harlem Ship Canal between 1913 and 1916, though the Bronx Historical Society maintains a small piece of it under

Marble Hill Avenue between West 228th and 230th Streets, in almost exactly its old position.

Kingsbridge Heights, and its neighbors to the west, Kingsbridge and Spuyten Duyvil, sprung up along some of the city's steepest cliffs. Some of the thoroughfares shown as streets on maps are in territory too steep for vehicular navigation, and steps were built to enable exit and entrance on foot.

SUBWAY: ④ to Kingsbridge Road; IRT ① to 231st Street

BUS: Bx32 to Jerome Avenue or West 195th Street, and West Kingsbridge Road; **Bx9** on West Kingsbridge Road; **Bx3** on University and Sedgwick Avenues; **Bx28** on East Kingsbridge Road or Jerome Avenue; **Bx1** to West 231st Street, or Heath and Sedgwick Avenues; **Bx10** to West 231st Street or Bailey Avenue

45 Kingsbridge Armory
Kingsbridge Road and Jerome Avenue

Believe it or not, the Kingsbridge Armory, on West Kingsbridge Road between Jerome and Reservoir Avenues, was at one time considered a prime NYC tourist attraction: In its heyday in the 40s and 50s it was home to bicycle races and boat shows.

The Armory was constructed from 1912 to 1917 by architectural firm Pilcher and

Tachau as a munitions storage area; when built, it supposedly was the largest armory in the world. The interior dirt drill-deck measured 300 × 600 feet. The Armory housed the 258th Field Artillery; the unit has its roots as a military escort for George Washington at his first inauguration. It is the largest of New York City's remaining armories.

Old Croton Aqueduct gatehouse, Goulden Avenue.

46 Jerome Park Reservoir
Reservoir and Sedgwick Avenues

The Jerome Park Reservoir was built in 1906. It was designed by Benjamin Church to serve the Croton Aqueduct system, and holds 773 million gallons of water at capacity. The Old Croton Aqueduct actually runs under Goulden Avenue, its eastern border, and its stones are visible in the reservoir wall from the avenue.

47 Kingsbridge Terrace Community Center
Summit Place and Kingsbridge Terrace

At Summit Place and Kingsbridge Terrace you will find the imposing former NYPD 50th Precinct station house, built by architects Arthur Horgan and Vincent Slattery in 1902, complete with a curved corner featuring four doric columns. Since 1976, it has been home to the Kingsbridge Heights Community Center; it was made an NYC landmark in 1986.

48 Bailey Avenue and West 231st Street

You will find a marvelous, porched Victorian-era building with cupolas on Bailey Avenue facing West 231st Street that looks like something out of a dream. Be sure to check out the small trefoils, each reversed from the other.

BRONX

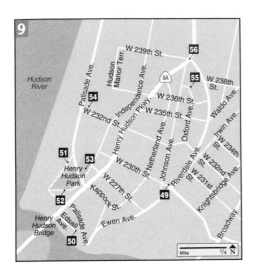

Spuyten Duyvil is tucked into the corner of the Bronx where the Hudson and Harlem Rivers meet. It's the first stop on the Metro-North Railroad beyond Marble Hill. It has been known as Speight den Duyvil, Spike & Devil, Spitting Devil, Spilling Devil, Spiten Debill, and Spouting Devil, among other spellings. In Dutch, "spuyten duyvil," the accepted spelling these days, can be pronounced two ways: one pronunciation means "devil's whirlpool" and the other means "spite the devil."

The Lenape Indians inhabited the land for hundreds of years before Europeans arrived; they called the banks of the creek *shorakapok* or "sitting-down place." After a few hundred years, the name has been pared down and exists as a street name: Kappock (pronounced kay' pock).

SUBWAY: ① to West 231st Street

BUS: Bx10 or **Bx20** on 231st Street, Johnson Avenue, Kappock Street and the Henry Hudson Parkway; **Bx7** on West 231st Street and Riverdale Avenue; **Bx9** on Broadway

49 Stepped Streets

West 230th Street, between Riverdale and Netherland Avenues

West 230th Street between Riverdale and Netherland Avenues may take the prize as lengthiest stepped street in the Bronx, and possibly all of New York City. The staircase is four blocks long and connects Riverdale, Johnson, Edgehill, and Netherland Avenues.

West 230th Street is just one of many stepped streets in the neighborhood: there are Godwin and Naples Terraces, Summit Place between Bailey and Heath Avenues, Cannon Place and Orloff Avenue at West 238th Street, and many other western Bronx spots. Some of these stepped streets preserve one-of-a-kind lamppost shaft designs.

50 Edsall Avenue

Johnson Avenue, west of Kappock Street

Rural in appearance, Edsall Avenue passes under the Henry Hudson Bridge twice, since it is a circular road emanating from Johnson Avenue. It is marked as a "mapped

Note the stained-glass windows: They are by Louis Comfort Tiffany.

Isaac Gale Johnson was an original Spuyten Duyvil resident, founding a Civil War–era foundry supplying ordnance to the Union side. By 1890, the Johnson family owned much of what is now Spuyten Duyvil, but by 1938, the factory buildings had been razed.

private street" to discourage intruders and traffic. There is no sidewalk, and it is lined with houses of varying age—some go back to the 1880s. Thomas Edsall, for whom the road is named, wrote *History of the Town of Kings Bridge* in 1887 and lived near here in an estate overlooking Spuyten Duyvil Creek.

51 Half Moon Overlook
Palisade Avenue, between Independence Avenue and Kappock Street

Half Moon Overlook, on Palisade Avenue, overlooks the Harlem and Hudson Rivers' confluence. It is named for explorer Henry Hudson's ship. The view isn't the only notable thing about it: The rough terrain below the plaza reveals an old house in ruin.

52 Edgehill Church
Independence Avenue, between Palisade Avenue and Kappock Street

Surprisingly, this majestic blending of disparate architectural styles was designed by Francis Kimball to be a modest chapel for workers of the now-vanished Johnson Iron Foundry at 2550 Independence Avenue.

53 Henry Hudson Park
Along Independence Avenue, north of Kappock Street

In Henry Hudson Park, you will find Karl Bitter and Karl Gruppe's 1939 memorial to the explorer and navigator, who sailed past Spuyten Duyvil in the *Half Moon* in 1609. A sixteen-foot statue of Henry Hudson is mounted on a 100-foot shaft that had been erected thirty years previously, on the 300th anniversary of Hudson's visit here.

Hudson and his son are shown bartering with local Native Americans in bronze relief on the base.

🐾 54 Wallenberg Forest

Palisade Avenue and West 232nd Street

Raoul Wallenberg Forest, on Palisade Avenue across from River Road, is named for the Swedish diplomat (1912–1947) credited with saving tens of thousands of Hungarian Jews from extermination by the Nazis during World War II by printing counterfeit passports and distributing them to Jews bound for the concentration camps. He also purchased as many houses, villas, and buildings as possible and adorned them with the blue and yellow of Sweden's flag, thereby making them neutral diplomatic property and safe havens for Jews.

His whereabouts became unknown in 1945. In 1957, documents were released stating he had died of a heart attack in 1947 in a Russian prison. Suspicions remain that he was killed by the KGB.

55 Tulfan Terrace

Oxford Avenue, near West 236th Street

In the 1920s, the architectural company Tully and Fanning built a short lane off Oxford Avenue north of West 236th Street, and named it for themselves ("Tul" and "Fan"). Its eastern end looks over a high hill from which all of Kingsbridge as far as the Jerome Park Reservoir can be spotted. It was lined on both sides by small, charming cottages, until the cottages on the south side were razed in 2004.

🚋 56 Bell Tower

Riverdale Avenue and West 239th Street

At Riverdale Avenue and West 239th Street (located in a particularly maddening traffic circle, hardly navigable for pedestrians) you will find the Riverdale Bell Tower, inscribed with the names of every person who served in World War I from Spuyten Duyvil and Riverdale.

In 1746, a massive bell was cast in Spain and shipped to a mission in Mexico. During the Mexican War, between 1846 and 1848, General Winfield Scott, known to friends and foes as "Old Fuss and Feathers," captured the bell as a spoil of war and brought it back to the U.S., where it was placed in a fire lookout tower at the Jefferson Market at Sixth Avenue and West 9th Street in Greenwich Village. In 1884, it was moved to a Bronx firehouse located at Riverdale Avenue and West 246th Street. It was removed from the firehouse in 1930 and placed here at architect Dwight James Baum's 500-ton stone tower. The bell and tower were moved 700 feet to the south in 1936, when the Henry Hudson Parkway was built.

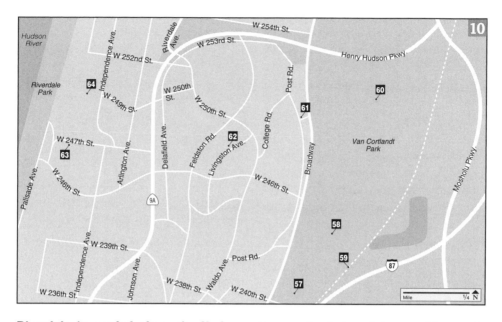

Riverdale is nestled along the Hudson River between Spuyten Duyvil to the south, Yonkers to the north, and Van Cortlandt Park to the east. With its curving, quiet lanes, spectacular views of the New Jersey Palisades, and beautiful estates, it seems to be more a part of suburban Westchester. The *New York Times* real estate section seems to agree: it has famously listed Riverdale separately from the rest of the Bronx for years. Yet, Riverdale has been a part of New York City since 1874, and the numbered street system that begins with East 1st Street in the Village extends to the city line at the Yonkers border at the highest numbered street in the series, West 263rd Street.

Much of Riverdale and Fieldston, the adjacent semiprivate neighborhood, were part of a forest owned by War of 1812–veteran Major Joseph Delafield. In 1829, he purchased 312 acres in the area and built a lime quarry and kiln. His son Edward constructed an elegant mansion that he named Fieldston Hill (which still stands on West 246th Street), and the major's grandsons brought in architect Dwight James Baum, who designed dozens of homes in Riverdale and Fieldston in different styles. Fiorello LaGuardia and John F. Kennedy (as a young boy) have also called the area home.

SUBWAY: ① to 242nd Street

BUS: Bx10 on West 231st Street and Johnson Avenue; **Bx7** along Riverdale Avenue; **Bx9** to Broadway and 231st Street; Bee-Line **1** and **2** to Broadway

57 Van Cortlandt Park
Broadway and Van Cortlandt Park South

The story of Van Cortlandt Park begins in 1699, when future NYC mayor Jacobus Van Cortlandt bought a large tract of the

BRONX

Frederick Philipse holdings in the northern Bronx. New York City obtained the property in 1888 and committed much of it to parkland.

Van Cortlandt Park is marked by rocky outcroppings made mostly of gneiss, a metamorphic rock with a distinctive banded texture. Streaks of mica can be found in the rocks, as well as quartz. Van Cortlandt Park's Northwest Forest contains the park's older-growth trees, featuring hickory, beech, cherry birch, sweetgum, red maple, and, of course, the incredibly tall and straight tulip trees. The 1997 John Muir Nature Trail as well as the Putnam Railroad and Croton Aqueduct Trails run through the park.

58 Van Cortlandt Mansion
Broadway and Manhattan College Parkway

This Georgian-style country house made in the fieldstone style was built in 1748 for Frederick Van Cortlandt. The vast athletic field north of the mansion was at one time the Van Cortlandt farm. George Washington used Van Cortlandt Mansion as a headquarters during the Revolutionary War.

The house is maintained by the National Society of Colonial Dames as a museum appointed with period Colonial and Federal collections. It is open to the public: call (718) 543-3344 for hours or go to www.vancortlandthouse.org.

Behind the mansion, you will find William Clark Noble's 1902 bronze of General Josiah Porter (1830–1894). General Porter was the first Harvard College graduate to

enlist in the Union army during the Civil War. As a captain, he commanded the 22nd Regiment of the New York State National Guard in the war. He rose to the rank of adjutant general in 1886.

59 "The Old Put"
Van Cortlandt Park at Broadway and Manhattan College Parkway

There's a trail in Van Cortlandt Park that was once a railroad. It can be reached by walking east through the park from the 242nd Street stop on the IRT subway line, the last stop. When you reach an overpass, climb onto it: you have reached what is now the Putnam Trail.

The Putnam Branch, or "The Old Put" as it's called, originally ran from Sedgwick Avenue in the Bronx north to Brewster, New York, on the New York Central commuter line, now called Metro-North. Passenger service ended on the line in 1958, and the last freight train rumbled on the long-gone tracks in 1980.

Follow the Putnam Trail north and you will arrive at the skeletal remains of the Van Cortlandt station. The Putnam once had a station here in the middle of the park. Just north of the old station, the trail crosses over Van Cortlandt Lake, the largest freshwater lake in the Bronx. The trail continues through the park and north into Yonkers.

On the left side of the trail as you travel north, you will see thirteen stone pillars. In the 1910s, before the Grand Central Terminal was built, it was decided to test different varieties of stone to see which could stand the weather the best: these pillars were used in the experiment. The second pillar from the left, made of Indiana limestone, contains the stone selected—not for its durability, but because it was cheapest.

60 Vault Hill

Van Cortlandt Park, east of West 251st Street

Roaming in Van Cortlandt Park, east of the Parade Grounds and athletic fields (including NYC's premier cross-country running course) that line the park's western edge at Broadway and just south of the Henry Hudson Parkway, you can find the original burial plot of the Van Cortlandt family: Vault Hill. NYC municipal records were hidden from the British here in 1776 by clerk Augustus Van Cortlandt (Frederick's son), and in 1781, George Washington lit campfires here to deceive the Brits while he marched to Yorktown to face Cornwallis in a decisive battle of the Revolution. By 1917, the region in view of the cemetery was being used as a training ground for World War I troops: doughboys dug trenches and hiked the surrounding hills. Most of the Van Cortlandt family's remains are now in Woodlawn Cemetery.

61 Hadley House

Post Road, north of West 251st Street

Brothers George and William Hadley built the center section of this two-story colonial on Post Road just north of West 251st Street in the mid-1700s, making it just

a little younger than the Van Cortlandt Mansion. In 1777, the Hadleys used the house as a garrison for a corps of volunteers serving the patriots' cause. In 1829, it became the property of Major Delafield, along with much of the rest of Riverdale and Fieldston.

In 1915, Dwight James Baum, who had a hand in so much of Riverdale's architecture, remodeled the Hadley house, adding wings to the north and south. Baum was careful to maintain the house's original features.

62 Indian Pond

Livingston Avenue, north of West 246th Street

Walk west on West 246th Street from Waldo Avenue and then turn north on Livingston Avenue, which is marked by a dead end sign. Don't mind the sign; just ascend the hill. You'll be treated to a small lake surrounded by a dirt walkway and benches. It's not on any map, and it is one of Riverdale's best-kept secrets. Locals call it Indian Pond.

BRONX

63 Dodge Mansion

West 247th Street, near Palisade Avenue

One of the most imposing mansions in a neighborhood full of them is the gabled, multi-chimneyed 1864 James Renwick–designed Dodge Mansion on West 247th Street, built for William Dodge, Jr., founder of the Phelps-Dodge mining company. The Dodge family helped found Columbia University Teachers College, and later turned the building over to the college. It has now become a Buddhist community house.

64 Wave Hill

Independence Avenue and West 249th Street

The Wave Hill Center for Environmental Studies was instituted by conservationist George Walbridge Perkins, who bought the twenty-eight-acre estate in the early twentieth century. The Perkins family gave Wave Hill to New York City as a gift in 1960. Now an urban garden and cultural center, it is a true getaway and contains some of New York City's best views of the marvelous New Jersey Palisades across the river. Wave Hill is approachable by car or on foot; only one street, West 249th, makes it through from the Henry Hudson Parkway all the way to the front gate at Independence Avenue.

The gardens' centerpiece is the imposing mansion built for William Lewis Morris in 1844 from locally quarried stone. Don't miss the mural in the Perkins Visitors Center by designer/author Maria Kalman depicting the grounds; art exhibits are a Wave Hill staple. The nearby Georgian Revival Glyndor House was constructed by the Perkins family after the original Glyndor was struck by lightning in 1926. Wave Hill is open to the public six days a week (except Monday) and is free on Tuesday. For information, call (718) 549-3200 or go to www.wavehill.org.

If your Wave Hill visit hasn't taken up the entire day, you may want to wander up Independence Avenue to West 252nd Street, then turn left and head down twisting, turning Sycamore Avenue to take a look at the landmarked Stonehurst house at 5225 Sycamore, built in 1858 for importer William Cromwell and sold in 1859 to paint manufacturer Robert Colgate. The house looks like its name, with stolid graystone construction.

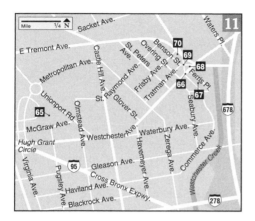

Parkchester, the Bronx's premier housing project, was built in 1941 by the Metropolitan Life Insurance Company on 110 acres. The complex boasted a bowling alley, the very first Macy's branch outlet, and three movie theaters in or nearby: the Loew's American (still there as a multiplex), the Palace, and the Circle.

Unionport was a mecca for German and Irish immigrants in the mid-to-late-1890s. After the eastern Bronx was annexed to NYC in 1895, the streets were renamed for local luminaries and settlers, and Unionport was absorbed into what's now known as Castle Hill. Unionport Road still runs as a main route from Castle Hill through Parkchester to Bronx Park. To Unionport's south is Castle Hill, so-called for a slight elevation noticed by seventeenth-century Dutch explorer Adrian Block, who thought it resembled a castle.

Westchester Square appears to be a small-town hub, clustering around the triangle formed by Westchester, East Tremont, and Lane Avenues. The "town" has recently celebrated its 350th anniversary, having been settled here, as Oostdorp ("east village") by the Dutch in 1654, and taken over by the British with the rest of New Amsterdam in 1664. It became a busy port along Westchester Creek, which has-

tened its development. By 1693, St. Peter's Episcopal Church was founded there; the parish is still in existence. During the Revolution, patriots dismantled a bridge over the creek, delaying British advancement (the present-day bridge carries East Tremont Avenue over the creek).

SUBWAY: ⑥ to Parkchester, Castle Hill Avenue, Zerega Avenue, or Westchester Square–East Tremont Avenue

BUS: Bx4 on Westchester Avenue; **Bx22** to Unionport Road or Castle Hill Avenue; **Bx36** or **Bx39** on White Plains Road; **Q44** to Cross Bronx Expressway; **Bx14** to Metropolitan Avenue or East Tremont Avenue; **Bx40** or **Bx42** to East Tremont Avenue; or **Bx8** to Williamsbridge Road

65 The Sculptures of Parkchester
Parkchester station, Westchester Avenue at Cross Bronx Expressway

A walk around Parkchester, called a "city within a city" by the *New York Times* when the project first opened, is an experience

BRONX

that will delight anyone with an interest in urban planning and a sharp eye for detail. Take the 6 train, exit at the Parkchester station, and you will find yourself at Hugh Grant Circle, named for a New York City mayor from 1890 to 1892. Look here on its south side for the façade of the old Circle Theatre, which is now an exercise studio. Cross into Parkchester and choose any street or pedestrian path.

Met Life chose Federal Seaboard Terra Cotta Corporation to provide Parkchester's ornamental appointments. The company supplied more than 500 statues of hula girls, accordion players, and farm animals, as well as elaborate designs for theaters and storefronts, some by renowned sculptor Joseph Kiselewski.

66 St. Peter's

Westchester and Commerce Avenues

St. Peter's Episcopal Church was built in 1856 by Leopold Eidlitz when this was an isolated country village along the Westchester Turnpike. It was rebuilt by the architect's son, Cyrus, after a fire in 1877. St. Peter's has existed as a parish since 1693, and is the third church to exist on this site; the churchyard contains many graves dating back to the early 1700s. Foster Hall, facing Westchester Avenue in the cemetery,

was built by Leopold Eidlitz in 1868, and is currently used as a community theater.

67 Ferris Cemetery

Commerce Avenue, near Westchester Avenue

The private cemetery of the Ferris family can be found on Commerce Avenue a short walk south of Westchester Avenue. According to Bronx historian John McNamara, John Ferris had moved to the village of Westchester by 1667 and James Ferris was running a mill in 1820. By 1839, Benjamin Ferris owned much of what is now Westchester Square.

68 Chair in the Square

Westchester Square at Lane and Westchester Avenues

At Westchester Square, there's always an empty seat. David Saunders' 8-foot-high sculpture, "The Seat," was installed in 1987. Under the chair is a bronze dictionary open to an entry on the birds of North America, and dictionary and chair are mounted on a granite boulder sporting a carved wild boar. A separate monument in the square to area residents who served in World War I was dedicated with a speech by area educator Owen Dolan in 1925. After Dolan's speech, by accounts a spirited, energetic one, he sat down and promptly dropped dead of a heart attack. Westchester Square Park was renamed for Dolan the following year.

69 Huntington Free Library

Westchester Square at Lane Avenue and Benson Street

On Lane Avenue between Benson Street and Westchester Avenue (officially #9 Westchester Square), note the small, dark brownstone building with an arched front door with an emblazoned "18" on one side and "90" on the other, indicating the date it was built. Over the arch, a chiseled sign says "Huntington Free Library and Reading Room." The architect was Frederick Withers, who also designed the Gothic Jefferson Market Library building in Greenwich Village.

The Library's Reading Room features a large map of Throgs Neck in the 1850s drawn by the Bronx historian John McNamara. Pipes for the reading room's original gas lighting are visible near a book stack.

The Reading Room, with its large collection of Bronx pictures and books, remains open weekdays by appointment at (718) 829-7770.

70 The White Elephant

Westchester Square and Ponton Avenue

The Bronx probably has more defunct theaters used for new purposes than any other borough. Many have become furniture outlets or storefront churches. The story goes, though, that a magnificently apportioned building between Ponton and Roberts Avenues on East Tremont Avenue was built as a theater, but never got to fulfill its builders' ambitions. It features glazed white brick and symbolic terra-cotta figures like the lyre and tragical mask over its front entrance. Locals call it "the white elephant."

Pelham Parkway was first proposed in 1881 by the New York Park Association in response to the success of Brooklyn's Ocean and Eastern Parkways, built in the 1870s by Olmsted and Vaux. The present-day parkway preserves the original urban greenway concept and is famed for its overhanging elm trees.

The pedestrian mall of Pelham Parkway is named for Jonathan "Yoni" Netanyahu, a Bronx-born commander of the Israeli hostage rescue force. He was the only soldier killed in freeing 105 hostages from hijackers on Air France Flight 103 in Entebbe, Uganda, on July 4, 1976. His brother became Prime Minister in 1996 in Israel's first prime ministerial election.

The name Morris Park is an echo of the old Morris Park Racetrack, which was here between 1890 and 1913 and was a former home of the Belmont Stakes. The adjoining "Bronxdale" replaced the area's former name, Bear Swamp, a reflection of the former wildlife.

SUBWAY: ② or ⑤ to Bronx Park East or Pelham Parkway

BUS: Bx8 on Williamsbridge Road; **Bx21** to Morris Park Avenue; **Bx22** or **Bx39** on White Plains Road; **Bx12** on Pelham Parkway

71 The Esplanade's Rail Stations
Morris Park and Pelham Parkway

The Esplanade covers the open cut of the old New York, Westchester, and Boston railroad line, now the IRT subway. Some of the old rail line's stations have been drafted into use as subway stops, though their railroad roots are still in evidence. At Paulding and Hone Avenues is the Spanish Colonial–inspired Morris Park station. Close inspection of the walls will reveal two caducei (snakes entwining a staff), a symbol of the old rail line. Another such symbol can be found on the concrete overpass at nearby Mathews and Brady Avenues.

Between Pelham Parkway and Mace Avenue, the Esplanade becomes a wide, grassy mall flanked by two roadways. You'll find the bright, gleaming Pelham Parkway station here, resembling a small-town way station rather than a stop on the largest subway system in the world.

72 Regis Philbin Avenue
Cruger Avenue, between Sagamore Street and Bronxdale Avenue

Regis (no one seems to call him Mr. Philbin) was born in the Bronx in 1933; his family lived on Cruger Avenue here in

Bronxdale. He was named for his father Frank's high school, a Jesuit academy on West 84th Street in Manhattan.

In 1992, the Department of Transportation named the block of Cruger Avenue between Sagamore Street and Bronxdale Avenue for Regis; the small, frame house where the Philbin family lived near Bronxdale still stands.

On the block today, you will find a subway el overpass, a junkyard, and several small buildings. Nearby Bronxdale Avenue, however, is lined with several magnificent Art Moderne–style high-rise apartment buildings.

Morris Park, Pelham Parkway, and Bronxdale

BRONX

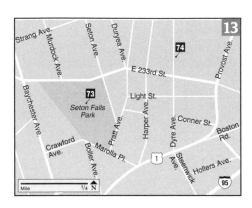

The nearer in the Bronx you get to *West*chester County, the further into *East*chester you penetrate. Founded in 1665, Eastchester is a neighborhood in the northeast Bronx that actually used to belong to Westchester County and didn't become a part of New York City until 1895. It's a quiet neighborhood of one- and two-family homes, a few apartment buildings, and massive Co-op City.

Freedomland, built on 205 acres of reclaimed swampland along the "V" limned by the New England Thruway and Hutchinson River Parkway, is one of New York City's great lost amusement parks. During its four-year run between 1960 and 1964, it took the title of America's largest such park and played host to millions of visitors. From 1968 to 1970, the massive Co-op City housing development was constructed atop Freedomland's ashes, featuring the Bronx's tallest buildings: thirty-five high-rise buildings, each thirty-five stories high, along with more than 200 smaller buildings in a self-contained environment with its own supermarkets, schools, and fire house.

SUBWAY: ⑤ to Baychester Avenue or Eastchester-Dyre Avenue

BUS: Bx30 on Boston Road and Conner Street; **Bx16** on East 233rd Street, Dyre Avenue and Boston Road

🎣 **73 Rattlesnake Brook in Seton Falls Park**
East 233rd Street and Baychester Avenue

Seton Falls Park is best entered from East 233rd Street east of where it meets Baychester Avenue. Winding through a short section of the park, much of which is set aside as a wilderness area, is Rattlesnake Brook, named for the venomous reptiles that used to live there.

74 Little Red Schoolhouse
4010 Dyre Avenue, north of East 233rd Street

Bronx's own "little red schoolhouse," P.S. 15, is at 4010 Dyre Avenue. The architectural gem designed by architect Simon Williams was built in 1877. It now serves as a community center.

Wakefield, just northwest of Eastches-ter, was a small town annexed by New York City in 1895. It was originally surveyed in 1855 and given the name of the house near Fredericksburg, Virginia, where George Washington was born in 1732. Woodlawn Heights, the triangle between Van Cortlandt Park, Woodlawn Cemetery, and the Bronx River, is home to a large Irish immigrant population. Katonah Avenue, its main drag, features a collection of small shops featuring imported items from the "old sod."

SUBWAY: ② to 233rd Street, Nereid Avenue, or Wakefield-241st Street

BUS: Bx41 to White Plains Road and East 241st Street, Baychester Avenue; **Bx16** to Jerome Avenue, East 233rd Street, Webster Avenue, East 238th Street, Nereid Avenue or Baychester Avenue; **Bx34** to Katonah Avenue; Bee-Line **40** to White Plains Road

75 Bissel Gardens

Bissel Avenue, between Bruner and Edson Avenues

Bissel Gardens, along the former Bissel Avenue between Bruner and Edson Avenues, was reclaimed from its former status as a dumping ground by the residents of Wakefield in 1994, led by Teresa LeCount with the aid of former Bronx Borough President Fernando Ferrer. Much of the produce grown here is used for local hunger-relief organizations. Over the years, Bissel Gar-

BRONX

dens has donated almost 4,000 lbs. of food to organizations such as God's Love We Deliver and area churches. A children's garden and farmer's market are also planned.

76 Garden Place

Alley off White Plains Road and East 240th Street

Known only to its dozen or so residents, Garden Place is a tiny dirt road wedged between White Plains Road and Furman Avenue south of East 240th Street in Wakefield. It is accessible only from a private right of way on White Plains Road; it's the only street in NYC that doesn't "officially" meet any other one. It lacks street signs, paving, regular garbage pickup, and snow removal, all because of a private easement. Decades ago, there may have been a garden here. All of the houses on Garden Place, save one, are accessible from Furman Avenue.

77 Indian Field

East 233rd Street, between Jerome Avenue and Van Cortlandt Park East

On August 31, 1778, seventeen Mohican Indians, led by Chief Abraham Nimham and fighting on the side of the patriots, were massacred after their defeat by Colonel Simcoe and his Queen's Rangers, who were fighting for the Crown. The Indians are commemorated at Indian Field in Van Cortlandt Park on East 233rd Street, east of Jerome Avenue.

The Mohicans were buried in Indian Field by the Devoe family, on whose land the battle was fought, and their gravesite is marked by a plaque and a cairn, a stone mound used in Scottish burials.

78 Woodlawn Cemetery

Webster Avenue and East 233rd Street

In 400-acre Woodlawn Cemetery, founded in 1863 and laid out by landscape designer J. C. Sidney (who also designed Philadelphia's Fairmount Park), there are many New York City luminaries: Herman Melville, Admiral David Farragut, musicians Miles Davis and Duke Ellington, and so many more. Much like its Brooklyn contemporary, Green-Wood Cemetery, Woodlawn is a product of the rural cemetery movement of the mid-nineteenth century that saw cemeteries designed like large, peaceful parks.

Call (718) 920-0500 or visit www.thewoodlawncemetery.org for hours or information.

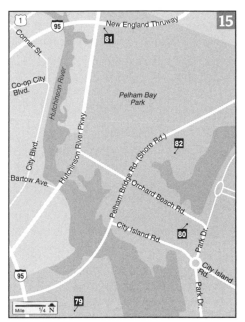

 **79** Bronx Victory Memorial
Pelham Bay Park

At over 2,700 acres, three times the size of Central Park, Pelham Bay Park stretches from the Bronx neighborhoods of Middletown and Spencer Estates on the south, to the Westchester County line on the north, and from the Hutchinson River and its namesake Parkway on the west, to Eastchester Bay and Long Island Sound in the east.

The Kazimiroff Nature Trail on Hunter Island (now a peninsula attached to the park by landfill) as well as the Siwanoy and Split Rock Nature Trails provide easy access to the park's wilder areas. The eastern section of the park facing Long Island Sound had been named Orchard Beach in 1905 for the orchards that grew on local estates.

SUBWAY: ⑥ to Pelham Bay Park

BUS: QBx1 to Bruckner Boulevard; **Bx12** to Pelham Parkway; Bee-Line **45** to Bartow-Pell Mansion along Shore Road (ask driver to stop)

A car, or lengthy walk from the subway, is necessary to visit Glover's and Split Rocks.

"Winged Victory," a beautifully gilded statue, tops this towering column located in the northern section of the southern part of Pelham Bay Park along the approach road connecting the New England Thruway to Pelham Parkway, near where it crosses the Hutchinson River and becomes Shore Road. The memorial was designed by architect John Sheridan and sculptors Belle Kinney and Leopold Scholz in 1932. Limestone reliefs depict marching soldiers, and the paths leading to the memorial are lined with lavish floral beds and hedges, but the star of the show is the brilliantly gold statue standing eighteen feet tall and weighing more than three tons. The memorial was renovated from base to tip in 2001 after decades of weathering and vandalism.

80 Glover's Rock
Off of Park Drive, near Orchard Beach

There's a large boulder on the side of Orchard Beach Road, midway between Bar-

BRONX

tow Circle at Shore Road and Park Drive near the beach, deposited here by the retreating glaciers at the close of the last Ice Age.

On this spot during the Revolutionary War in October 1776, Colonel John Glover (1732–1797) and his 14th Continental Regiment, largely made up of militia from Marblehead, Massachusetts, engaged the British during the Battle of Pell's Point and took heavy casualties, allowing a retreating General Washington to escape.

Glover's Rock is marked by a tablet erected in 1960 by the Bronx Historical Society, replacing an earlier one dedicated in 1901 by the Daughters of the American Revolution.

81 Split Rock

Hutchinson River Parkway and Shore Road

Walk along the Split Rock Trail that runs west along Orchard Beach Road from Bartow Circle and north along the Hutchinson River Parkway deep into Pelham Bay Park, skirting the Split Rock Golf Course. Just below the junction of the Hutch and the New England Thruway, cross the service road into the triangle formed by the service road, the parkway, and the expressway. You will see a large rock that looks as if it has been cleft in two by lightning.

Pioneer settler Anne Hutchinson's farm was located just over the river; peering through the "split" enables you to see where it once stood (in the winter when there's less foliage). Anne and most of her family were killed in a Siwanoy Indian raid in 1643 by a sachem named Wampage.

82 Bartow-Pell Mansion

Shore Road, north of City Island Road

Englishman Thomas Pell, a physicist, purchased a vast tract of more than 9,000 acres of land (most of what is now eastern Bronx) from the local Siwanoy Indians in 1654. Descendants of the Pells occupied the tract for nearly 150 years. By 1813, the acreage was sold out of the Bartow-Pell family (Ann Pell had married John Bartow), but in 1836, John's grandson Robert reacquired the property and, in 1842, built the mansion that is there today.

NYC bought the house from the Bartows in 1888. In 1915, the mansion underwent a complete restoration by the International Garden Club, Inc., which has continued to maintain the grounds, now numbering nine acres, as a public garden to this day. In 1946, the mansion opened as a museum exhibiting furniture and paintings from the nineteenth century. The Bartow-Pell Mansion welcomes the public: call (718) 885-1461 for directions and hours.

City Island Avenue's "skyscraper"

Located on a spit of an island in Eastchester Bay in the extreme northeast Bronx, City Island looks like a transplanted New England fishing village seemingly dropped into the New York metropolitan area. City Island was privately owned, first by the Pell family and then by the Palmer family, from 1654 until it became a part of the town of Pelham, in Westchester county, in 1819. The island became a part of New York City in 1895.

Benjamin Palmer, who owned the island in 1761, thought of it as a potential commercial rival to New York City, and so it picked up a new nickname (it previously had been called Great Minneford's Island). Of course it never rivaled New York City as a seaport, but it did develop thriving seaside industries. Palmer's group laid out streets and established two ferries to the mainland. Palmer, a staunch supporter of the Revolution, engaged the ire of the British, who plundered the island in 1776. Three years later, Palmer and his family were captured and forced to leave the island for Manhattan; he never returned to City Island.

City Island is chock-full of antique shops, art galleries, and terrific seafood res-

taurants, most of them arrayed along City Island Avenue. Its street grid is arranged much like a fish skeleton, with City Island Avenue as the spine and the twenty-four streets intersecting it as the bones, making exploration on foot easy.

SUBWAY: ⑥ to Pelham Bay Park; connect there to:

BUS: Bx29 on City Island Avenue

83 City Island Bridge
City Island Avenue and Sutherland Street

The City Island Bridge was first opened on July 4, 1901, replacing a previous wood

BRONX

bridge that had charged tolls. As far back as 1977, the 1,470-foot swing bridge was beginning to show its age, and plans were drawn in the late 1990s to reconstruct it. The new City Island Bridge will be NYC's first major cable-stayed bridge; smaller examples of the newly popular style can be found on pedestrian bridges spanning Twelfth Avenue and West 46th Street and the FDR Drive and East 63rd Street.

84 High Island
View from King Avenue and Terrace Street

High Island is a small island off the northeast shoreline of City Island. In the early days of the twentieth century, the island was home to a year-round community of bungalow dwellers, but they were displaced in the early 1960s with the construction of a 541-foot-high antenna tower.

85 Pelham Cemetery
King Avenue and Tier Street

Pelham Cemetery, on King Avenue between Ditmars and Tier Streets, is New York City's only waterside cemetery, the final resting place of generations of City Islanders.

En route to the cemetery from City Island Bridge, walk down Minnieford and King Avenues and take in the many beautiful Victorian-era homes painted in brilliant colors, many having an enviable view of Long Island Sound.

86 Hart Island
Visible from Pelham Cemetery

Hart Island is easily visible from City Island; probably the most unrestricted view is from Pelham Cemetery. Hart Island has been home to New York City's burial grounds for its unknown and indigent since 1869 when the island was purchased by the city from the Hunter family. Looking across the strait separating the two islands you will see a large white cross.

Known to city residents as the "potter's field," the burial ground is officially called City Cemetery by the Department of Corrections. It maintains the site, and, with the help of prison labor, handles the interments. More than three-quarters of a million people have been buried on Hart Island.

Hart Island is also an architectural graveyard; some of its decaying buildings can be spotted from City Island, including an abandoned Catholic church, a greenhouse, and memorial obelisks devoted to now-disinterred Civil War Union soldiers. There's a thirty-foot-high concrete monument with gold letters spelling "Peace" that was erected in 1948.

87 City Island Museum
Fordham Street and King Avenue

The City Island Historical Nautical Museum is at 190 Fordham Street, in City Island's old P.S. 17, with artwork and exhibits chronicling the island's near-250-year-old history of shipbuilders, fishermen, and

America's Cup yachtsmen. The museum owns one of the world's largest collections of maritime-themed books, as well as many beautiful watercolors of Orchard Beach, City Island, Hunter Island, and other local sites by Professor Harold V. Walsh, painted in the 1930s.

The museum is open Sundays from 1:00 PM to 5:00 PM and by appointment. Call (718) 885-0008 for more information.

88 Mooncurser Records

City Island Avenue and Schofield Street

Mooncurser Records at 229 City Island Avenue has a collection of more than 100,000 albums and singles (mostly big band, jazz, and Latin) as well as more than 30,000 piano rolls. The place also serves as a museum of recordings, with wall displays of movie posters, music memorabilia, musical instruments, and antiques hanging from the rafters. *In the summer of 2006, at press time for this book, Mooncurser Records unfortunately closed.*

89 Execution Rock Lighthouse

Off City Island and Belden Street

Looking from the southern end of City Island Avenue, you will see a brown-and-white striped lighthouse with an adjoin-

ing two-story keeper's house. It is known as Execution Rock Lighthouse, named for a Revolutionary War legend of the torture and murder of American prisoners by their British captors.

Execution Rock Lighthouse was built in 1850 when it was determined that the lighthouse at nearby Sands Point was insufficient during foggy or stormy weather. It was manned until 1979, and has been automated since then.

BRONX

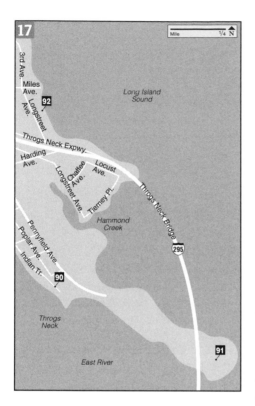

southeastern redoubt, was named for a very early British settler, John Throckmorton, who arrived in the peninsula capped by Fort Schuyler in 1642. The peninsula, or "neck" (cf. Little Neck in Queens), was bestowed an abbreviation of his lengthy name and Throgmorton Avenue, also a tribute, is a variant spelling. Locals spell "Throggs Neck" with a double "g," but the Department of Transportation signage resolutely sticks to one "g." However Throgs Neck is spelled, it is a peaceful, tranquil area with a couple of private communities that enjoy terrific views.

SUBWAY: None. Connections to the **Bx8**, **Bx40**, and **Bx42** can be made by taking the ⑥ to Westchester Square–East Tremont Avenue

BUS: Bx40 and **Bx42** to East Tremont Avenue, Harding Avenue, and Pennyfield Avenue; **Bx8** to Throgs Neck Expressway and Harding Avenue

90 Silver Beach

Between Throgs Neck Boulevard and Fern Place

This small seashore neighborhood can be reached by a walk along Indian Trail, which meanders along the East River shore from Throgs Neck Boulevard to Jasmine Place, past summer cabins along a cliff which affords terrific views of the nearby Throgs Neck Bridge. Here, homeowners possess

Eastern Bronx was once peppered with small crossroads like Stinardstown, centered at today's Westchester Avenue and St. Theresa Avenue; Middletown, along today's Middletown Road—though no one is sure which two landmarks or towns it was in the "middle" of; and Country Club, so named for the former twenty-six-acre Westminster Country Club. The nearby Spencer Estates was the home of William Spencer, a benefactor of the New York Public Library.

A clutch of local streets in Spencer Estates south of Pelham Bay Park have "electric" names: Radio, Watt, Ampere, and Ohm. This is a reminder of the contribution Isaac Leopold Rice (1850–1915), the president of Electric Storage Battery Company and founder of Forum Publishing, made when his land was donated to create part of Pelham Bay Park.

Throgs Neck, mainland Bronx's most

the buildings in which they live, but not the property on which they stand; a similar situation exists in nearby Edgewater Park. In these riverside, or soundside (depending on what side of the Throgs Neck Bridge you're on), neighborhoods there's a conscious attempt to de–New Yorkify the surroundings. In Silver Beach, the street names can be found on wooden boards nailed onto the telephone poles, and the streetlamps aren't the standardized New York City issue. It all combines to impart a rather surreal effect.

91 Fort Schuyler
At the end of Pennyfield Avenue

This fort named for Revolutionary War general Philip Schuyler at the tip of a peninsula jutting into the junction of the East River and Long Island Sound under the Throgs Neck Bridge was built between 1833 and 1851 as part of the "third system" of harbor fortifications. The first two "systems" were initiated during the Revolution and War of 1812, while the third was enacted as a preemptive means of stopping any enemy vessels with designs on New York City.

Since 1986, Fort Schuyler has been the setting for the Maritime Industry Museum, which offers one of the world's largest collections of maritime industry material. Featured is an exhibition called "Evolution of Seafaring," from the ancient Phoenicians until the present, as well as a realistic model of the Brooklyn Navy Yard in

its peak years (1942–1944). The Maritime Museum is funded, staffed and maintained with voluntary contributions and support. For hours and information, call (718) 409-7218 or visit www.maritimeindustrymuseum.org.

92 Park of Edgewater
North of Throgs Neck Expressway along Eastchester Bay

New York City's most obscure Main Street is located in the private Bronx neighborhood of Park of Edgewater, aka Edgewater Park, which is wedged north of the Throgs Neck Expressway and south of Eastchester Bay. The Park of Edgewater is so obscure, in fact, that it wasn't even represented correctly on maps until the 1980s. Like Silver Beach Gardens, Park of Edgewater residents own their homes but not the property they're built upon. It has been thus since about 1910, when bungalows were built on the former seaside estate of the Adee family. During their early years, the bungalows were just wooden tents with canvas tops, without heat or electricity; kerosene stoves were used for cooking. Today they have been completely modernized and are occupied year-round.

On foot, the Park of Edgewater is best accessed from Pennyfield Avenue, which is the only vehicular or pedestrian crossing of the Throgs Neck Expressway in the area.

a.

a. *This terra-cotta lunette can be found over a doorway on West 14th Street, between Seventh and Eighth Avenues.*

b. *This gnome winks at passersby from an apartment building at Irving Place and East 19th Street.*

c. *This gnarled gnome is one of two guarding an office building door on West 29th Street, between Seventh and Eighth Avenues.*

b.

c.

d. *A couple of painted giraffes have lunch on this East 19th Street lunette.*

e. *A gate on West 21st Street between Seventh and Eighth Avenues depicts the climactic scene from film pioneer Georges Méliès' 1902* A Voyage to the Moon.

f. *Caryatids, female torsos mounted on bases, can be found at many NYC brownstone doorways, such as this one on St. Mark's Place, just west of Second Avenue.*

Brooklyn's

relationship with New York City, which it joined in 1898, at times has been characterized as prickly, with Brooklyn maintaining an independent spirit and an autonomous nature. The original vote for consolidation into the five-borough plan was only passed by a slim margin. In the 1970s, motorists driving on Shore Parkway just east of the Verrazano Bridge were greeted by a sign placed on the side of the road by Sebastian Leone, the borough president at the time, which read "Welcome to Brooklyn, the country's fourth largest city," as if Brooklyn had never joined the other boroughs. So it's always felt as if Brooklyn has had a shotgun wedding with New York City, with its own distinctive "Greenpernt" accent, its own cuisine (think cheesecakes from Junior's and candy-store egg creams), and its own lore, with a built-in nostalgia for stickball and the Brooklyn Dodgers.

It is likely that Brooklyn preserves more Colonial-era architecture than any other borough. Manhattan and the Bronx have only a handful of buildings remaining from the time of the Revolutionary War, while Queens and Staten Island are oases in an increasing sea of planned developments. In Brooklyn, many older structures have been carefully absorbed into the fiber of its housing stock; in Flatbush and Flatlands, there are quite a number of homes dating back to the 1700s that stand among

their fellows, redecorated over the years so that they are nearly indistinguishable from homes built after World War II.

In the 1990s and early 2000s, Brooklyn experienced a modern renaissance as Sunset Park continued its transformation into a thriving Chinatown, and neighborhoods like Fort Greene, Williamsburg, DUMBO, and Cobble Hill blossomed into recharged communities by an influx of young profes-

sionals and artists. From a *Forgotten New York* perspective, some aspects of the neighborhoods' older traditions and touchstones have sadly been buried or removed due to all the new development. In 2005, Red Hook Lane, a downtown Colonial-era path, was designated for elimination to make way for new office buildings, and both the Williamsburg waterfront and Coney Island were scheduled for major changes.

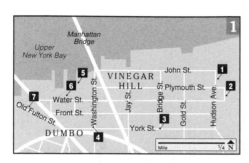

Beginning in the late 1990s, the dark, Belgian-block-lined streets between the Brooklyn and Manhattan bridges, commonly known as DUMBO, or "Down Under the Manhattan Bridge Overpass," were transformed into a vibrant neighborhood with pricey condominiums, delis, hardware stores, pizzerias, and even gourmet chocolatiers. Before then, though, this was a gritty, grimy manufacturing and warehousing district (Robert Gair introduced corrugated cardboard here in 1890).

SUBWAY: 🅕 to York Street

BUS: B61 to Navy, York, or Gold Streets; **B25** to Old Fulton, Front, Main, or Water Streets

1 Vinegar Hill
Hudson Avenue and Water Street

Vinegar Hill is an enclave located east of DUMBO and north of the Farragut Houses. It is a charming little area marked by brownstone buildings and Belgian-block streets that haven't yet been asphalted. It was unfortunately decimated by the construction of the nearby Brooklyn-Queens Expressway and the Farragut Houses south of York Street in the 1940s and 1950s, and just this tiny area remains.

Vinegar Hill was created in 1800, when John Jackson purchased its land from the Sands brothers (for whom Sands Street is named). Jackson actually hoped to attract Irish immigrants in an era when Irish were otherwise unwelcome. He named his tract Vinegar Hill after the site of a fierce battle in the unsuccessful Irish rebellion of 1798. Most of its residences were built between the late-1820s and the 1850s; the latter ones reflect the Italianate style.

2 Navy Commandant's House
Little Street, east of Hudson Avenue

The Naval Commandant's House, now a crown jewel of the Brooklyn Navy Yard, is visible behind a locked gate from Evans and Little Streets in Vinegar Hill. It was built between 1806 and 1807, and is purportedly the design of Boston's Charles Bulfinch, who designed Faneuil Hall and the State House in Boston.

3 Eskimo Pie/Thomson Meter Building
110 Bridge Street at York Street

The Thomson Meter Building at Bridge and York Streets was designed by Beaux Arts–schooled Louis Jallade in 1908. It represents one of Brooklyn's earliest examples of concrete construction, though its real claim to fame lies in its exuberant use of brilliant, richly colored terra-cotta along the roof. Look closely and you will see at the building's corners the remnants of stylized letters T and M (one corner on York Street preserves them intact). Thomson Meter moved to headquarters on Washington Street in 1927, and Eskimo Pie moved in. In February 2004, the Thomson Meter Building was designated an NYC landmark.

4 Manhattan Bridge Vista
Washington and York Streets

A look north on Washington Street from just north of York presents a gorgeous view of the eastern tower of the Manhattan Bridge. By a happy accident, the Empire State Building can be seen through the two legs of the tower.

Walk a couple of blocks to Jay and Plymouth Streets, and look west. A similar view of the Brooklyn Bridge's eastern tower presents itself. No other neighborhood in New York City features such wonderful views of not one but two major bridges.

5 Jay Street Connecting Railroad
Plymouth and Main Streets

The Jay Street Connecting Railroad operated as Brooklyn's smallest waterfront railway from 1904 to 1959. The role of this

small railroad was to move freight cars from carfloats on the East River to the industrial buildings and warehouses where they would be loaded and unloaded; you can still see a few abandoned tracks going into buildings. The JSCR filled about the same role as the old High Line on Manhattan's West Side. The railroad was built by the Arbuckle Brothers Coffee Company in the early 1900s to facilitate the transport of goods among its various factory and warehouse buildings. Eventually, the Arbuckles made a profit by expanding the railroad further and having it serve other businesses in the area. The little railroad thrived until the mid-1950s, even after the Arbuckles had sold off most of their waterside properties.

The old JSCR yards are now occupied by a vast Con Edison plant as well as the new Empire-Fulton Ferry State Park, completed in 2003. It is part of a plan to eventually make the entire Brooklyn waterfront between the Manhattan Bridge and Atlantic Avenue landing a large park.

6 Empire Stores

Water Street, between Dock and Main Streets

The Arbuckle Brothers produced America's first national coffee brand, Ariosa, which remains available, complete with a traditional piece of peppermint candy in the bag. The Arbuckles were also sugar importers, and early on, they kept their coffee from getting stale by glazing it in sugar. In the 1930s, large ads for another Arbuckle brand, Yuban, were painted on the exterior of the brick Empire Stores, a series of warehouses along Water Street west of Main Street—one of the region's original warehouses still standing.

Immediately to the west of the Empire Stores, at Water and Dock Streets, is the hollowed remnant of a tobacco inspection warehouse that is now a part of Empire-Fulton Ferry State Park.

7 Long Island Safe Deposit Company ⋀

Old Fulton and Front Streets

One of Brooklyn's most impressive cast-iron building façades is the Long Island Safe Deposit Company building, 1 Front Street at Old Fulton Street, which dates to 1868 and was designed by William Mundell. The construction of the Brooklyn Bridge made life difficult for businesses on lower Fulton Street, and Long Island Safe Deposit was no exception; it closed in 1891. Its presence is a testimony to how this part of town was formerly one of Brooklyn's business hubs. Its subsequent decline was symptomatic of the neighborhood's status after ferry service ended in 1924. In recent years, the building has been restored to much of its old glory.

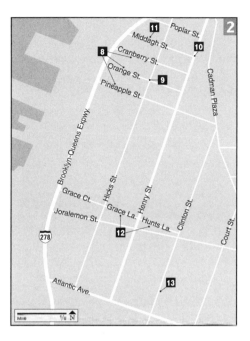

Brooklyn Heights can at times feel more like a sibling of Manhattan than a part of Brooklyn; however, its architecture and down-home vibe firmly connect it to the rest of Kings County. Originally, "the Heights" looked out over Manhattan from a high cliff. The hill is now hidden by the Brooklyn-Queens Expressway, which, in the 1950s, was planned to cleave right through the area, forcing the demolition of some of Brooklyn's prime architecture. Fortunately, Robert Moses, New York's "master builder," was prevailed upon to angle the highway along the waterfront and depress it below street level. This enabled engineers to place a pedestrian plaza above the BQE from Remsen Street north to Orange Street. The walkway is alternately known as the Promenade and Esplanade, and commands what are arguably the most spectacular views of downtown Manhattan.

SUBWAY: ② or ③ to Clark Street; Ⓜ or Ⓡ to Court Street; Ⓐ or Ⓒ, to High Street; Ⓐ, Ⓒ, or Ⓕ to Jay Street

BUS: B25, B26, B38, B41, B51, or **B52** to Cadman Plaza West

🚋8 Pineapple, Orange, and Cranberry

Fruity Streets: Pineapple, Orange, and Cranberry Streets

Before the IRT subway arrived in 1908, Brooklyn Heights was one of the more secluded areas in Brooklyn that only the very wealthy could afford. Jealousies and disputes arose among the moneyed gentry. The story goes that in the decade prior to the Civil War, a local resident, Mabel Middagh Hicks, in a disagreement with her aristocratic neighbors, tore down the street signs bearing the names of the offending families, and hastily installed signs bearing the names of her favorite fruits and trees: Pineapple, Orange, Cranberry, and Willow. When Brooklyn authorities restored the original street names, she struck again and changed them back. This tug-of-war eventually resolved itself in the lady's favor, and the streets retain plant names to this day.

The more likely story is that they were simply named by early-nineteenth-century landowners and Mabel Hicks' relatives by marriage, the Hicks brothers, John and Jacob. Each brother bore the middle name Middagh, their mother's maiden name. There is a Middagh Street and, of course, a Hicks Street in Brooklyn Heights. An 1816 map of Brooklyn Village compiled by Jeremiah Lott as well as William Hooker's Pocket Plan of 1827, already show the streets in question as Pineapple, Orange, Cranberry, and Willow.

The three "fruit streets" are, for the most part, quiet, shady streets with brick or brownstone town houses. Cranberry Street, in particular, offers an iconic view of downtown Manhattan at its western end.

BROOKLYN

9 Church of the Pilgrims

Orange and Hicks Streets

Orange Street, between Hicks and Henry Streets, is dominated by the Plymouth Church of the Pilgrims, where Henry Ward Beecher preached from the church's opening in 1849 until 1887. Beecher, a lecturer and writer as well as a pastor, attained a preeminence almost equal to Abraham Lincoln's at the height of the Civil War, and even endorsed products, which well-known ministers did in the era. His sister, Harriet Beecher Stowe, wrote *Uncle Tom's Cabin*. Henry Ward Beecher is commemorated by not one but two statues in Brooklyn Heights: one in Cadman Plaza that used to be closer to City (now Borough) Hall, and one in the garden court next to Plymouth Church.

10 The Candy Men

Henry and Middagh Streets

A very large ad painted on the corner of a building at Henry and Middagh Streets promotes "Peaks Mason Mints"; it is the former home of the Mason, Au & Magen-heimer Candy Company. According to advertisement researcher Walter Grutch-field, the company was in business here between 1892 and 1949, and was founded by confectioners Joseph Mason and Ernest Von Au in 1864. The company produced Mason Peaks and Mason Mints candies.

11 To Let: Flats

Middagh Street, west of Fulton Street

Note the ad painted across the street from the Peaks Mason sign. It reads "To Let: Flats, James R. Ross & Co. Real Estate." Its age is revealed in its usage: We haven't called apartments "flats" in the U.S. for several decades.

12 Brooklyn Heights Mews

Hunts Lane and Grace Court Alley

Grace Court Alley at Hicks Street, just south of Remsen Street and Hunts Lane on Henry Street between Joralemon and Remsen Streets were originally true mews—yards or streets lined by buildings originally used as stables. After the horseless carriage gained popularity in the first years of the twentieth century, the stables were converted to residences. Hicks Street and Grace Court is also the site of Richard Upjohn's Gothic Grace Church, built from 1847 to 1849.

Love Lane, between Henry and Hicks Streets just north of Pierrepont Street, is what remains of an ancient Indian trail that led down to the East River. Its smaller

Grace Court Alley

tributary, College Place, was named for the long-vanished Brooklyn Collegiate Institute for Young Ladies, which was built nearby on Henry Street in 1822.

13 The Ghostly Gentleman of Clinton Street

169 Clinton Street at State Street

Brooklyn Heights' leafy lanes have been a mecca for renowned literary figures. Most famously, Walt Whitman's *Leaves of Grass* was published on Fulton and Cranberry Streets, and W. H. Auden, Truman Capote, Hart Crane, Norman Mailer, Carson McCullers, Arthur Miller, Henry Miller, and Thomas Wolfe have all lived in the neighborhood.

There was one writer whose time in Brooklyn Heights was most decidedly a depressing period in his life. Howard Phillips (H. P.) Lovecraft (1890–1937), although read mainly by pulp fiction fans in his lifetime, is now considered by some crit-

ics second only to Edgar Allan Poe (whose time in NYC was also less than cheerful) in horror storytelling. His stories imagine a universe rife with hostile forces utterly indifferent to the everyday cares and desires of man. Lovecraft was born in Providence, Rhode Island, and lived most of his life there except for a two-year sojourn here in Brooklyn Heights, which was, at the time, a down-at-heel part of town.

In 1924, Lovecraft would marry in New York and move to his wife Sonia's home in Brooklyn, in an apartment at 259 Parkside Avenue. After a year, they would move to 169 Clinton Street. Sonia then moved to the midwest to set up a business, leaving Lovecraft alone in Brooklyn, which he came to dislike intensely. Born into aristocracy in New England, but subject to increasing poverty due to trouble selling his stories and lack of employment, he disdained New York's maddening crowds. There is more than a hint of racism in his screeds complaining about New York's cosmopolitan makeup, and this resentment asserted itself in two stories he wrote in 1925 during his "exile" in Brooklyn: "He," a story of a mysterious stranger who provokes attacks by spirits of Native Americans, and "The Horror at Red Hook," a lurid story of idol worship. "Red Hook," in particular, reads like an atlas of Brooklyn: protagonist Robert *Suydam*, his wife Cornelia *Gerritsen*, and his dwelling, on *Martense* Street, are all from Brooklyn street names.

Downtown Brooklyn is generally ac-cepted as the commercial strip along Fulton and Livingston Streets and between Boerum Place and Flatbush Avenue. Brooklyn's commercial strip has never actually had a real name; my parents always referred to it as "downtown" when we took our periodic visits on the B37 bus down Third Avenue from Bay Ridge to Fulton Street. It is bordered on the west by Brooklyn Heights, the south by Boerum Hill, and to the east by Fort Greene. It's hard to say exactly where the northern boundary is; there is no precise line of demarcation to distinguish what is in Fort Greene and what's "downtown." I've decided to let the Flatbush Avenue Extension, built in 1909 from Flatbush Avenue and Fulton Street to allow Flatbush Avenue to connect to the Manhattan Bridge, to be the neighborhood arbiter on the north and east.

SUBWAY: ②, ③, ④, or ⑤ to Borough Hall or Nevins Street; ② or ③ to Hoyt Street; Ⓐ, Ⓒ, or Ⓕ to Jay Street–Borough Hall; Ⓐ, Ⓒ, or Ⓖ to Hoyt-Schermerhorn; Ⓜ or Ⓡ to Lawrence or Court Streets

BUS: Many Brooklyn bus routes make

their way here, including the **B25**, **B26**, **B38**, and **B52** along Fulton Street; **B54**, **B57**, **B61**, and **B67** along Jay Street; and **B37**, **B41**, **B45**, and **B67** along Livingston Street. Consult a Brooklyn bus map, available for free from the MTA, for exact routes, or go to www.mta.info.

🚋 14 Fulton Street's Old Department Stores

Fulton Street, between Adams Street and Flatbush Avenue extension

Until the 1970s and 1980s, Fulton Street was home to a number of large department stores, Abraham & Straus, Marshalls, A.I. Namm & Son, Frederick Loeser & Company, E.J. Korvette, and many more. Most of their façades are still there, and if you look closely, their names can still be found right there on the buildings.

a. A&S was begun in 1865 as Wechsler & Abraham—a partnership between dry-goods salesmen Joseph Wechsler and Abraham Abraham. In 1893, Abraham partnered with the Straus family of Macy's fame, which gave the store a new moniker. In the 1990s, A&S was folded into Macy's under the Federated Department Stores banner. The many buildings that comprised A&S are still here on Fulton Street.

b. The impressive wraparound building on Fulton and Lawrence Streets once had its own name, as witness the interlocking letters "OC" on its façade. The store was once known as Oppenheim Collins.

c. Adolph I. Namm opened a dry-goods store in Manhattan in 1876 and moved it to Brooklyn in 1886. Namms was on Fulton Street until 1957; the Namms name is still readily visible on its former

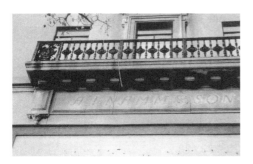

building's façade on Fulton and Hoyt Streets in the outlines of a former sign.

d. Another trace of Fulton Street's department store heritage can be found in the IND Hoyt-Schermerhorn Street subway complex, where you can catch the A, C, or G, but not the L, which here stood for Frederick Loeser & Company department store, which had a number of branches. Loeser's was situated in a block-wide building bounded by Elm Place, Fulton, Bond, and Livingston Streets from the late nineteenth century until the building was sold in 1950.

15 Cadman Plaza
Montague Street north to Middagh Street

Downtown Brooklyn's aspect was changed forever, and Fulton Street lost much of its old personality, when entire blocks just east of it were razed between 1950 and 1960 to make way for Samuel Parkes Cadman Plaza, which served to add green space to downtown Brooklyn. Samuel Parkes Cadman (1864–1936) was a Methodist minister and leader of the Central Congregational Church in Brooklyn from 1901 until his death.

Cadman Plaza provides views of the Manhattan Bridge from the steps of Borough Hall, and allows a vista looking toward the beautiful U.S. Post Office building on Tillary Street. However, there's a kind of forced stillness about Cadman Plaza; it just seems like a plot of green that has been deposited into a neighborhood that didn't really ask for it.

16 Brooklyn Fire Headquarters
Jay Street, north of Willoughby Street

This magnificent double-towered, triple-turreted former fire department headquarters on Jay Street, just north of Willoughby, contrasts with the rather less exuberant office buildings surrounding it. Built in 1892 by Frank Freeman, it is a prime example of the Romanesque Revival movement popular at that time. It is now used as housing for some of the people who were displaced by the construction of MetroTech. The arched doorway once had the words "Fire Headquarters" carved into the stone. The building served as Brooklyn's fire department headquarters for just six years, until Brooklyn consolidated with Manhattan as part of the New York City system. After that, it was New York City's most magnificent firehouse for over eight decades.

17 New York and New Jersey Telephone Company Building
Willoughby Street, near Lawrence Street

It's just another beautiful Beaux Arts building on Willoughby and Lawrence Streets, right? A closer look pays off. The "TC" carved above the door stands for "Telephone Company." This used to be the New York and New Jersey Telephone Company building, built in 1898. Architect Rudolph Daus cleverly designed the structure with telephones carved all over it—the old-fashioned 1898 type. The building contains many cartouches (scroll-like ornaments) and arched windows just below the roof, and a porthole window is accentuated by a portrait of Mercury, the Roman messenger god.

18 Former Gage & Tollner
Fulton Street, near Smith Street

Charles Gage and Eugene Tollner's venerable Brooklyn restaurant at 372-374 Fulton Street, just west of Smith Street, opened in 1879 and had occupied its Fulton Street

brownstone building since 1892. Gage & Tollner was known for its first-class seafood dishes, but over time the restaurant found it harder to attract customers, despite hiring a string of acclaimed chefs. The space is now a T.G.I. Friday's.

A manhole on Atlantic Avenue is the only entrance to an old LIRR tunnel.

19 Atlantic Avenue Tunnel
Below Atlantic Avenue, between Court Street and the East River

Unbeknownst to most, an abandoned Long Island Rail Road tunnel runs for a couple of blocks below Atlantic Avenue in Brooklyn Heights. But this isn't just any tunnel . . . it was abandoned for 140 years with virtually no one knowing about its existence. It was built in 1844, and was used in passenger service for fourteen years, ending in 1859, and was a part of the Long Island Rail Road's main branch, from Brooklyn to the North Fork of Long Island.

By the 1860s, the tunnel had been filled in and pretty much forgotten about, except for an occasional article or two published over the decades. In 1979, rail historian Bob Diamond, then a teenage engineering student, heard a rumor on a radio show that there might be a tunnel under Atlantic Avenue. Diamond scoured through newspapers published in Brooklyn during the nineteenth and early-twentieth centuries, and found an article about the tunnel in the July 23, 1911, *Brooklyn Eagle*. He was able to find the tunnel's only entrance, a manhole cover at Court Street and Atlantic Avenue, and set to work with a group of volunteers to hollow out an entrance to the lengthy underground tunnel.

Diamond formed the Brooklyn Historic Railway Association in 1982 to restore the tunnel. The association won the tunnel a place in the National Register of Historic Places, and the Transit Museum occasionally hosts tours of the tunnel for the public: for information, call (718) 694-1600 or go to www.nycsubway.org.

Fort Greene extends roughly from the
Flatbush Avenue Extension east to Carlton
Avenue, and from Farragut Houses/Brook-
lyn Navy Yard south to Atlantic Avenue.
Clinton Hill runs from Carlton Avenue east
to about the Pratt Institute area at Clas-
son Avenue, where it melts into Bedford-
Stuyvesant; no exact boundaries have been
mapped, and if you live on, say, Adelphi
Street and you want to be considered a
Fort Greener, no one's going to object.

The two neighborhoods play host to architectural marvels, with street after street
lined with brownstone mansions built by
industrialists and other magnates.

SUBWAY: Ⓖ to Fulton Street and Clinton-
Washington Avenue Stations

BUS: B57 or **B69** on Flushing Avenue;
B69 on Vanderbilt Avenue; **B61** on Park
Avenue; **B54** to Myrtle Avenue; **B38** on
DeKalb and Lafayette Avenues; **B52** on
Fulton Street and Greene Avenue

🚌20 Duffield and Concord Streets

*North and east of the Flatbush Avenue
Extension*

Like Vinegar Hill to the north, there's a
pocket of nineteenth-century Brooklyn
wedged between the Manhattan Bridge

approach and the Brooklyn-Queens Expressway, with brownstones, single-family
homes, and tree-lined streets.

On Concord Street, just east of Flatbush
Avenue, there's a small dormered house, a
neat picket fence, and an almost absurdly
small car parked in the front yard. The car
is a Didik Long Ranger, a hybrid gasoline/
electric–powered vehicle designed in the
mid-1980s by Frank Didik, the owner of
both the house and the car. The house itself
is among the oldest in the neighborhood.
It was built in 1762 and is surrounded by a
stone wall dating to about 1820. The house
is rumored to have participated in the Underground Railroad in the pre–Civil War
era.

21 Brooklyn Navy Yard

*Along Flushing Avenue, between Navy
Street and the Brooklyn-Queens Expressway*

The New York Naval Shipyard, also known
as the Brooklyn Navy Yard, stretches along

Flushing Avenue from Navy Street east to the Brooklyn-Queens Expressway. Its entrances are carefully guarded, though walking along Flushing Avenue will give you glimpses of what's inside. Robert Fulton's steam frigate the *Fulton* was built here and launched in 1815, as well as the battleship *Maine* and the first angled-deck aircraft carrier, the *Antietam*.

The Navy Yard at its peak, just before World War II, employed 10,000 workers. It has five miles of paved streets, four dry docks (including the nation's oldest, constructed in the 1840s), two steel shipways, and six pontoons for salvage work. The Navy Yard was decommissioned in 1966 and is now a center for private manufacturing and industrial parks; however, it is still closed to the public.

Sadly, apart from the Commandant's House on the northern end of the complex abutting Vinegar Hill, most of the Navy Yard's old officers' quarters, some dating from the mid- to late-nineteenth century, have been allowed to deteriorate. They look out over Flushing Avenue between Navy Street and Carlton Avenue, their windows ivied and hollow. In 2006 they were slated for demolition.

At the eastern end of the Navy Yard on Flushing Avenue near the Brooklyn-Queens Expressway, you'll find the Brooklyn Navy Motion Picture Exchange. The BNMPE was a depot from which movie prints and projectors were shipped out for entertainment and instruction on ships and at naval bases.

22 Fort Greene Park
Between DeKalb and Myrtle Avenues

Fort Greene Park forms a thirty-acre quadrilateral of green between DeKalb and Myrtle Avenues on the north and south, St. Edward Street and Brooklyn Hospital on the west, and Washington Park on the east. It is named for a fort built in 1776 by Gen-

eral Nathaniel Greene (1742–1786) at what is now the park's central summit.

Walt Whitman, editing the *Brooklyn Daily Eagle* from 1846 to 1848, pressed for a public park in the area, and in 1847, Washington Park, named for the president, began development. Whitman lived nearby, at 99 Ryerson Street, in a building that is still standing.

Washington Park was designed by Olmsted and Vaux, and was officially opened in 1850; in 1897 the park was renamed for Fort Greene. By then, the area had become a handsome residential neighborhood. The two-block stretch of Cumberland Street lining Fort Greene Park's eastern side retains the Washington Park name.

23 Prison Ship Martyrs Monument
Fort Greene Park

During the Revolutionary War, the British anchored eleven prison ships in Wallabout Bay (the body of water west of Williamsburg) and allowed more than 11,000 prisoners to die in their holds.

There were early monuments to those who became known as the "prison ship

martyrs." Some of their remains were buried in the vicinity of the Navy Yard in 1808 and interred in Washington (now Fort Greene) Park in 1873. The current monument, a 148-foot doric column, was designed by McKim, Mead, and White in 1908. The monument originally featured a staircase and an elevator to its summit, where there was a lighted brasier and observation deck. The elevator was broken in the 1930s and was finally removed in the 1970s. The Prison Ship Martyrs Monument, however, remains one of Brooklyn's more striking landmarks, visible from any part of the neighborhood. The remains of the prison ship martyrs are interred under the monument.

24 Signs of a Former Time

Auburn Place, east of St. Edward Street, and Willoughby Avenue, east of Flatbush Avenue

By pure chance, Fort Greene has preserved a couple of key examples of street signage used decades ago.

Mounted on a pole on the north side of Willoughby Street, just west of Ashland Place, is what could be Brooklyn's last humpbacked street sign, a style first

installed in the 1910s. (The "humps" originally showed the cross streets.) The old humpback marks the now-eliminated intersection of Willoughby Street and Hudson Avenue.

Continue down Willoughby Street, then turn left at St. Edward Street, cross Myrtle Avenue past the twin-towered Church of St. Michael and St. Edward and, turning right on Auburn Place, note

the pair of porcelain-coated signs marking the long-gone intersection of Auburn
and North Elliott Places. The porcelains
are slightly more common than the hump-
backs, though less than a dozen remain in
place on Brooklyn streets.

25 Caroline Pratt Ladd House ◅
229 Clinton Avenue

The Caroline Ladd Pratt House is possibly
the choicest of the many luxurious buildings that line Clinton, Washington, and
Vanderbilt Avenues in the Clinton Hill section.

Charles Pratt, the founder of Astral Oil,
made his fortune in kerosene and founded
a prestigious art school, the Pratt Institute.
He built four homes in Clinton Hill as
wedding gifts to his first four sons. Three
remain standing: 229 and 241 Clinton Av-

enue, now the residence of the Bishop of
Brooklyn; and 245 Clinton Avenue, now St.
Joseph's College.

26 Cathedral Preparatory Seminary
Atlantic and Washington Avenues

Cathedral Preparatory Seminary was built
by the Brooklyn Diocese in 1914 and was
originally a seminary where young men
would be trained for the priesthood. It's
a magnificent Flemish Gothic building at
Washington and Atlantic Avenues, with
crosses, gargoyles, and two magnificent
spires. An intimidating iron gate protects
what looks like a moat. It was converted
to residences after the Brooklyn Diocese
closed the Brooklyn campus of Cathedral
Prep in 1985.

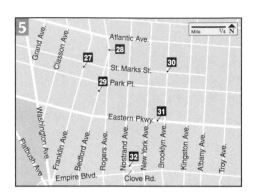

SUBWAY: **B**, **Q**, or **S** to Prospect Park; Franklin Shuttle (**S**) to Prospect Park, Botanic Garden, or Park Place; **3** to Franklin, Nostrand, Kingston, or Crown Heights–Utica Avenues

BUS: **B41** on Flatbush Avenue; **B43** on Empire Boulevard; **B45** on Washington Avenue, Sterling Place, or St. John's Place; **B48** on Classon and Franklin Avenues; **B49** on Bedford and Rogers Avenues

Prospect Heights, on the eastern side of Prospect Park, is a handsome mix of brownstone buildings, along with row and carriage houses built after the park was completed. The southern end of the district is known as Lefferts Gardens, named for the Lefferts family whose ancestral home still stands in Prospect Park just off Flatbush Avenue. James Lefferts sold 600 lots of the family's land to developers in 1894, but stipulated that single-family residences had to be built there, according to a specific set of designs and materials. The legacy of these restrictions is one of Brooklyn's finest residential neighborhoods.

Crown Heights is clustered along Eastern Parkway between Bedford and Albany Avenues. It is on high ground relative to surrounding regions, hence its name, and was first settled by Dutch farmers in the mid-1600s. After Olmsted and Vaux completed Eastern Parkway that ran through the area, limestone houses and elegant mansions began to appear, many of which remain. Crown Heights today is home to sizable Lubavitcher Hasidic and Caribbean populations. West Indians make the annual Labor Day parade along the parkway a must-see celebration.

27 Franklin Shuttle

West of Franklin Avenue, between Fulton Street and Montgomery Street

The Franklin Shuttle is a subway line the MTA allowed to deteriorate for decades. It's also the site of the worst subway accident in the 100-year history of the system, and it runs past breweries, industrial sites, and hospitals it has long outlived.

The Shuttle is a remnant of the Brooklyn, Flatbush, and Coney Island Railroad, first operated in 1877 from downtown to Coney Island. Over the years, the BF&CI was incorporated into Brooklyn's network of elevated railroads. New York City's worst subway crash, the Malbone Street Wreck, occurred near Prospect Park in 1918. Intriguing remnants of the line's past as an at-grade railroad can be found along the route.

a. On Prospect Place, one of the old utility poles that carried electric power on the old Brighton Beach Railroad stands just east of the trestle. Just inside the fence next to the pole, ancient tracks that are likely the last remnants of the old Brooklyn, Flatbush and Coney Island Railroad can be seen.

b. At Park Place, the street dips below street level; here the Shuttle begins a slow descent into an open cut to join the Brighton Line. Between Sterling and Park Places, the Shuttle makes its upward journey on a ramp that had connected it to the old Fulton Street El. When the grade crossing was eliminated in 1905, Park Place was depressed to allow traffic to continue uninterrupted. This placed the roadbed as much as three feet under the sidewalk, so steps and railings were built to allow entrance and exit to the street. When the station was rebuilt in the 1990s, the street underneath it wasn't touched: the 1905-era steps are crumbling away and their railings are in a rusty, collapsing condition. Some of the staircases retain their original 1905 fencing.

c. The hastily erased words "Consumers Park Brewery" can still be found on the massive brick building along Franklin Avenue south of Montgomery Street. The brewery was in business between 1897 and about 1920. Ebbets Field stood one block east of the brewery from 1913 to its demolition in 1960.

28 U. S. Grant
Bedford and Rogers Avenues

While President Ulysses S. Grant, an Ohioan by birth, is entombed on Manhattan's Upper West Side, his most striking memorial is here in Prospect Heights. William Partridge's 1896 bronze equestrian statue stands in a triangle surrounded by striking architecture: the Imperial Apartments with its Corinthian columns at 1198 Pacific

Street on Bedford Avenue, and the 1890 Union League Club, now a senior citizens center, at Bedford and Dean Streets (look closely for stone portraits of Lincoln and Grant in the spaces between the arches).

29 Studebaker Showroom
Bedford Avenue and Sterling Place

This neo-Gothic masterpiece at 1469 Bedford Avenue is one of the great former Studebaker showrooms scattered around town. It was built in 1920 by architectural firm Tooker and Marsh. The distinctive Studebaker script and wagon-wheel logo are prominent on the corner façade.

30 Brooklyn Children's Museum
Brooklyn and St. Mark's Avenues

Before 1899, there were no museums in the world devoted to kids. The Brooklyn Children's Museum at 145 Brooklyn Avenue was incorporated in that year and occupied the former William Newton Adams House on St. Mark's Avenue, and then the L. C. Smith Mansion next door until 1967,

BROOKLYN

when the buildings were demolished. The present facility opened in 1977 and occupies the space below Brower Park, with 15,000 feet of exhibition space, due to expand to 102,000 feet after a renovation by Rafael Viñoly.

31 Eastern Parkway

Between Washington and Utica Avenues

Eastern Parkway runs east from Grand Army Plaza at Flatbush Avenue, and forms the dividing line between Crown Heights and Bedford-Stuyvesant. The grand parkway was conceived as a twin of Olmsted and Vaux's Ocean Parkway, featuring two wide greenways running parallel to the main roadway, originally serving horses and carriages.

The architects originally envisioned that Eastern Parkway would be a link in a chain of grand boulevards and parks, like the Baron Haussmann plan in Paris. But on Eastern Parkway, the greenery ends at Ralph Avenue, while the roadway continues northeast on the Eastern Parkway Extension to Brooklyn's Broadway, built later when automobiles replaced carriages.

32 Malboneville

Clove Road and Malbone Street

After the Malbone Street subway wreck in 1918, the city decided to rename Malbone Street to expunge the horrible memory of the crash, and so it was rechristened Empire Boulevard, after New York City's namesake, the Empire State.

In so doing, a link to area history was severed. Malbone Street, when laid out in the 1830s, ran through Malboneville, named for its prominent founder, Ralph Malbone, a downtown Fulton Street grocer who became wealthy through real estate speculation. He bought land along Clove Road, an old road that in the Colonial era stretched from the heart of the village of Bedford at the Brooklyn and Jamaica Turnpike (now straightened as part of Fulton Street) and Cripplebush Road (now Bedford Avenue) and ran south and west, joining Flatbush Turnpike (Flatbush Avenue) at what is now Lincoln Road.

A glimpse of old Malboneville can still be seen just east of the busy intersection of Nostrand Avenue and Empire Boulevard. Here, Clove Road *still* intersects Malbone Street. This is a small, two-block section of Clove Road, which in the 1800s was a busy stagecoach route to southern Brooklyn. A tiny, one-block stretch of Malbone Street is still here because it was isolated when the rest of the street was straightened in the early 1900s.

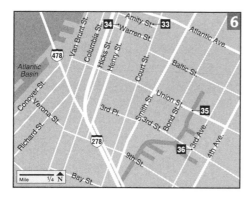

Cobble Hill, Boerum Hill, Carroll Gar-dens, and Gowanus are neighborhoods south of Atlantic Avenue, from Third Avenue west to the East River, and north of the Gowanus Expressway and Gowanus Canal. These neighborhoods feature block after block of Brooklyn's most expressive and diverse residential architecture. Cobble Hill is Brooklyn's second-largest Italian-American enclave (after Bensonhurst), while emerging Gowanus, closest to its namesake's canal, is the former haven of the Mohawk Indians who worked on Manhattan's skyscrapers from the 1930s to the 1960s and beyond.

Boerum Hill lost just a bit of its quirkiness in 2003, when the last of artist Jerry Johnson's tongue-in-cheek public service advertisements at Nevins and Atlantic Avenues were painted over. Past Johnson billboards touted the importance of insisting on plates while dining out, and suggested that one should "dress right to get a better shake out of life." Smith Street has seen a rapid influx of swank bistros but, thankfully, much of its local flavor hasn't been sacrificed.

SUBWAY: F or **G** to Bergen or Carroll Streets

BUS: B75 on Court and Smith Streets; **B71** on Union and Sackett Streets; **B61** on Columbia Street

 **33 Jennie Jerome**
197 Amity Street

Two houses in Cobble Hill claim to have been the birthplace of Jennie Jerome (1854–1921), the mother of British statesman Winston Churchill. Her true birthplace, 197 Amity Street, is unmarked, though its residents report that a plaque is planned, while a house at 426 Henry Street has a marker that claims it to be her home. The building at 426 Henry Street *does* have a Jerome family connection: Her parents, Leonard and Clara, lived there *before* the woman who would be known as Lady Randolph Churchill was born. Her father was financier Leonard Jerome, who organized the American Jockey Club and built the Jerome Park Racetrack in Kingsbridge Heights in the Bronx in 1865.

Jennie Jerome was a magazine editor in an age when few "respectable" women worked, and, interestingly, had a tattoo of a snake around her left wrist. She wedded three times; her first marriage to Lord Randolph Spencer Churchill in 1874, whom she met on a visit to Britain, produced Winston and his brother, John.

BROOKLYN

34 Workingmen's Cottages

between Warren Place and Baltic Streets, east of Hicks

Warren Place, just east of the BQE, dates from an era when new, fashionable housing was actually built for people not necessarily of well-to-do status.

The Warren Place Workingmen's Cottages were financed by Alfred Tredway White in 1878. Twenty-six of forty-four brick cottages face Warren Place, a narrow pedestrian walkway. White was a firm believer in building low-cost model housing and was instrumental in the founding of the Brooklyn Botanic Garden. The cottages are twenty-four feet high, but only eleven feet wide and thirty-two feet deep. White also conceived the delicately balconied Tower Apartments next door that front on Hicks Street and the BQE.

35 Carroll Street Bridge

Crossing Gowanus Canal

The Carroll Street Bridge spanning the increasingly less-toxic Gowanus Canal is one of just four retractile bridges remaining in the U.S., and is one of Brooklyn's oldest, having been built in 1889 by the Brooklyn Department of City Works. In a retractile bridge, two sections roll on wheels set on steel rails and pull away, or retract, from each other, opening the bridge to allow shipping to pass.

In a rare moment of levity, the Department of Transportation has preserved the message of an original sign posted when the Carroll Street Bridge opened in 1889. It says, "Any person driving over this bridge faster than a walk will be subject to a penalty of five dollars for each offense." Of course, the sign originally referred to the drivers of horses.

36 Third and Third: Litchfield's Improvement

Third Avenue and 3rd Street

At the corner of Third Avenue and Third Street in Gowanus is a magnificent little building with ornate trimmings and ionic columns by the door. It was designed in 1872 by William Field for a concrete manufacturer and later became the headquarters of the Brooklyn Improvement Company, founded by Edwin Litchfield for the express purpose of dredging the Gowanus Creek. Litchfield owned much of the property between here and Prospect Park and built, with the aid of architect Alexander Davis, an Italian-style villa at what would become Prospect Park West and Fifth Street in 1854.

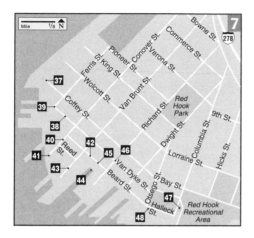

Red Hook is undergoing a major face-lift. Damaged and decrepit housing is being rehabilitated and new construction is already underway. At this writing, a new Fairway supermarket had opened as well as new piers for cruise ship lines. Red Hook presents many different faces: its industrial and shipyarded waterfront, its side streets with modest brick and frame homes, its empty lots, and the nearby hum of the Brooklyn-Queens Expressway.

SUBWAY: None. **B77** bus is available from the Smith–9th Street Station (**F** or **G**)

BUS: B61 on Van Brunt Street; **B77** on Lorraine, Coffey, and Van Dyke Streets

37 Louis Valentino, Jr. Pier
Coffey Street, west of Ferris Street

From old Pier 39 at the foot of Coffey Street, Red Hook residents enjoy a great view of the Statue of Liberty. Rebuilt in the late 1990s,

Upper New York Bay, New Jersey, Governors Island, and lower Manhattan are also well in view. Louis Valentino, Jr. Pier is named for a heroic firefighter who sustained fatal injuries in a Canarsie blaze in 1996.

38 Unusual Pavement
Van Dyke Street, between Conover and Ferris Streets

Some paving stones can be found in the pavement on Van Dyke Street between Conover and Ferris Streets, where the concrete has worn away. Strangely it seems to have been laid purposely in semicircles. My guess is that the workmen, kneeling down to pave the street back in the 1800s, bricked the streets as far as they could reach . . . forcing them to work in a circle.

Pier 41 viewed from Conover Street

39 Pier 41
Van Dyke Street, near Conover Street

Pier 41, also known as the Merchant Stores, was developed by Daniel Richards as a shipping and warehousing center in the late 1870s. For many years it was home to Morgan Soda, which distributed the White Rock brand. Presently, Pier 41 is home to Flickinger Glassworks and the famed Steve's Authentic Key Lime Pies. It's best seen from the new pocket park facing the water at Conover and Reed Streets.

BROOKLYN

40 Sunny's Bar ➤
Conover Street, near Reed Street

Sunny Balzano's bar on Conover Street between Beard and Reed Streets has been a Red Hook waterfront institution for three generations. As the Red Hook docks became silent when the shipping industry moved across the harbor to New Jersey, Sunny and his uncle John discovered that a new clientele of artists and musicians from nearby Williamsburg was coming to the bar. After John passed away in 1994, Sunny ran it as a nonprofit club featuring musicians and local performers, opening Friday nights only, though after acquiring a new liquor license and renovating the bar, Sunny has been able to open a couple more nights a week. It's well worth a visit to evoke memories of Red Hook's maritime past.

For information and hours call (718) 624-4719 or consult www.waterfrontmuseum.org.

41 Hudson Waterfront Museum
Conover and Reed Streets

At the end of Conover Street, you'll find Lehigh Valley Railroad Barge #79, a 30' × 90' railroad barge built in 1914 with a wood exterior, the last of its kind still in existence. During New York's era as a world-class port, it transported goods across the harbor. Maryland native David Sharps rescued Barge #79 in 1985 after it had been abandoned in eight feet of mud near Edgewater, New Jersey; it took eight years of toil to make it seaworthy. Since 1994, it's been a maritime museum and classroom, and a home for art, exhibition, and concert space, as well as a center for parties and weddings.

42 Beard Street Warehouse Pier
Beard Street, near Van Brunt Street

The Brooklyn waterfront, from Greenpoint to Red Hook, was an incredibly bustling shipping area for over a century, with warehouses employing thousands of workers. Only a few of the old warehouses remain: the Arbuckle brothers' Empire Stores in DUMBO and the buildings here at the end of Van Brunt Street.

The brick structures between Van Brunt and Conover Streets west of Reed Street, known collectively as the Beard Street Warehouse, were built by William Beard and Jeremiah and George Robinson in 1869.

The seven-and-a-half-acre Beard Street Warehouse complex consists of twenty-one attached structures built from Manhattan schist salvaged from railroad projects and the Montague Street grading and paving, as well as ballast stones from European vessels. One story has it that the enterprising Beard would charge the ships 50 cents per cubic yard to empty their stones into the nearby basin before taking on cargo for a return trip.

The warehouse contains dozens of individual "stores" that have housed an incredible variety of businesses, including ad agencies, costume designers, and medical-supply distributors. Its public harbor esplanade has recently been shored up and once again provides magnificent views of the harbor. Check out its indoor walkway for tantalizing glimpses of the beehive-like activity within.

43 Red Hook/Van Brunt Stores
480 Van Brunt Street

This historic warehouse built by William Beard in the 1860s has become an artists' colony, with a number of galleries run under the umbrella of the Brooklyn Working Artists Coalition, which you can visit at www.bwac.org. Each May, the pier is the site of the Waterfront Arts Festival. The building is divided into sections by 12- to 16-inch thick brick walls and is supported by massive, square, yellow pine posts supporting heavy girders. Its interior is fascinating not only for the art shows, but as a representation of unaltered Civil War–era construction.

 44 Lightship *84*
Off the Beard Street Pier

The New York Water Taxi landing at Beard and Richards Streets provides a glimpse of Lightship *84*, or rather, just its two masts— the ship sunk in 1997, a victim of neglect.

Lightship *84* was built in 1907 in New Jersey, and did its duty replacing the lighthouse at the St. John's River in northeast Florida beginning in 1929. The 135-foot vessel later served lightship patrol in New York harbor until 1965. Since then, it has served as a floating school in Maryland,

The huge dome of the Revere Sugar Refinery's granary and the masts of the sunken Lightship 84 show a glimpse of Red Hook's wonderful strangeness.

was purchased by the *Intrepid* Sea, Air & Space Museum, and was sold again to developers intending to refit it as a restaurant, but those plans fell through. By 1997, the lightship, which had never had its leaks fully repaired, sunk into the waters of Erie Basin. In recent years, Lightship *84* has been an unofficial training site for police scuba divers.

45 Revere Sugar Refinery
Beard Street, between Van Brunt and Richards Streets

The Revere Sugar Refinery's huge domed granary can be seen from all over the neighborhood. The company, once owned by Antonio Floriendo, known as the "Banana King of the Philippines," declared bankruptcy in 1985, and the refinery has been idle since. The refinery is best seen from the Beard Street Pier, accessible by a short walk from Beard and Reed Streets.

46 Brooklyn Clay Retort and Fire Brick Works ➤
Richards and Van Dyke Streets

This long, low building on the corner of Richards and Van Dyke Streets has a distinctive exterior, consisting of 20-inch-thick stones, reminiscent of some churches. It was originally the storehouse of the Joseph K. Brick Company, founded in 1854

to produce items used in gaslighting. Brick originated the fire clay retort, a device used to produce gas used for illumination. The structure was restored in 1996 and was the first designated landmark building in Red Hook.

47 Grain Elevator Terminal
Columbia Street, near Halleck Street

This massive concrete silo, built in 1922 at Columbia and Halleck Streets, was once the processing center for grains used for breweries and distilleries. The terminal closed when shipping in Red Hook gave way to New Jersey containerization beginning in the 1950s. With its fifty-four joined concrete silos, it has been described as looking like "concrete ladyfingers." Today, the soccer field in front of the terminal has

it as an impressive backdrop, dance companies have used it as a staging area, and it's been used as scenery in movie shoots. It's best viewed from the field at Columbia and Bay Streets.

48 Todd Shipyards
Halleck Street, between Otsego and Columbia Streets

The Todd Shipyards, also known as New York Shipyards, front along Beard and Halleck Streets west of Columbia and contain the largest dry dock on the East Coast; they now stand idle. The *Monitor*, the first ironclad vessel from the Civil War era, was repaired here. In the mid-2000s, demolition of the Shipyards commenced so that an Ikea branch could be built in its place.

Williamsburg presents many faces, from immigrants' homes featured in *A Tree Grows in Brooklyn* . . . to a heavily industrial and abandoned waterfront . . . to a Hasidic community . . . to a mix of artists, hipsters, and Polish families. Teddy's Bar & Grill on Berry Street is one of Brooklyn's oldest taverns, while new clubs and restaurants have sprung up along Bedford Avenue and side streets. Grand plans to transform the waterfront area with new parks and housing may wash away the present riverfront wasteland.

SUBWAY: Ⓛ to Bedford Avenue or Lorimer Street

BUS: B61 (to Bedford, Driggs, or Wythe Avenues); **B59** to Grand Street and Kent Avenue; **B44** to Bedford and Lee Avenues; **B39** from Delancey Street, Lower East Side, across Williamsburg Bridge to Washington Plaza at South 5th Street)

49 Williamsburg Houses
Between Leonard Street and Bushwick Avenue, north of Scholes Street

Public-housing projects usually disappoint; they tend to be depressing and dismal buildings without personality. Some, like Stuyvesant Town or Parkchester, rise above the rest, and then there's a very special case in Williamsburg.

Williamsburg Houses, occupying twelve blocks and approximately twenty-three acres between Maujer Street on the north, Scholes Street on the south, Leonard Street on the west, and Bushwick Avenue on the east, was one of the very first housing projects built in NYC, completed in 1938 before the more typical "boxes-in-a-park" pattern took hold. The apartment buildings were constructed by the Williamsburg Associated Architects, which comprised Richmond Shreve (a member of the team that designed the Empire State Building) and Swiss architect William Lescaze, in a streamlined "International" style. The Williamsburg Houses pioneered the "superblock" concept, as Stagg and Ten Eyck Streets were truncated and their roadbeds given over to pedestrian traffic. Never before had streets been closed to accommodate housing.

50 The City Reliquary ➤
307 Grand Street at Havemeyer Street

Dave Herman's collection of NYC artifacts he calls The City Reliquary began to take shape in 2004 when he, with the indulgence of his landlord, painted directions to local Williamsburg attractions on this building. Then, using the building's former corner storefront with glass display cases on two sides, he added some interesting and offbeat historical artifacts, including:

BROOKLYN

- A pair of "devil's nuts," an aquatic fruit found in the Hudson River. The nuts, named for their two-horned appearance, are edible and turn up in some ethnic food shops.
- Metalwork salvaged from the Williamsburg Bridge's extensive renovations begun in the 1980s (and still ongoing).
- A stone removed from Fort Greene Park in preparation for the construction of the Prison Ship Martyrs Monument in 1908.
- A plate numbered "7843," originally on an R-26 subway car that plied the IRT as early as 1959, and a metal strap from the same car.

Dave also has an eclectic collection of material that won't fit in the store windows but takes up space in his basement, including a life-size dancing hula girl mannequin, old typewriters, subway maps, and Pez dispensers. Dave and the City Reliquary opened a storefront in nearby 370 Metropolitan Avenue in 2006.

51 Domino Sugar Plant ⋎
Kent Avenue and Grand Street

According to local legend, when the recently shuttered sugar refinery was humming, the smell of caramelized sugar could be detected all over the neighborhood. The plant, prominently seen from the J, M, or Z trains on the Williamsburg Bridge, shut down in 2004 after about 150 years in business. The red neon Domino sign will likely be removed and the building's future remains unknown.

52 Williamsburg Art and Historical Center ➤
Broadway and Bedford Avenue

The former Kings County Savings Bank built in 1867 is now one of the focal points for Williamsburg's burgeoning art community, but it's a uniquely handsome struc-

detail like the stylized "KC" and "SB" on the door and the coral-shaped decorative stonework.

53 Williamsburg Savings Bank Dome
Broadway and Driggs Avenue

At Broadway and Driggs is the gorgeous green-and-white dome of the Williamsburg Savings Bank, built between 1870 and 1875 by George Post. The bank is unfortunately marred by the overbearing signage of its current owner, HSBC.

54 Williamsburg Trust Company
South Fifth Street and Driggs Avenue

One more beautiful domed building can be found at Driggs Avenue and South Fifth Street: the Williamsburg Trust Company, built in 1905 by Helmle and Huberty. It is now a Greek Orthodox church, and its whiteness dazzles in the sun. Across the street, Henry Shrady's statue of George Washington depicts him on horseback at Valley Forge. He appears cold and weary, yet determined.

ture in its own right. Architectural critic Francis Morrone has called it "probably the finest Second Empire–style building in Brooklyn." Second Empire architecture, so-called because it arose during the "second empire" of Louis Napoleon in France, features sloped mansard roofs. Look for the recently revealed "KC Savings Bank" lettering on the roof, as well as incredible

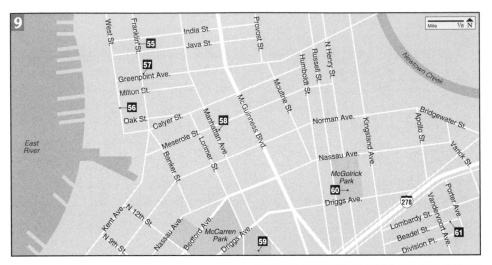

Greenpoint, called the "garden spot of Brooklyn" by the *Brooklyn Eagle* many years ago, rests at the borough's northernmost point. Queens' Long Island City is just a short skip over Newtown Creek. This Polish/Hispanic community has a magnificent manufacturing past: it was a former center for printing, petroleum refining, and iron and glass making. The firm that became Corning got its start here.

Wander through Greenpoint's streets, especially Manhattan, Nassau, and Meserole Avenues, for Polish delicacies, and don't miss the magnificent Gothic St. Anthony of Padua Church, with its 240-foot spire at Manhattan Avenue and Milton Street.

SUBWAY: Ⓖ to Nassau or Greenpoint Avenue

BUS: **B61** or **B43** on Manhattan Avenue; **B24** on Greenpoint Avenue

55 Astral Apartments

Franklin Street, between Java and India Streets

This handsome, distinctive apartment building was built by Charles Pratt as living quarters for workers at his Astral Oil Works. The company's slogan was, "The holy lamps of Tibet are primed with Astral Oil." The family founded Pratt Institute, one of NYC's most prestigious art schools, in Clinton Hill.

The Astral takes up the entire frontage on Franklin Street and has nearly a hundred apartments. Its distinctive three-sided bays, arched entrances, and recessed arch reaching the fifth floor are rare features. A center courtyard admits air and light to all apartments that don't have a street-side exposure. According to legend, actress/comedienne Mae West was born here.

₰ 56 The Desolation of West Street

Between Milton and Oak Streets

In a few short Greenpoint blocks, you can take in gentility, gentrification, and desolation. The Greenpoint Terminal Warehouse on West Street between Milton and Oak was a tangled mass of nineteenth-century industrial loft buildings bridged by rusting, deteriorating overpasses; it burned down in a ten-alarm fire in May 2006. One remnant can be found on West Street, lined on both sides by sidewalks composed of wooden blocks. As far as I know, NYC has no other remaining wooden-blocked sidewalks.

57 Eberhard Faber Pencils

Greenpoint Avenue at Franklin Street

Eberhard Faber, the scion of a Bavarian pencil-producing family, arrived in the U.S. from Germany in 1848, and after his first Manhattan factory burned down in 1861, he relocated the business to Greenpoint in 1872. The Faber company finally moved to Pennsylvania in 1956. The man-

ufacturer is recalled by a large sign facing the East River painted on its original building at 37 Greenpoint Avenue at West Street, and by the huge yellow terra-cotta pencils on its newer Art Deco building next door. The former pencil factory itself on Franklin Street is recognizable by a distinctive yellow star-in-diamond symbol.

58 Bomelstein's Clock

Manhattan Avenue near Meserole Avenue

Bomelstein's Clock was in ruins for many years, but it has since been restored and is telling time once again. The old Bomelstein name has been removed, however, since the jeweler moved out many years ago.

59 McCarren Park Pool

Driggs Avenue and Lorimer Street

Opened as a Works Progress Administration project in 1936, the McCarren Park Pool in Greenpoint, Brooklyn, was the last of eleven pools built in New York City during the Depression. Mayor La Guardia, at its opening-day dedication noted that "no pool anywhere has been as much appreciated as this one." Unfortunately, no one has actually swum here since 1984. In 2005, the pool was cleaned up and is now used as a performance space.

McCarren Park itself was developed between 1903 and 1905, and is named for Patrick McCarren, state legislator and Williamsburg Bridge promoter in the late nineteenth century. Just outside McCarren Park is the magnificently onion-domed

BROOKLYN

Russian Orthodox Cathedral of the Transfiguration, on Driggs Avenue and North Twelfth Street, built by architect Louis Allmendinger between 1916 and 1921.

60 Monsignor McGolrick Park

Driggs Avenue and Russell Street

This park, bounded by Russell and Monitor Streets and Nassau and Driggs Avenues, was originally named Winthrop Park, but was renamed in 1941 for a beloved pastor of nearby St. Cecilia's Church, Msgr. Edward McGolrick. The park contains a crescent-shaped shelter pavilion designed in 1910 by famed architectural firm Helmle and Huberty, as well as two magnificent monuments: a striking bronze memorial to Greenpointers who served in World War I, sculpted in 1923 by Carl Heber, and the John Ericsson monument by sculptor Antonio de Filippo, dedicated in 1938. Engineer Ericsson built the *Monitor*, the U.S.'s first ironclad vessel, at Greenpoint's Continental Iron Works in 1861. The vessel engaged the Confederate states' *Merrimac* at Hampton Roads in 1862.

61 Brownstone Haven

Beadel Street, between Vandervoort and Porter Avenues

It's a hike but it's worth it. From the subway station at Nassau and Manhattan Avenues, strike off east on Nassau, using willpower to avoid the ethnic delis jammed with mouthwatering kielbasas. Walk through Monsignor McGolrick Park, then bear south on Kingsland Avenue until you're in an absolute no-man's-land of industry. Avoiding the junkyard dogs, turn left on Beadel Street, head east two blocks, and cross Vandervoort Avenue. You will find one block of the tidiest, neatest, most well-maintained brownstone and brick buildings you could ever hope to see—an oasis in this land of tractor trailers. The massive KeySpan Gas Works lies just behind this brief respite.

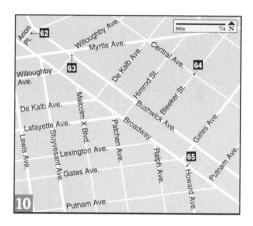

Bushwick became a neighborhood of stately churches and mansions built for brewers and other professionals in the mid-nineteenth century, but during the 1977 blackout, much of the neighborhood was burned and looted. After recent stabilization took place, Bushwick and its immediate neighbor to the northeast, Ridgewood, are now quite similar with block after block of well-kept, uniform attached houses. But today, the two neighborhoods maintain a strict independence from each other.

Until the 1920s, the Brooklyn-Queens border cut in a straight line through streets, homes, and, in some cases, living rooms. NYC then drew up a zigzag border to remedy the situation. Today, Ridgewood is in Queens, and Bushwick is in Brooklyn.

SUBWAY: **J**, **M** to Flushing Avenue, Myrtle Avenue, Kosciusko Street, or Gates Avenue; **L** to Jefferson Street, DeKalb Avenue, or Myrtle–Wyckoff Avenues; **M** to Myrtle Avenue, Seneca Avenue, Forest Avenue, or Fresh Pond Road

BUS: **B13** or **B57** to Flushing Avenue; **B38** on DeKalb and Seneca Avenues; **Q54** on Metropolitan Avenue; **B46**, **B47**, or **Q24** on Broadway

62 Arion Mannerchor
Arion Place, near Broadway

On Arion Place near Broadway is the hulk of the old Arion Hall, home of the Arion Society, Bushwick's foremost German singing society. It later became a mansion and then a catering hall, but these days, it's something of a handyman's project. The building is rich with detail of its musical past with German initials at the very top and lyre-shaped ironwork on the fire escapes.

63 Dr. Cook and the Bushwick Avenue Mansions
Bushwick and Willoughby Avenues

Was Dr. Frederick A. Cook the first explorer to reach the North Pole? Or was he, as some detractors assert, a fake? After Cook returned to the U.S. in 1909, the public in New York City seemed to fall squarely in the pro-Cook camp. Ultimately, Cook lost in court to Admiral Robert Perry, who is

BROOKLYN

Cook Mansion

now recognized as the first to discover the North Pole. Cook's mansion and several others survive along Bushwick Avenue.

a. Cook lived in a now-abandoned mansion at 670 Bushwick Avenue at Willoughby Avenue. It originally belonged to William Ulmer, whose brewery still stands on Beaver Street between Locust and Belvidere Streets, a few blocks to the northwest.

b. The residence at 959 Bushwick, one in a row of brownstones, was home to John Hylan, NYC mayor from 1918 to 1925.

c. At 1001 Bushwick Avenue is a recently restored shingle-style home, built for a Charles Lindemann in 1890. A short walk to 1080 Greene Avenue and Goodwin Place reveals a deteriorated ruin with many of its original features.

d. Of all Bushwick's streets, Linden Street is particularly gracious. The crenellation on the mansard roof at the northwest corner at Bushwick Avenue has been allowed to remain, while the town houses in the Queen Anne style on the north side of Linden have their original iron fences.

64 St. Barbara's
Central Avenue and Bleecker Street

St. Barbara's Church ranks among Brooklyn's tallest buildings; its gleaming white spires can be spotted throughout Bushwick. It was named for the daughter of brewer Leonard Eppig, and built by the Parfitt Brothers architectural firm between 1888 and 1892. The only brownstone church in Brooklyn, it originally boasted Tiffany stained-glass windows, but those were replaced in 1914 with windows by Alexander Locke.

65 RKO Bushwick
Howard Avenue and Broadway

When you get off the El at the Gates Avenue Station at Broadway, you have only to walk up the street about a block or so to be transported back to a time when showbiz

was really *showbiz* . . . a time when entertainment meant more than just a movie and an overpriced candy bar. That's because the proud, old RKO Bushwick Theatre is still standing at the triangular corner of Broadway and Howard Avenue.

The 2,000-seat theater's exterior features a flock of terra-cotta trumpeting angels, with the initial "B" festooned with musical instruments on the corner entrance. It was built by showman Percy Williams with William McElfatrick as architect, and first opened as a vaudeville house on September 11, 1911. The Bushwick later became part of the RKO organization, but it showed its last picture in 1969 and stood in ruin for more than three decades, until its interior was completely rebuilt for the ACORN High School for Social Justice in 2003. Its rococo exterior was mostly preserved in the renovation.

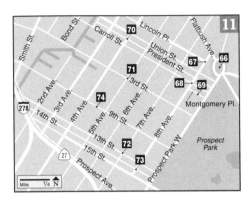

ment, needs no introduction, but there are a couple of tidbits about it that you may not have known. It has a working elevator, for example, and there are two reliefs on each side of the arch by artists William O'Donovan and Thomas Eakins: one of Ulysses S. Grant and another of Abraham Lincoln that is said to be the only known portrait of Lincoln on horseback. General William Tecumseh Sherman laid the cornerstone in 1889 and the arch was completed in 1892.

Park Slope, literally a sloped neighbor-hood next to a park, features an amazing collection of attached brownstone buildings that are meticulously maintained by their owners. In most cases, no two are the same, and where they are, you don't mind, since they come from an era when craftsmanship was paramount in the consideration of what constituted a livable space. There are buildings here from the Victorian era that are mini-castles in their execution. While it is one of the most chronicled of Brooklyn's neighborhoods, there are a few features here that have missed being captured by its admirers.

SUBWAY: ② or ③ to Bergen Street, Grand Army Plaza, or Eastern Parkway–Brooklyn Museum; 🄵 to 4th Avenue–9th Street, 7th Avenue, or 15th Street–Prospect Park

BUS: **B41** or **B67** on Flatbush Avenue; **B63** on Fifth Avenue; **B65** on Bergen Street; **B67** on Seventh Avenue; **B69** to Eighth Avenue and Prospect Park West; **B71** on Union Street; **B75** on 9th Street

b. The top of the monument depicts Columbia, an allegorical symbol of America, riding triumphantly in a four-horse chariot known as a quadriga. Frederick MacMonnies created stylistic, semi-realistic battle scenes depicting the Army and Navy on each side of the arch.

66 Lincoln on Horseback and Other Grand Army Plaza Sights

Soldiers and Sailors Monument, Flatbush Avenue and Eastern Parkway

a. The triumphant arch at Grand Army Plaza, the Soldiers and Sailors Monu-

c. Inside the oval of Grand Army Plaza, note the 1932 Bailey Fountain sculpted by Eugene Savage, the fourth fountain to be built in this spot. It depicts

a rather annoyed-looking Neptune surrounded by conch-blowing mermen and sculpted representations of Wisdom and Felicity.

Grand Army Plaza

At the park entrance is Frederick MacMonnies' bronze depiction of James Stranahan. Prospect Park is, in good part, the brainchild of railroad builder Stranahan, who headed a board of commissioners selected by New York state in 1859 to investigate areas to build a public park in Brooklyn similar to Manhattan's Central Park.

Scattered around Grand Army Plaza are these other memorials:

a. Henry Baerer's 1896 rendering of General Gouverneur Warren. He holds a pair of binoculars, as befits this army engineer known for fortifying Little Round Top at the Battle of Gettysburg against Robert E. Lee in July 1863.

b. NYC's only public memorial bust depicting a gynecologist, Dr. Alexander Skene, a president of Long Island College Hospital from 1893 to 1899 and inventor of thirty-one surgical instru-

ments. The bust by sculptor J. Massey Rhind was placed here in 1905.

c. A small relief, sculpted by Augustus Saint-Gaudens, on a boulder dedicated to Henry Maxwell, another former president of Long Island College Hospital; he also served as Brooklyn Park Commissioner in 1884.

d. MacMonnies' equestrian study of General Henry Slocum. The general commanded forces at Bull Run and Gettysburg and took part in Sherman's March to the Sea.

67 Montauk Club
Eighth Avenue and Lincoln Place

The Montauk Club is a slice of Victoriana that would be pretentious if it weren't so enjoyable and fun to view when walking past. The club itself was established in 1889 as a "gentleman's social club." A plaque at the front entrance describes its 1891 building as modeled by architect Francis Kimball after the Ca' d'Oro in Venice. There is a lengthy frieze above the third floor depicting the "exploits of the Montauk Indians," as the plaque puts it, in terra-cotta. On the second floor arch, you'll find another frieze showing the club's founders laying the cornerstone. The club occupies only the lower two floors, while co-op apartments occupy the others. The Montauk Club has an open house the first Friday of each month: call (718) 638-0800 or visit www.montauk-club.com for details.

BROOKLYN

68 Thomas Adams House

Eighth Avenue and Carroll Street

In the 1860s, exiled Mexican President Antonio López de Santa Anna stayed with a photographer named Thomas Adams in Staten Island. Santa Anna suggested that Adams might be able to make a fortune off chicle, a gummy substance Mexicans had been extracting from sapote trees and chewing for centuries. Santa Anna believed the chicle could be combined with rubber to make better carriage tires, but that turned out not to be true. After a year, Adams was stuck with a warehouse full of chicle and was bewildered about what to do with it: Then he remembered what Santa Anna had mentioned about chewing it.

By 1888, Adams was wealthy enough from the manufacture of chewing gum to commission C. P. H. Gilbert to build a grand Romanesque house on Eighth Avenue and Carroll Street. Its entrance arch is reminiscent of the Astral Apartments in Greenpoint, but this one is more intricately carved. The Adams mansion also features two polygonal towers, a triangular panel above the entrance, and dormer windows.

69 Montgomery Place

Between Eighth Avenue and Prospect Park West

If you only have a short time to spend in Park Slope, this is the block you should visit. Most of the buildings were developed for realtor Harvey Murdock between 1888 and 1892, and designed by C. P. H. Gilbert in the Romanesque Revival style. Of special note are 11, 19, and 47 Montgomery. Eleven is Murdock's own house in a rustic style, 19 has particularly interesting semicircular arches, and 47 is built from red sandstone by R. L. Daus, one of a handful *not* done by Gilbert.

70 Brooklyn Lyceum

Fourth Avenue and President Street

New York City used to feature dozens of public baths. This one, at 227 Fourth Avenue, formerly New York Public Bath No. 7, is a Beaux Arts terra-cotta extravaganza constructed by Raymond Almirall between 1906 and 1910. It features massive arched windows, and separate entrances for men and women. Look high above the windows for carved terra-cotta wyverns.

In the 1990s, Eric Richmond converted the crumbling structure into a theater space, café, garden and gift shop and renamed it the Brooklyn Lyceum. The Lyceum boasts three theaters: one tiny and two massive. For shows, call (718) 866-gowanus or www.gowanus.com.

71 The Old Stone House

Fifth Avenue and 3rd Street

What we now call the Old Stone House was originally built in 1699 by Dutchman Klaes Arents Vecht. The house remained in the Vecht family until just prior to the American Revolution, when it was rented to Isaac Cortelyou; his father, Jacques, bought the property in 1790.

Officially known as the Vecht-Cortelyou House, the Old Stone House played a pivotal role in the American Revolution. On August 27, 1776, during the Battle of Brooklyn, about 900 American troops retreated from what is now the Green-Wood

The Old Stone House received a thorough makeover in 1996 with new plumbing, wiring, and roofing installed. Maryland state flags wave at the Old House, in honor of the Maryland regiment.

Visit the Stone House in Byrne Park at Fifth Avenue and 3rd Street. It's open weekends: call (718) 768-3195 for hours, or go to www.theoldstonehouse.org.

72 Ansonia Clock Factory
Seventh Avenue and 13th Street

Ansonia shelf clocks are still very collectible today, with their expert craftsmanship and accurate timekeeping. The firm moved to Brooklyn in 1879; its original factory there burned down immediately, but the second is still here. Active clock production at Ansonia Clocks ended around 1930 when the machinery was sold off to a Russian manufacturer. Recently, the factory was divided into apartments and renamed Ansonia Court.

73 A Little Bit of Gettysburg
Eighth Avenue and 14th Street

The 14th Regiment Armory at Eighth Avenue and 14th Street was designed by William Mundell and built between 1891 and 1895. The U.S. Army's 14th Regiment was organized in the 1840s and was known as the Red-Legged Devils, since their dress uniforms were based on the flamboyant Zouave style favored by the French at the time, and featured bright blue jackets and red pants.

A small plaque to the right of the front door marks what is purportedly a small stone removed from the battlefield at Gettysburg, Pennsylvania. The stone was donated by 14th Regiment veterans and now bears the carved phrase: "All of which I saw, part of which I was."

Cemetery, hoping to track northward. General William Alexander, also known as Lord Stirling, led a company of 400 Maryland troops that engaged British General Charles Cornwallis's force of 2,000 grenadiers and cannoneers at the Stone House to cover the retreat. While many of the Americans were able to escape, Stirling was captured and 259 of the Maryland troops were killed. George Washington, observing the battle from what is now Cobble Hill, is said to have uttered, "What brave fellows I must this day lose."

The house continued on with the Cortelyou family until 1850 when it was sold to Edwin Litchfield, who allowed the house to literally sink into ruin. The house was demolished in 1897, though its original construction was so strong that Gatling guns had to be used to force the old stones apart.

The house found an angel in Brooklyn Borough President John J. Byrne. The Old Stone House's original foundations and bricks were rediscovered, and Byrne, in one of his final acts before his death in 1930, ordered its reconstruction in a park posthumously named for him in 1933.

74 The Second Empire Music School

271 9th Street, between Fourth and Fifth Avenues

On the outskirts of Park Slope on 9th Street between Fourth and Fifth Avenues, edging toward the Gowanus Canal, stands a magnificent stucco house, a textbook Second Empire–style with a slanted mansard roof, moldings, bay windows, and, best of all, a cupola open on three sides. It's been the home of jazz musician and teacher Charles Sibirsky since 1981. When it was built, Park Slope was open country.

Directly in back of the house is the old Charles Higgins ink factory, now divided into apartments, accessible via a charming cul-de-sac on 8th Street. The inkmaker, though still going strong, moved out about thirty years ago.

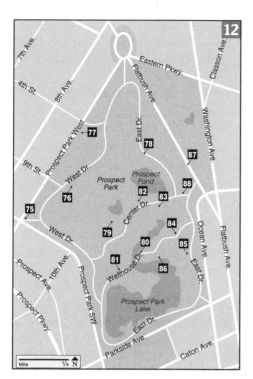

Prospect Park is perhaps the pinnacle of Olmsted and Vaux's career: a brilliant study in landscape architecture; a true urban retreat.

If you're not familiar with every detail to be found in the park, take along *The Complete Illustrated Guidebook to Prospect Park and the Brooklyn Botanic Garden*, published by Silver Lining Books and containing incredibly detailed maps. For information on Prospect Park events, check prospectpark.org.

SUBWAY: ② or ③ to Grand Army Plaza; ⒡ to 15th Street–Prospect Park; Ⓑ, Ⓠ, or Franklin Shuttle(s) to Prospect Park; Ⓠ to Parkside Avenue

BUS: B16 on Ocean Avenue; **B41** on Flatbush Avenue; **B68** on Prospect Park Southwest; **B69** on Prospect Park West; **B71** on Eastern Parkway

75 Acanthus Columns, Bartel-Pritchard Square

Bartel-Pritchard Square, on Prospect Park's western edge, is the dividing point between Park Slope and Windsor Terrace. It was once a major trolley interchange. Bartel-Pritchard isn't really a "square" at all: It's a traffic roundabout in the British tradition. It was named for two local residents, young American soldiers, Emil Bartel and William Pritchard, who were killed in France in 1918 during World War I combat. Another roundabout, more logically named Park *Circle*, is at the park's southwestern entrance at Parkside Avenue, Ocean Parkway, and Coney Island Avenue.

At Prospect Park's entrance at Bartel-Pritchard, you will find two massive columns. Inspired by the 400 B.C. Acanthus Column of Delphi, they feature granite acanthus leaves snaking around the columns and on the capital, topped by bronze lanterns. They were designed by Stanford White in 1906.

76 Tennis House

Constructed by the architects Helmle, Huberty, & Hudswell in 1910 along Long Meadow, south of Prospect Park West and the 9th Street entrance, the Tennis House is a limestone-bricked, colonnaded building with distinctive Guastavino roof tiling.

There are no tennis courts left in Prospect Park (though there are in the nearby Parade Grounds), but the Tennis House was built as a shelter and a locker room for participants in lawn tennis. It has been restored and is presently the home of the Brooklyn Center for the Urban Environment (BCUE). It is open from 9:00 AM to 5:00 PM weekends and 10:00 AM to 5:00 PM weekdays. Call (718) 788-8500 or go to www.bcue.org for details.

77 Litchfield Villa

Edwin Litchfield's villa, facing Prospect Park West on the park grounds near 5th Street, was here before Prospect Park, and it predates most of the rest of the neighborhood. The villa was completed in 1857 by architect Alexander Jackson Davis. Litchfield owned all the land from about 1st to 9th Streets, and from the Gowanus Canal to about Tenth Avenue, which at one time did go through here, at least on paper. The city of Brooklyn acquired the territory for Prospect Park, which was built around the house. The villa was constructed in Italianate style and named Grace Hill, for Litchfield's wife. It's a great area to walk around, picnic in, and admire the ornate architecture with its arches, corinthian columns, and porch supports with carved corn and wheat motifs. Go on in, it's open for visitors as the Brooklyn HQ of the NYC Department of Parks and Recreation.

78 Battle of Brooklyn Remnants

What would become Prospect Park was once the setting of an outright rout of American Revolutionary forces by the British, Scottish Highlanders, and Hessian mercenary troops early on the morning of August 27, 1776. A ragtag group of volunteer soldiers were dug in on a hill in what is now the eastern section of Prospect Park, south of Grand Army Plaza, waiting for the world's mightiest fighting force to approach. But British General Henry Clinton devised a plan that would have his soldiers sneak up behind the colonists and take them by surprise. Completely flummoxed, the colonists fled Battle Pass toward the Old Stone House at Gowanus Creek. There, a brave Maryland regiment stood their ground, engaged the British, and helped many of the Brooklyn troops to flee.

Except for East Drive, this heavily wooded part of the park must look much as it did that day in 1776. Two markers along East Drive, just north of Prospect Park Zoo, point out the sites of the rebel defenses and Valley Grove House, a tavern that stood near the battle site. Another monument marks the spot where colonists felled a large white oak tree across the Old Flatbush Road in a futile attempt to stop the onrushing British forces.

79 Quaker Cemetery

Quaker Hill, along Center Drive near the park entrance at Prospect Park Southwest and 16th Street, holds a cemetery that was established by the Society of Friends before Prospect Park was built. Burials here date to the 1820s. The park was simply built around the cemetery and no trace now remains of the cross streets that surrounded it. Actor Montgomery Clift (1920–1966) was buried here at his mother's request. The cemetery is somewhat hidden in a wooded area off the main drive; there are no large monuments or tombs, per Quaker custom.

80 Lookout Hill and the Maryland Monument

The Maryland Monument, a simple granite shaft with a sphere at its apex, designed by Stanford White, is at the foot of Lookout Hill at the bottom of a staircase along Wellhouse Drive in a relatively inconspicuous area. It is a tribute to the Maryland regiment who aided the patriots at the battle of Brooklyn. It was erected August 17, 1895, at the 119th anniversary of the battle.

81 Well House

Walking west on Wellhouse Drive from the Maryland Monument, you are soon within view of Prospect Park Lake. Note the small stone-and-brick structure on your right. It is the Prospect Park Well House. Built in 1869, it once housed engines and machinery that pumped 750,000 gallons of water a day into a reservoir. After city water entered the park, the reservoir and smokestack were torn down and the well was covered over.

82 Ravine

Prospect Park's answer to Central Park's Ramble, the Ravine is an entirely artificial, planned construction, though its waterfalls, forests, and timber and rock bridges meld together seamlessly to form an out-of-city experience.

The Ravine is accessed from a number of entrances from the Long Meadow on the north and Nethermead on the south, via the timber Esdale and Falkill Bridges and the stone Nethermead Arch, which is the only bridge in Prospect Park that spans a park path, a bridle path, *and* a waterway. The Ravine is punctuated by the Ambergill Falls. The park's architects originally constructed waterfalls in the park in the 1860s, but erosion and neglect eliminated them until a 1990s restoration.

83 Music Pagoda, Binnenwater, and Boathouse

From the Ravine, follow the park path under the Nethermead Arch. Note the trefoils (three-lobed designs resembling shamrocks) on the railing. You will see the second of Prospect Park's two lengthy meadows before you: Nethermead. The path takes you past the timber bridge spanning Binnenwater, which flows south from Ambergill Falls under Nethermead Arch.

You have arrived at the Music Pagoda, an octagon-shaped structure built in 1887. Its base consists of rocks and boulders that were removed from Sullivan Hill, which lies east of the Ravine along Long Meadow. Until the 1960s, the Pagoda was a major concert and theater venue, but the park's concert organizers now use the Bandshell, built by Robert Moses in 1939, near Prospect Park West and 10th Street.

Binnenwater forms another impressive artificial waterfall south of the Pagoda. It, too, has undergone a revival, with Binnen Pool's original parameters having been restored after years of burial under swamps and fallen trees.

From Binnenwater, note the shining, white Boathouse, built in 1905 by Helmle, Huberty, & Hudswell, recently polished to near perfection and given a new lease on life as the kid-friendly Audubon Center. Stop in and check out the birdwatching exhibits and grab a snack. You can sit on the deck and watch the pleasure boats cruise under Lullwater Bridge, Prospect Park's one and only cast-iron span.

84 Camperdown Elm and Cleft Ridge Span

Just past the Boathouse and Lullwater Bridge, you will find what appears to be a large shrub surrounded by an iron fence. The rare Camperdown Elm is a ground-hugging elm tree that grew from a cutting of a creeping Scotch elm at the Camperdown House in Dundee, Scotland, in 1872. By the mid-1960s, the tree was in danger of dying, but was rescued at the encouragement of Brooklyn poet Marianne Moore, whose tribute to the tree was published in *The New Yorker* in 1967. Prospect Park is home to many other rare botanical species; *Tree Trails in Prospect Park* by George Kalmbacher is the definitive guide, and *New York City Trees*, by Edward Sibley Barnard, covers all of NYC.

Cleft Ridge Span, directly in front of the Camperdown Elm, is the newest of Prospect Park's arched bridges, having been completed in 1872. The intricately molded

interior was among the first concrete products to be mass-produced.

85 Oriental Pavilion

Olmsted and Vaux made sure to provide unique vistas at the ends of many of their Prospect Park arches. Near Grand Army Plaza, Endale and Meadowport Arches "open" to the Long Meadow.

The Cleft Ridge Span is no different. It "opens" to two of Prospect Park's original music venues, the mysterious-looking Oriental Pavilion and the Concert Grove. The Pavilion was completed in 1874 and consists of eight cast-iron posts, painted colorfully in a Middle Eastern pattern, supporting a complex roof that flares outward on the edges, providing a large area of shade. The underside of the Pavilion features a beautiful stained-glass octagonal skylight.

86 Concert Grove

Directly in front of the Oriental Pavilion, down a short set of steps, is Concert Grove, a formal European-style garden designed to look out over a small island in Prospect Park Lake containing a performance stage.

There were large areas for carriages to park on each side of the Grove. It turned out that the acoustics weren't the best, and concerts moved to the Music Pagoda and, ultimately, the Prospect Park Bandshell. The stage area was torn up, the island attached to the mainland by fill, and the Wollman Rink was installed in its place.

However, the formal garden remains, with busts of Ludwig van Beethoven, Edvard Grieg, Wolfgang Amadeus Mozart, Carl Maria von Weber (Mozart's cousin by marriage), and Irish writer Thomas Moore. With his back to the composers, looking out over the skating rink, is H. K. Brown's massive bronze study of Abraham Lincoln.

87 Lefferts Homestead

Near the Willink Entrance at Flatbush and Ocean Avenues and near the Prospect Park B/Q subway station are a couple of early Brooklyn relics that have found their way into Prospect Park for different reasons.

Lefferts Homestead is one of Brooklyn's many old Dutch houses. It was built by the Lefferts family in an area east of the park along the Old Flatbush Road at about where Flatbush Avenue and Maple Street are now. Peter Lefferts had arrived in New Netherland in 1660, and purchased a farm in this area in around 1675, and passed the property on to his son John. By

1777, John's son Peter had constructed this gabled, shingle-roofed building featuring a six-columned porch and dormer windows. The Lefferts family continued to occupy it until 1918, when the city took it over and moved it to its present location. It's now used as a children's museum.

Just to the rear of the Lefferts Homestead you will find the Prospect Park Carousel, built in 1951 but containing parts of two earlier designs by Charles Carmel dating back to 1915 and 1918. The B&B Carousell in Coney Island has details dating to the same era. Note the lion, giraffe, and deer mixed in with the fifty-one painted ponies.

88 Flatbush Toll House

Also near the Willink Entrance, south of the Lefferts Homestead and Carousel, is a small green structure that looks a lot like a ticket kiosk.

It's an early version of a tollbooth. It was used to collect fares on the Old Flatbush Turnpike, which generally followed the route of today's Flatbush Avenue. After New York City consolidation in 1898, the practice of collecting tolls was dropped. In the 1950s, the structure was restored (it is mostly wood) and placed in its current location which is not far from its original position at the intersection of Flatbush and Lefferts Avenues.

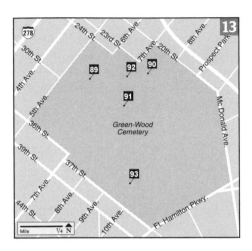

James Ives, painter and inventor Samuel Morse, newspaperman Horace Greeley, Henry Ward Beecher, Tammany politician William Marcy "Boss" Tweed, New York Governor DeWitt Clinton, and Charles Lewis Tiffany and his son, Louis Comfort Tiffany.

Excellent guides to use when walking Green-Wood's paths are the two slim volumes produced by cemetery historian Jeffrey Richman, *The Green-Wood Cemetery: Walk #1: Battle Hill and Back* and *Walk #2: Valley and Sylvan Waters*. They can be purchased at the office at the main gate or online.

I have included the cemetery road and section numbers where the graves can be found as noted on the map of Green-Wood available for free at the main office. The main gate is open from 8:00 AM to 4:00 PM: call Green-Wood at (718) 768-7300 or visit www.green-wood.com.

SUBWAY: Ⓡ to 25th Street; walk 1 block to the entrance gate on Fifth Avenue

BUS: B63 on Fifth Avenue; **B16** along Dahill Road to entrance at Fort Hamilton Parkway and McDonald Avenue

Green-Wood Cemetery (not "Greenwood") was founded in 1838 on 478 acres of rolling acreage. Its first landscape architect was David Bates Douglass, who rode on horseback all over northern Brooklyn with Henry Pierrepont, one of the founders of Brooklyn's parks system, in order to select the optimal area. The cemetery's peaceful, quiet expanse permits spectacular views of Manhattan in its north and northwestern sections, as its peaks and valleys were graded and flattened only slightly by its creators. This was among the first "rural" cemeteries in New York; most burial grounds in the city prior to this had been associated with churches, with the better-off buried under churches in vaults, the rest in churchyards.

Enter the cemetery through the Gothic Revival red sandstone main gatehouse at Fifth Avenue and 25th Street, designed by Richard Upjohn between 1861 and 1863, with its rich details: a double arch, three spires, religious reliefs with a Resurrection theme, and a bell that rings to announce every funeral procession. Also note that a colony of monk parrots has made its home in the central tower.

Among Green-Wood's thousands of burials are industrialist and educator Peter Cooper, engravers Nathaniel Currier and

89 The Prentiss Brothers
Lake Avenue, Section 88

Baltimore natives Clifton and William Prentiss both served and died for their country. In 1862, with the USA and Confederate States at war, Clifton joined the Union army and later rose to the rank of brevet (or temporary) colonel. His younger brother, William, however, sympathized with the South and joined the army of the Stars and Bars. Clifton, shocked, swore he would never again speak to his brother.

On April 2, 1865, General U. S. Grant led a final assault on Robert E. Lee's intricate system of fortifications at Petersburg, Virginia, the culmination of a nine-month siege. The Army of the Potomac was finally able to break through. A week later, Lee surrendered at Appomattox at Wilmer McLean's farm, the very place the first battle of the war had been fought in July 1861.

It was Clifton Prentiss who led the assault on Petersburg on that April morning. He received a bullet in the lung. As it happened, William was there on the Confederate side and he, too, received an injury: a shell fragment in his knee necessitating an amputation. Both men were taken to a field hospital where, after some intransigence on Clifton's part, they were reunited. They were brought to Armory Square Hospital in Washington, D.C., where they were aided by none other than Walt Whitman, who was working as an army nurse. The brothers' wounds were too severe for recovery: William passed away in June, Clifton in August. The brothers are interred side by side in a Green-Wood meadow, united as they were not during their lifetimes.

90 Minerva
Border Avenue, Section J

Charles Higgins was a wealthy ink manufacturer whose mansion on 9th Street in Park Slope and adjoining factory are still standing. It was a dream of his to commemorate the Revolutionary Battle of Brooklyn. On August 27, 1920, he unveiled "Minerva and the Altar of Liberty" in front of his mausoleum, which had already been

completed nine years before his death on the spot where one of the bloodiest skirmishes had taken place. The Roman goddess of battle was sculpted by Frederic Wellington Ruckstall. She faces the harbor, and her left hand is raised in tribute to the Statue of Liberty, which is directly visible from this spot through trees which are carefully pruned to preserve the view.

91 Charlotte Canda
Greenbough and Fern Avenues, Section 92

Frenchman Charles Canda (1792–1866) was a wealthy owner of a girls' school and a major in Napoleon's army. His beloved daughter, Charlotte, was a victim of a carriage accident as she and the family were traveling home after her seventeenth-birthday celebration. The horses pulling the carriage bolted and she was thrown and killed.

Charlotte had been educated in the finest of New York City's schools and was an accomplished artist: She had drafted a plan for a cemetery monument for a recently deceased aunt. Her father took the plans and built one of Green-Wood's most magnificent early monuments, dedicated in 1848 and sculpted by John Frazee and Robert Launitz.

Off to the right of Charlotte's monument you will see a smaller stone. Buried here is her fiancé, Charles Albert Jarrett de la Marie, who committed suicide after learning of her death. Because Charlotte's grave was on ground consecrated by the Roman Catholic Church, as one who committed suicide, he could not be buried alongside her.

92 Jane Griffith
Hydrangea Path, Section 106

What is likely the most poignant monument in Green-Wood is Charles Griffith's monument to his beloved wife, Jane. It depicts a young man going off to work in the morning at the front door of a wisteria-covered townhouse. He leans on a partially opened gate, while his clearly adoring wife beams. Her hands are folded in a relaxed fashion. A small dog sits on the steps to her left, and a horsecar and driver is shown on the right side of the sculpture. The inscription at the top reads simply: "Jane, My Wife."

The sculpture depicts the last conversation of Jane and Charles Griffith at 109 West 13th Street on August 4, 1857. When Charles returned later that evening, Jane was dead of what physicians said was heart disease. She was forty years old. Devastated, Charles commissioned an Italian-American sculptor, Patrizio Piatti, to create the monument. Charles is said to have visited his wife's monument weekly for twenty-five years until his own death in 1882. He was laid to rest at Jane's side.

93 The Dietzels' Train
Sassafras Avenue, Section 206

In the cemetery's southwestern section, near Seventh Avenue and 37th Street, you will find a large, four-columned memorial topped by an angel, with a large, wide base with the chiseled names of the deceased. Look closely between the columns, and you will see what appears to be a derailed locomotive: the steam engine in front with its cowcatcher, and a pair of passenger cars behind, the second of which is off the tracks.

Braid manufacturer Oscar Dietzel and his wife, Maggie, were on their way home on the Long Island Rail Road from a Manhattan Beach, Brooklyn, outing on August 26, 1893. The train had almost reached the ferry stop at Long Island City when disaster struck: A train from Rockaway Beach was mistakenly permitted on the same track by an errant switchman, and it plowed into the last car of the train near the Laurel Hill Station, killing sixteen passengers, including the Dietzels.

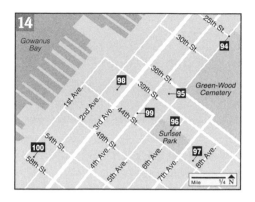

Sunset Park and Borough Park are two neighborhoods along the western edge of Brooklyn between the waterfront on the west, Green-Wood Cemetery on the north, McDonald Avenue on the east, and 65th Street on the south. Sunset Park fades into Borough Park at about Ninth Avenue. In just twenty years, the stretch along Eighth Avenue has become one of NYC's three Chinatowns (along with the one in Manhattan and one in Flushing, Queens). The area nearest the water has a distinctly Hispanic flavor, and Borough Park is one of NYC's three Hasidic Jewish strongholds, along with Crown Heights and southern Williamsburg.

Thirty to forty years ago, Sunset Park and its neighbor to the south, Bay Ridge, boasted a considerable Scandinavian population, primarily Norwegian (*Nordisk Tidende* was to be found on most newsstands), and a number of Danish bakeries lined Fifth Avenue. The Scandinavian legacy is preserved by the annual Norwegian Day Parade, and by the Lutheran Medical Center on Second Avenue and 54th Street (founded in 1883 by a Norwegian Lutheran nurse, Sister Elizabeth Fedde, noted on the 53rd Street BMT subway station signs).

SUBWAY: Ⓡ to 36th, 45th, or 53rd Street; Ⓓ to Fort Hamilton Parkway; Ⓕ to Church Avenue

BUS: B11 on 49th and 50th Streets; **B16** on 13th and 14th Avenues; **B23** on 16th Avenue; **B35** on 39th Street; **B37** on Third Avenue; **B63** on Fifth Avenue; **B70** on 39th Street and Eighth Avenue

94 Weir Florist
Fifth Avenue and 25th Street

The McGovern-Weir greenhouse, across the street from Green-Wood Cemetery at Fifth Avenue and 25th Street, stands out

BROOKLYN

like a jewel in this otherwise nondescript Brooklyn region. Not technically in Sunset Park, which really begins further south at 39th Street, this is pretty much a neighborhood without an agreed-upon name. According to legend, the greenhouse, sporting a wrought-iron "Weir" at the top (with "McGovern," his partner's name, added later) originally appeared in the St. Louis, Missouri, World's Fair in 1904.

James Weir opened the floral business with plant nurseries and greenhouses in Yellow Hook, in what is now Bay Ridge, in the 1850s. After a yellow fever epidemic struck the area, taking a heavy toll, Weir proposed renaming Yellow Hook as Bay Ridge, since it was built along a hill facing Upper New York Bay. The region formally approved the name change in 1853.

95 Spanish Bricks
441 37th Street, between Fourth and Fifth Avenues

The story goes that the set of bluish paving stones presently embedded in the sidewalk in front of 441 37th Street were brought over by the Spanish during their era of conquest in the New World sometime in the 1500s. At one time, much of 37th Street was paved with these stones, but in the 1980s, the city had them removed and returned to Spain. A few were left behind, and have been placed here.

96 Sunset Park
Between Fifth and Seventh Avenues, and 41st and 44th Streets

Sunset Park was named for the spectacular sunsets that can be seen from here. The park offers views of Upper New York Bay, Jersey City, Manhattan, Staten Island, and, on those rare perfectly clear days, New Jersey's Watchung Mountains.

97 Finnish Co-op
816-826 43rd Street, near Eighth Avenue

A relic of Sunset Park's Finntown, marked "Alku Toinen" ("New Beginning") at 816-826 43rd Street, near Eighth Avenue, was the very first nonprofit co-operative apartment built in the U.S., constructed by the Finnish Home Building Association in 1916. In the early-to-mid-twentieth century, 10,000 Finns were among the Scandinavians living in Bay Ridge and Sunset Park, finding work along the docks.

98 Bush Terminal

28th to 50th Streets, between Second and Third Avenues

The white-painted monoliths fronting Third Avenue between 29th and 36th Streets were constructed by architect William Higginson in the first three decades of the twentieth century for industrialist Irving T. Bush. There are fifteen lofts in total, each six to eight stories in height, on 200 acres of land. Bush Terminal had a waterfront railroad and eighteen deep-water piers. Bush Terminal is being converted by Industry City Associates into a home for broadband services providers.

99 Sunset Park Stables

4302 Fourth Avenue

The southwest corner of Fourth Avenue and 43rd Street, in the shadow of St. Michael's Church's lofty campanile, is a magnificent ruin: a relic of when local police precincts maintained their stables here. This Romanesque example was built around 1890. Also, check out 43rd Street between Fourth and Fifth Avenues for some prime Brooklyn brownstones.

100 Elvis Presley and the Long Island Rail Road

Brooklyn Army Terminal, 58th Street and First Avenue

Elvis Presley isn't a name you'd normally associate with the Long Island Rail Road, or even Sunset Park or Brooklyn, for that matter. (Elvis almost always traveled by plane or by pink Cadillac.) Actually, what may be the only occasion Elvis spent in Brooklyn was one of the more celebrated incidents in his life: the day he shipped out to Germany as an Army draftee in September 1958. He traveled by train along with other recruits from Fort Hood, Texas, and the last leg of his route took him along the Long Island Rail Road Bay Ridge Branch to the Brooklyn Army Terminal, along the Narrows facing Second Avenue between 58th and 65th Streets. The Terminal maintains an exhibit in the front lobby commemorating Elvis's arrival and departure.

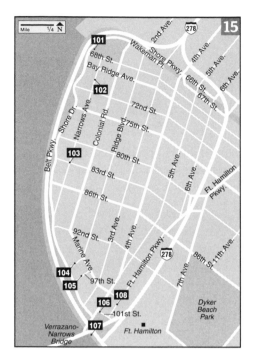

When I was a kid, they built the Verrazano-Narrows Bridge in my backyard. I spent my first thirty-five years in Bay Ridge and witnessed the destruction of much of the neighborhood to clear space for the bridge's approach road, followed by the gradual rise of its incredible towers. I ate sundaes at Hinsch's Confectionary, the ice cream shop still dispensing sugary treats at Fifth Avenue and 86th Street; had my knuckles rapped by the nuns at St. Anselm's School, and was shooed across the street by the moviemakers shooting *Saturday Night Fever* in 1977. I left in 1993 for Flushing, Queens, but in a sense, I never left Bay Ridge.

Since the Gowanus Expressway opened in 1964, Bay Ridge has been easily defined as everything between the expressway, the water, and the bridge. Its immediate neighbors to the southeast, Dyker Park and Bensonhurst, stretch off to Stillwell Avenue, the border with Gravesend. The neighborhoods' neat, orderly streets are lined with

detached homes as well as magnificent brownstones.

SUBWAY: Ⓡ to Bay Ridge Avenue, 77th, 86th or Bay Ridge–95th Street

BUS: B1 on Bay Ridge Avenue, 13th Avenue, or 86th Street; **B4** on Bay Ridge Parkway; **B16** on Fort Hamilton Parkway, 86th Street, or Shore Road; **B37** on Third Avenue; **B63** on Fifth Avenue; **B64** on 86th Street, 14th Avenue, or Bath Avenue; **B70** on Seventh and Eighth Avenues

101 Owl's Head Park
Colonial to Shore Roads, between 68th Street and the Belt Parkway

Owl's Head Park is Bay Ridge's largest public park, and its high hill provides a prime viewing spot during Brooklyn's occasional tall ship parades. The park was created from the estate of Eliphalet Bliss (1836–1903). In 1867, he founded the machine shops that became the E. W. Bliss Company and the United States Projectile Company. His estate, Owl's Head, featured an observatory known as the Bayard Tower. He willed the property to New York City, provided it be used for parkland; the mansion and tower were razed in 1940.

102 Revolutionary Cemetery
Narrows Avenue and Mackay Place

The smallest cemetery in Brooklyn, the "Revolutionary Cemetery," was founded in 1725 by Dutch immigrant William Harmans Barkaloo. A plaque erected in 1962 on the protective gate indicates that several Revolutionary War veterans are buried here. Some historians say that Barkaloo's sons, Harmaus and Jacques, fought in the Revolutionary War's Battle of Brooklyn on

the side of the Americans. The last burial here took place in 1848. This is the only family plot in Brooklyn not part of a larger cemetery.

103 Gingerbread House ⋀
Narrows Avenue and 83rd Street

The private residence at Narrows Avenue and 83rd Street just across from Fort Hamilton High School is probably the most extreme example in NYC of the Arts and Crafts school of architecture, with its playful, ornate style. It appears to have been built out of boulders and has a simulated-thatch roof. Known to Bay Ridgeites as "the Gingerbread House," it is more properly called the Howard E. and Jessie Jones House, after its original owners. The architect was J. Sarsfield Kennedy (who later designed Prospect Park's Picnic House); it was built from 1916 to 1917.

104 Farrell House
119 95th Street, near Shore Road

This 1847 Greek Revival wood house was built by Joseph S. Bennett when most of

Bay Ridge was just forests and meadows. It originally overlooked the harbor from Shore Road, but was moved to its present spot in 1913. According to the Brooklyn Historical Society, it is officially known as the James Farrell House, after its owner from 1890 to 1912, a Tammany Hall politician.

105 Shell Mansion/Fontbonne Hall
Shore Road and 97th Street

At one time, Shore Road was lined with mansions and private homes like the one on the corner at 99th Street. It is now Fontbonne Hall, a Catholic school for girls, but according to legend, it used to belong to actress/singer Lillian Russell. The mansion was bought by the Sisters of St. Joseph in 1937. Until that time it was called Shell

Mansion. Rumor has it that it had been used as a casino and speakeasy.

106 Rodman Gun at John Paul Jones Park
Fourth Avenue and 101st Street

John Paul Jones Park, also known as Fort Hamilton Park and Cannonball Park, is the site of one of the only two Rodman guns ever produced. In 1864, Fort Hamilton tested this new cannon, designed by Captain Thomas Jefferson Rodman, weighing fifty-eight tons and firing shot weighing 1,080 pounds up to four and a half miles. A derrick had to be used to load the cannon. It was judged to be ineffective after it failed two trials, and, ultimately, it found a home in the park.

Fort Hamilton is now NYC's only re-maining active military base, after the recent decommissioning of Fort Totten in Bayside, Queens. It serves as a military induction center and is home to more than 1,500 military personnel. Its Harbor Defense Museum, located in its caponier, is open to the public by appointment.

107 Denyse Ferry Wharf
Waterfront, near 4th Avenue Belt Parkway entrance

There's a small outcropping of stones and a concrete jetty jutting into the water just southeast of the Verrazano-Narrows Bridge, accessible from the sidewalk along the 4th Avenue Belt Parkway entrance that leads to a shoreline bike path. It used to be a more important pier and once actually had direct access from the Belt Parkway, which roars past a few feet away, as well as from Fort Hamilton.

In the Colonial era, local property owner Denyse Denyse ran a ferry to Staten Island from the slip, which was close to his home. The British and their Hessian and Scottish compatriots under General William Howe chose the Denyse Ferry Wharf as the place to land in New Utrecht for a major offen-

Denyse Ferry Wharf in 1964

Bay Ridge

sive on August 22, 1776, after massing 437 ships off Sandy Hook by July 12. When the war finally ended in 1783, the British also evacuated by the Denyse Ferry.

108 Church of the Generals
Fort Hamilton Parkway and 99th Street

Though the present structure dates only to 1890, there has been a St. John's Episcopal Church here since 1834, when soldiers garrisoned at Fort Hamilton built the first St. John's. The nearby Roman Catholic parish, St. Patrick's, originated the same year.

Captain Robert E. Lee was stationed at Fort Hamilton from 1841 to 1846. An engineer by training, he took charge of building fortifications. He served as vestryman at the church from 1842 to 1844. Major Thomas J. "Stonewall" Jackson was also a parishioner during his own Fort Hamilton command between 1848 and 1850 after his stint in the Mexican War, and he was baptized in the church in 1849 (he would later join the Presbyterian Church). Nearby Jackson Court, an alley on 101st Street, may or may not be named in his honor.

BROOKLYN

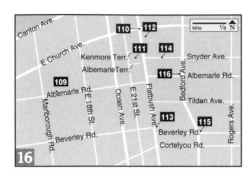

Kolle House

Flatbush takes its name from the Dutch term for "wooded plain," and was first settled by the Dutch as early as 1652 after acquiring the land from the Canarsee Indians. It was a sleepy small town until the Brooklyn, Flatbush, and Coney Island Railroad arrived in 1878; the railroad is now the Brighton subway line. Developers arrived in the 1890s and built large communities whose handsome dwellings still line Flatbush's side streets.

SUBWAY: **F** to Church Avenue, Ditmas Avenue, or 18th Avenue; **Q** to Beverly Road, Cortelyou Road, Newkirk Avenue, or Avenue H; **2** or **5** to Church Avenue, Beverly Road, or Brooklyn College–Flatbush Avenue

BUS: B23 on Cortelyou Road; **B35** on Church Avenue; **B8** on 18th and Foster Avenues; **B68** on Coney Island Avenue; **B41** on Flatbush Avenue; **B49** on Bedford and Rogers Avenues; **B44** on Nostrand and New York Avenues

109 Prospect Park South
Albemarle and Buckingham Roads, south of Church Avenue

When walking down any street between Albemarle and Beverly Roads and Stratford Road and East 19th Street, you'll find Victorian mansions of every conceivable size, color, and style. This is no mere accident: the region, known as Prospect Park South,

was developed by upstate New Yorker Dean Alvord, who purchased a parcel of land in Flatbush from the estate of Luther Voorhies and the Dutch Reformed Church in 1898. Alvord, with the aid of architect John Petit, set about building sumptuously appointed buildings. By 1898, Flatbush had evolved into a well-established community that boasted good schools, and the Brooklyn Rapid Transit Company offered easy transport to Manhattan via the Brooklyn Bridge.

Alvord's idea was to extend Prospect Park south and adapt it to residential use. He buried utility lines underground and paved the streets in an age when many roads were still dirt or Belgian-blocked. Streets were given British-sounding names, and brick fence-posts bearing the interlocking Prospect Park South monogram can still be seen on many intersections.

The more fanciful buildings are along Albemarle Road between Argyle and Buckingham Roads, and along Buckingham, between Albemarle Road and Church Avenue. Of note are the Japanese-style Kolle House at 131 Buckingham Road, and the temple-like Minton House at 1510 Albemarle Road.

110 Flatbush Dutch Reformed Church
Flatbush and Church Avenues

There's been a church at the corner of Flatbush and Church Avenues since 1654, the

Revival row houses that are not all quite the same: every set of windows on each building is different from the other. The alleys' residents zealously maintain their property. Windows and doors are each painted a separate color from their neighbor's.

very beginnings of the village. Flatbush Dutch Reformed has had three incarnations: a wood structure built on orders from Governor General Peter Stuyvesant in 1654, a stone building in 1699, and the current one dating to 1798 built from Manhattan schist. The churchyard goes back to the church's first incarnation and contains stones inscribed in both English and Dutch. Among the many stained-glass windows are a few by Louis Comfort Tiffany.

111 Albemarle and Kenmore Terraces
East 21st Street, south of Church Avenue

The otherwise nondescript block of East 21st Street, between Church Avenue and Albemarle Road, rewards visitors with two gorgeous cul-de-sacs dating from 1916 to 1918, Albemarle and Kenmore Terraces. The two lanes are around the corner from the Flatbush Reformed Dutch Church and, together, they have been designated a historic district.

Albemarle Terrace is lined on both sides, and Kenmore Terrace on one, by Georgian

112 Erasmus Hall Academy
Flatbush Avenue, south of Church Avenue

Erasmus Hall, named for Dutch philosopher Desiderius Erasmus, presents two historic buildings in one location at Flatbush and Church Avenues. Its white clapboard Federal-style building, constructed in 1787, housed the private academy instituted by the Reformed Dutch Church across the street. The older building isn't visible from the street, however, since it is surrounded by the Gothic, fortress-like Erasmus Hall High School, constructed in 1905. The original academy was funded by several founding fathers, including Alexander Hamilton and Aaron Burr, and became a high school in 1896. It boasts famous alumni such as Barbra Streisand, Beverly Sills, and Neil Diamond. The historic academy, known by students and faculty as "the white house" can usually only

BROOKLYN

be glimpsed from the iron gate guarding the high school, but it does contain a small museum. Call (718) 856-3571 for hours.

Loew's King's

113 Flatbush at the Movies
Church Avenue, near Flatbush Avenue

Flatbush is home to a number of theaters that have been shut down or converted for other uses. The Kenmore, on Church Avenue just across the street from the Flatbush Dutch Reformed Church, was the most recent to close. It had been opened in 1928 and later fell under the RKO Keith banner.

Loew's Kings, on Flatbush Avenue and Beverly Road, is one of those gigantic, Baroque-style movie palaces whose fortunes have gone from riches to rags. The Kings was built in 1929, and could hold more than 3,600 theatergoers. In addition to the ornate décor common to Loew's theaters around town, the Kings has a basketball court in the basement, built for the Flatbush Avenue Theater Ushers League.

The old Farragut Theater, on Flatbush Avenue and Farragut Road, was a movie

palace from 1919 to 1959, seating about 1,600. It served as a bowling alley from 1959 to 1963, and then was converted to a YMCA.

114 Flatbush Town Hall
Snyder Avenue, between Flatbush and Bedford Avenues

This Rococo, towered building is a relic of Flatbush's status as a town on its own before being absorbed into the city of Brooklyn in 1894, and then the City of New York in 1898. Flatbush Town Hall was built by John Y. Culyer in 1875, in a style known as Ruskinian Gothic, after John Ruskin, a Victorian critic and writer who championed the Gothic style after visiting Europe in the mid-eighteenth century. The building served as the 67th Police Precinct until 1972.

115 Ebinger's Bakery
Albemarle Road and Bedford Avenue

Arthur Ebinger's Bakery is spoken of in hushed, reverential tones by Brooklynites of a certain age. I remember the company's

Hall featuring the words "Ebinger Baking Co." emblazoned on the façade, is still here, though the company's scrumptious baked goods haven't been sold for many years.

116 Art Deco Sears
Bedford Avenue and Beverly Road

At Beverly and Bedford is a huge Art Moderne monolith. This stark, sculpted tower, with "Sears Roebuck and Co" spelled out in huge blue and white letters at the top, has been here since 1932 (a photo mounted inside shows First Lady Eleanor Roosevelt turning a ceremonial key to open the store), and was the first retail Sears location in New York City.

green boxes with diagonal black lines, its V-shaped counter in its 86th Street, Bay Ridge branch, and its small cakes coated on all sides by rich icing, as well as its butter cookies, drizzled with frosting in every conceivable color in the rainbow. Ebinger's Bakery, in an imposing brick building on Bedford Avenue and Albemarle Road with painted-over windows across from Town

17

Foster Ave.
Glenwood Rd.
117
Avenue H
Brooklyn College
118
Avenue J
Ocean Ave.
Bedford Ave.
Bay Pkwy.
Washington Cemetery
Avenue L
Locust Ave.
120
Avenue M
14th St.
17th St.
119
Avenue N
McDonald Ave.
Ocean Pkwy.
Coney Island Ave.
Avenue P
121
Snyder Ave.
Mile ¼ N

"Midwood" is an Anglicized form of a Dutch name, Midwout, that means "between the villages," because it was midway between Flatbush and Gravesend. The southern end of Midwood contains a collection of oddly angled streets that break the grid pattern. The streets were once part of a very old small town called South Greenfield. The four southwest-to-northeast roads were given woodsy names: Locust, Chestnut, Elm, and Cedar, while the two northwest to southeast were named for water: Bay and Ocean. South Greenfield was so named because it was located south of the older village of Greenfield, which became today's Parkville, centered along Foster and McDonald Avenues.

SUBWAY: Ⓠ to Avenue M or Kings Highway

BUS: B49 on Ocean Avenue; **B68** on Coney Island Avenue; **B9** on Avenues M and N; **B82** on Kings Highway

117 The Little Station That Could
Avenue H and East 16th Street

The present B/Q subway line tracks between Prospect Park and Brighton Beach were originally a part of the Brooklyn, Flatbush, and Coney Island Railroad, which ran between Prospect Park and the Brighton Beach Hotel beginning in 1878. The station house at Avenue H and East 16th Street had been the office for Fiske Terrace, an early real estate development in the area. The stop opened in 1907 after increasing population in the area necessitated a new station. It is the only station remaining from the time when steam trains ran the Brighton Line at grade.

In 2003, the MTA announced plans to tear down the Brighton building in favor of a more modern station house, but public outcry, as well as a NYC Landmarks Preservation Commission designation, caused the MTA to scrap the plan. The quaint station, with its eaves and porch, will be a part of the subway scene for years to come.

118 Parrots of Brooklyn College
Campus Road

These aren't your usual pigeons perched in a tree on Campus Road near Brooklyn College. Parrots have nested in this vicinity since the end of the 1960s. Either a couple of pet birds got loose, or a shipment of parrots from Argentina (where they are from) got lost. Birders know these parrots as Monk or Quaker parrots. They are regarded as highly intelligent and trainable, and they have adapted brilliantly to New York City's occasionally brutal climate: the tropical birds have developed some tricks, such as nesting near warmer power lines and transformers.

The best place to view them is Campus Road between East 22nd and East 23rd Streets. The parrots prefer to build nests in tall floodlight stanchions along Brooklyn College's athletic field.

✒119 NBC studios

Avenue M and East 14th Street

This imposing building is windowless because it contains mechanically lit soundstages. In the 1950s, Steve Allen and Perry Como headlined TV shows here, and one of the 1980s' most popular programs, *The Cosby Show*, was taped here between 1984 and 1992 (although Dr. Huxtable's brownstone exterior was shot on St. Luke's Place in Greenwich Village). Today it continues to facilitate the TV and movie business.

120 Vitagraph Smokestack

Locust Avenue and East 15th Street

Smokestacks seem to preserve ancient advertising even more effectively than ads painted on walls, which are subject to graffiti and obstruction. Often a company name will actually be shown on smokestacks lettered in darker bricks than the others, making the name nearly impos-

sible to erase. A good example is the one on Locust Avenue just west of the Brighton Line trestle. It's clearly labeled "Vitagraph" on its eastern edge.

Vitagraph Studios produced hundreds of films in the surrounding neighborhood, which was still open country in the 1910s. Warner Brothers purchased the studio in 1925 and turned out shorts under the Vitaphone banner until 1939. The Shulamith School for Girls now occupies the Vitagraph Studios site.

✒121 Ocean Parkway Milestones ➤

On Ocean Parkway, near Avenue P and at Neptune Avenue

Just south of Avenue P on Ocean Parkway is a mile marker dating back to the early days of the road. Marked "3," it notes the third mile from Ocean Parkway's northern terminus at Prospect Park. When Olmsted and Vaux built Ocean Parkway between 1874 and 1876, they envisioned a six-milelong extension of their earlier creation, Prospect Park. When first laid out, Ocean

Parkway was a direct route for pedestrians and mounted traffic, as well as buggies and wagons, to get to the Coney Island shore from the park. Milestones like this were probably placed at every mile of the six-mile route. This one, as well as the five-mile marker at Neptune Avenue, can still be seen along the parkway.

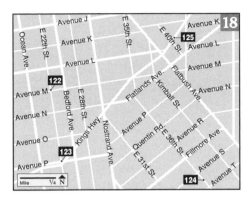

East Flatbush and Flatlands comprise block upon block of neat, well-kept detached homes, broken up by the occasional shopping strip or apartment building. Their southern flank, Mill Basin, is the home of Brooklyn's first "modern" mall, Kings Plaza, built in 1970. East Flatbush and Flatlands have been settled since the mid-1600s, and a few of its ancient homes built by Dutch settlers are still hidden among the ones built after World War II, when the neighborhood started attracting families.

SUBWAY: None, though you may transfer to the **B6**, **B41**, or **B44** buses at the Flatbush Avenue IRT station from the ② and ⑤ trains, the **B2** or **B7** at the B/Q Kings Highway station, and the **B3** at the B/Q Avenue U station

BUS: B6 on Glenwood Road and Avenue H; **B8** on Avenue D; **B7** on Kings Highway; **B41** on Flatbush Avenue; **B44** on Nostrand Avenue; **B46** on Utica Avenue; **B47** on Ralph Avenue; **B2** on Avenues R and S; **B3** on Avenue U

122 Van Nuyse–Magaw House
Avenue M and East 22nd Street

Johannes van Nuyse originally built this house at what was the western edge of his father's farm in open country between 1800

and 1803. In 1916, George Case moved it to its present site at 1041 East 22nd Street and added its dormer windows. There is a plaque between the corner windows marking it as a historic building. Another house belonging to both the Magaw and Van Nuyse families is still standing at 1130 East 34th Street, near Avenue K.

123 Henry and Abraham Wyckoff House
Avenue P and East 22nd Street

Kings Highway was used as a conduit for British troops during the Revolution (the Brits burned Flatlands to the ground in 1776), and this residence, built in 1766 just to its south, was seized and used to garrison Hessian troops, who carved graffiti into a glass door that has been preserved.

124 Hendrick I. Lott House
1940 East 36th Street, between Avenues S and T

Johannes Lott built a small house on his Flatlands property about 1720, on land first settled by Dutchman Hugh Aerens as far back as 1636. In the 1700s, Gerritsen Creek still flowed nearby. Johannes bequeathed the house to his son, also named Johannes, who became a colonel in the Kings County militia and fought in the French and Indian War. His son,

BROOKLYN

Hendrick I. Lott, inherited the small house and farm, and built a much larger addition in 1800 for his bride, Mary. The house remained in the Lott and Suydam families until 1989, when Ella Suydam, great-great-great-great-granddaughter of Johannes Lott, passed away. Evidence that the Lotts housed slaves in the building was discovered by Brooklyn College researchers, though records show that the family freed their slaves long before slavery was outlawed in New York State in 1827.

125 Flatlands Dutch Reformed Church

Kings Highway and East 40th Street

Like the Flatbush Dutch Reformed Church, this church was established by order of Peter Stuyvesant. It is the third church building on the site, and was built in 1848, though its ancient cemetery dates back to the 1600s.

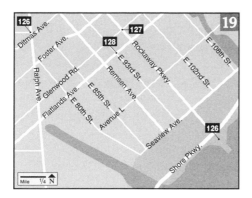

Canarsie is named for the indigenous Canarsee Indians. The etymology is in dispute, but some scholars say it means "fenced land" or "fenced place." Years of warring with the invading Dutch forced the Canarsees east, and today most of their descendants can be found at the Poospatuck Reservation, near Patchogue in eastern Long Island.

Canarsie was the most remote of Brooklyn neighborhoods for many years; it was cut off by Paerdegat Basin and Jamaica Bay from wagon and foot traffic, and few roads reached it from the north. It was not truly developed into a full-fledged community until postwar construction in the 1950s. Canarsie still has a number of old farm roads, now narrow lanes interrupting the street grid.

SUBWAY: Ⓛ to Canarsie–Rockaway Parkway

BUS: B6 on Flatlands Avenue and Glenwood Road; **B17** on Remsen and Seaview Avenues; **B42** on Rockaway Parkway; **B82** on Flatlands Avenue; **B102** on Avenue M

rived in America in 1637. By 1652, he was living in New Amersfoort (Flatlands) and became a supervisor on a farm belonging to Peter Stuyvesant, governor of New Netherlands, acquired some property, and became a town magistrate. He built this house along the now-defunct Canarsie Lane in 1652; at the time it was situated on one of the higher hills in town, which was later leveled. When the British took over in 1664, the house became the property of the Duke of York, but later reverted to the Wyckoff family, which occupied it well into the twentieth century.

By the mid-1970s, the house was in poor repair, its restoration beyond the means of the Wyckoff family. Fortunately, federal funds were allocated, and between 1979 and 1982, the architectural firm John Milner Associates restored the house to approximate its appearance in 1820 when it was last renovated. Today, the Wyckoff House is thriving as a museum and community center.

Visitors are quite welcome. Check out www.wyckoffassociation.org or call (718) 629-5400 for hours.

126 Pieter Claesen Wyckoff House
5816 Clarendon Road at Ralph Avenue

This is the oldest house in New York City and in New York State.

Pieter Claesen Wyckoff (1625–1694) ar-

127 Trolley Remnants
Rockaway Parkway and Glenwood Road

The BMT Canarsie line operated, via a trolley that ran past the backyards of Canarsie homes at grade, all the way to Seaview Avenue. Though it was discontinued in 1942,

BROOKLYN

its legacy can still be made out with a flock of trolley poles, some of which are mounted with old-style mercury streetlamps, at the subway-and-bus terminal on Rockaway Parkway and by other poles on the parkway and on nearby Glenwood Road.

128 Canarsie's Log Cabin
Flatlands Avenue and East 93rd Street

There's a genuine log cabin in Canarsie. It was built by the Lloyd Doubleday family sometime in the 1930s and was originally an ice cream parlor; it is now home to a real estate office.

129 Canarsie Pier and the Belt Parkway Bike Path
Rockaway Parkway and Jamaica Bay

Always a prime fishing haven, Canarsie Pier, at the foot of Rockaway Parkway, was built at the same time the Belt Parkway reached Canarsie in 1939, replacing Golden City, a former amusement park, as Canarsie's premier recreation spot. It was completely renovated in the 1990s, and is now part of the national Gateway Recreational Area.

Formerly in disrepair, the bike path along Jamaica Bay has been repaved and renovated from Howard Beach to Knapp Street in Sheepshead Bay, and is accessible from the pier.

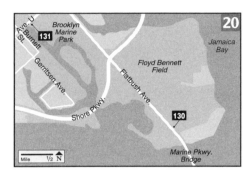

These remote areas of Brooklyn com- prise much of its remaining wide-open space and are some of the few locations that offer solitude in this busy borough.

SUBWAY: None. Bus connections can be made from the ② or ⑤ to Flatbush Avenue, the ⑤ to Avenue U, or the ⑥ to Avenue U

BUS: Q35 on Flatbush Avenue; it crosses Marine Parkway Bridge to Rockaway peninsula; ask bus driver for Floyd Bennett stop; **B3** on Avenue U; **B31** on Gerritsen Avenue

Flight Tower

🗿130 Floyd Bennett Field

Flatbush Avenue, between the Belt Parkway and Marine Parkway Bridge

Floyd Bennett Field makes up a large part of southern Brooklyn, east of Flatbush Avenue, south of the Belt Parkway, north of Jamaica Bay. Constructed on the site

of Barren Island, Floyd Bennett Field was New York City's first municipal airport and was completed in 1930. In the nineteenth and early twentieth centuries, Barren Island was home to glue factories (as reflected in the names of nearby bodies of water: Dead Horse Inlet and Dead Horse Bay).

The airport's namesake, Floyd Bennett, was born in Warrensburg, New York. In 1925, he accompanied Admiral Richard Byrd on the MacMillan Expedition to the Arctic. On May 9, 1926, Byrd and Bennett made history by being the first men to fly over the North Pole, winning the Congressional Medal of Honor. Bennett died, suffering from pneumonia, while flying to aid a stranded flight crew on Greenley Island, Quebec.

Though it's a national historic site, Floyd Bennett Field can appear to be desolate at times. Former administrative buildings and hangars have deteriorated, though the main hall, now known as the Ryan Visitor Center, is welcoming and well-maintained. The tower is still manned and busy, and cargo aircraft still use its runways. For information, call (718) 338-3799 or visit www.geocities.com/floyd_bennett_field.

131 Marine Park

Avenue U, between Burnett and East 33rd Streets

To the west of Floyd Bennett Field can be found the vast (about 800 acres) Marine Park. Until a few years ago, Marine Park was mostly wilderness, but nature trails that lead directly to the shore are now maintained.

The trail, along Gerritsen Creek, on the west side of Burnett Street, invites parkgoers to observe a wealth of flora and fauna, and enjoy a new saltwater marsh nature center.

BROOKLYN

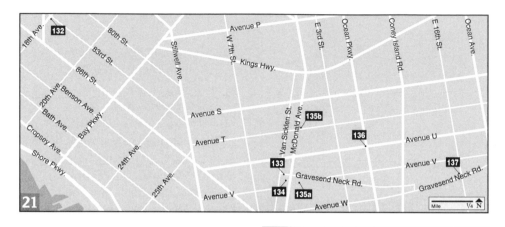

Bath Beach is located along Gravesend Bay between the Bay Eighth Street (Exit 5) and Cropsey Avenue (Exit 6) exits of the Belt Parkway. In the late 1890s, Bath Beach was home to yacht clubs and seaside villas for the wealthy (the neighborhood takes its name from an English resort town). There's no beach to be found there these days, though you can find some sand at low tide in the vicinity of Exit 5 along the waterside bike and jogging path.

Neighboring Gravesend is much, much older than Bath Beach. The original town was first settled in 1643, making it not only the oldest settlement in Brooklyn, but the oldest in Long Island, and retains its original square boundaries. Willem Kieft, Dutch provincial governor of New Netherland, donated a small tract of land in what became Gravesend to a British immigrant, Lady Deborah Moody, and her son, Sir Henry, in 1643.

SUBWAY: **D** or **M** to 18th Avenue, 20th Avenue, Bay Parkway, or 25th Avenue; **N** to Avenue U or 86th Street; **F** to Avenue U or Avenue X

BUS: B8 on 18th Avenue; **B1** on 86th Street; **B6** or **B82** on Bay Parkway; **B64** on Bath Avenue; **B3** on 25th Avenue and Avenue U; **B4** on Stillwell Avenue and 86th Street

📯132 Reformed Church and Liberty Pole

Eighteenth Avenue, between 82nd and 84th Streets

The heart of New Utrecht, one of Kings County's original six towns, was the New Utrecht Reformed Church. The first Reformed Church in town was founded around 1699, and the original building stood at what today would be Sixteenth Avenue at about 84th Street. This church no longer stands, but its ancient churchyard can still be found there.

A "newer" church was built in 1828, at

what would become Eighteenth Avenue and 84th Street and contains some stones from its predecessor, along with Tiffany-style stained glass. The adjacent shingle-style Parish House, built in 1885, still stands on 84th Street.

To harass the British, or to signal their defeat, Colonial patriots erected "liberty poles" on which the new American flag was flown. The first such pole in New Utrecht was raised here in 1783 to celebrate American victory. Six poles have been placed here in succession; this latest pole was placed in 1946.

1643, the first year of the settlement. Lady Moody, according to legend, is buried in an unmarked grave somewhere within, although the oldest stone in the cemetery is dated 1676, and no stone has been found bearing her name. Next to Old Gravesend Cemetery, Van Sicklen Cemetery is weedy and overgrown, seemingly betraying any attempt at upkeep.

133 Lady Moody House
27 Gravesend Neck Road

There's a debate going on about whether or not the house at 27 Gravesend Neck Road, just east of Van Sicklen Street, actually was the home of Lady Deborah Moody. If it was, it would make the house one of New York City's oldest, since she died in 1659. Brooklyn historical records have Sir Henry Moody, Deborah's son, selling the property on which the house stands in 1659 to Jan Jansen ver Ryn. It passed through various hands before winding up with the Van Sicklen brothers, John and Abraham, who may also have built the house in 1770. In either case, this is one old house.

134 Graveyards of Gravesend
Gravesend Neck Road, near McDonald Avenue

The Old Gravesend Cemetery across the street from the Moody house dates to

135 Charles Ryder, Ryder–Van Cleef, and Samuel Hubbard Homes
Village Road North, near Avenue U

On Village Road North, just south of where it meets Avenue U, you will find a couple of ordinary-looking homes, but they come with very old pedigrees.

a. At 32 Village Road North is the Charles Ryder home, reportedly built around 1788. It was originally located at McDonald Avenue and Gravesend Neck Road and served as a school when President George Washington visited it in 1789. At 38 Village Road North is the Ryder–Van Cleef House, originally located at 22 Village Road North. It was moved in 1928 to make way for a playground that is still there. The house was built around 1840 by Lawrence Ryder, and was owned later by his son-in-law John Van Cleef.

b. At 2138 McDonald (formerly Gravesend) Avenue, north of Avenue T, is the Samuel Hubbard House. It was built around 1750, most likely by the Johnson family (an extinct lane in Gravesend was called Johnson's Lane). The two-story wing at the left side of the house was added in 1925.

⛏136 That Thing at Ocean Parkway and Avenue U

Ocean Parkway and Avenue U

It's big, it's ornate, it's rusting, and I hadn't a clue what it might be. It's on the north-east corner of Ocean Parkway and Avenue U. After I looked far and wide for the answer, Oscar Israelowitz, in his *Flatbush Guide,* provides the information: It's the air vent for the sewage pumping station beneath the intersection.

The city is full of air vents that appear in dozens of different designs. They usually take the form of a shaft with air holes at the top. Most are steel, but the older ones, like this one, are painted iron and can be quite thick and "busily" designed.

137 The LIRR in Gravesend

Gravesend Neck Road and East 16th Street

There are some bricked-up, fenced "steps to nowhere" on the East 16th Street side of the (Gravesend) Neck Road Station. They used to lead to the Long Island Rail Road, specifically the Neck Road Station of the LIRR Manhattan Beach line, which ran here until the early 1920s. There are also remnants of a spur to the old Sheepshead Bay Race Track, which was east of here from 1886 to 1910, just south of the Avenue X station.

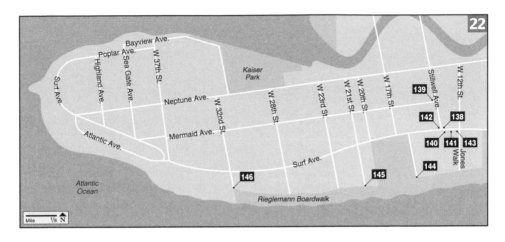

What Brooklyn kid hasn't been to Coney Island? Its roller coasters, rides, games and honky-tonk atmosphere made it Brooklyn's premier seaside recreation era from the 1910s through the 1960s. But by the time I got there in the early 1960s, Coney's classics, Luna Park and Dreamland, had long disappeared, and Steeplechase Park was on its last legs. Coney was well past its prime, but still featured a lot more echoes of the old days than it does now. The Half Moon Hotel, Thunderbolt Roller Coaster, Playland amusement area, and the Catholic Youth Organization day camp on West 26th Street were all still there; all are gone now. In 2005 came news of a vast new entertainment development that threatens to wipe out even more of Coney's remaining legacy.

SUBWAY: Ⓓ, Ⓕ, Ⓝ, or Ⓠ to Coney Island–Stillwell Avenue

BUS: B36 on Surf Avenue; **B64** on Stillwell Avenue; **B74** on Mermaid Avenue; **B82** on Cropsey Avenue; **B68** on Neptune Avenue

The Coney Island Mermaid Parade is held every June.

138 All's Well That's Stillwell
Stillwell and Surf Avenues

In 2005, a bright new subway terminal opened, featuring a tall, arched roof admitting sunshine, replacing an ancient shed that had been allowed to deteriorate almost from the day it opened in 1920. In fact, the builder, Granite Helmar Construction, has included working solar paneling in the design. Classic sea green and red BMT signs from the façade of the old station were removed, repaired, and replaced in their old positions. A new 370-foot glass-brick wall mural by artist Robert Wilson, "My Coney Island Baby," featuring silk-screened archival images celebrating the characters and entertainments of historic Coney Island, has been installed. The dank, dismal atmosphere has disappeared.

139 Terminal Hotel
Mermaid and Surf Avenues

Coney Island remains home to some old seaside resort hotels, some functioning, some not. The Terminal Hotel became terminal long ago, but the 1903 Surf Hotel, on

Surf Avenue and Henderson Walk, is still in business, now known as the Shore Hotel.

140 Henderson's Dance Hall
Surf and Stillwell Avenues

The building on the southeast corner of Stillwell and Surf Avenues, stretching south to Bowery Street and housing Faber's Fascination (where I spent hours on the pinball machines in the 1970s) and the adjoining "Shoot the Freak" was built in 1899 as a dance hall by Fred Henderson. The building was gutted in a 1903 fire, rebuilt, but then cut back in 1923 when Stillwell Avenue was widened. Until 1984, the building housed Lily Santangelo's House of Wax.

141 Popper Building
Surf Avenue, east of Stillwell Avenue

Herman Popper and his brother built this building as a distillery and later, a tavern, in 1904. Unfortunately, it's been "assaulted" by garish signage. By 2002, an art gallery occupied the top floor.

the 1980s; only its original mansard roof can be made out.

 144 Thunderbolt and Playland

Boardwalk and West 16th Street

According to Coney Island historian Charles Denson, Playland began life as Silver's Penny Arcade in 1930, and a former "change boy," Alex Elowitz, bought it in 1957. The Elowitz family ran Playland for the next twenty-four years, and closed it in 1981. The old building has remained empty ever since. Taking a peek inside, you can make out 1950s-era murals by cartoonist Larry Milliard. Next to Playland, the deteriorating Thunderbolt roller coaster stood for many years, closed in 1983, and was finally razed in 2000. It was built atop the old Kensington Hotel. The building became the home of Fred Moran and companion May Timpano, who lived under the roller coaster for decades. It inspired Alvy Singer's family's house in Woody Allen's *Annie Hall*.

Across the street from Playland, on the northwest corner of Surf Avenue and West 16th Street, embedded in the sidewalk in

142 Loew's/Shore Theater

Surf and Stillwell Avenues

Originally a theater featuring live shows and first-run movies on Surf and Stillwell Avenues, Loew's Theater, built in the 1920s, featured a Nedick's on the ground floor by the 1960s and offices on the upper floors. It was once the second tallest building in Coney Island, next to the now-demolished Half Moon Hotel. Coney Island's high-rise developments are now much taller than either.

By the 1970s, Loew's, by then known as the Shore Theater, was home to X-rated grind-house films. Nedicks gave way to a succession of businesses like the Kansas Fried Chicken and Gayway Bar and Grill; these days, not much is happening.

143 Grashorn Building

Surf Avenue and Jones Walk

This plain, maroon structure is the oldest building on Surf Avenue, having been built in the 1880s by Henry Grashorn as a hardware store. Its shingles, clapboard siding, and dormer windows were all removed in

front of yet another empty lot used for school bus parking, you can make out the name of Seven Seas, a restaurant that stood there years ago.

145 Sweet Childs o' Mine

Surf Avenue and West 12th Street, and Boardwalk and West 21st Street

Coney Island featured two branches of the old Childs Restaurant chain, one of the first restaurant chains in the country, whose heyday came in the first three decades of the twentieth century. At the southwest corner of Surf Avenue and West 12th Street, the old Childs is an Italian Renaissance classic. It's been compromised over the years, but its distinctive eaves and brackets on the roof have survived. It's the present home of the Coney Island Museum and the Sideshow by the Seashore.

The Childs on the boardwalk and West 21st Street is an otherworldly apparition that has to be seen to be believed. Graffiti demons can't mar its grandeur. It was built by architects Ethan Dennison and Frederic Hirons in 1924 with an exterior of soft stucco and four marble columns emphasized by four multicolored rondels depicting: King Neptune; a Venetian galleon; the *Golden Hind*, the flagship of Queen Elizabeth's fleet; and two fish swimming in rough seas. This Childs branch closed in the 1950s and later became a candy factory. In 2003, it was, thankfully, declared a landmark and will not share the fate of the almost equally ornate Washington Baths, which stood on its left side for many years.

146 Bungalows

Boardwalk and West 32nd Street

At one time, the streets between Surf Avenue and the boardwalk featured a number of summer bungalows (similar to the situation at Rockaway Beach). Over the years, the bungalows fell out of use and the streets either became abandoned or had housing projects constructed on them. The remnants of one such bungalow colony still can be found from West 32nd to West 33rd Streets, between the boardwalk and an alley called Sea Place.

Sheepshead Bay resembles a small fish-ing village with its rows of boats lining Emmons Avenue, taking amateur fishermen and grizzled seadogs out to the Atlantic in search of bluefish and crabs. In the late 1800s, and for a few decades more, the town, along with its neighbors, Manhattan Beach and Oriental Beach, attracted summer vacationers and later, residents. In fact, Victorian seaside hotels, the Sea Beach Palace and the West End Hotel, gave their names to the steam railroads that brought Brooklynites to their doors. (Another hotel, the Van Sicklen, had a station on the Culver Line named for it, but it was renamed Neptune Avenue after the nearest thoroughfare, in the 1990s.) After the Sheepshead Bay Racetrack closed in 1910, streets were cut through and residential housing filled in. The north side of Emmons Avenue features Lundy's Restaurant, Pip's Comedy Club (famed for helping introduce many of the greats, including Adam Sandler and Jerry Seinfeld), Roll-n-Roaster, and some bait-and-tackle shops, but most of its grand old mansions have been torn down.

Walk down Brighton Beach Avenue under the El and experience the sights and tastes of Little Moscow, a haven for Russian immigrants over the last few decades.

Then follow Emmons Avenue past the party boats, grab some seafood lunch at Lundy's, cross the rickety wood bridge to Manhattan Beach, and make a day east of Coney Island.

SUBWAY: Ⓑ or Ⓠ to Sheepshead Bay Road or Brighton Beach

BUS: B4 on Neptune and Emmons Avenues; **B1** on Brighton Beach Avenue; **B36** on Avenue Z; **B68** on Coney Island and Brighton Beach Avenues; **B49** on Sheepshead Bay Road, West End Avenue, or Oriental Boulevard

147 Wood Bridge
Over Sheepshead Bay, from Emmons Avenue south to Shore Boulevard

Spanning Sheepshead Bay is a picturesque wood bridge with a low fence that looks as if you could easily jump over it into the bay, or even get knocked into the waters below if sufficiently jostled. The bridge has a very old pedigree: It was first opened by Long Island Rail Road king Austin Corbin in 1880. After a few false starts (Corbin kept closing the bridge since he thought "undesirables" would frequent his development, the then-exclusive Manhattan Beach), it has been continuously open since. It's called the Ocean Avenue Bridge, even though it's a block west of Ocean Avenue.

The bridge was lit by mini-versions of the old Belt Parkway "woodie" poles; faux "bishop's crook" fixtures were installed in the late 1990s.

148 Guardhouses
West End Avenue and Oriental Boulevard; Shore Boulevard and Exeter Street

Two small structures that look like toll-booths can be found in Manhattan Beach,

one at Oriental Boulevard and Westend Avenue, the other at Shore Boulevard near the Ocean Avenue pedestrian bridge.

These were never tollbooths, though. These structures are reminders that this used to be a private neighborhood (like Sea Gate to the west) called Manhattan Beach Estates, opened in 1906. When it was still a private development, guards posted at these gatehouses allowed only residents and expected guests to enter the area.

149 Emmons Avenue Mansion
Emmons and Dooley Streets

The former Poole Lane, between Emmons Avenue and the Belt Parkway near East

21st Street, has been mostly obliterated by a housing project for senior citizens. The lane ran alongside this building, Emmons Avenue's last remaining grand seaside mansion, with a beautiful double-decker porch.

150 Alleys of Sheepshead Bay
Haring, Brown, and Batchelder Streets, north of Emmons Avenue

Sheepshead Bay still has many bungalows on its eastern end, which have tiny alleys interspersed between them; Brighton Beach, to the west, has similar tiny pedestrian ways between its one- and two-family homes. Brighton Beach's alleys lost their names decades ago, and are now called Brighton First Place, Road, Terrace, etc., but in Sheepshead Bay, the alleys have kept their character.

Most of the alleys came into existence during a building boom between 1920 and 1926. Sheepshead Bay for a while was known as Brooklyn's gold coast, with dozens of extravagant hotels and restaurants. Eventually, the magnates and nabobs moved east, and cheaper bungalows and taverns replaced the more extravagant dwellings.

In 1920, a developer named Robert Densely bought land north of Emmons Avenue, east of East 29th Street, and west of Batchelder Street, which was mostly a marsh. He dredged sand from the bay and built one-story, bungalow-type homes on the lots, with the alleys located between the buildings named for friends of Densely and building executives with whom he dealt: thus, Canda, Hitchings, Lincoln, Dunn, Gunnison, Stanton, Lake, Mesereau, and Losee have passed into the Brooklyn street directory.

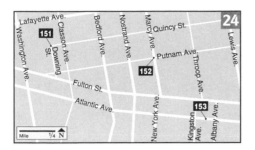

Myrtle and Willoughby Avenues; **B44** on Bedford and Nostrand Avenues; **B48** on Franklin and Classon Avenues; **B52** on Greene and Gates Avenues

Bedford was a Brooklyn farming com-munity first settled in 1677 by British governor Richard Nicolls, who founded the settlement at the junction of two former Indian trails. After the Revolutionary War, the land was gradually divided into lots, and houses began to appear, though the farmland hung on in some areas until after the Civil War. The opening of the Brooklyn Els on Lexington and Myrtle Avenues in the 1880s provided a whole new building boom. The last two decades of the nineteenth century and first two of the twentieth gave rise to the area's distinctive brownstone architecture. Gradually, Bedford and the neighboring community to the east, Stuyvesant Heights, were referred to as one large neighborhood, Bedford-Stuyvesant, which today stretches from roughly Washington Avenue on the west to Broadway on the east, and from Flushing Avenue on the north to Atlantic Avenue in the south.

Walk Jefferson Avenue between Nostrand and Tompkins Avenues, or MacDonough, between Tompkins and Stuyvesant Avenues, and you will find some of the best brownstone architecture Brooklyn has to offer.

SUBWAY: **C** to Franklin, Nostrand, Kingston-Throop, or Utica Avenues; **G** to Clinton–Washington, Classon, Bedford–Nostrand, or Myrtle–Willoughby Avenues

BUS: B25 on Fulton Street; **B26** on Putnam Avenue and Halsey Street; **B38** on

151 Broken Angel
Quincy and Downing Streets

This building looks like something Frank Gehry or Sir Norman Foster might dream up, but on a smaller budget. It is the creation of artist Arthur Wood, who purchased the building in 1979 and added a full two stories of brickwork, arches, mirrors, and masonry to a four-story building. He calls the artwork "Broken Angel."

152 Boys' High ➤
Marcy Avenue and Putnam Avenue

Irish architect James Naughton built the block-long Boys' High School at Marcy and Putnam Avenues from 1891 to 1892, with its imposing corner towers and rich terracotta details. Authors Norman Mailer, Jack Newfield, Isaac Asimov, and NBA Phoenix Suns star Connie Hawkins attended school

BROOKLYN

Agate Court

153 Alice and Agate Courts
Atlantic Avenue, between Kingston and Albany Avenues

here. Boys' High's towers are of two distinct designs: one is a tall, squarish tower with thin windows, and the other is a more traditional conical tower that seems to match the rest of the building more. Its roof is pleasantly uneven, with cornices, flagpoles, dormers, arches, and moldings.

Huddled against the shadow of the El along the north side of Atlantic Avenue between Kingston and Albany Avenues are two charming cul-de-sacs called Alice and Agate Courts. Filled with charming row houses, the two alleys stand out along a road filled with gas stations and auto-repair shops. The two courts date to about 1890.

Brownsville and East New York are neighborhoods of eastern Brooklyn delineated in great part by the Bay Ridge branch of the LIRR. In the north, Brownsville runs from East New York Avenue, on the Bedford-Stuyvesant border, south to its border with Canarsie at the railroad; East New York begins at the railroad and continues east to the Queens line at Ozone Park, with the neighborhoods of Highland Park and Cypress Hills to its north, and Jamaica Bay on its south.

Though Dutch immigrants established some homes and farms in Brownsville and East New York in the 1700s, the area did not gel as a community until the early-to-mid-1800s. East New York was developed by John R. Pitkin, a Connecticut merchant beginning in 1835, while Brownsville is named for Charles S. Brown, who subdivided the area in 1865. The area reached its zenith in the early twentieth century when Pitkin Avenue became one of Brooklyn's premier shopping streets, and it retains its vibrancy even today.

SUBWAY: ③ to Rockaway Avenue, Junius Street, Pennsylvania Avenue, or Van Siclen Avenue; ❶ to Sutter, Livonia, or New Lots Avenues

BUS: B14 on Pitkin, Dumont, and Sutter Avenues; **B15** on New Lots Avenue; **20** or **B83** on Pennsylvania Avenue; **B60** on Rockaway Avenue

154 Loew's Pitkin Theatre
1501 Pitkin Avenue at Saratoga Avenues

The magnificent Loew's Pitkin, taking up an entire block on the avenue between Legion Street and Saratoga Avenue, was built in 1929 by Thomas Lamb and seated 2,827 patrons. Unfortunately, like so many of the grand theaters of the era, it went out of business in the 1960s and has pretty much been left to deteriorate.

155 Holy Trinity Russian Orthodox Church ➤
400 Glenmore Avenue

An onion-domed fantasy rising from the horizon as you pass on the elevated L train, the Holy Trinity Russian Orthodox Church at New Jersey and Glenmore Avenues looks even better up close. Surprisingly, it was built in 1935, but appears to be much older.

BROOKLYN

156 Fortunoff's Sign
Livonia and Pennsylvania Avenues

Fortunoff's got its start more than eighty years ago in East New York. Amazingly, a painted sign advertising its old presence can still be found here on Pennsylvania Avenue (Granville Payne Avenue), just south of Livonia. "The Source" was opened under the El in 1922 by Max and Clara Fortunoff as a household appliance store.

157 New Lots Reformed Church
New Lots and Schenck Avenues

The oldest building in East New York, this church was built in 1823 by local Dutch farmers, because of the inconvenience of traveling by wagon to the former nearest church, Flatlands Dutch Reformed on Kings Highway. It's a simple, country church and churchyard. The street in back of the churchyard, McClancy Place, used to be called, fittingly enough, Repose Place.

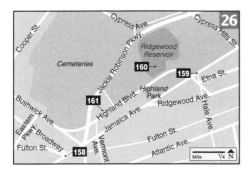

Highland Park and Cypress Hills were first settled in the early 1800s along the tolled Jamaica Plank Road, now called Jamaica Avenue, while Highland Park itself was opened in 1903. Cypress Hills is also known as City Line: Prior to the 1898 consolidation, the City of Brooklyn ended here at the Queens County line.

SUBWAY: ① to Broadway Junction, Van Siclen Avenue, Cleveland Street, Crescent Street, or Cypress Hills; Ⓐ, Ⓒ, or Ⓛ to East New York

BUS: Q24 on Atlantic Avenue; **Q56** on Jamaica Avenue

158 Broadway Junction
Fulton Street at Broadway and Jamaica Avenue

Although demolition and redesign have been chipping into it for many years, Broadway Junction, where Brooklyn's Broadway, Fulton Street, and Jamaica Avenue all meet, remains a haven—perhaps a heaven—for Brooklyn's train buffs. Three elevated lines all came together here, accompanied by an IND subway line and Brooklyn's second largest train yard, *and* a Long Island Rail Road line. Of the elevated lines, only two, the Canarsie L and Nassau Street–Jamaica J remain; the Fulton Street Line had succumbed to competition from the IND line below it by 1950. Many of the streets in the vicinity of Jewell Square (as the junction is officially known) provide great views of the "big iron" elevated structure.

159 National Cemetery
Jamaica Avenue and Hale Street

There are a total of seventeen cemeteries in Cypress Hills on either side of the Brooklyn-Queens border. It's a hilly area, where a glacier was stopped cold thousands of years ago, depositing debris in its advance, accounting for the hills in the middle of Brooklyn and Queens. Each and every one of the more than 21,000 stones at National Cemetery at Jamaica Avenue and Hale Street bears the cross that appears on the gravestones of military veterans.

Cypress Hills National Cemetery is one of the original fourteen National Cemeteries. Its site had already been established before its national designation, as part of the larger Cypress Hills Cemetery. More than 7,000 Civil War veterans, Union and Confederate, are buried at Cypress Hills National. Only the Gettysburg and Arlington Cemeteries contain more Civil War veterans killed at Gettysburg than does Cypress Hills National. Private Alfred Mitchell was the first Union interment. Twenty-two Congressional Medal of Honor recipients, marked by gold-lettered marble headstones, are here.

Three members of the 7th U.S. Cavalry

BROOKLYN

who survived the battle of Little Big Horn, June 25, 1876, are interred at Cypress Hills National, including Italian-born John Martin (Giovanni Martini), who had served in his youth under Giuseppe Garibaldi and was the only survivor of General Custer's company at the battle. Nine other nations, Argentina, Brazil, Canada, France, Italy, Poland, Russia, Spain, and the U.K., claim interments in the cemetery, including twenty-five French sailors who died while on duty in American waters in World War I, and British Revolutionary War soldiers whose remains were transferred to Cypress Hills National in 1909, the earliest war dead in the cemetery.

160 Ridgewood Reservoir
Vermont Place and Highland Boulevard

Ridgewood Reservoir, along Vermont Place north of Highland Boulevard, straddles the border of Brooklyn and Queens just south of the Jackie Robinson Park-

way. The reservoir was built in 1856 and was used in Brooklyn and Queens' water supply for more than 100 years. It was decommissioned in 1959, but was used as a backup sporadically for the next thirty years, finally ceasing all operations in 1990. At its peak, it held more than 154 million gallons of water. Its fifty acres were added to NYC's 28,800 acres of parkland in 2004. The best view of the reservoir can be found along the jogging track next to the Jackie Robinson Parkway east of Vermont Place.

Close-up at Grand Army Plaza showing General Grant on horseback. See page 86.

161 Highland Boulevard ≺
Between Bulwer and Vermont Places

A clutch of impressive mansions peer down from the high hill along Highland Boulevard to East New York. On clear days, you can see all the way to Jamaica Bay. A walk along the boulevard, on Sunnyside Avenue, a block south, and some streets at the bottom of the hill such as Arlington Avenue and Ashford Street, will reveal surprising remnants of when the area was thought of as a suburban retreat.

a. b. c.

d.

e.

a. *The private enclave of Forest Hills Gardens in Queens has its own unique set of lampposts and street signs. This one on Ascan Avenue is the only one to sport an orange fire alarm signal.*

b. *This short bishop's crook lamppost can be found on Steinway Street in Astoria. It still carries the frames for two "humpback" street signs in common use from the 1910s through the 1960s.*

c. *This Type 24M lamppost, colloquially known as a Corvington, stood guard on Rockaway Boulevard in Rosedale, Queens, for perhaps seventy-five years before being removed in 2002.*

f.

g.

h.

d. *This is the only twin bishop's-crook lamppost in NYC. It was installed in the late 1990s on Irving Place and East 18th Street, across from Pete's Tavern.*

e. *Many of Robert Moses's NYC and Long Island parkways, which date back to the 1920s, featured wood-masted poles like this rare one in Bayside, Queens.*

f. *Twin-masted cast-iron poles were often used to illuminate wide roadways and important intersections. This one, on Amsterdam Avenue and Hamilton Place in Manhattan, is the only one remaining with this type of heavier base and finials on the mast.*

g. *From the mid-1920s through the late 1950s, many NYC street corners featured long arm traffic light masts with an automobile wheel design in the scrollwork. This one is still there on the 86th Street Transverse Road in Central Park.*

h. *Legions of these reverse-scrolled cast-iron poles, known as Type Fs, once lit NYC's side streets, as well as stretches of Seventh and other avenues. This is one of two that can still be found on the pedestrian bridge at the Belt Parkway and 27th Avenue in Brooklyn.*

Manhattan

is the cultural center and lifeblood of the five boroughs: The world's financial and entertainment capital, with miles and miles of shopping, the Chrysler and Empire State Buildings, the punks in the Village, the jazz of Harlem . . . it's all here. But Manhattan also has acres and acres of untrodden forests, alleys dating back to the days of peglegged Dutchmen and tricornerhatted Tories, flocks of rusted 100-year-old lampposts, abandoned subway stops, statues depicting unremembered heroes, relics of forgotten wars, remnants of post roads from the 1700s, and a Hollywood-style sidewalk of fame.

For its first 150 years or so, New York City was confined to the southern tip of Manhattan Island, and was originally a Dutch trading outpost featuring a fort, first called Fort Amsterdam and then British Fort George. The city blossomed as one of the world's great ports with the Hudson and East Rivers meeting at the Battery. Later, the depth of the bedrock allowed Manhattan to grow as high as its great architects could dream.

Construction of New York's City Hall was completed in 1812. Few thought the city would advance much farther north than where the Post Road to Boston branched from Broadway. North of City Hall, Manhattan was a collection of small towns, such as Bloomingdale, Harmansville, and Yorktown. The year before City Hall opened, a blueprint called the Commissioners' Plan was approved, and drawn up by surveyor John Randel Jr., instituting the island's street grid system, and development gradually spread uptown.

Deep within the bustling grid that begins at Houston Street and continues for more than 200 numbered streets uptown, amid the winding, rambling lanes of Greenwich Village, and even in the clean geometry of Midtown, there are places that evade detection. ✍

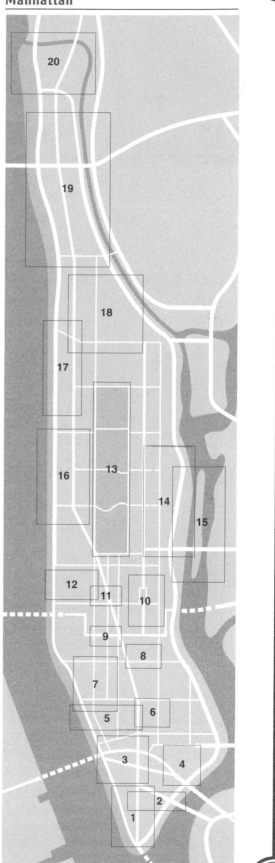

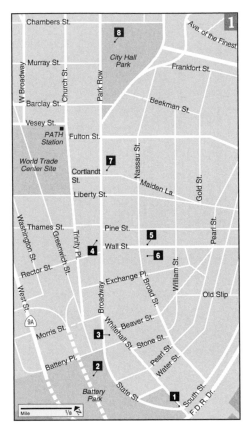

In lower Manhattan, traces of the past can be found in its street names. Broad Street was the widest street in the area other than Broadway, and it got that way because tall-masted Dutch ships once sailed down the middle; the waterway was paved over in the 1700s, leaving an especially wide roadway. Old Slip, Peck Slip, and Market Slip were once waterways where ships "slipped" in to dock. Bridge Street crossed the Broad Street canal, while Wall Street commemorates a wall built of timber and earthwork by the Dutch in 1652 to keep marauding Brits and Indians out. Though the wall was dismantled in 1699, terra-cotta plaques depicting it can be seen in the Lexington Avenue Wall Street station serving the 4 and 5 trains.

SUBWAY: ① to South Ferry or Rector Street; ② or ③ to Wall Street or Ful-ton Street; ④ or ⑤ to Bowling Green, Wall Street, or Fulton Street; Ⓐ or Ⓒ to Broadway–Nassau, Ⓔ to World Trade Center; Ⓡ or Ⓦ to Whitehall, Rector, or Cortlandt Streets, or to City Hall; Ⓙ, Ⓜ, or Ⓩ to Broad or Fulton Streets.

BUS: M1 or **M6** to Broadway and Trinity Place; **M9** to Water Street, State Street, or Battery Park City; **M20** to Battery Park City; **M15** to Water Street

1 Peter Minuit Plaza
Whitehall and South Streets

Peter Minuit (1580–1638) is reputed to have purchased the whole of Manhattan Island in 1626 from the Lenape Indians for goods valued at 60 Dutch guilders. The actual transaction likely took place at Shoko-ropack Rock in today's Inwood Hill Park, almost as far removed from Peter Minuit Plaza as you can get and still be in Manhattan. Minuit served as New Netherland's third Director General for the next seven years after the deal took place.

2 Battery Park Control House
Battery Park at State and Bridge Streets

The subway station at Bowling Green is among the more unusual in the city. It is the site of one of NYC's more unfortunate subway décor makeovers and the location of one of New York's last remaining above-ground station houses.

Bowling Green Station opened on July 10, 1905. Its architects, George C. Heins and Christopher LaFarge, lined its coved (indented) walls with elaborate name tablets and lengthy, mosaic "tapestries." In 1978, the original designs were covered in oceans of burnt orange, a favorite color of subway renovators in the 1960s and 1970s.

Heins and LaFarge also designed Battery Park's two "control houses" in which fares were taken. One of them remains just south of Bowling Green at State and Bridge Streets. Upon entering it, note the word "Entrance" above the interior north doorway. Subways once had designated entrances and exits, and passengers were expected to use their respective passages in or out, hence the term "control house." The Battery Park Control House achieved official NYC landmark status in 1973.

 **3 Bowling Green**

Broadway and Whitehall Street

Bowling Green, where State Street meets Whitehall Street and Battery Place, is where Broadway begins. There's a continuous road beginning here that runs all the way north to Rensselaer County (north of the Bronx, the road is known as the Albany Post Road, after its original use for mail carriers), and if you include New York State Route 9, the road goes all the way to the Canadian border, just north of the town of Champlain. Bowling Green was indeed used for lawn bowling, starting in 1732 when, by order of the city council, it became NYC's first public park. In the early 1770s, it was surrounded by an iron fence topped by crowns; a gilded statue of George III was erected in the center of the green. When the patriots declared independence in 1776, the statue was pulled down and, according to legend, melted down for ammunition. The fence, without its crowns, is still there.

4 James Leeson's Grave

Trinity Cemetery at Broadway and Wall Street

There's a curious set of symbols displayed on the top of James Leeson's tombstone in Trinity Cemetery at Broadway and Wall Street. Leeson, who died in 1794, left behind an elaborate stone on which Masonic symbols such as a compass and hourglass are carved. At the top of the stone are a series of boxes and partly rendered boxes, some with one dot, some with two, and others blank. For over a century, the significance of these marks was debated. Was it a secret message or just ornamental filigree?

First, to find Leeson's grave: Look for the stone with the unusual markings at the top just to the left of Soldier's Monument in the north end of the cemetery just in front of Broadway.

In 1889, the *Trinity Record* (Trinity Church's newspaper of the period) announced that they had solved the mystery, and it was fairly easy to figure out. Simply set up three tic-tac-toe boards, nine squares each, and place the letters A, B, C, D, E, F, G, H, I in the first, K, L, M, N, O, P,

Q, R, S in the second, and T, U, V, W, X, Y, Z in the third, leaving the last two squares blank. Then, place one dot on each letter in your first tic-tac-toe board, two in your second, and none in your third. (Count I and J as one square: in Colonial-era orthography, the two letters were the same.) Using this system, Leeson's final dispatch is spelled out quite clearly. The inscription says, "Remember Death."

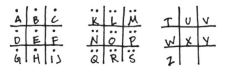

James Leeson's cryptogram

The oldest stone in the cemetery is right up front—you can spot it through the fence from Broadway. Richard Churcher was only five when he passed away in 1681. He's recalled by a short, informally cut stone. A "reward" of sorts can be found on the back of the stone: a skull and crossbones, a popular motif on gravestones of the period. This was a burying ground even before the first Trinity Church was raised in 1696; the present Trinity was finished in 1846.

5 Federal Hall and the Map of Ohio

Nassau and Wall Streets

The Federal Hall National Memorial, at 26 Wall Street where it meets Broad and Nassau Streets across the way from the New York Stock Exchange, is an imposing Greek Revival building resembling the Parthenon in Athens. It takes its name from the old Federal Hall, which served as New York City's first City Hall from 1701 until 1812. On April 30, 1789, George Washington took his oath as president just about where his imposing statue by John Quincy Adams Ward would be installed in 1883. The first Federal Hall gradually fell into disuse and disrepair, and it was sold and subsequently demolished in 1812. Thirty years later, in 1842, the U.S. Customs House was built on the spot. The building then became the second Federal Hall.

Intriguingly, there is a plaque on the Nassau Street end depicting the state of Ohio. With all the history that has occurred here since 1701 . . . why Ohio? The plaque commemorates the Ohio Company of Associates, consisting of former Revolutionary War officers and Massachusetts soldiers that was formed in 1786 to plan the purchase and settlement of lands along the Ohio River.

6 The Bombs of Wall Street

Wall and Broad Streets

On September 16, 1920, a bomb exploded in front of 23 Wall Street, the longtime offices of J.P. Morgan Inc., causing thirty-three deaths and 400 injuries.

When 23 Wall Street was constructed in 1913–14, the Morgan name was so well-known that it was considered unnecessary to mark the building with it. The exterior of 23 Wall Street is pockmarked on the Wall Street side: these marks were produced by flying debris from the explosion, and they have since remained unrepaired.

Investigations centered on known Sicilian, Romanian, and Russian terrorist groups, but no sure leads developed and the FBI dropped the case in 1940. It is widely surmised that the blast was done by anarchic terrorists bent on destroying a building symbolic of American capitalism. The Bolsheviks had taken Russia by force two years earlier.

7 Broadway's Sidewalk Clock

Broadway and Maiden Lane

One of Manhattan's most unique and beautiful monuments gets stepped on thousands of times each day.

William Barthman Jewelers store's sidewalk clock on Broadway and Maiden Lane was embedded there in 1899. It has been attacked by vandals and trodden on for years but it keeps on ticking (with the help of an electric motor). Barthman first set up shop in the financial district in 1884. An organization known as the Maiden Lane Historical Society set up a plaque at Barthman's in 1928 depicting what Broadway and Maiden Lane looked like that year. In 1946, the NYPD estimated that 51,000 people stepped on the clock each day between 11:00 AM and 2:00 PM.

8 City Hall Subway Station

Located under City Hall Park

The world's most gorgeous ex–subway station is located at the south edge of the loop that turns Lexington Avenue IRT local 6 trains around to the south of the Brooklyn Bridge Station. It's been closed to the public since 1945, but can be seen by staying on the 6 local after the end of the line riding southbound as it loops around to enter the Brooklyn Bridge Station northbound, provided the conductor allows you to do so.

City Hall Station was designed by the architectural firm of Heins and LaFarge, who built the subway's oldest stations back in the early 1900s. The construction included such features as arches, vaulted ceilings, and polychromatic tiles. Elegant chandeliers supply light and are supplemented by vaulted skylights of amethyst glass—which are still visible from City Hall Park, in a section of it now closed to the public. Arched stairways led from street level to the mezzanine, where tickets could be purchased. Tokens were never available at the City Hall Station since it was closed before tokens were adopted.

The wide turns a modern subway train has to take as it wends through City Hall Station make for large gaps between the platform and the cars. That, and the gradually declining use of the station, sealed the station's doom as an active subway stop in 1945.

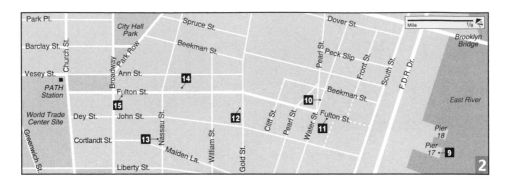

Nineteenth- and early-twentieth-century pictures of South Street show sloops, square-riggers, clipper ships, and many other classes of vessels docked right next to the street, which formerly abutted the East River. The Fulton Fish Market, NYC's primary seafood wholesale market, and a large part of the neighborhood's history, moved to Hunts Point in the Bronx in 2005, after a tenure here of more than 170 years. It's gone now, as are Sweet's and Sloppy Louie's restaurants (however, the old Paris Bar and Grill at South Street and Peck Slip still stands as it has since 1873, as does the oldest NYC restaurant, the Bridge Café, at Water and Dover Streets, dating back to 1794).

New York City's preeminence as a world-class seaport is in the past, but remaining here are a trove of seventeenth- and eighteenth-century buildings, Belgian-blocked streets, and, of course, the South Street Seaport Museum at Pier 17 that includes sailing ships refitted as water-borne museums and training centers, such as the *Wavertree* (built in 1885), the *Peking* (1911), the *Pioneer* (1885), the *Lettie G. Howard* (1893), and the *W.O. Decker* (1930).

If Pier 17's touristy vibe is a bit much, stroll the streets of the immediate seaport area, Pike Slip, Beekman, Water, and Front Streets, many of which have been marvelously re-bricked, and see the ancient buildings, some of which go back to the 1790s

(the Joseph Rose House at 273 Water Street was built in 1773, making it the third-oldest building in Manhattan). An indispensable guide to the area is Ellen Fletcher's *Walking Around in South Street*, published by the South Street Seaport Museum; contact the Museum at (212) 748-8590 or visit www.southstseaport.org.

SUBWAY: ② or ③ to Fulton Street

BUS: M9 on Pearl Street; **M22** to Frankfort Street

9 Lightship
Pier 17, South Street Seaport

One of NYC's few remaining floating lighthouses, or *lightships*, the *Ambrose* (LV87) (the nomenclature differentiates it from two other lightships named *Ambrose*), served the Port of New York, the Coast Guard, and Fort Hancock, New Jersey (as an examination ship) from 1908 to 1966. It was one of three such lightships patrolling the Ambrose Channel, the southern entrance to New York Harbor off the coast of New Jersey. Lightships were employed where the seabed was sandy or otherwise inhospitable for construction of a light-house, but by the 1960s and 1970s, most lightships had been replaced by automated towers. According to *Lighthouses of New York* author Jim Crowley, in 1921, the *Ambrose* (LV87) was the first lightship to use a radio fog beacon. In 1968, the *Ambrose* (LV87) was permanently docked at Pier 17 and has served as a floating museum ever since.

tall pole at the apex originally had a metal ball that, when signaled by a telegraph at the National Observatory in Washington, D.C., would drop at noon daily: that feature is currently being restored.

11 Schermerhorn Row
Fulton Street, between Water and South Streets

Ship chandler (an entrepreneur supplying onboard equipment) Peter Schermerhorn Jr. built this row of Georgian buildings on Fulton Street, between Water and South Streets, between 1810 and 1812. However, he first had to fill in the land: Front Street, as its name implies, was the approximate original shoreline. The original Fulton Ferry, which ran between Manhattan and Brooklyn's Fulton Streets, began to supply potential customers in 1814, and, in that year, the first storefronts appeared on what would come to be called Schermerhorn Row. The mansard roofs and dormer windows near South Street were added in the 1860s; many additions have been made over the years. Schermerhorn Row was restored in 1983 as part of the Historic District construction. The South Street Seaport Museum has recently opened Schermerhorn Row's upper rooms as gallery space.

10 Titanic Memorial
Water and Fulton Streets

New York City has formal, informal, and completely accidental homages to those who died in the sinking of the R.M.S. *Titanic* on April 15, 1912. On the corner of Fulton and Water Streets stands the Titanic Memorial Lighthouse, dedicated exactly one year after the sinking and originally placed atop the Seamen's Church Institute, a former fourteen-story building at South Street and Coenties Slip. In 1967, the Seamen's Institute moved and the building was later demolished. The lighthouse, fortunately, was preserved and by 1976, it had been installed at its present location. The

12 Excelsior Power Company
Edens Alley at Gold Street

Gold Street weaves through lower Manhattan, reminding us that this part of the

city was built long before the automobile. It was named for a flower, the celandine, called "*gouwe*" by the Dutch. The British, who had a talent for boiling down Dutch names for easier pronunciation, eventually Anglicized the name to Golden Hill.

At 33 Gold Street, just south of Fulton Street, architect William Grinnell constructed the Excelsior Power Company building in 1888. Its huge, gorgeous blue-green cast-iron sign with its intricate lettering has been pretty much undisturbed since. The building originally housed coal-fired electric generators.

Next to the cast-iron sign, a 1910-era wall-bracket lamp, with original metal scrollwork and incandescent luminaire, can still be found. Opposite the building, note the tiny, brick-paved alley that dog-legs around to Fulton Street. Until 1842 (no one knows when it originally appeared), it was known as Eden's Alley, but between 1842 and 2000 it was called Ryders Alley. In 2000, a compromise of sorts was reached when the portion facing Gold Street was re-designated as Edens Alley and the portion facing Fulton Street retained the Ryders name.

13 Ben and . . . George?
Nassau Street, south of John Street

By some accounts, this building at 63 Nassau Street was built in the 1860s by an early giant of cast-iron architecture, James Bogardus (1800–1874). His use of cast-iron to cover building exteriors later led to steel-frame construction. In the Soho area, you'll find dozens of distinctive buildings with such cast-iron cladding. A short street near Fort Tryon Park in far upper Manhattan is named for Bogardus, far from his architectural innovations.

Of note here are the patriotic depictions of Ben Franklin. The empty spaces between the two Franklins used to contain two similar portraits of George Washington.

14 K & E
Fulton Street, east of Nassau Street

At 127 Fulton Street you will find the Keuffel & Esser Building. It was built in 1893 by the architectural firm DeLemos and Cordes, who went on to create the Siegel-Cooper and Macy's department store buildings farther uptown. Above the ground-floor storefront here, you can see the cast-iron detailing: renderings of drafting implements and for some reason, a winged wheel.

Established in 1867, Keuffel & Esser is a company that manufactures compasses, transits, surveying equipment, and other instrumentation—and it is still going strong. The company built the magnificent Clock Tower Building on 3rd and Adams Streets in Hoboken in the 1890s, as well as this distinctive Fulton Street exterior.

15 The 1890s Meet the 1970s
Fulton Street, east of Broadway

On Fulton Street, just east of Broadway, is an original chiseled "Subway" sign installed in the 1930s when the IND opened its Broadway-Nassau Station (the IND complement to the Fulton Street subway complex). Close by are several historical artifacts all rolled into one: an angular 1970s modern front was grafted onto what

looks like an 1890s Beaux Arts building! At one time, no doubt, the two lamps at the top lit up. The "facsimile" and "typewriter" ads look quaint as we head into the middle of the first decade of the twenty-first century.

Known as the Lower West Side before the 1960s, these Manhattan neighborhoods have gone from farmland (1700s) to fashionable residences (early 1800s) to sweatshops hidden behind gorgeous cast-iron fronts (late 1800s). Later, light industry (cardboard, tool, and die makers) occupied these blocks until the mid-1900s, when artists began to occupy the area's spacious lofts. In the 1960s, Soho residents beat back a Robert Moses proposal to build an expressway over Broome Street that would have connected the Manhattan Bridge to the Holland Tunnel. Since then, real estate has been on an upswing, with fashionable restaurants and galleries lining West Broadway, Spring, and the rest of the area's streets. Best of all, the magnificent cast-iron fronts have been mostly preserved. Many of them now contain expensive luxury apartments.

SUBWAY: ① to Chambers, Franklin, or Canal Streets; Ⓐ or Ⓒ to Chambers or Canal Street; Ⓒ or Ⓔ to Spring Street; Ⓡ or Ⓦ to City Hall, Canal Street, or Prince Street

BUS: M6 to Broadway and Sixth Avenue; **M20** to Hudson and Varick Streets; **M21** to Spring Street or Houston Street and Sixth Avenue; **M22** to Chambers Street

16 The Strange Medallion of Harrison Street
Harrison Street, west of Greenwich Street

There's a pedestrian overpass spanning two sections of Independence Plaza above Harrison Street, just west of Greenwich Street. The bridge carries a highly stylized medallion that recollects a lost highway, waterfront, and railroad.

In 1974, Independence Plaza, a large residential complex, rose on land formerly occupied by the Washington produce market. At the same time, the West Side Highway (officially called the Miller, after the Manhattan borough president when the road was built in the early 1930s) was falling apart due to neglect. The section of the road spanning Harrison Street was closed in 1973 and demolished by the mid-1980s.

The highway originally featured Machine Age–style entablatures above every cross street, featuring a highly stylized eagle, as well as signs denoting the cross street (and the pier opposite the cross street). The Harrison Street frieze denotes Pier 23, which was owned by the Baltimore and Ohio Railroad, now a part of CSX. It was saved and placed on this overpass when Independence Plaza was built.

17 Duane Park
Duane and Hudson Streets

Duane Street splits in two in Tribeca, with one half ending at Hudson Street and the other half continuing east into the Foley Square area. Between the two halves, you'll find Duane Park, a spot that has been green since the very beginnings of New York City. It was originally part of a Dutch farm dating back to the mid-1600s that was once owned by the Duke of York of England, who gave it to Trinity Church, which owned vast amounts of property in lower Manhattan. The church sold it to New York City for the grand total of 5 dollars in 1797.

 18 Hudson Street Compass
Hudson and Thomas Streets

A compass is embedded in the sidewalk in front of a brick building on the east side of Hudson Street at Thomas Street. It's a concrete circle with a metal arrow pointing at true north, shown by a metal "N." The compass was likely placed on the sidewalk when the building was constructed many decades ago.

19 Staple and Collister
Staple and Collister Streets

Staple Street is a short alley extending two blocks from Duane Street Park north to Harrison Street, just west of Hudson. Its one unmistakable feature is the huge footbridge that spans over it. According to Tribeca historian Oliver E. Allen, the footbridge appeared at some time between 1900 and 1910, and was built to span two buildings owned by New York Hospital. An "NYH" frieze can still be spotted at the top of a brick building at Staple and Jay Streets.

Collister Street, which runs between Beach and Laight Street west of Hudson, has no grand signature like the Staple Street footbridge, but there's a secret or two to be rooted out. Take a look at the top of the building on the northeast corner of Collister and Hubert Streets: There's a sculpture of a dog's head, surrounded by the words "American Express Co." American Express had a longtime NYC headquarters in what is now Tribeca, at Jay and Hudson Streets. This was one of their stables, topped off with the company's old logo, a rendering of a bulldog. A second canine depiction can be found on Laight and Collister Streets, and yet another on a former American Express building way downtown on Trinity Place.

20 Yankee Ferry
West and North Moore Streets

New York City's oldest ferryboat is located on Pier 25 at West Street near North Moore. According to the *Downtown Express*, a local newspaper, the *Yankee* was built in 1907 and was originally named the *Machigonne*. In its nearly 100 years of ser-

vice, it has ferried tourists to the Statue of Liberty and immigrants from Ellis Island. After 1947, it was rechristened the *Yankee* and was moved to Rhode Island, where it saw service between Providence and Block Island. It was brought to Tribeca in 1990 by former owner Jimmy Gallagher, who lived onboard for more than seventeen years. In 2003, the *Yankee* was purchased by Richard and Victoria MacKenzie-Childs, who reportedly plan to restore it. In 2006, the *Yankee* was displaced for Hudson River Park construction but is expected to return.

21 African Burial Ground

Duane and Elk Streets

Workers excavating a construction site on Duane Street, east of Broadway, in the fall of 1991 stumbled upon human remains interred in wooden boxes about twenty-five feet below street level. A search through property maps revealed that this area was a former burial ground for African Americans enslaved in the early 1700s. In 1993, this small patch of land was declared a national historic landmark.

22 The Sidewalk Subway Map

Greene Street, near Spring Street

In front of the SoHo Building, at 110 Greene Street, between Spring and Prince Streets, you will find NYC's most unusual subway map. Entitled "Subway Map Floating on a New York Sidewalk," it was cre-

ated in 1986 by Françoise Schein, a Belgian artist and architect. The schematic runs the length of the building—87 feet long and 12 feet wide. Embedded in concrete are half-inch-wide stainless-steel bars representing the IRT, IND, and BMT lines, with colored disks indicating subway stops. The project cost an estimated $30,000 to produce and won the City Art Commission Award for the best art project of that year.

23 Sixth Avenue Medallions

Sixth Avenue, north of Canal Street

An unusual lamppost treatment along Sixth Avenue appeared in the early 1960s when member countries in the Organization of American States were represented by medallions mounted on then-new octagonal aluminum poles. (Sixth was "renamed" Avenue of the Americas by Mayor Fiorello La Guardia in 1945.)

Throughout the years, the Department of Transportation has gradually winnowed out the medallions; an entire section of them was eliminated around 1992 when a flock of new retro bishop's crook lampposts were installed. Today, the medallions have two strongholds: Soho/Greenwich Village and a few blocks on Sixth Avenue, just south of Central Park.

24 Charlton-King-Vandam
West of Sixth Avenue

At the northwest corner of Sixth Avenue and King Street, you can see some very old houses. They are part of the Charlton-King-Vandam Historic District and comprise some seventy-two Federal and Greek Revival houses. Many of them were built as early as the 1820s by fur magnate John Jacob Astor on land sold to him in

1817 by Aaron Burr. Astor saw a profitable real-estate investment at Richmond Hill, and built dozens of row houses on Charlton, King, and Vandam Streets, and luckily, most have survived to the present.

The Lower East Side of Manhattan is
roughly defined by East Houston Street
on the north, the East River on the east
and south, and by the Manhattan Bridge
and the Bowery on the west. In the eighteenth and early-nineteenth centuries, the
area was primarily countryside and farmland, attracting prominent merchants and
wealthy landowners such as Henry Rutgers and James De Lancey, whose names
still are prominent on local street signs.
George Washington had a mansion at
3 Cherry Street, on a site now serving as
an anchorage for the Brooklyn Bridge. In
subsequent decades came immigrants:
first the Irish, escaping the potato famine
of the 1840s and British repression in the
1860s; then the Germans, in such numbers that the area became known as Klein-
deutschland ("little Germany"); and later,
Eastern Europeans, many of them Jewish,
escaping persecution in their homelands.
The neighborhood still contains relics of
lost streets, banks lost to hubris, and long-
forgotten political campaigns.

SUBWAY: ⓕ to Second Avenue, Delancey
Street, or East Broadway

BUS: M22 on Madison Street; **M14A** on
Grand Street; **M9** on East Broadway, Essex,
and Clinton Streets; **M15** on Allen Street;
M103 on Bowery

25 Jarmulowsky's Bank
54 Canal Street

At the southwest corner of Canal and Orchard Streets stands a grand twelve-story
building with faux ionic columns on its
curved corner. Bas-reliefs above the doorway flank a broken clock. The building's
name is proclaimed in Roman-style lettering over the door: "Jarmvlowsky's Bank Est
1873."

In 1873, Sender Jarmulowsky started
a bank with his own savings for fellow
Lower East Siders. For its first few years,
Jarmulowsky's Bank was a success, and he
hired the architectural firm of Rouse &
Goldstone to build it a magnificent building. Jarmulowsky passed away shortly after the building opened, believing he had
started an institution that would pass the
test of time. When the Great War broke out
in 1914, many of his depositors withdrew
their funds and sent them to relatives in the
old country, causing the bank to crash.

26 Eldridge Street Synagogue
12 Eldridge Street

Towering above the surrounding tenement
buildings is the Eldridge Street Synagogue;
the architectural firm Herter Brothers
completed it in 1887. The Eldridge Street
Project has been restoring the building
slowly over the past few years. From the

exterior, you can marvel at the Moorish architecture and giant stained-glass window; the twelve roundels of the window represent the twelve tribes of Israel. Inside, note the centrally located bimah, or reader's platform, with its elaborate brass fixtures that were originally illuminated by gas; and the hand-carved walnut Ark of the Torah. The Synagogue is open for tours. Call (212) 219-0888 ext. 206, or visit www.eldridgestreet.org for information.

27 Tenement Museum
Orchard and Broome Streets

Lower East Side residents of the late 1800s and early 1900s would be a little surprised, and more than a few would be somewhat bemused, to discover that their apartments had been converted into a museum. The building at 97 Orchard Street, just north of Broome, was at one time rented by seamstress Nathalie Gumpertz, garment presser Abram Rogarshevsky, and the Confino and Baldizzi families, all representing different eras in its long history. Originally constructed in 1867 without gas, hot water, or flush toilets, it is similar to most of the other tenements in the area. Owners only installed these amenities after housing laws were passed around the turn of the twentieth century. The building is open seven days a week for guided tours. Visit the Lower East Side Tenement Museum office and retail store at 108 Orchard Street. For more information, call (212) 431-0233 or visit www.tenement.org.

28 Ancient Poster Art
Orchard and Broome Streets

A couple of billboards were removed from a wall at Orchard and Broome Streets during renovation of the former Tenement Museum Visitors' Center and store, and a small piece of New York City history was revealed. You can now spot old posters

urging the re-election of Mayor Vincent Impellitteri, who served between 1950 and 1953, and Assemblyman Louis DeSalvio, who served between 1941 and 1979. You can also make out ads for a rally supporting the Israel Orphan Asylum and Hersh's Sacramental Wine, evidence of the Jewish flavor the neighborhood had in the 1950s. The Lower East Side Tenement Museum intends to preserve these relics.

29 Henry Street Settlement ➤
Henry Street, south of Grand Street

Walking down Samuel Dickstein Plaza, an extension of Pitt Street, south of Grand Street, you pass by a building with a back porch. Houses with back porches were more common in Manhattan in 1827, when 263, 265, and 267 Henry Street, now part of the Henry Street Settlement, were built.

In 1893, Lillian Wald started the Visiting Nurse Service in the Lower East Side with philanthropist Jacob Schiff—an institution that is still going strong today. Wald also started the Henry Street Settlement, an organization bringing a wide range of arts and social services to its community.

The Henry Street Settlement has grown to encompass eighteen buildings. Oddly, both Lillian Wald and Jacob Schiff had NYC thoroughfares named for them, but both have fallen into disuse: Lillian Wald Drive had been East Houston Street between Avenue D and the FDR Drive, while the middle lane of Delancey Street, between Bowery and the Williamsburg Bridge, had been known as Schiff Parkway.

30 Wondrous Vista

East Broadway, near Clinton Street

New York's skyscrapers are so massive that they make for unexpected views in places you might not expect them to pop up. A look down East Broadway from about Clinton Street reveals the Woolworth and Municipal Buildings, appearing like the mad dreams of a wedding cake confectioner.

31 A Tarnished Sheriff's Star

Broome near Lewis

There's a service alley leading off to the east from Columbia (Kazan) Street, just north of Grand Street near the Williamsburg

Bridge. Walk up the alley a short distance, and on your left, a lone rusted "bishop's crook" lamppost appears. You'll have to make a bit of an effort to see it in spring or summer, because it stands in a clump of trees at the rear of a playground. It's at the northwest intersection of what was once Broome and Sheriff Streets. Not only is it an increasingly rare cast-iron lamppost remnant . . . it signifies a neighborhood that is no longer there.

Years ago, the Lower East Side was lined with rows and rows of tenement buildings. The streets bore names like Sheriff, Cannon, Mangin, and Goerck (the latter two named for the surveyors and architects who had a hand in NYC's street-grid plan in the early 1800s), Tompkins (named for a New York state governor and U.S. vice president), and Scammel (named for Colonel Alexander Scammel, a Revolutionary War hero from New Hampshire who was captured and killed by the British in 1781). Except for the occasional street like Lewis Street, which has been allowed to survive, most traces of these streets, and the tenements that were built on them, are now gone.

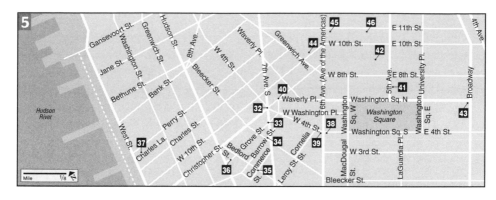

Greenwich Village conjures up visions

of goateed, black-clad hipsters in coffeehouses, but it actually had a long history before the writers, revolutionaries, and bohemians made it their enclave in the early twentieth century.

The original Greenwich Village was a Canarsee Indian fishing village called Seppanikan (some accounts spell it Sapokanican), centered around a stream they called Manetta, meaning "devil water." It became known as Minetta Brook; Minetta Street is located over the brook today. The site was later occupied by the Dutch, whose governor Wouter Van Twiller made it a tobacco plantation. When Manhattan Island was taken over by the British, they called it Greenwich, possibly for the London suburb which is now the starting point for the world's longitude.

When NYC adopted a rigid grid plan for its streets in 1811, Greenwich Village was allowed to maintain its rather confusing street pattern, largely because it had been isolated from the rest of the city by a yellow fever and cholera epidemic in the early 1800s. The street pattern of the Village is largely the same as it was in the late 1700s and early 1800s, with winding paths better suited for foot traffic than automobiles.

SUBWAY: ① to Christopher Street–Sheridan Square; Ⓐ, Ⓑ, Ⓒ, Ⓓ, Ⓔ, Ⓕ, or Ⓥ to West 4th Street; Ⓝ, Ⓡ, or Ⓦ to 8th Street

BUS: M20 to Hudson Street and Seventh Avenue South; **M5** or **M6** on Sixth Avenue; **M8** on Christopher Street and West 10th Street; **M3** or **M5** on Fifth Avenue

32 Hess Estate Triangle

Seventh Avenue South and Christopher Street

Embedded in the sidewalk at the venerable Village Cigars shop at Seventh Avenue South and Christopher Street and trod upon by hundreds of feet each day yet barely noticed is a marker that reads: "Property of the Hess Estate which has never been dedicated for public purposes."

There used to be a five-story residential building on Christopher Street called the Voorhis. It was condemned in the 1910s to make way for the IRT subway, which extended Seventh Avenue south from Greenwich Avenue. However, the Voorhis' owner, David Hess, refused to surrender this small

MANHATTAN

plot to the city to become part of Seventh Avenue South's new sidewalk. The Hesses created this mosaic to let everyone know of their small (*very* small) victory against the city.

Village Cigars moved to its present corner site in 1922, and bought the 500-square-inch property from the Hesses for $1,000. The mosaic has stayed put, while Village Cigars has become an iconic symbol of the neighborhood.

cupies the site was constructed. In 1806, he had moved to New York City, residing on Church, Herring (now Bleecker), and finally, Grove Streets. He lived at 59 Grove for only about a month before his death. He was buried at his farm in New Rochelle, but his bones were eventually dug up and moved to London by political activists (Paine had no heirs to prevent such a thing). No one knows where Paine is buried now.

In 1923, the Greenwich Village Historical Society installed a plaque at 59 Grove Street commemorating the revolutionary.

33 Thomas Paine and Greenwich Village
59 Grove Street

What can a piano bar named Marie's Crisis at 59 Grove Street in Greenwich Village possibly have to do with Thomas Paine, the Revolution-era rabble-rousing pamphleteer?

Marie's Crisis is named for Thomas Paine's 1776 treatise, "The Crisis." It followed up on the themes of his earlier "Common Sense," which laid out, in logical terms, why America had to break from England. ("Marie" is Romany Marie, who was the proprietor of several tearooms in Greenwich Village in the early 1900s.)

But why is Paine honored here? Paine died in 1809 in a small, wood-framed house that had been on this property before the brick building that presently oc-

34 The Village Volcano
Seventh Avenue South and Barrow Street

The Village Volcano looks like a natural rock formation, and while there are bigger natural outcroppings that resemble this one in upper Manhattan and the Bronx, this "volcano" is purely artificial. It was "installed" in 1982 by Christie Powers of the Buffalo Roundhouse restaurant: there was a steam leak in the sidewalk, prompting Powers to construct a volcano from cement and tar and plop it on the leak as a gag. Powers and the Roundhouse are long gone. The "volcano" is still there, but it's likely to remain dormant for the foreseeable future.

35 Isaacs-Hendricks House
Bedford and Commerce Streets

The oldest house in Greenwich Village is at 77 Bedford Street. Known as the Isaacs-Hendricks House, it was built in 1799 (before most of the Village streets had been laid out). Large sections of it, including the brick facing, were added in 1836, and the third floor is practically "new," since it was added in 1928. It is a former farmhouse owned by Harmon Hendricks, a copper merchant who supplied Robert Fulton with materials for boilers that powered the historic *Clermont* steamboat in 1807. Next door, in a house so narrow it rates only half an address, is 75½ Bedford Street, a house only 9½ feet wide. There used to be stables inside the block adjacent to the Isaacs Hendricks House, and the narrow building was constructed in 1873 on what used to be the carriage entrance. Famed poet Edna St. Vincent Millay lived in that house briefly from 1923 to 1924.

36 Grove Court
Grove Street, near Hudson Street

When it was constructed between 1848 and 1852, Grove Court, located on the bend of Grove Street between Seventh Avenue South and Hudson Street, was a revolutionary concept in urban home construction. In the pre–Civil War period, no respectable family would live in a house not fronting on the street. So, Samuel Cocks, co-owner of a grocery at 18 Grove Street, decided to build housing for tradesmen and laborers that would make excellent customers for his shop. At the time, Grove Court was nicknamed "Mixed Ale Alley."

Grove Court has changed character since then. It's now among the most exclusive Village streets. Guarded by a gate, keys are available only to those who own homes in the street; visitors need to be buzzed in. The Georgian-style homes are fronted by a red brick sidewalk.

37 Charles Lane and Sing Sing
Between West and Washington Streets

The Newgate State Prison (remembered in the mosaics of the IRT Christopher Street subway station) was opened at the foot of Christopher Street in 1797 and, as unlikely as it sounds now, the prison spurred development and residences and businesses began to be built near it. Some of those houses still stand. The prison moved upstate in 1828 to Ossining where it became known as Sing Sing. A Belgian-blocked lane that ran along the north wall of the prison is still there, now called Charles Lane. *Gravity's Rainbow* and *Mason & Dixon* author Thomas Pynchon is a former resident.

38 Golden Swan Park

Sixth Avenue and West 4th Street

This vest-pocket garden commemorates the Golden Swan Café, also known as the Hell Hole, a sawdust-floored dive with a weather-beaten stuffed swan in the back room; Eugene O'Neill was a regular patron in the mid-1910s. The Hell Hole was demolished in 1928.

39 The Original "21"

359 Sixth Avenue

At 359 Sixth Avenue you will find an 1832 Federal-style building; you may remember the restaurant facing the street in the 1980s as McBell's. In 1922, it was a speakeasy called the Red Head. It subsequently moved to Washington Place and then uptown to 52nd Street, where it put on airs and became the 21 Club.

40 Northern Dispensary at Waverly and Waverly

Waverly Place and Christopher Street

Due to a geographical quirk, the triangular Northern Dispensary has two walls facing Waverly Place and the other wall facing Grove and Christopher Streets. Here, Waverly Place runs northwest to its ultimate ending at Bank Street, but a short spur continues on to Grove Street. So, Greenwich Village not only features the odd occurrence of West 4th Street intersecting with West 10th, 11th, 12th, and 13th Streets; Waverly Place also intersects Waverly Place! From 1831 to the late 1980s, free medical treatment was available at the Dispensary.

41 Washington Mews

Fifth Avenue, north of Washington Square

Washington Mews, between Fifth Avenue and University Place just north of Washington Square, features stables that have all been converted to residences. The houses on the south side of the alley built in the 1930s are younger than the original stables on the north side. Also, see nearby Mac-Dougal Alley for a similar layout. While London has many such "mews," this is the only so-called one in NYC.

42 Hotel Griffou

19-23 West 9th Street

In 1877, a boarding house on West 9th Street, between Fifth and Sixth Avenues, was opened by a French widow, Madame Marie Griffou. It became a hotel accommodating immigrants, including many French and Spanish artists, and continued the bohemian tradition as a friendly outpost for artists and writers who may not have been welcomed elsewhere with open arms. The hotel was an inspiration for American authors such as William Dean Howells, who set his novels *A Hazard of New Fortunes* (1890) and *The World of Chance* (1893) in the NYC European enclave. Historian and author Thomas A. Janvier, a Philadelphian who went on to write the engaging NYC guidebook *In Old New York*, also was a Griffou regular in the 1880s, as was Mark Twain.

By the turn of the century, things had wound down, with the proprietor in poor health. Upon her death in 1905, the Hotel Griffou closed. The building narrowly escaped demolition in 1929 (thanks to the onset of the Depression), and its ground floor has been home to a succession of restaurants, among them Nat Simon's Penguin, Marylou's, and Ocean's 21.

**43** **Treffurth's**
Broadway and Waverly Place

Cast your gaze skyward at a grand old red-bricked building at the east side of Broadway and Waverly Place. You'll see the word "Treffurth's" spelled out in the florid, expressive lettering of a bygone era. Treffurth's was a restaurant on this site, apparently during the same era this building was built in 1882.

44 Patchin Place and Its Gaslamp
Off West 10th Street, near Sixth Avenue

Seemingly straight out of a 1930s Berenice Abbott photo, Patchin Place has barely changed in over a hundred years. Its neighbor is oddly angled Milligan Place, which fronts on Sixth Avenue. Named for original property owner Samuel Milligan's land surveyor, Patchin Place, on West 10th Street, just west of Sixth Avenue, is more conventionally laid out than its partner in that it's a straight cul-de-sac without

Milligan's odd angles. Famous residents of Patchin Place have included poet e. e. cummings and authors John Reed and Theodore Dreiser.

Patchin Place also contains, at its very end, a rare New York City artifact. Thousands of small lampposts were lit by gas in the late 1800s and even after the introduction of electrified streetlighting in the early 1890s. Only two of these old curbside gaslamps still survive: this one, which has been fitted with an electric fixture, and a lone holdout bereft of a luminaire on Broadway and West 211th Street in Inwood.

45 The Half Cemetery
West 11th Street, east of Sixth Avenue

Triangular Shearith Israel Cemetery can be found on West 11th Street. It had been here long before the area's street grid was laid out, and when West 11th Street was cut through, half of the cemetery was eliminated. The remains were disinterred and brought uptown to another Shearith Israel Cemetery on West 21st Street, just west of Sixth Avenue.

Just west of the cemetery, the apartment building on the southeast corner of Sixth Avenue and West 11th Street, built in 1915, stands in place of a roadhouse built in 1830 called the Old Grapevine. Village locals would congregate here to exchange gossip. During the Civil War, a certain phrase was adopted that inferred that certain information was being distributed through back channels that only insiders would know. The phrase was, of course, "I heard it through the grapevine."

46 The Odd Townhouse
18 West 11th Street, west of Fifth Avenue

Henry Brevoort built seven houses numbering 14 through 26 on West 11th Street in 1844. Most (except for 20) have been altered to some degree, but 18 has been changed beyond recognition. That's because the original 18 is no longer there; it was destroyed by a bomb in March 1970.

Five members of the Weathermen, a domestic terrorist group in the 1960s, had set up a bomb factory in the basement of 18 West 11th Street, purportedly aiming to destroy a hall at Fort Dix in New Jersey. But on March 6, 1970, some of their dynamite accidentally exploded. Three Weathermen were killed; two, Cathlyn Wilkerson and Katherine Boudin, escaped and avoided capture for more than a decade. Actor Dustin Hoffman and his family resided at 16 West 11th Street at the time; their apartment suffered extensive damage.

Eighteen West 11th Street was reconstructed in 1978 by architect Hugh Hardy, featuring a façade that swings 45 degrees from the street line, as a subtle reminder of the blast long ago. In a homey touch, the current owners keep a Paddington Bear in the window and change its outfit to match whatever the current weather happens to be.

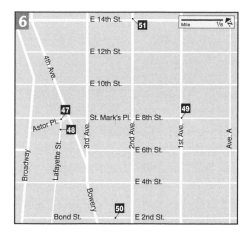

The East Village, much of it originally a part of the Stuyvesant family farm, has been home to German, Polish, and Ukrainian immigration over the decades, and Loisaida (the region between Avenues A and D) is New York City's chief downtown Latino enclave. At Astor Place and Cooper Square stands Cooper Union, where Abraham Lincoln gave a speech that kickstarted his presidential campaign in 1860. Other neighborhood highlights include McSorley's Old Ale House on East 7th Street; New York's primary Indian restaurant row on East 6th Street; historic St. Mark's Church-in-the-Bowery on Second Avenue and 10th Street, dating to 1799; and Tompkins Square Park, between East 7th and 10th Streets and Avenues A and B.

SUBWAY: ⑥ to Astor Place; Ⓛ to First Avenue

BUS: M1 on Lafayette Street; **M103** to Bowery; **M15** on First and Second Avenues; **M14A** on Avenue A and East 14th Street; **M9** on Avenue B; **M21** on Avenue C and East Houston Street; **M14D** on Avenue D and East 14th Street; **M8** on St. Mark's Place and East 9th or 10th Streets

47 St. Mark's Place Mosaics
Along Astor and St. Mark's Places

Many lampposts of the East Village have been festooned with psychedelic crockery. What mad home-decorator has glued broken plates, cups, dishes, sea shells, and even broken toys in the form of mosaics to the lower parts of lampposts, signs, and traffic lights? And why?

East Village artist and Vietnam veteran Jim Power has been decorating these lampposts for nearly twenty years. He has also decorated local hot spots such as the Coffee Shop, the Scrap Bin, Alcatraz, and the Megador. An installation from the early 2000s at the southeast corner of Cooper Square and Astor Place recalls former theaters in the area, such as the Fillmore East and the Eden. As a rule, the crockery goes up to about chest height on the decorated lampposts. Power, in recent years, has adorned building fronts and has produced

MANHATTAN

several mobiles in Tompkins Square Park. He has also made mosaic-themed tables for local cafés.

Anarchic in concept and execution, Powers's mosaics defy the NYC Department of Transportation's usual disdain of nonstandard equipment. As old mosaics drop off the lampposts, Power occasionally does a new installation. In the late 1980s and early 1990s, the mosaics were relatively themeless and nondescript, but after the events of September 11, 2001, a greater sense of purpose seemed to define the mosaics, as tributes were worked into the themes.

48 Colonnade Row
Lafayette Street, south of Astor Place

The landmarked Colonnade Row on today's Lafayette Street was built in 1833 by architect Seth Geer as a development known as La Grange Terrace. It originally consisted of nine houses, of which only four remain today. When first built, the houses were occupied by socialites of the era: Astors, Vanderbilts, and Washington Irving. But while the rich occupied La Grange Terrace, the imprisoned built it. Convicts from Sing Sing in upstate Ossining quarried marble from Westchester and cut it in preparation for construction, prompting riots from local stonecutters.

49 You Can See All the Stars on St. Mark's Place
St. Mark's Place and First Avenue

Everyone has heard of Grauman's Chinese Theatre in Hollywood, where generations of film stars have signed their names and set their handprints in wet concrete. It turns out we have our very own version of Grauman's Chinese right here in the East Village.

Theatre 80, at 80 St. Mark's Place used to be the kind of place where they ran

movies from the golden era of Hollywood, the 1930s to the 1950s, and served you coffee in china cups and cake on real porcelain. Former actor/singer Howard Otway bought the former speakeasy and decided to turn it into a revival house in 1971. His dream was realized in August of that year when he threw an old-fashioned Hollywood premiere party to celebrate the opening. He invited several old-time Hollywood stars, and had them make their marks on the new sidewalk outside the theater. Other celebrities joined in over the next decade and, by 1980, Joan Crawford, Joan Blondell, Allan Jones, Ruby Keeler, Gloria Swanson, Myrna Loy, Kitty Carlisle, and Dom Deluise had all visited and managed to leave mementoes. When the sidewalk was repaired in the 1990s, the fate of the stars' signatures was in doubt, but the theater managed to preserve them by moving them slightly.

50 The New York Marble Cemeteries
East 2nd Street, between Bowery and First Avenue

East Second Street boasts two small, well-maintained cemeteries: one visible from the street and one hidden from view. New York Marble Cemetery, organized in 1830, and New York City Marble Cemetery, from 1832, are not two locations of the same cemetery, but separate organizations. New York Marble Cemetery is located within the block bounded by the Bowery, Second Avenue, and East 2nd and East 3rd Streets,

and its only public reminder is a locked gate emblazoned with the cemetery's name on Second Avenue. There are no headstones there: the interred, in vaults, are identified by inscriptions inlaid on tablets on the perimeter wall.

New York City Marble Cemetery fronts on East 2nd Street, between First and Second Avenues. President James Monroe was briefly interred here. Preserved Fish, of the famed New York City family, occupies a vault here. "Preserved" is a traditional Quaker name.

51 "The Senate" in NYC

East 14th Street and Second Avenue

There's a grand old apartment building at 235 Second Avenue that has a tale to tell about the United States Senate in the waning years of the nineteenth century. A close look at the stonework over the entrance nearest to East 15th Street reveals the words "The U.S. Senate" chiseled into the concrete.

So what's going on? Take a look at the entrance closest to East 14th Street. You'll find, in much smaller carved letters, the words "The W.M. Evarts." William Maxwell Evarts was a Republican senator from New York in the years from 1885 to 1891. Perhaps the architect was a Republican, or an Evarts supporter.

MANHATTAN

BUS: M11 on Ninth and Tenth Avenues; **M20** on Seventh and Eighth Avenues; **M14A** or **M14D** on 14th or 15th Street; **M23** on 23rd Street

Thomas Clarke, a retired British seaman, bought acreage in this area (roughly between West 14th and 23rd Streets, and Seventh Avenue west to the river), naming it for Chelsea Hospital in London, a facility corresponding to NYC's Sailors' Snug Harbor, a home for retired sailors. His son was academician Clement Clarke Moore, of " 'Twas the Night Before Christmas" fame.

After Clarke's farm was subdivided and streets laid through, the area was home to slaughterhouses and glue factories on its western flank, and was served by what would become the New York Central Railroad. Its tracks ran down the middle of Eleventh Avenue, giving it the sobriquet "Death Avenue" for its many accidents. The elevated structure known as the High Line replaced it in the 1930s. Chelsea's eastern section fared much better, as rows upon rows of genteel brownstone buildings were constructed in the late 1800s, many of which survive today. The neighborhood's anchor is the magnificent Chelsea Hotel, built in 1884, treasured not only for its cast-iron balconies, but for its literary and musical clientele, from Mark Twain and O. Henry to Janis Joplin and Sid Vicious.

SUBWAY: ① to 14th, 18th, or 23rd Streets; **C** or **E** to 23rd Street

52 General Theological Seminary

Ninth Avenue, between West 20th and West 21st Streets

If you work on Manhattan's west side and need a breather from hectic office life, the perfect solution can be found on Ninth Avenue between West 20th and West 21st Streets. Enter the Episcopal Church's General Theological Seminary, founded in 1817, through a relatively bland, modern exterior, sign in at the desk, and pass through another set of doors into New York City as it looked in the last days of the nineteenth century, with wide, spacious grassy lawns surrounded by red-bricked buildings.

The oldest structure, the West Building, dates to 1836, while the quadrangle's central focus is the Chapel of the Good Shepherd, with a 116-foot-tall tower. Architect George Coolidge Haight designed and built the various Gothic Revival buildings between 1883 and 1902. The Seminary grounds had been an apple orchard owned by Clement Clarke Moore, who was Professor of Oriental and Greek Literature, as well as Divinity and Biblical Learning at the General Theological Seminary. Moore donated part of his property to the Seminary. He anonymously published the holiday poem "A Visit from St. Nicholas" in a Troy, New York, newspaper in 1823; he did not publish it with a by-line until 1844. Moore's depiction of Santa Claus in the poem, combined with Thomas Nast's accompanying illustrations, helped to solidify the Jolly One's present image.

53 Chelsea Market

Ninth and Tenth Avenues at West 16th Street

A former National Biscuit Company cookie factory (where the Oreo was first produced) taking up the entire block between Ninth and Tenth Avenues and West 15th and 16th Streets was turned into the Chelsea Market in 1997 as a wholesale food center. Even if you're *not* in the mood for the many treats available here, just a walk around is worth the visit for the crazy-quilt, art-gallery vibe with exposed-brick walls, odd sculptures, and even an urban waterfall.

54 A Gate to Remember

Eleventh Avenue and West 14th Street

Take a walk down Eleventh Avenue south of the Chelsea Piers, past West 14th Street. You'll see a semicircular tower of rusting metal at the remains of Pier 54. Lettering on the crossbar, just below the arch, reveals the words "White Star." This is where the White Star Lines berthed grand passenger ships that sailed the Atlantic Ocean. White Star leased the pier from its owner, Cunard Lines ("Cunard" is superimposed over "White Star" on the outside gate, and wind and rain have exposed both names as

time went on). Cunard itself was bought by Carnival Cruise Lines in 1998. One of the spectacular ocean liners that would have used this gate in its heyday was the *Titanic*, though the liner was actually due to arrive at nearby Pier 58, if fate had not intervened.

55 High Line to Nowhere

West of Tenth Avenue, between Gansevoort and West 34th Streets

In 1934, NYC built two viaducts: the West Side Elevated Freight Railroad to carry train traffic, and the Miller Elevated Highway to serve automobiles. The Miller was more commonly known as The West Side Highway. The elevated freight railroad was designed to pass through, or just beside, the buildings whose businesses it served, such as the National Biscuit Company (still standing as Chelsea Market), Armour Meat Packers, and the Manhattan Refrigerating Company (presently divided into apartments).

The freight railroad never caught on. It was first sabotaged by the Depression, and then trucking became the primary means of transporting goods within NYC. The section of the railroad south of Bank Street was torn down in the 1960s, while sporadic service continued on the line north of Bank Street until 1980. The trestle stayed in place, for the most part, until the mid-1990s when a section south of Gansevoort Street was torn down. Some buildings that remaining portions of the High Line went through had their openings bricked up, although the old Bell Labs Building (now called Westbeth) between Bank, Bethune, Washington, and West Streets, still has a recognizable gap in it, with a short, rusty section of the High Line poking through at Washington and Bank. A conversion of the old High Line into a park has been championed by an organization known as Friends of the High Line, and construction began in early 2006.

The Ehrlich Brothers store closed in 1911 and the building passed to Chicago merchants J.L. Kesner Company. Architects Taylor & Levi added new storefronts with Arts and Crafts style pilasters and terra-cotta by Hartford Faience Company. The Kesner Company left in 1913, only two years later, but the Ks are still there.

57 "The Corner"

Sixth Avenue and West 24th Street

The building on the southeast corner of Sixth Avenue and West 24th Street features two tablets calling it "The Corner." The name is also plainly visible on the cornice at the top of the structure. This is the last remnant of a larger entertainment center in the Madison Square area, built as an annex to a hall known as Koster & Bial's vaudeville theater. One of the conductors was a young Victor Herbert, who would go on to write "Babes in Toyland," among many other works. For many years, Billy's Topless occupied the ground floor; perhaps Herbert would have been amused.

56 Ehrlich Brothers "K"

Sixth Avenue and West 22nd Street

The Ehrlich Brothers Emporium was built by William Schickel in 1889 on Sixth Avenue between West 22nd and 23rd Streets. Its ground floor now houses a Burlington Coat Factory store. Oddly, the building features mosaic and terra-cotta Ks in the building façade on Sixth Avenue. Why "K"?

Madison Square Park has been a potter's field, an arsenal, and a military parade ground. Until 1844, a major wagon route to Boston originated here. The park was named for President Madison and was opened to the public in 1847. At first, it was the centerpiece of one of NYC's most exclusive residential neighborhoods. Broadway between Union and Madison Squares emerged as a commercial center in the late 1800s, and the construction of the Fuller (Flatiron) Building in 1902 sealed the deal. The first two Madison Square Gardens, built in 1879 and 1890, respectively (the latter designed by Stanford White), overlooked the square. According to some sources, Alexander Cartwright formalized the rules of baseball and created the Knickerbockers, the first professional baseball team, here in 1846.

Gramercy Park is the only privately owned park in Manhattan. Since it was laid out in 1831, only adjacent-property holders have been able to enter. Today, only residents of surrounding buildings have keys to the gate; the rest of us can look through its wrought-iron fence. The neighborhood was originally a marshy area known as the Crommissee Vly (or Valley), a part of the Stuyvesant family's holdings. The land was later purchased by developer Samuel Ruggles, who turned it into one of NYC's premier residential areas in the 1830s and 1840s. The Players and National Arts Clubs, as well as the statue of famed Shakespear-

ian actor Edwin Booth in the center of the park, are reminders of the glittering cultural demimonde that flourished here in the late eighteenth and early nineteenth centuries.

SUBWAY: ⑥ to 23rd Street; Ⓡ or Ⓦ to 23rd Street

BUS: M2, **M3**, or **M5** on Fifth Avenue; **M1**, **M2**, or **M3** on Park Avenue South; **M101**, **M102**, or **M103** on Lexington and Third Avenues; **M23** on East 23rd Street

58 Teddy Roosevelt's Birthplace
East 20th Street, between Broadway and Park Avenue South

Theodore Roosevelt (1858–1919) is the only U.S. president born in New York City. His boyhood home at 28 East 20th Street has been appropriately preserved, or rather, its site has.

The house presently occupying the property was built in 1923 as a faithful reconstruction of Roosevelt's home between 1858 and 1872. After the original house was demolished in 1916, the Women's Roosevelt Memorial Association rebuilt the house using architectural details from an identical house next door, which has since disappeared. The building is a National Historic Site, and five of its rooms have been appointed with period furnishings, much of it courtesy of the Roosevelt family, and a small museum contains some of TR's papers, documents, and diaries. It is open to the public: call (212) 260-1616 for hours.

59 Madison Square Park Statues
East 23rd Street and Fifth Avenue

Take a stroll through Madison Square Park and you will happen upon statues of luminaries who wielded great power in their era but are not necessarily household names anymore.

a. Senator William Henry Seward's (1801–1872) main claim to fame is that he engineered the sale of Alaska from Russia to the U.S. in 1867. But he was also a powerful government figure: governor of New York from 1838 to 1843, U.S. senator from New York (1849–1861), and Abraham Lincoln and Andrew Johnson's Secretary of State (1861–1869). Randolph Rogers's sculpture was installed here in 1876.

b. Described as a forceful, charismatic, and flamboyant orator, Roscoe Conkling (1828–1888) was a New York senator between 1867 and 1881 after two stints at the House of Representatives. In 1876, Conkling lost in a squeaker to Rutherford B. Hayes for the Republican presidential nomination. In March 1888, Conkling was caught outdoors near Union Square at the worst of the famed blizzard of that year and died from exposure. John Quincy Adams Ward's statue of the senator was installed here in 1893.

c. Admiral David Farragut (1801–1870) was the greatest naval commander of the Civil War. At the height of the successful battle for Mobile Bay, Farragut was lashed to the mast of his ship so he could see farther into the distance. Noticing that the bay was booby-trapped with mines, Farragut chose to enter the bay anyway, shouting "Damn the torpedoes! Full speed ahead!" (In the naval parlance of the day, a mine laid at sea was called a torpedo.) The Farragut Memorial by Auguste Saint-Gaudens was first located at Fifth Avenue and East 26th Street in 1881. In 1935, it was moved to its present location at the park's northern end.

d. With his muttonchop sideburns, President Chester Alan Arthur (1829–1886) looked the very model of a modern U.S. president in the Victorian Age, which he was between 1881 and 1885. He was elected as James Garfield's vice president and assumed office when Garfield was assassinated. His statue, sculpted by George Bissell in 1899, is near the park's northeastern end at East 26th Street and Madison Avenue.

60 General Worth
Fifth Avenue and East 25th Street

The General William Jenkins Worth Monument, on the triangle formed by Broadway, Fifth Avenue, and East 25th Street, is not only a memorial to the general (1794–1849), but is also his gravesite. It was created by sculptor James Batterson in 1857, when his remains were transferred here. The iron gate surrounding the obelisk is famed among connoisseurs of cast iron.

General Worth rose to the rank of captain during the War of 1812, was elevated to the rank of major in the Indian wars, and was promoted brigadier general during the Mexican War. He died of cholera in 1849 in Texas; subsequently, the city of Fort Worth was named for him.

61 The Stars of Madison Square Park

Fifth Avenue, north of East 23rd Street

For more than 80 years, two Madison Square Park poles have been topped by illuminated stars.

a. The pole on Fifth Avenue, just north of East 23rd Street, known as the Eternal Light Memorial Flagpole, honors the military heroes of World War I and was designed by architect Thomas Hastings. It was erected in 1918 and the star was illuminated in 1923.

b. Another star can be found on East 23rd Street, just east of Fifth Avenue. The Star of Hope was first erected in 1916 to commemorate the first Madison Square tree lighting, the U.S.'s first community Christmas tree, four years earlier. The twenty-two-bulb star sits atop a 35-foot-tall pole.

62 Little Church Around the Corner

East 29th Street and 5th Avenue

The Episcopal Church of the Transfiguration at 1 East 29th Street was founded by Reverend Dr. George Houghton in 1848, and in the following year, this small brick church appeared at what was the city's northern edge. Houghton, an abolitionist, made the church a sanctuary for blacks fleeing the Draft Riots of 1863 and a stop on the underground railroad. The church has been a favorite of actors since 1870, when thespian Joseph Jefferson requested a funeral for his friend George Holland at a neighboring Episcopal church. Upon learning Holland was an actor, the church refused Jefferson, telling him to seek out the "little church around the corner." A stained-glass window depicts Joseph Jefferson in a role as Rip Van Winkle, leading the enshrouded Holland. Today, the church and parsonage boast a charming garden, an oasis from bustling Fifth Avenue.

63 Broadway Alley

between East 26th and 27th Streets, just west of Third Avenue

Broadway Alley is Manhattan's last dirt road, on a block where Herman Melville spent his last years. It is lit by one of NYC's few remaining cast-iron wall lamps. Some scattered Belgian blocks indicate it was paved years ago. There is one remaining residence: 8 Broadway Alley.

MANHATTAN

MANHATTAN

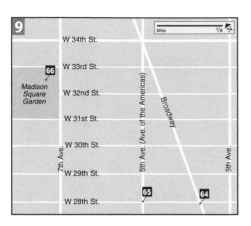

Most people who have commuted into NYC from New Jersey or Long Island, or perhaps taken the train from other parts of the country like Washington, D.C.; Boston; or Chicago in the past thirty-five years, have thought of Penn Station as the basement under Madison Square Garden on West 33rd Street—a large basement, with shops, newsstands, and ticket booths, but still a basement.

Between 1910 and 1964, though, a great monument to travel existed here. The largest building ever erected for rail travel, Pennsylvania Station, commissioned by Pennsylvania Railroad President Alexander Cassatt, and built by architectural firm McKim, Mead and White, stood between West 31st and 33rd Streets and Seventh and Eighth Avenues—over eight acres. It was truly a temple of transportation.

With the 277-foot-long waiting room designed to resemble the Roman Baths of Caracalla and the Basilica of Constantine, the grand edifice used 500,000 cubic feet of granite; was supported on 650 steel columns; required the digging of tunnels over 6,600 feet long under the Hudson River; and required the demolition of more than 500 buildings and the removal of over 3,000,000 cubic yards of soil and bedrock. It had a 150-foot-high ceiling.

The ups and downs of public transpor-

tation took their toll on the station over the years after World War II, and both the Pennsylvania Railroad and its grand station began their decline. Concessions to the modern age, like neon signs and illuminated advertising, as well as deferred maintenance which left a thin layer of dirt over what were once magnificent pink marble columns, left Penn Station, which was only half a century old in 1960, looking a lot older than its actual age.

It was decided as early as 1955, when the "Pennsy" sold its air rights above the building, that Penn Station would soon be torn down. Though the building was meant to last for centuries, it stood for just fifty-three years, leaving few relics behind.

SUBWAY: ①, ②, or ③ to 28th Street or 34th Street; Ⓐ, Ⓒ, or Ⓔ to 34th Street; Ⓑ, Ⓓ, Ⓕ, or Ⓥ to 34th Street; Ⓝ, Ⓠ, Ⓡ, or Ⓦ to 34th Street

BUS: M5 on Fifth and Sixth Avenues; **M6** or **M7** on Broadway and Sixth Avenue); **M20** on Seventh and Eighth Avenues; **M16** or **M34** on 34th Street

64 Tin Pan Alley
Broadway and West 28th Street

Change has come to the stretch of Sixth Avenue between West 23rd Street and Herald Square in the last five years. Condos have sprouted like spring dandelions, forcing the razing of many old buildings. Thus far, the Flower District centered on

West 28th Street, but running up Sixth Avenue between West 26th and 28th Streets, has weathered the change. West 28th Street between Broadway and Sixth Avenues was formerly known as "Tin Pan Alley," the epicenter of songwriting in NYC in the early twentieth century. George Gershwin sold Fred Astaire songs here when Fred and sister, Adele, were a fledgling song-and-dance act, and the William Morris Agency was located here in its early days. The last remnant of Tin Pan Alley is a commemorative plaque on the sidewalk on West 28th Street, just east of Broadway, mostly unnoticed because of street vendors, who set up directly on top of it.

65 Childs Restaurant

Sixth Avenue and West 28th Street

The McDonald's on Sixth Avenue and 28th Street has fortunately preserved an old seahorse-festooned façade, which marks it as a former Childs Restaurant branch. There is still a beautiful terra-cotta Childs building on the Coney Island boardwalk, and you can always recognize former Childs restaurants scattered all around the city by their seahorses.

66 Penn Station Remnants

West 33rd Street and Sixth Avenue

The old Penn Station is not completely gone. If you poke around long enough in the basement of Madison Square Garden, which is what the "new" Penn Station became, you can find a hint or two of the old magnificent Penn still there. And you can even find a couple of remains in broad daylight, too.

a. Possibly the most intriguing relic of the old Penn Station is part of an original track indicator in the baggage area near Track 1. These ornate indicators were hallmarks of the old Penn, standing 16

feet high and complementing the ornate fencing and banisters. The aluminum signs were painted bright red. The track number appeared in the semicircular area on top. The numbers on the bottom were used to show the departure time.

b. Twenty-two three-ton eagles appeared on Penn Station's exterior, each created by the noted sculptor Adolph A. Weinman, whose sculptures personifying Night and Day graced a 7-foot-wide clock on Penn Station's exterior at Seventh Avenue and West 32nd Street. Two of the eagles were rescued and placed outside the new entrance. Others can be found in Kings Point and Hicksville, and as far away as Philadelphia.

c. Some of the staircases still have the original brass banisters and X-shaped molding. A small area of the original Penn Station can be found when you walk toward the front of the downtown IRT local platform. A ledge containing original brass banisters and tiled arches (with the addition of modern light-

ing) is at the top of the staircase leading down to the token booth. Through soaped-up windows can be glimpsed more arches in an area used for storage.

d. Probably the only extant remnant of the old Pennsylvania Railroad in the station—besides the names Pennsylvania Station and Pennsylvania Hotel across the street—is a painted sign that can be seen in the passenger concourse (known as the Hilton Passageway) behind the Long Island Rail Road Station. The concourse somehow escaped renovation when the rest of the LIRR Station was renovated from 1992 to 1994.

To see these artifacts and more, there's a Penn Station tour the third Monday of every month at 12:30 PM meeting at the tourist information booth in the station's rotunda. For further information, call (917) 438-5123.

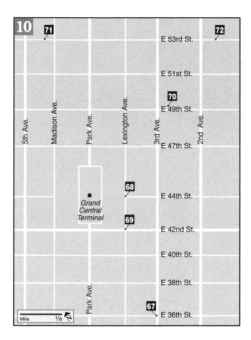

Station serves nationwide routes. The terminal was in danger of demolition in the 1970s before a group of preservationists led by Jacqueline Kennedy Onassis helped save it. After a lengthy period of neglect, it has undergone extensive renovations, first the interior in the 1990s, and the exterior was completed in 2005.

Just across from the Lexington Avenue terminal entrance is the best-known Art Deco edifice in the country, the Chrysler Building. When it opened in 1930, it was briefly the world's tallest building. Its eastern end, seen from East 42nd Street, east of Lexington, is built on a slant, since old property lines followed the long-vanished Eastern Post Road there.

Murray Hill, in the East 30s, East of Park Avenue, is an isolated patch of beautiful attached buildings along tree-lined streets, a tribute of sorts to squire Robert Murray, who constructed a country home here before the Revolution. Its northern counterpart, Turtle Bay, in the East 40s, likely takes its name from a Dutch term meaning "bent blade," probably referencing the shape of the shoreline. It is somewhat hard to believe it now, but slaughterhouses along the waterfront had to be razed in the 1940s to make way for the United Nations complex on First Avenue.

There have been two Grand Central Terminals where the current one stands on East 42nd Street and Pershing Square. By 1869, Commodore Cornelius Vanderbilt acquired control of all railroads going into NYC and set about building a vast depot on East 42nd Street and train yards stretching up Fourth Avenue, north of his new terminal. He built here since steam railroads had been banned south of 42nd Street (in fact, remnants of the old New York and Harlem Railroad can still be found under Park Avenue between East 32nd and 39th Streets—an old railroad tunnel was converted to auto traffic). The present magnificent complex replaced the old one in 1913, and is the hub of a vast facility containing a passenger station, power plant, steam and water mains, luggage storage, and dozens of track loops and layup tracks.

Grand Central Terminal once served railroads that reached a large swath of the country. Today, in a somewhat ironic turn of events, Grand Central Terminal serves only commuter railroads, while the much more downscale (since 1964) Pennsylvania

SUBWAY: ④, ⑤, or ⑥ to Grand Central–42nd Street; ⑥ to 33rd or 51st Streets

BUS: M101, M102, M103 on Lexington and Third Avenue; **M15** on First and Second Avenue; **M1** on Park Avenue South; **M34** on 34th Street; **M42** on 42nd Street; **M1, M2, M3,** or **M4** on Fifth on Madison Avenue; **M5** and **M6** on Fifth or Sixth Avenues; **M27** and **M50** on 49th and 50th Street

MANHATTAN

67 Sniffen Court

East 36th Street, west of Third Avenue

Nestled in prosperous Murray Hill on East 36th Street is one of two alleys (along with Broadway Alley) in the midtown area. Sniffen Court was constructed sometime between 1850 and 1860 by architect John Sniffen and consists of ten handsome brick carriage houses protected behind a locked iron gate. The carriage houses were used as stables until the 1920s when they were converted into living spaces. The rear wall features plaques of horsemen created by artist Malvina Hoffman, who lived in Sniffen Court for more than forty years. The court was used for the cover of the Doors' 1967 album *Strange Days* in a surreal photo employing circus performers.

68 Graybar Building Rats

Lexington Avenue and East 43rd Street

The Graybar Building abuts Grand Central Terminal as well as the Grand Hyatt (formerly Commodore) Hotel on Lexington Avenue across the street from the Chrysler Building.

Above one of the entrances at East 43rd Street, a handsome canopy provides shelter for people waiting for taxicabs. But what

are those bumps on the struts holding the marquee in place? Those aren't bumps—those are rats! A close look will also reveal eight rats' heads surrounding each hawser (the lines holding the canopy) as they reach the Graybar Building.

The Graybar was originally named the Eastern Offices Building. It was designed with a lighthearted feel by the architectural firm of Sloan and Robertson, and was opened in 1927 at the height of the Art Deco period. The Graybar's architects wanted to emphasize NYC's status as a great port, and chose to use rats, so often found on sailing ships of yore, to emphasize a maritime theme.

69 Chanin Building

East 42nd Street and Lexington Avenue

The Chanin Building at 122 East 42nd Street is one of New York's more flamboyant Art Deco creations. Like the Graybar, it was designed by Sloan and Robertson and opened in 1929. Grilles and bas-reliefs in the lobby, designed by sculptors René Chambellan and Jacques Delamarre, are a stop on any architectural student's itinerary. The Chanin Building exterior features a gold-colored bas-relief running around the façade. A close look reveals flounder, sand dollars, kelp, chambered nautiluses, starfish, as well as octopuses, jellyfish, and bass. They are supposedly arranged in evolutionary order.

🐾 70 Amster Yard

East 49th Street near Third Avenue

Sure, it might *look* like an ordinary building front on East 49th Street between Second and Third Avenues, but this passageway, now known as Amster Yard, dates all the way back to 1830 or earlier. On this site, the stagecoach to Boston began its route on a now-vanished road called the Eastern Post Road. Later in the century, tenements were built here, and an alley between them was gradually covered with refuse until James Amster Associates, a design firm, took it over and remodeled it in the mid-1940s. Amster himself lived on the property until his death in the 1980s.

In 2002, Spanish cultural center Instituto Cervantes acquired the property and immediately discovered that it had become unfit for habitation. They razed the building and rebuilt it from scratch, but also restored Amster Yard and added an art gallery and a charming garden. The complex is to remain open to the public so that all New Yorkers can enjoy this heretofore hidden cul-de-sac.

🐾 71 Berlin Wall

East 53rd Street, near Madison Avenue

The Berlin Wall came down in November 1989 after twenty-eight years. Some 360 segments of the wall were offered for sale by a state-owned foreign trade enterprise of the German Democratic Republic, AHB Limex-Bau Export-Import in 1990. Eighteen sections of the wall wound up in the U.S., including two in NYC: here on East 53rd Street, in the courtyard across the street from my publisher HarperCollins' offices, and also at the *Intrepid* Sea, Air & Space Museum on West 46th Street and Twelfth Avenue. Other chunks are at the Ronald Reagan and George H. W. Bush Presidential Libraries. The men's bathroom at the Main Street Station Hotel and Casino in Las Vegas also has a piece.

72 East 53rd Street Houses

East 53rd Street, east of Second Avenue

A pair of French Second Empire clapboard houses built by Robert and James Cunningham in 1866 have somehow survived at 312 and 314 East 53rd Street, on a block otherwise dominated by brownstone buildings which came along about twenty years later. In 1866, they were located in the city's northern reaches and were likely surrounded by fields and forests.

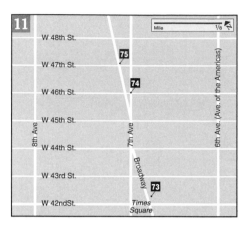

M50 to Broadway or Eighth Avenue and West 49th or 50th Street; **M42** on 42nd Street; **M10** or **M20** on Broadway, Seventh, and Eighth Avenues

No greater neighborhood transforma-tion has taken place over the last twenty years than in Times Square. Pornography, peepshows, and prostitution have been replaced by glitzy new and renovated buildings, huge neon signs (continuing a tradition dating back to Times Square's earliest days), and restaurants, alongside the area's dozens of theaters.

In the late 1800s, the lengthy junction of Broadway and Seventh Avenue was home to dozens of carriage manufacturers and horse traders. When the *New York Times* moved uptown to the Times Tower occupying the triangle formed by Seventh Avenue, Broadway, and West 42nd Street in 1904, the city changed the name of Longacre Square to commemorate the move: Longacre Square was so-called for a London square that was also home to the carriage trade. The square's old name survives in the Longacre Theater, built in 1913 at 220 West 48th Street.

SUBWAY: ①, ②, ③, Ⓝ, Ⓠ, Ⓡ, or Ⓦ to 42nd Street; Ⓑ, Ⓓ, Ⓕ, or Ⓥ to 42nd Street; ⑦ to Times Square–42nd Street; Ⓢ shuttle from Grand Central to Times Square–42nd Street

BUS: **M6** or **M7** on Broadway, Sixth, or Seventh Avenues; **M104** on Broadway, Eighth Avenue, and 42nd Street; **M27** or

73 Subway Doors to Nowhere
Subway shuttle platform, Times Square

Next time you are taking the Times Square Shuttle to Grand Central Station, walk toward the northern end of the platform on Track 1. You'll find a locked door with the word "Knickerbocker" above it.

Behind the door is a staircase which used to lead up to the rear lobby of the old Knickerbocker Hotel at 1466 Broadway, at the southeast corner of West 42nd Street. There was a lower level nightclub/dancehall/restaurant. Underneath the stair is a subway power/communications manhole; also in back of the wall are sidewalk vaults that belonged to the hotel, which opened in 1905 and closed in 1921. Its bar was once known as the "42nd Street Country Club." In 1912, a bartender named Martini di Arma di Taggia is said to have mixed a drink with gin and vermouth which found favor with John D. Rockefeller, and the martini was born.

Another relic can be spotted from the platform on Track 1. On the opposite end from the Knickerbocker door, near the corridor connecting the platform with the concourse, observe the black area near the ceiling. If you look closely, you'll find what looks like an archway. It used to be a door leading directly to the Times

Tower. The Times Tower has functioned as a glorified billboard since the 1960s, but a vestige of its former grandeur can be seen in this old subway stop, which is named for the newspaper whose offices you could once walk right into from one of its platforms.

74 Leading Ladies

Seventh Avenue and West 46th Street

The I. Miller Building was built from 1927 to 1929, and is nearly unrecognizable underneath the video billboards and garish scaffolding advertising a chain restaurant. In a previous era, Israel Miller's shoe store was long patronized by theater people.

A closer view of the I. Miller Building along West 46th Street will prove to be a glimpse into the Great White Way's past. In 1927, the I. Miller company took a public vote to determine the most popular theater actresses of the day, with the idea of placing statues of them above their new Seventh Avenue store. The results came in, and sculptor Alexander Stirling Calder was chosen to depict them in some of their most famous roles: Ethel Barrymore as Ophelia, singer-dancer Marilyn Miller as Sunny, Mary Pickford as Little Lord Fauntleroy, and soprano Rosa Ponselle as Bellini's Norma.

75 Father Duffy

Duffy Square, West 47th Street and Broadway

Father Francis Duffy of Most Holy Trinity Church on West 42nd Street near Broadway served with the Fighting 69th, a mostly Irish regiment, in World War I. He was severely wounded and received the Distinguished Service Cross for bravery on the battlefield.

His monument in Duffy Square, the triangle formed by Broadway, Seventh Avenue, and West 47th Street featuring Father Duffy in his World War I uniform standing in front of the Celtic cross, was dedicated in 1937.

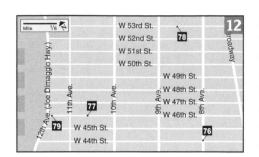

Hell's Kitchen, the area west of Eighth Avenue, between West 42nd and 59th Streets, used to be one of the city's most notorious slums. It was a rough district and a battleground for gang supremacy all the way into the twentieth century. In recent decades, the neighborhood has made great strides of improvement, and Ninth Avenue especially is now known as one of the ethnic food centers of the city. Despite efforts of real-estate agents to rename the area "Clinton" or "Times Square West," the names haven't stuck and Hell's Kitchen it remains.

SUBWAY: **A**, **C**, or **E** to 42nd Street or 50th Street

BUS: **M10** or **M20** on Eighth Avenue and Broadway; **M42** on 42nd Street; **M50** on 49th and 50th Streets; **M11** on Ninth and Tenth Avenues

76 Cameo Appearance
Eighth Avenue and West 44th Street

The Playpen Theatre at Eighth Avenue and West 44th Street, part of Times Square's fading red-light district, is notable for be-

ing the former Cameo—one of Manhattan's last remaining vaudeville houses. A close inspection reveals two "cameos": female figures, perhaps playful depictions of Greek mythological Muses, on either side of the entrance; one holds a film canister and the other a camera. The Playpen neon sign still shows the Twin Towers.

77 Clinton Court
West 46th Street, west of Tenth Avenue

A locked gate between 422 and 424 West 46th Streets hides a secret: a hidden alley which leads to a post–Revolutionary-era carriage house formerly belonging to George Clinton, New York Governor from 1777 to 1795. The house at 422½ West 46th Street has been here since at least 1800, if not longer. The house was built when the area was open country.

78 Omega Oil and the Missing El
West 53rd Street, east of Ninth Avenue

Omega Oil, an all-purpose liniment supposedly good for "weak backs," was one of the city's most ubiquitous outdoor advertisers (along with Fletcher's Castoria) for the first two decades of the twentieth century. This ad, on West 53rd Street, east of Ninth Avenue, is one of many still seen in Manhattan and the Bronx. It's also important because it marks the passage of the Sixth Avenue El, which ran down West 53rd Street as it connected with the Ninth Avenue El. The Omega sign was positioned so that El riders could see it as they went by.

79 Cable-Stayed Bridge
Twelfth Avenue and West 46th Street

Cable-stayed bridges superficially resemble suspension bridges, but cables tie the load directly to the bridge's tower instead of the traditional suspension bridge, whose

cables ride across the towers to support the load from either end. One of NYC's few examples is a 287-foot-long, 59-foot-high pedestrian bridge crossing Twelfth Avenue at West 46th Street at the *Intrepid* Sea, Air & Space Museum. It was designed by architect Barbara Thayer and completed by the New York State Department of Transportation in 2002.

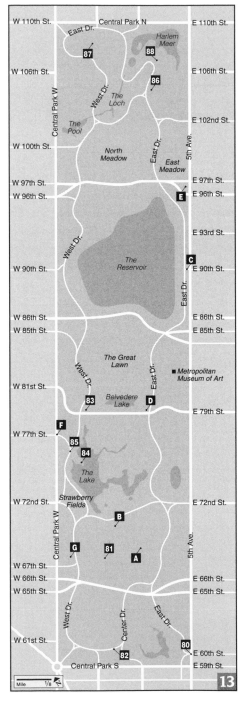

the park's manicured lawns, ponds, brooks, and rolling hills, to its "wild" areas like the Ramble. The park is even more of a miracle when you consider that this was the pair's first large-scale project.

Every feature in Central Park is unique and not repeated elsewhere in the park; its 843 acres can be discovered and rediscovered every time you walk through it. With that kind of acreage, there's no wonder there are plenty of wonderful park features that can easily be overlooked.

SUBWAY: Ⓐ, Ⓑ, Ⓒ, Ⓓ, ①, ②, or ③ to 59th Street–Columbus Circle; Ⓝ, Ⓡ, or Ⓦ to Fifth Avenue–59th Street; Ⓑ or Ⓒ to 72nd, 81st, 86th, 96th, and 103rd Streets

BUS: M10 or **M20** to Eighth Avenue, Broadway, or Central Park West; **M5**, **M7**, or **M104** to Broadway and Central Park South; **M1**, **M2**, **M3**, **M4**, or **M30** to Fifth Avenue or Madison Avenue; **M2**, **M3**, or **M4** to Central Park North

80 Lombard Lamp
Fifth Avenue and 60th Street

This five-luminaired lamp with its cherubic attendants at the park entrance on Fifth Avenue and 60th Street was donated by Hamburg, West Germany, in 1979, and is a replica of an ornate lamp found in the German seaport at the Lombard Bridge. The plaque reads: "This Lombard Lamp is presented to the people of New York City and by the people of the Free and Hanseatic City of Hamburg so that it may forever brighten a bridge of friendship in human relations, trade and commerce." In the same year, a second Lombard Lamp replica was donated to Chicago and placed in its Lincoln Square neighborhood.

The Lombards, or Langobards, were a Germanic tribe that originated in southern

The genius of Central Park's chief creators and designers Frederick Law Olmsted and Calvert Vaux is apparent whenever you stroll through Central Park, from

Cop Cot, near Central Park South and Sixth Avenue

Central Park has a number of shelters made entirely of timber. This one near Central Park South is known as Cop Cot (Anglo-Saxon for "hilltop cottage").

Sweden and worked their way down into Italy in the early medieval period, naturalizing in the process and giving their name to the northern Italian region of Lombardia. Their name, the Langobards, referred to their lengthy beards.

81 Lighting the Way

Lamps throughout park

Cast-iron lampposts designed by architect Henry Bacon (who also designed the Lincoln Memorial) in 1907 are standard issue throughout Central Park, as well as in parks citywide. They occasionally make appearances on side streets, too. For some years now, the city has marked most of Central Park's lampposts with embossed, numbered metal plaques. The first two or three digits correspond to the cross street you would be on if that street extended through the park. So, a post reading "6102" is located where 61st Street would be.

The park's 1960s-style octagonal-shaft poles have been given the same treatment, with cross streets emblazoned with white numbers. Some of them also bear a W, C, or E, corresponding, respectively, to the western, central, or eastern part of the park.

83 Swedish Cottage

West Drive, above 79th Street Transverse

The Swedish Cottage was built in 1876 as part of Sweden's entry in the U.S. Centennial Exhibition in Philadelphia that year. It was taken apart and reassembled in Central Park the following year. It has found use as a storage shed, a public restroom, an entomology research lab, a Civil Defense headquarters, and, since 1947, as a marionette theater. It is just west of the American Museum of Natural History on Central Park West.

84 Hernshead

West Drive, near West 76th Street

A short peninsula juts into Central Park Lake at about West 76th Street, affording stellar photo opportunities. Hernshead is Anglo-Saxon for "heron head," but according to birdwatchers, wading birds like herons and egrets stay away from Hernshead for the most part. A curving path takes you through a maze of flowering vegetation until you are lakeside, which affords a good view of the massive San Remo Apartment towers, built in 1929.

🐚85 Ladies' Pavilion

West Drive, near West 76th Street

The crown jewel of Hernshead is undoubt-edly the Ladies' Pavilion, which dates back to 1871 and was designed by Jacob Wrey Mould, who also moulded the stone cre-ations at Terrace Bridge. It was originally a trolley car shelter at Columbus Circle, but after years of rust and neglect (a past theme in Central Park), it was taken apart, repaired, and reassembled in the early 1970s.

The Ladies' Pavilion is so named be-cause it took the place of the former La-dies' Shelter, which gave women skating at the Ladies' Pond site the opportunity to change from shoes to skates without losing their dignity: a glimpse of stocking would have been shocking at the time. It was likely moved to Hernshead in 1913.

86 Green's Private Bench

Behind the Conservatory Garden, East 105th Street and Fifth Avenue

Climbing the Great Hill from Central Park West and West 103rd Street, you follow a

pathway for a while, pass the Pool through Glen Span Arch, walk along a babbling brook known as Montayne's Rivulet, and when you are in sight of Huddlestone Arch and the Lasker Rink, take a sharp detour to the right, climb some steps, and you'll find an isolated bench smack in the middle of nowhere overlooking East Drive.

The bench is a memorial to lawyer and preservationist Andrew H. Green (1820–1903), who in large part was responsible, in his capacity on the fledgling Central Park Board of Commissioners, for the Olmsted-Vaux Central Park plan being effected. He also played an important role in the formation of the Metropolitan Museum of Art, the American Museum of Natural History, the Central Park Menagerie (the Zoo), and the New York Public Library.

Tragically, Green was shot and killed by a deranged gunman in 1903. In 1929, this bench, along with five newly planted trees, were dedicated to Green; the bench was moved to its present location in the early 1980s.

🔫87 The Blockhouse

Below Central Park North

On the northern edge of Central Park, near Warrior's Gate at Adam Clayton Powell Jr. Boulevard, the hills are steep, and rough-hewn staircases ascend as high as a two- or three-story building. This part of the park is known as the Cliff and is one of the natural aspects that Olmsted and Vaux al-lowed to remain while building the park in the 1850s.

A chain of major military batteries was installed in upper Manhattan during the early days of the War of 1812: Fort Clinton, Fort Fish, a battery at McGown's Pass, Nutter's Battery, and Blockhouse Number One were located in what would later become Central Park. When it was built, this Blockhouse had a sunken roof with a large cannon that could be fired in any direction. The five fortifications in what would become Central Park had more than 2,000 militiamen garrisoned.

 **88 McGown's Pass**

Along East Drive, near West 106th Street

McGown's Pass was named for a tavern run by Scotswoman Catherine McGown and her family from 1759 into the 1840s.

The tavern was on an old Manhattan road called Old Harlem Road; no trace of it remains, but a road it intersected, Harlem Lane, is today called St. Nicholas Avenue above Central Park, from 110th Street north. The pass, located about midway on the southern edge of what would become the Harlem Meer, was occupied by British and Hessian mercenaries in 1776 and held until the end of the war in 1783. McGown's Tavern, which was located south of the pass, was purchased by the Sisters of Charity in 1847 and became a religious community center called Mount St. Vincent. The Sisters decamped to Riverdale in the Bronx in 1860, and the site once again became a tavern and was renamed once again for McGown. It was razed in 1917.

Who Are Those Guys?

In Central Park you'll find quite a few representations of the famous and no-longer-quite-as famous. There are statues of the usual suspects, like Christopher Columbus (there's a monument to him in Columbus Circle and another one at the southern end of the Literary Walk), William Shakespeare, Hans Christian Andersen, Ludwig van Beethoven, and Alexander Hamilton, but, perhaps, you might not know these guys:

a. FITZ-GREENE HALLECK (1790–1867)

Fitz-Greene Halleck wrote romantic and satirical light verse. Little-read today, he was considered the most important and talented American poet of his time—he was called "The American Byron"—and indeed, he is the first American poet to be honored with a sculpture in Central Park or anywhere else. Halleck's statue, sculpted by James W. A. MacDonald and installed in 1876, can be found on the east side of the Literary Walk as you go north.

b. JOHANN VON SCHILLER (1759–1805)

German playwright and philosopher Johann Christoph Friedrich von Schiller's is the oldest portrait sculpture in Central Park: the C. L. Richter work near the Schaumburg Bandshell at the north end of Literary Walk first appeared in 1859 to celebrate the centennial of Schiller's birth.

Schiller, who wrote the plays "William Tell," "Don Carlos," and "Wallenstein," was a champion of human rights and liberty, and also of German unification and reform. He was a close friend of fellow playwright Johann Wolfgang von Goethe, who is memorialized in Bryant Park, and Ludwig van Beethoven, whose statue stands nearby. His life was tragically cut short by tuberculosis when he was forty-six.

c. JOHN PURROY MITCHEL (1879–1918)

Known as "The Boy Mayor"—the youngest NYC chief executive to date—John Purroy Mitchel was elected in 1913 at the age of thirty-four. After losing his bid for reelection in 1917, he was killed while training for the aviary corps in World War I in a freak accident: He fell out of his plane after apparently not sufficiently tightening a seat belt. Adolph Weinman's bust, coated in gold leaf, was installed at the park entrance at Fifth Avenue and East 90th Street in 1926.

d. LADISLAUS JAGIELLO (1351–1434)

Ladislaus Jagiello, Grand Duke of Lithuania, became king of Poland as Ladislaus II in 1386. He established Christianity as a state religion in Lithuania, and his reign is regarded as a revival of learning and literature in eastern Europe as it slowly emerged from the dark ages. Ladislaus's forces assisted Polish, Lithuanian, Russian, and Tatar troops in the defeat of the Teutonic Knights at the Battle of Tannenberg in Prussia in 1410.

Jagiello's statue at the east end of Turtle Pond, was sculpted by S. K. Ostrowski and originally appeared at the Polish pavilion at the first NYC World's Fair in 1939. A gift from Poland, it was moved to its present site in 1945.

e. ALBERT THORVALDSEN (1770–1844)

This is the only statue in New York City that is a self-portrait, and one of two statues of a Dane, the other being Hans Christian Andersen's at Conservatory Lake.

Thorvaldsen was born to an Icelandic family who had emigrated to Copenhagen. He is considered the leading Neo-Classical sculptor of the nineteenth century. His self-portrait, cast in 1839, was presented to the U.S. as a gift from Denmark on the occasion of the 50th anniversary of his death and was installed here in 1894 on a park pathway just north of Fifth Avenue and East 96th Street.

f. ALEXANDER VON HUMBOLDT (1769–1859)

In a fitting location, Explorer's Gate at Central Park West and West 77th Street, you'll find Gustaf Blaeser's portrait of explorer and author Alexander von Humboldt. He traveled widely in South America and Asia and produced the five-volume work *Cosmos*, a study of the physical universe which was left unfinished at his death. Von Humboldt was also an ardent abolitionist and favored independence for Spain's South American colonies. A chance meeting with Simón Bolívar in Paris in 1804, it is said, helped inspire Bolívar's subsequent revolutionary efforts. Many towns and counties throughout the U.S. are named for Humboldt, and it's likely that Brooklyn's Humboldt Street is as well.

g. GIUSEPPE MAZZINI (1805–1872)

You will find this heroic bust of Giuseppe Mazzini by Giovanni Turini, installed in 1876, on West Drive, just north of Tavern on the Green at West 67th Street. Mazzini was a writer, philosopher, and passionate proponent of a united Italy. In 1831, he organized the Young Italy movement, which Giuseppe Garibaldi (memorialized by sculptor Turini in Washington Square Park) joined.

For all of his patriotism, Mazzini was exiled from Italy for much of his life. Even after unification was achieved, he was disappointed in the ruling monarchy, earning disfavor, and only reentered Italy in disguise as a traveling salesman toward the end of his life.

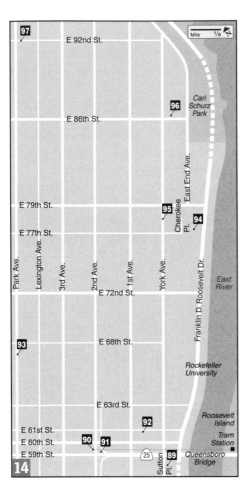

The Upper East Side is a common term for the three neighborhoods between East 59th Street, East 110th Street, Central Park, and the East River: Lenox Hill, the area highlighted by Lenox Hill Hospital on Lexington Avenue between East 76th and 77th Streets; Yorkville, originally a small settlement centering around Third Avenue and East 86th Street that became a major German enclave in the late 1800s and early 1900s (York Avenue is not named for the neighborhood it passes through, but rather for World War I hero Sergeant Alvin York); and Carnegie Hill, between Third and Fifth Avenues, from East 86th to 96th Streets, named for steel magnate and philanthropist Andrew Carnegie's mansion

at Fifth Avenue and 91st Street, now the Cooper-Hewitt National Design Museum. Along the upscale neighborhood's "Museum Mile" on Fifth Avenue can be found the Metropolitan Museum of Art, the Guggenheim, and the Jewish Museums, as well as the Museum of the City of New York.

SUBWAY: ⑥ to 59th, 68th, 77th, 86th, or 96th Streets

BUS: M31 on York Avenue and East 57th Street; **M15** on First and Second Avenues; **M98, M101, M102,** or **M103** on Third or Lexington Avenues; **M1, M2, M3,** or **M4** on Madison or Fifth Avenue; **M57** on 57th Street; **M66** on 67th or 68th Street; **M30** or **M72** on 72nd Street; **M79** on 79th Street; **M86** on 86th Street; **M96** on 96th Street

89 Sutton Square and Riverview Terrace
East 58th Street, east of Sutton Place

The view of the Queensboro Bridge from East 58th Street, east of Sutton Place, is unparalleled in the borough, and was featured in Woody Allen's 1979 movie *Manhattan*. Known officially as Sutton Square, East 58th Street doesn't quite come to a dead end here, since Riverview Terrace extends north from here for a few feet. With a pair of stone goats flanking its entrance, Riverview Terrace is still paved with red brick and has a set of expensive townhouses overlooking the East River.

90 Tramway
Second Avenue and East 60th Street

New York City's only tramway was constructed in 1976 as a temporary means to shuttle residents of the then-new Roosevelt Island housing developments to and from

Manhattan. When a subway stop on Roosevelt Island was opened in 1989, the tram was so popular it remained in operation.

The tramway is unique as the only aerial commuter tram in the U.S. It was designed by Vonroll of Switzerland, and travels a distance of 3,100 feet. Since it actually rises above the Queensboro Bridge, it provides excellent views of that structure, as well as panoramic views of the surrounding area for miles, but the trip takes only about four minutes.

Trolley entrance kiosk

91 Relics of the Queensboro
Second Avenue at the Queensboro Bridge

The southern side of the Queensboro Bridge plaza at Second Avenue and East 59th Street features an ornate, Beaux Arts lightpole stanchion, with four opaque globular lamps surrounding one mounted on the central shaft, facing up. The lamp used to have a partner at the northern side of the bridge, but it disappeared some years ago. The lamp's base is four-sided, and four of New York City's boroughs are represented in stone on the base, all except Staten Island. The missing borough's absence is as much a mystery as the whereabouts of the lamppost's former partner. Staten Island joined New York City in 1898, along with Brooklyn, Queens, and the Bronx, eleven years before the bridge opened.

Trolley service was maintained on the Queensboro until 1957 as a special service to Welfare, now Roosevelt, Island. One of the trolley's five ornate Beaux Arts–style entrance kiosks, featuring Guastavino tiling and ornate exterior trim, survived until the early 2000s, while another has been placed near the tram terminal on Roosevelt Island after years of duty as the entranceway at the Brooklyn Children's Museum.

92 Mount Vernon Hotel Museum
East 61st Street, west of York Avenue

A stone building with a two-level white porch is the remnant of an estate purchased in 1796 by William Stephen Smith and his wife, Abigail, the daughter of President John Adams. The main mansion was lost in an 1826 fire, while the carriage house, the building that remains today, was employed as lodging for northerly travelers and people wishing a day in the country, between 1826 and 1833. It remained in private hands until 1924, when it was purchased by the Colonial Dames of America, refitted with historical effects, and rechristened as a museum in 1939. There is a quiet outdoor patio out back. The Mount Vernon Hotel and Museum is open to the public. For more information, call (212) 838 6878 or visit www.mvhm.org.

93 7th Regiment Armory
Park Avenue and East 67th Street

New York City still has a handful of imposing armories scattered around town, and the 7th Regiment Armory, completed in 1879 by architect Charles Clinton, with additions in 1909 and 1931, might well be the most fascinating. The armory is the only remaining building in the country constructed using a wrought-iron truss system developed by Robert Griffith Hatfield. Its design, consisting of the Administrative Building and a 50,000-square-foot Drill Room, was inspired by the original Grand Central Depot on East 42nd Street. The Drill Room was built to withstand the footfalls of thousands of drilling soldiers and even Army tanks.

The entrance gate on Park Avenue is wide enough to allow a four-abreast marching formation through the massive oak doors. Just inside, you will find halls lined with military-themed exhibits; the halls are also leased for use by antique and book fairs. The more lavish rooms, designed by Louis Comfort Tiffany and Stanford White, are closed to the public, but are used for corporate-sponsored events.

94 The Cherokee
East 77th Street and the FDR Drive

I had always been under the impression that Cherokee Place, between East 77th and 78th Streets, near the FDR Drive, was cut through when the Drive was constructed here in the early 1940s, but the short alley has actually been here since 1912. It was named for the Cherokee Club, an East 79th Street headquarters of the powerful Democratic Party organization, Tammany Hall.

The Cherokee Club is still there, but is now an apartment building.

What truly dominates Cherokee Place, and has since 1912, is the former Shively Sanitary Tenements (now Cherokee Apartments) with its distinctive balconies facing the river. Before today's treatments for tuberculosis, it was thought that the best way to treat "consumption" was with plenty of light and air. The Shively Tenements were conceived with that thought in mind by Dr. Henry Shively, a leading physician in the treatment of tuberculosis at the Clinic of the Presbyterian Hospital. Mrs. William K. Vanderbilt sponsored the project, which was built by architect Henry Atterbury Smith from 1909 to 1912. Every apartment in the building had a balcony and floor-to-ceiling windows, and each apartment could be accessed from staircases from the inner courtyard, built with seats so those afflicted with TB could rest on their way up.

95 Avenue A? Up Here?
York Avenue and East 77th–78th Streets

Why is a public school on York Avenue between East 77th and 78th Streets marked "Avenue A" on the York Avenue side? If you want to catch a glimpse of some former names of New York City thoroughfares, just look up at building corners around town. You will definitely be in for some surprises.

As originally laid out in the Commissioners' Plan of 1811, York Avenue was called Avenue A all the way uptown. Between the Queensboro Bridge and East 92nd Street, Avenue A was renamed soon after World War I in honor of hero Sergeant Alvin York. Other cut-off portions of Avenue A are named Asser Levy Place, Sutton Place South, Sutton Place, and Pleasant Avenue.

🔓 96 Henderson Place
East 86th Street, near York Avenue

Henderson Place is its very own landmark district. A dead end north of East 86th Street near East End Avenue just south of Gracie Mansion, it is home to twenty-four Queen Anne–style row houses built in 1883 by the firm of Lamb & Rich (who also built Sagamore Hill, Teddy Roosevelt's Oyster Bay home) for developer John Henderson. Alfred Lunt and Lynn Fontanne, the famed husband-and-wife acting couple, lived on Henderson Place for a number of years.

97 East 92nd Street Houses
East 92nd Street, east of Park Avenue

Sequestered along quiet East 92nd Street, east of Park Avenue, are a trio of grand wooden houses with porches, unique to the Upper East Side. They are remnants of the old village of Yorkville, which was settled a number of years earlier than the surround-

ing districts. The house at 120 East 92nd Street, built by Catherine Rennert, dates to 1871, while 122 was built in 1859 by customs house officer Adam Flanagan. A third wooden house can be found on the other side of Lexington Avenue at 160 East 92nd Street. According to author and architectural critic Christopher Gray, the construction of wooden houses was outlawed south of 86th Street in 1866, and south of 155th Street in 1888.

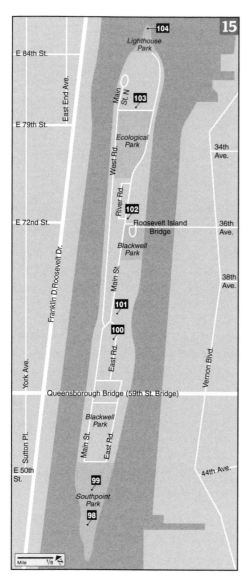

Located in the East River between Man-hattan and Queens, two-mile-long Roosevelt Island has been the home since 1973 of a small town of about 8,300 people in the midst of a huge city. Native Americans called the island Minnehanak ("Long Island"), and the Dutch called it Varkens ("Hog Island"). But it has gone under a variety of names in English: Blackwell's Island in 1686, then Welfare Island in 1921, and finally Roosevelt Island in 1973; a substantial memorial to Franklin Delano

Roosevelt was supposed to occupy the island's southern tip, but the plans were scratched when the architect passed away. In 1828, the first of the island's lengthy succession of asylums, penitentiaries, and hospitals opened; its isolation in the East River gave NYC a convenient place to stash dangerous or contagiously ill people.

By the 1920s and 1930s, the Island had become a bizarre fiefdom of gangsters serving time in the neglectful tenure of Joseph McCann, who ran Blackwell Penitentiary. The mobsters were able to have all the comforts of home smuggled in, and lived like kings amid the deteriorating, squalid conditions surrounding them. The penitentiary was closed and moved to Rikers Island in 1935.

By the 1930s, the era of institutionalization on Welfare Island was winding down. Goldwater Memorial Hospital, named for Dr. S. S. Goldwater, Commissioner of Hospitals, opened in 1939 and Bird S. Coler Hospital, named for the consolidated NYC's first comptroller, in 1952. The rest of the island was in ruins by this time.

Various proposals for parks and residential development, which would include a subway connection, began to circulate in the 1960s. Finally, a plan envisioned by legendary architect Philip Johnson and John Burgee was decided upon. The Urban Development Corporation, inaugurated in 1969, hired developers and construction began. Roosevelt Island was built up with high-rise developments and a promenade on the eastern and western sides of the island. No dogs were allowed on the island at first, and cars were discouraged (they were allowed only in the parking garage near the bridge; buses transported people up and down Main Street, one of two named streets in the development).

Though it is technically a part of Manhattan, the only way to get there by motor-ized vehicle is from a bridge at 36th Avenue and Vernon Boulevard in Astoria, Queens. Since 1976, the only tramway in NYC has run from Second Avenue and East 60th Street and, since 1989, the subway travels to one of the deepest stations in the system located here.

SUBWAY: 🄵 to Roosevelt Island

BUS: Q102 from Astoria; the Roosevelt Island Operating Corporation offers local bus service on the island.

🎐98 Smallpox Hospital
Southpoint Park

Ruins of the Smallpox Hospital, built in 1856 by James Renwick Jr. on the southern tip of the island, have recently been made more accessible to public view. Though the ruin remains fenced off, it is occasionally open as "Southpoint Park." Visitors can view it from the outside, but the interior has yet to be made safe for the public. Unusually, it is well-lit at night and its ghostly outline can be seen from Manhattan Island after dark.

In the 1850s, smallpox was a dangerously transmittable illness, and its sufferers were quarantined here. In the late 1800s, North Brother Island became NYC's quar-

antine center, and the hospital became a nurses' residence. It has been gradually deteriorating since the 1950s.

99 Strecker Laboratory
Southpoint Park

The Strecker Laboratory, a premier facility for bacteriological research in the 1890s, was constructed as an adjunct to the old City Hospital in a Romanesque Revival style by architects Frederick Withers and Walter Dickson. Since it closed in the 1950s, it had been allowed to collapse for nearly forty years despite its landmarking in 1975. In 2000, the laboratory was renovated and restored.

100 Blackwell Farmhouse
Main Street

Roosevelt Island's first permanent resident was Captain John Manning, a disgraced British naval officer who had allowed Fort Amsterdam (on Governors Island) to fall to the Dutch in 1673. Upon Manning's death, the island was passed on to his stepdaughter, Mary, and her husband, Robert Blackwell, and the island stayed in the Blackwell family until 1823, retaining the name "Blackwell's Island" for decades after that.

The oldest building on Roosevelt Island is the Blackwell Farmhouse, built in 1794. In 1828, the farmhouse was purchased by the city, and it later became the administrative center for the succession of institutions that sprung up on Blackwell's Island beginning that year.

101 Chapel of the Good Shepherd
Main Street

The oldest church on Roosevelt Island, the Chapel of the Good Shepherd (Episcopal) was built in 1889 by Frederick Clarke Withers and was restored when new development came to the island in the early 1970s. It was originally a gift from banker George Bliss to the Episcopal City Mission Society to serve patients and inmates on the island.

102 Episcopal Church of the Holy Spirit
River Road, facing Manhattan

It turns out that Roosevelt Island's other old church is also an Episcopal church: the Episcopal Church of the Holy Spirit, located on the west side, mid-island, facing Manhattan. Built in 1924 from island-quarried gneiss as a chapel for Metropolitan Hospital with an attached rectory for the hospital's chaplain, it stood abandoned between 1955 and 1975 after Metropolitan moved to Manhattan. It has subsequently been the Redeemed Christian Church of God and Dayspring Church. The deepest section of Water Tunnel No. 3, connecting upstate Kensico Reservoir to NYC's water supply, is being built directly underneath the chapel.

 # 103 Octagon
South of Lighthouse Park

What is known today as "The Octagon" in the island's northern end, just below Light-house Park, is a remnant of Blackwell's Island's first insane asylum, constructed in 1839 and opened in 1841. On a New York City visit in the mid-1840s, Charles Dickens decried the treatment given inmates there. Elizabeth Cochrane, writing under her nom de plume Nellie Bly, feigned mental illness to gain admission, and wrote an exposé on the asylum in 1887. The building was renovated and renamed Metropolitan Hospital in 1894, and remained in that capacity until the mid-1950s, after which most of it was demolished. The remaining section languished in disrepair for decades, but in 2005, "the Octagon" was being restored with a new dome as part of a new apartment complex named for it.

104 Lighthouse Park
Lighthouse Park

Lighthouse Park, at the island's northern tip, is named for the lighthouse built by architect James Renwick Jr. in 1872, who also built the island's Smallpox Hospital. It replaced a small fort built by Thomas Maxey, a patient in the nearby insane asylum. A plaque carved by another patient, John McCarthy, who claimed to have assisted in its construction, is reported to have been here until the 1960s when it was stolen.

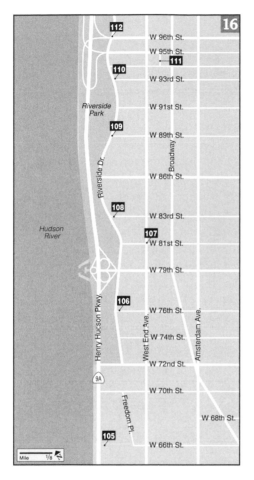

What is now Manhattan's Upper West Side was settled in the late seventeenth century and named Bloomingdale, a transliteration of the Dutch term for "vale of flowers." A farm road was established through the small town as early as 1705, and after 300 years, what is now Broadway is still the area's main drag. Later, villages like Harsenville, established by farmer Jacob Harsen where West 70th Street is now, harbored future French monarch Louis Philippe and statesman Talleyrand during their French Revolution exile. Charles Apthorp's 1764 mansion, where Columbus Avenue and West 91st Street are now, is remembered by the grand, richly ornamented Apthorp Apartments at Broadway and West 79th Street. Edgar Allan Poe lived in a cottage in 1843–44 on what is now West 84th Street. When Central Park was laid out by Olmsted and Vaux in the 1850s, an entire community, Seneca Village, located along what would have been Seventh and Eighth Avenues, between West 81st and 89th Streets, was forced to disperse. A village of approximately 1,600, it was one of NYC's first strongholds of African-American property owners after its establishment in the 1820s.

After the coming of the Ninth Avenue El (running up Columbus Avenue), elegant mansions and row houses appeared. Riverside Drive above 72nd Street, built in 1880, allowed vistas of the river and New Jersey beyond. Riverside Park, Manhattan's longest—stretching from West 72nd to West 125th Streets—was built between 1875 and 1900 using an original plan by Frederick Olmsted. By the 1920s, the plan was compromised as the park became a de facto train yard, accommodating the railroad tracks along the Hudson riverbank. Parks Commissioner Robert Moses rebuilt and expanded the park between 1934 and 1937. He also shaped the Upper West Side in the 1960s by condemning 15 acres between Columbus Avenue, Broadway, Amsterdam Avenue, and West 62nd through 66th Streets to create Lincoln Center for the Performing Arts. The American Museum of Natural History arrived in the Upper West Side at its present location on Central Park West from West 77th to West 81st Streets in 1874; the adjoining Hayden Planetarium followed in 1935, and its successor, the Rose Center for Earth and Space, opened in 2000.

SUBWAY: Ⓐ, Ⓑ, Ⓒ, Ⓓ, ①, ②, or ③ to 59th Street–Columbus Circle; ① to 66th, 72nd, 79th, 86th, and 96th Streets; ② or ③ to 72nd or 96th Streets; Ⓑ or

MANHATTAN

C to 72nd, 81st, or 96th Streets, and Cathedral Parkway

BUS: **M10** on Central Park West; **M7** or **M11** on Columbus and Amsterdam Avenues; **M104** on Broadway; **M5** on Riverside Drive; **M72** on 72nd Street; **M79** on 79th and 81st Streets; **M86** on 86th Street; **M96** on 96th Street; **M4** to 110th Street–Cathedral Parkway

105 West Side Railroad Remnants

West Side Highway, south of West 72nd Street

The stretch of Riverside Park on the Hudson River, the site of the old West Side Rail Yards between West 59th and West 72nd Streets, is now open to the public. While Amtrak passenger trains still run underground, freight trains used to rumble to and from barges that floated produce across the Hudson. This was, as most waterfront areas in New York had been, a vital area for shipping and commerce. Those days are gone, but twisted, decaying wreckage remains.

A gantry, a hinged bridge spanning the gap between land and barge, would be moved up and down depending on the tide; railroad cars would be hoisted from the tracks to the barge, then floated out. The New York Central Railroad, who owned this bridge, was the only railroad with direct freight access to NYC. With most railroads terminating on the waterfront in New Jersey, the railroads had to transport their freight in railroad cars (on car floats) and on barges across the Hudson to small, self-contained freight yards up and down the Hudson, East, and Harlem Rivers.

The barges and piers aren't the only remains here: an old warehouse appears to be "sagging" into the Hudson River. Long ago, a fire bent and twisted the beams; it looks like a carnival ride from hell. Also, a truncated exit at West 72nd Street is the last remaining piece of the old Miller Highway, which was torn down in sections beginning in 1973. Here, above the pedestrian entrance at West 72nd Street, are the last examples of the highway's unique lampposts and railings.

106 Riverside Drive Horse Trough

Riverside Drive at West 76th Street

At Riverside Drive and West 76th Street you'll find a marble basin featuring an ea-

gle; a coat of arms; decorative, Beaux Arts carvings; and water plants (mostly algae, to be honest) languidly floating around.

The fountain was built by Robert Ray Hamilton, a real estate broker and sportsman who paid for its construction sometime in the 1890s. The fountain was completed in 1906 by the architects Warren and Wetmore, who would go on to build the second Grand Central Terminal. The large basin, it is thought, was made so that it would be convenient for the horses who pulled the many carriages and coaches that filled the streets in this era, just before the advent of the automobile. Riverside Drive was built as a leisurely drive in the country, and its twists and turns still give it a somewhat suburban character.

107 Calhoun School

West End Avenue at West 81st Street

Architect Costas Machlouzarides designed the Calhoun School Learning Center at 433 West End Avenue in 1975 with a distinctive quirk: He provided two giant picture windows shaped like television screens on each exposed side.

108 Mount Tom

Riverside Drive and West 83rd Street

There's an outcropping of rock at Riverside Drive and West 83rd Street known as Mount Tom, rising impressively from the park path surrounding a stone slab commemorating those who perished in the Warsaw Ghetto and the subsequent transport of Polish Jews to the Treblinka concentration camp between 1940 and 1943.

Edgar Allan Poe's favorite neighborhood spot was here at Mount Tom. Poe lived in a farmhouse at what is now 215 West 84th Street; there he completed "The Raven," and it's believed he also wrote the poem "To Helen" on Mount Tom. From Riverside Drive, you can recognize the outcropping by the portion of the Riverside Park fence that is painted white. There are pebbled paths that lead you to the rock.

109 Soldiers and Sailors Monument

Riverside Drive and West 89th Street

This unheralded columned monument to the nation's Civil War dead was designed by Stoughton and Stoughton and erected in 1902. It is ringed by twelve 36-foot-tall columns. Twisting, winding Riverside Drive is quite unlike Manhattan's other north-south arteries, and architects have

MANHATTAN

taken full advantage of its frequent bends to create magnificent apartment buildings and monuments along its route.

110 Joan of Arc

Riverside Drive at West 93rd Street

This statue of the fabled French saint at Riverside Drive and West 93rd Street was sculpted by Anna Huntington in 1915, one of her first works in a very long career that lasted into the 1960s. Fragments of the cathedral at Rheims and the tower at Rouen, where Joan was executed, are embedded in the pedestal. Though New York City has many statues of people on horseback (Manhattan has eleven scattered around the borough), this is the only historic female figure so enshrined.

111 Pomander Walk

West 94th and 95th Streets, west of Broadway

Pomander Walk is the only Manhattan thoroughfare named for a stage play. The play—itself named for a London alley—ran briefly in 1910 and starred one Dorothy Parker. This Parker was *not* the later doyenne of the Algonquin Round Table, though the actress and the writer were contemporaries.

The alley and its row of twenty-seven small town houses were constructed in 1922 and have pretty much stayed unchanged since then. In 1920, nightclub proprietor

Thomas Healy acquired the property and built Tudor-style buildings on each side. He meant to tear down the buildings after a few years and construct a hotel. That plan never came to fruition, and this reminder of an earlier age has survived various challenges over the years. Pomander Walk is open only to residents, but it can be seen from the gate facing West 94th Street.

112 Riverside Swastikas

Riverside Drive at West 96th Street

Two terra-cotta swastika-shaped symbols can be found on the upper corners of a residential building at 243 Riverside Drive, at West 96th Street, which was built about 1914. The swastika, formerly a symbol of good fortune and prosperity, was co-opted and forever corrupted by the National Socialist Party of Germany in the 1920s. The building, according to the *AIA Guide to New York City*, is called the Cliff Dwellers Apartments. Other friezes on the building depict mountain lions, buffalo skulls, and rattlesnakes that symbolize Arizona cliff-dwelling Native Americans (this building overlooks hilly Riverside Park across the street). Other swastikas can be found on buildings around town.

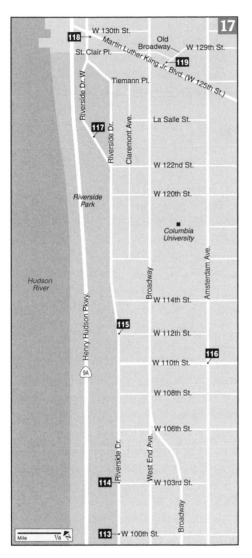

SUBWAY: ① to 96th, 103rd, 110th, 116th, and 125th Streets; Ⓐ, Ⓑ, Ⓒ, or Ⓓ to 125th Street; Ⓑ or Ⓓ to 116th Street

BUS: M4 or **M104** on Broadway; **M60** on Amsterdam Avenue and West 125th Street; **M18** on West 116th Street and Manhattan Avenue; **M5** on Riverside Drive; **M11** on Amsterdam Avenue

Of all of Manhattan's former self-contained villages, such as Harsenville, Yorkville, and Seneca Village, Manhattanville has retained more of a singular identity than the others. Indeed, its old street pattern, centered on slanting West 125th (formerly Manhattan) Street, predating the overall street grid, has been retained. This village was founded in 1806 in a deep valley whose location was propitious for cross-island travel to and from the older village of Harlem to the east. The valley necessitated the construction of two of Manhattan's great steel bridges: the Riverside Drive Viaduct, carrying the drive above Twelfth Avenue, built in 1900, and the railroad bridge spanning West 125th Street and carrying the IRT subway, completed in 1905. For those not used to traveling through this part of town by subway, it's quite surprising to emerge into the daylight at 125th Street, only to descend into the depths once again. Subway engineers deemed it more advisable to bridge the valley rather than tunnel deeper under it.

Morningside Heights arose at the site of the Revolutionary War Battle of Harlem Heights in the mid-1800s. Though the town was initially slow to develop because of the presence of the Bloomingdale Insane Asylum in the nineteenth century, it eventually became home to Columbia University (much of the present campus was designed by Charles McKim), the Cathedral of St. John the Divine, and Riverside Church.

🔥113 Firemen and Fire Horse Memorials
Riverside Drive at West 100th Street

Seemingly hidden on Riverside Drive between West 100th and West 112th Streets are a number of memorials and monuments.

The Firemen's Memorial, designed by H. Van Buren Magonigle and sculpted in

MANHATTAN

1912 by Attilio Piccirilli, is a large marble slab surrounded by an approach of steps, two balustrades, and allegorical figures representing Sacrifice (shown as a woman embracing the body of her dead husband) and Duty (shown as a mother standing by a fire hydrant, holding a fireman's coat and hat and embracing a child). The slab supports a bas-relief of a fire wagon pulled by three galloping horses.

A bronze memorial to the horses that pulled fire wagons is embedded in the walkway at the top of the steps—it is the only permanent memorial to horses in NYC.

114 Franz Sigel

Riverside Drive at West 106th Street

Major General Franz Sigel (1824–1902) overlooks Riverside Drive at West 106th Street. Sigel, born in Baden, Germany, served in the German military until 1852, when he emigrated to the U.S., and became a journalist. Joining the U.S. army at the outbreak of the Civil War, he helped suppress Missouri's secession and went on to fight in Virginia and West Virginia. He was defeated by General John C. Breckinridge at the Battle of New Market, Virginia, in May 1864—a skirmish that is commemorated by the Virginia Military Institute to this day because ten cadets were killed in the fight. After the war, Sigel went on to work in public relations and journalism in Baltimore and New York City.

Sigel's statue was unveiled amid great

fanfare in 1907. The sculpture, by Viennese artist Karl Bitter, was designed to be seen by passing boats in the Hudson, like other statues on Riverside Drive. In the century to follow, though, lush vegetation has grown to obscure that view. The general is also remembered by Sigel Park in Concourse Village in the Bronx.

115 Samuel Tilden

Riverside Drive and West 112th Street

In the election of 1876, which wound up with a popular vote in near-deadlock, the Republicans formed the majority of the commission that was appointed to determine the vote of three key southern states. As a result, Republican Rutherford B. Hayes went to the White House and New York Democrat Samuel Tilden (1814–1886) returned home. He governed New York State, helped create the New York Public Library, fought the extension of slavery, and prosecuted the Tweed Ring. Tilden lived near Gramercy Park and also on his estate, Greystone, in Yonkers. He actually set aside $50,000 of his fortune for this memorial statue to be built after his death, but due to squabbles between sculptor William Partridge and the executors of Tilden's will, the statue didn't appear until 1926. It's inscribed with the motto: "I Trust the People."

116 Peace Fountain

Amsterdam Avenue and West 110th Street

Greg Wyatt's Peace Fountain, installed adjacent to the Cathedral of St. John the Divine in 1985, has been described as both whimsical and disturbing. It depicts the archangel Michael triumphant bestride a defeated demon. Giraffes, representing peace in Wyatt's iconography, gambol on stylized moon and sun figures, while a giant crab rests on a double-helix-shaped pedestal. Surrounding the fountain, you

will find bronze animal sculptures constructed by New York City schoolchildren.

♟ 117 Who *Is* Buried at Grant's Tomb?

Riverside Drive and West 123rd Street

It's not who you think. The last resting place of the 18th President, Ulysses S. Grant, and his wife, Julia, on Riverside Drive on the Upper West Side has been the subject of NYC's most infamous, and silliest, riddle over the years. The correct answer is that nobody is buried under the monument . . . Grant and his wife are, however, *entombed* here and are not six feet under. (That's why it's Grant's Tomb, not Grant's Grave.)

But if you take a short walk up Riverside Drive, you *will* find a grave. Look for a small monument, standing by itself, surrounded by an iron fence.

Five-year-old St. Clair Pollock was playing on the rocks overlooking the Hudson River on the Pollock property, and fell to his death on July 15, 1797. When the Pollocks later sold the property, his father (perhaps his uncle; records are unclear) made the request that St. Clair's grave, which was on the property, would always be respected. A small stone urn remains marked, "Erected to the memory of an amiable child." St. Clair is also commemorated with the very short St. Clair Place, which runs between the Hudson River and West 125th Street under the Riverside Drive Viaduct, about a half mile to the north.

🚋 118 125th Street Streetcars

Twelfth Avenue and West 125th Street

Here and there throughout the city where the pavement has worn down, brief glimpses of New York's former widespread streetcar network can be seen. In Manhat-

MANHATTAN

tan, local laws prohibited unsightly overhead trolley wires, so street railways had to take power from electric conduits located beneath the pavement. Streetcars had thin arms, called ploughs, that extended into a below-pavement channel containing a charged rail with up to 600 volts (the same juice that subway third rails of today carry). The rail was placed between the two tracks that carried the wheels.

For a number of reasons, among them esthetic ones, New York decided to phase out streetcars in favor of buses in the 1930s. NYC's last streetcar run was in the late 1940s, though hybrid trolley buses (buses that took power from overhead wires but didn't run on tracks) remained in some parts of Brooklyn until the early 1960s.

On West 125th Street, under the massive Riverside Drive Viaduct where the pavement has worn away leaving the old block paving exposed, is a curving set of tracks with an extra line in the middle, the conduit slot, marked "3 Ave" in spots. Most surface lines in NYC became a part of the Third Avenue Railroad System by the late 1890s, and so insulator and manhole covers would carry the name "Third Avenue."

119 Old Broadway
Broadway and West 125th Street

Broadway in upper Manhattan follows the path of an ancient trail known in colonial days as Bloomingdale Road. It started at about where Madison Square is now, at Fifth Avenue and East 23rd Street (before these streets were mapped or cut through of course) continuing along the present path of Broadway to West 86th Street, where it veered east, running between today's Broadway and Amsterdam Avenue. At West 104th Street, it again assumed Broadway's present route until West 107th Street, where it turned northwest until meeting the present path of Riverside Drive, following it to West 116th. Here it turned northeast again, crossing Manhattan Street (today's 125th Street) as Old Broadway. From West 133rd Street, it ran slightly east of the present Broadway, to Amsterdam and West 144th Street (today's Hamilton Place is another remnant), and ended at St. Nicholas Avenue and 147th Street.

As the area became more populated, and Bloomingdale Road was straightened and widened in the 1870s into the Broadway we know today, a bend in the road between West 125th and 133rd Streets was left over and that became Old Broadway. In the 1960s, Old Broadway was separated into two pieces by the Manhattanville Houses.

As early as 1658, Dutch farmers had
established a settlement here, ultimately
supplanting an earlier Native American
settlement that had sprawled along the
Harlem River where the streets in the 110s
and 120s are now. Their village was named
Nieuw Haarlem, after the west Netherlands
city. In 1776, the village was the setting
for the Battle of Harlem Heights, in which
the colonists scored a key victory over the
British.

When a railroad and elevated public
transportation was extended north to Harlem in the 1880s, a feverish building boom
was triggered, producing block after block
of new apartments and tenements. In the
decades after the subway and El were built,
Harlem was home to many Eastern European Jews who had moved uptown from the
cramped tenements of the Lower East Side.
After World War I, they moved elsewhere,
and Harlem became a mecca for the city's
families of African descent, fleeing from
prejudice not only in other parts of the city
but from the southern and western states.
In the Roaring Twenties, Harlem became a
political and cultural capital for literature,
painting, and jazz in the movement known
as the Harlem Renaissance. The Depres-

sion and following decades proved devastating to the area, but by the turn of the
twenty-first century, investment in the area
put Harlem on the upswing again with
new and renovated housing and a revitalized artistic community.

Hamilton Heights is a small area just
north of the City University of New York
campus (whose Shepard Hall, built on a
high hill, is one of New York City's great
edifices) consisting of beautiful row houses
clustered along Convent Avenue and Hamilton Terrace, between West 141st and West
145th Streets.

Harlem proper runs from about Fifth
Avenue (and from the Harlem River further
uptown) west to St. Nicholas Avenue and
Sugar Hill, and from Central Park North
to West 155th Street. East of Harlem, from
East 106th Street to the East River, we find
Spanish and East Harlem, while west of St.
Nicholas Avenue are Manhattanville and
Hamilton Heights. Sugar Hill runs along
Edgecombe Avenue, from West 145th to
155th Streets. In the early twentieth cen-
tury, it was home to prominent figures,
including future Supreme Court Justice
Thurgood Marshall.

SUBWAY: ① to 116th, 125th, 137th, or
145th Street; Ⓐ, Ⓑ, Ⓒ, or Ⓓ to 125th
Street; ② or ③ to 125th Street; ④, ⑤,
or ⑥ to 125th Street; ② or ③ to 116th
or 135th Street; ⑥ to 116th Street; Ⓓ or
Ⓒ to 116th or 135th Street

BUS: M101, M102, or **M103** on Lex-
ington or Third Avenue; **M1** on Fifth and
Madison Avenues; **M7** or **M102** on Mal-
colm X Boulevard; **M2** on Adam Clayton
Powell Jr. Boulevard; **M10** on Frederick
Douglass Boulevard; **M3** on St. Nicholas
Avenue; **M18** on Convent Avenue; **M11,**
M100, or **M101** on Amsterdam Avenue;
M4 on Broadway; **M5** on Riverside Drive,

MANHATTAN

West 135th Street, and Broadway; **M116**, **M18**, or **M104** on 116th Street; **M100**, **M101**, **M60**, or **Bx15** on 125th Street; **M11** on West 135th Street, **Bx33** on East 135th Street; **Bx19** on West 145th Street

📖120 Harlem's Fire Tower

Fifth Avenue and East 120th Street

Marcus Garvey Park, set on an outcropping between East 120th and East 124th Streets, interrupts the northern progress of Fifth Avenue, which runs south from here all the way to Washington Square Park, and from 124th Street north to the Harlem River.

Long before the street grid marched north, land here was set aside for a park: Mount Morris Park was opened in 1842. In 1973 it was renamed for early-twentieth-century nationalist Marcus Garvey. The park is surrounded on three sides by magnificent brownstone buildings, some in faded magnificence and in need of repair.

Before electric lights, radios, or fire alarms, a series of bell towers were set up on high hills throughout the city to alert firefighters when a fire broke out. Blazes were fought by volunteer fire departments which were poorly coordinated and orga-

nized, until 1865, when the New York State Legislature replaced the volunteer companies with the Metropolitan Fire Department. (The Fire Department of New York would succeed it in 1870.) A telegraphic alert network was set up in 1874 that rendered the bell towers unnecessary.

Marcus Garvey Park is crowned by the last remaining fire bell tower in the city. What is now known as the Mount Morris Fire Tower was built by Julius Kroehl in 1857. Doric columns supported a platform and observatory (now removed). A spiral staircase ascends to what was the observatory, and the bell hangs from bowed iron girders. Many of the bell towers were made of wood and did not stand up to the elements over the years. This one was made of cast-iron, based on earlier towers by James Bogardus, a pioneer in the use of cast-iron in building.

🔫121 Blumstein's

West 125th Street near Adam Clayton Powell Jr. Boulevard

Blumstein's is probably the most recognizable sign on 125th Street other than the Apollo Theater marquee. Its namesake department store at 230 West 125th is gone now, but its old building and four-story-high sign remain. Blumstein's was not without controversy during its long tenure. The store was established by German immigrant Louis Blumstein in 1898. In its early days, Blumstein's refused to hire African-American workers until a boycott in 1934 served to call attention to such practices. After Blumstein's was finally integrated, it actually became the first store to employ an African-American Santa Claus and use dark-skinned mannequins.

122 Astor Row: Porches in Manhattan

West 130th Street, near Fifth Avenue

Comprising the southern side of West 130th Street between Fifth and Lenox Avenues, Astor Row, built by architect Charles Buek between 1880 and 1883, features a rarity in Manhattan: houses with porches!

Located on land owned by William Astor (great-grandson of fur entrepreneur John Jacob Astor and scion of his real estate empire), Astor Row is made up of twenty-eight brick houses, some attached, some not. Not all the Astor Row houses are in terrific shape, but, since 1992, great strides have been made toward rehabilitating them. In that year, the NYC Landmarks Conservancy, in association with the Landmarks Preservation Commission and the Abyssinian Development Corporation, began the ongoing project to reverse the deterioration and restore this unique stretch of houses.

123 Renaissance Ballroom

Adam Clayton Powell Jr. Boulevard and West 137th Street

The brick building on the corner of Adam Clayton Powell Jr. Boulevard and West 137th Street was a mecca of Harlem nightlife in the 1930s in its incarnation as the Renaissance Ballroom. The "Renny" offered dancing, cabaret acts, and the finest bands of the era, including those of Vernon Andrade, Fletcher Henderson, and Chick Webb. The theater was originated in the early 1920s by entrepreneur William Roche.

The adjoining Renaissance Casino was the home court of the 1920s Harlem Rennies, the first all-black professional basketball team, which racked up a 2,588–592 record against other local competition. Today, the Renny awaits rehabilitation. It still has an ancient neon sign reading "chow mein" and "chop suey." When the Renny was built, they were still considered foreign and exotic.

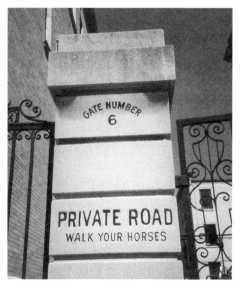

124 Striver's Row

West 138th and 139th Streets, between Adam Clayton Powell Jr. and Douglass Boulevards

Called "two of the most spectacular streetscapes in New York City" by the authors of *Touring Historic Harlem*, these 146 row houses and three apartment buildings were built by developer David King Jr. in 1890.

Appointed with elegant woodwork and modern plumbing (still in its infancy in NYC in 1890), the King Model Homes employ designs from the most illustrious architects of the period. Subtle variations in each building break up monotony as does the presence of handsome iron gates that open up to allow access to service alleys—very unusual in New York City. But in the days before horseless carriages, the alleys also served as a place to park your mount. Note the original "walk your horses" signs.

In the 1920s and 1930s, the King Model Homes were the residences of several prominent Harlemites, notably Vertner Tandy, the first commissioned African-American architect in New York State; W. C. Handy, the "father of the blues," composer and compiler of African-American folk music traditions; Fletcher Henderson, the jazz pianist and orchestra leader; and Harry Wills, a top heavyweight contender who never got to fight for the title due to racism in the boxing hierarchy.

125 Hamilton's House

Convent Avenue and West 141st Street

Tucked tightly into a cramped space at 287 Convent Avenue just north of West 141st Street is a house that the first U.S. Treasury Secretary, coauthor of the *Federalist Papers*, and *New York Post* cofounder Alexander Hamilton called home from 1802 until his death in a duel with political rival Aaron Burr in 1804. The house originally occupied a 32-acre plot about 350 feet to the southeast, but when the city's street grid system reached this far north in 1879, Hamilton Grange lay in the roadbed of West 143rd Street and so was moved to its present location.

The National Parks Service acquired the Hamilton Grange National Memorial in 1962, and has continued operating it as a museum (as it has been run since 1933). The NPS proposes moving it from its tight quarters into an airier location in St. Nicholas Park a block to the south. Call (212) 283-5154 or visit www.nps.gov/hagr for hours.

126 Mega Omega Oil Signs

Frederick Douglass Boulevard and West 147th and 148th Streets

Omega Oil ads took the cake when it came to large, legible, colorful, and gorgeous building-side advertisements. Back in the early 1900s, "wall dogs" labored for days to create these ads, some as large as this one which stretches for four stories on Frederick Douglass Boulevard between West 147th and 148th Streets. This large ad probably tried to catch the attention of riders on the Ninth Avenue El, which rumbled past here until about 1940.

 127 Macy's Uptown

West 148th Street between Frederick Douglass and Adam Clayton Powell Jr. Boulevards

Recognizable in this "wall dog" ad are the words "Uptown Stables" and "Orders for Goods Taken Here." Less legible are the words on top, which say "R.H. Macy & Co."

This ad most likely dates to the 1880s. In that era, Macy's, which was founded in 1857, was still located on West 14th Street

Harlem and Hamilton Heights

and Sixth Avenue downtown. The company would not move to its present location in Herald Square until 1902. Founder Rowland Hussey Macy was a Nantucket seaman aboard the *Emily Morgan* whaling ship; a tattoo he picked up at a port of call, a red, five-pointed star, still serves as the department store's symbol and indeed is front and center here. This ad is likely the oldest outdoor Macy's ad still detectable in NYC.

128 Bunny Theatre
Broadway and West 147th Street

The Bunny Theatre recollects early-twentieth-century comic actor and theater impresario John Bunny (1863–1915). Bunny appeared in more than 100 silents in a little over five years, including a filmed version of Winsor McCay's "Little Nemo" (1911) and Charles Dickens' "Pickwick Papers" (1913). Bunny's exuberant style and 300-pound girth made him a fan favorite; he was so well-known that many of his pictures billed him in the title, a novel practice in that era.

In the Bunny Theatre's later years, it was renamed the Nova. Sadly, it closed in 2003 and became a ninety-nine-cent store, with its marquee removed, but its stone rabbits remain, along with the word "Bunny" chiseled at the top.

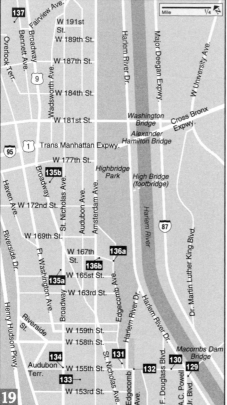

Washington Heights, the area from West 155th Street north to Fort Tryon Park, and from river to river, is named for Fort Washington, located on the high hills in the present Bennett Park on Fort Washington Avenue between West 181st and 183rd Streets. The region featured many forts—four in upper Manhattan and Fort Lee across the Hudson—that unsuccessfully tried to prevent the British from accessing New York harbor via the Hudson River in 1776.

After the Revolutionary War, Washington Heights, with its amazing views of the New Jersey Palisades across the Hudson, was dominated by mansions and country estates, remnants of which can still be made out along the Henry Hudson Parkway. Washington Heights' main tourist attraction, The Cloisters, opened in Fort Tryon

Park in 1938 after John D. Rockefeller purchased the former Cornelius Billings mansion and built a medieval art museum after the mansion burned down. Castle Village, consisting of five thirteen-story towers containing 580 apartments, was built on the site of Paterno Castle, a former Xanadu at what is now Cabrini Boulevard and West 181st Street. Charles Paterno's manse contained a mushroom cellar, a swimming pool surrounded by birdcages, and a master bedroom that measured 20 × 80 feet. Its 7-acre site was surrounded by woods and greenhouses.

SUBWAY: Ⓑ or Ⓓ to 155th Street; Ⓒ to 155th Street, 163rd Street–Amsterdam Avenue; Ⓐ or Ⓒ to 168th Street; Ⓐ to 175th Street; ① to 157th, 168th, 181st, and 191st Streets

BUS: **Bx6** to 155th Street and Riverside Drive; **M2** to 155th Street and Edgecombe Avenue or 165th Street; **M3** or **M18** on St. Nicholas Avenue; **M100** or **M101** on Amsterdam Avenue; **M5** or **M100** on Broadway; **M4** on Broadway and Fort Washington Avenue

129 Lampposts: Harlem Nocturne
Adam Clayton Powell Jr. Boulevard and West 153rd Street

A set of unique lampposts, still standing but no longer functional, used to light an underpass that brought traffic from Adam Clayton Powell Jr. Boulevard under the Harlem River Drive at West 153rd Street. They seem to be related to no other NYC lamppost genus or species—they're in a class of their own: an evolutionary midway point between the Beaux Arts cast-iron posts and the more utilitarian Whitestone or Triborough Bridge twinlamp designs.

According to the Friends of Cast Iron

Architecture, these poles originally had octagonal-shaped glass luminaires. Sometime in the 1940s or 1950s, these were replaced by the "teardrop" or "cuplight" luminaires that dominated NYC streets in the 1950s, before the greenish-white mercury lamps took over in the early 1960s.

There's also a group of similar but not quite the same posts on Riverside Drive from West 155th to 158th Street. These lamps apparently *have* been allowed to keep their original eight-paned octagonal luminaires.

130 155th Street Viaduct

Between Adam Clayton Powell Jr. Boulevard and Edgecombe Avenue

The 155th Street Viaduct carries traffic from the Macombs Dam Bridge high over a bluff to the northern end of Sugar Hill at Edgecombe Avenue. Robert Macomb constructed a dam in 1814 for a gristmill where 155th Street meets the Harlem River, for which he charged a toll. However, the dam flooded upstream meadows in Manhattan, obstructed river traffic, and was deemed a public nuisance by the courts after it was forcibly breached by annoyed shippers in 1838. A wood bridge was constructed and remained until the present Macombs Dam Bridge, and the accompanying 155th Street Viaduct, were built by Alfred Boller in 1895.

The viaduct was given a complete renovation at the turn of the twenty-first century that provided new fences that are close replicas of the lacy old ones, and the span, along with the Macombs Dam Bridge, was painted a light buff color, similar to the one of the bridges sported when first built in 1895.

131 The Giants' Last Stand

Edgecombe Avenue, north of West 155th Street

The New York Giants played in a number of stadiums named the "Polo Grounds" through much of the twentieth century; the first in the series actually did play host to polo matches. When owner Horace Stoneham pulled up stakes and moved the team to San Francisco in 1958, the latest Polo Grounds, located on Frederick Douglass Boulevard and West 155th Street, stood empty for four years, but was then employed for a couple of years by the fledgling New York Mets. It was torn down after the 1963 season.

In Edgecombe Park, along Edgecombe Avenue north of 155th Street on Coogan's Bluff, a fly ball's distance away from where the Polo Grounds used to stand, you'll find a rusted, abandoned staircase. If you dare to climb down on it to a landing, you'll find a plaque on which is inscribed: "The

John T. Brush Staircase, presented by the New York Giants." The rest has been erased by time. The staircase allowed fans exiting after a game access up the high hill to the trolleys.

John Tomlinson Brush bought the New York Giants in 1902. When the Giants won the National League pennant in 1904, he agreed with manager John McGraw that the Giants shouldn't play the "junior circuit" American League champion Boston Pilgrims (later called the Red Sox) because of an ongoing disagreement with AL president Ban Johnson. The World Series would be played every year thereafter until 1994 (when it wasn't held due to a strike). Brush was on a train bound for California in 1912 when he suddenly passed away; he had suffered from ill health for some time. The staircase was likely presented by the Giants shortly after Brush's death.

132 Hooper Fountain
Edgecombe Avenue and West 155th Street

The unusual fountain at Maher Circle, at West 155th Street, Edgecombe Avenue, and St. Nicholas Place, was a gift from civil engineer/newspaperman/entrepreneur John

Hooper. In his will, made public upon his death in 1889, he appropriated funds for the construction of two public fountains that had to include horse troughs as well as drinking fountains. Both fountains were built in 1894: the one here was designed by George Martin Huss at Maher Circle, and the other in Brooklyn at Flatbush and Sixth Avenues in Park Slope disappeared long ago.

The design features a trough topped by an ionic column with a human-scale drinking fountain, while the column is topped by a spherical lantern topped by a weather vane.

133 Trinity Cemetery
Broadway and West 155th Street

In the mid-1800s, Trinity Cemetery expanded uptown to the northern boundary of the city, deemed by the Commissioners' Plan of 1811 to be West 155th Street. It was thought at the time that the city would never expand north of that, and so the cemetery would be located at the city's northern boundary.

This section of Trinity Cemetery was originally part of naturalist John James Audubon's farm. He is buried in the cemetery's rolling hills (his grave can be recognized by a tall Celtic cross), along with author/poet Clement Clarke Moore. Carolers serenade the "A Visit from St. Nicholas" author on Christmas Eve.

134 Audubon Terrace
Broadway and West 155th Street

Audubon Terrace, located on land formerly held by John James Audubon, is an underappreciated mixture of Beaux Arts and American Renaissance architecture. It is home to Boricua College, the Hispanic Society of America, and the American Academy of Arts and Letters. Formerly, Audubon Terrace was home to the Mu-

seum of the American Indian, which has relocated to the Customs House in Bowling Green (and larger digs on the Mall in Washington, D.C.), the American Geographical Society (now relocated to Milwaukee), and the American Numismatic Society, now on Fulton and William Streets downtown. Audubon Terrace was commissioned at the behest of railroad heir Archer Huntington in 1907; his wife Anna sculpted the Terrace's statue of El Cid, the legendary eleventh-century Spanish knight.

135 Audubon Ballroom and Loew's 175th Street Theatre
Broadway, between West 165th and 166th Streets; West 175th Street

a. The Columbia Presbyterian Medical Center demolished much of Thomas Lamb's magnificent 1912 Audubon Theatre and Ballroom at Broadway between West 165th and 166th Streets, where Malcolm X was tragically assassinated in 1965, but preserved the building's Broadway frontage on the renamed Mary Woodward Lasker Biomedical Research Building. Over the front entrance on Broadway, the theater's magnificent multicolored terra-cotta lunette, featuring the head of Neptune, an oared galleon, and a torch- and anchor-bearing mermaid, was recreated by artist Susan Quimby in 1994.

b. Further up Broadway, another Thomas Lamb creation, Loew's 175th Street

Theatre is considered by many architects and cinephiles to be the greatest of the more than 120 theatres he designed in the U.S. One of Loew's five "Wonder Theatres" in the New York area, built to showcase MGM studio movies, its exterior features Indo-Chinese motifs on the exterior and, unlike most of NYC's other old theaters, its interior is in a Mayan style, featuring a palatial staircase; a goddess statue surmounted by an aurora borealis has been retained by the theater's current owner, Christ United Church.

136 Morris–Jumel Mansion and Sylvan Terrace
Edgecombe Avenue and West 167th Street

a. The oldest private home in Manhattan stands on a high hill at Edgecombe Avenue and West 160th Street. The Morris-Jumel Mansion was built around 1760 by a British colonel, Roger Morris, who was married to Mary Philipse (some say Mary had previously turned down a proposal from George Washington). Morris's estate, Mount Morris, covered vast tracts of Harlem acreage, some of which would become Mount Morris

MANHATTAN

Park, now called Marcus Garvey Park. During the Revolutionary War, Morris, a loyalist, was forced to vacate the mansion and return to England. It then became a headquarters for Washington in the autumn of 1776. While President in 1790, Washington had a formal dinner in the mansion with John Adams, John Quincy Adams, Thomas Jefferson, and Alexander Hamilton. After passing through several owners, the mansion was purchased in 1810 by a wealthy French emigrant, Stephen Jumel, and his wife, Eliza. They redecorated the house in the French Empire style it retains today. It has been preserved as a monument since 1904.

b. The adjoining Jumel and Sylvan Terraces are notable for retaining street paving stones and for Sylvan Terrace's uncannily well-preserved wooden row houses constructed in 1882. They sport paint schemes current to when they were built along the original Jumel Mansion carriage drive. Actor/activist Paul Robeson lived on Jumel Terrace for a time.

The mansion welcomes the public. Call (212) 923-8008 or visit morrisjumel.org for details.

Sylvan Terrace

137 Bennett Avenue Rocks

Bennett Avenue, from West 190th Street to Broadway

The highest point in Manhattan, and the second-highest point in New York City (second only to Todt Hill in Staten Island), is on Bennett Avenue in Washington Heights. It's among the weirdest sites in Manhattan, too, because of the exposed cliffs made of schist that occur frequently in this part of the city. They are a legacy of the great glaciers that descended from the north during the last ice age and stopped at about the middle part of Long Island. Walk along Bennett Avenue between West 190th Street and Broadway for an incredible view of the cliffs: in winter, when snow and ice encrust the outcroppings, you'll think you're in an Ansel Adams photograph.

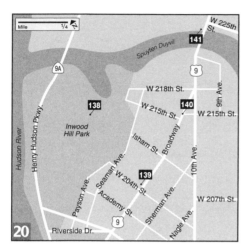

Manhattan Island's northernmost out-post is the site of the only natural woods remaining on the island. Here, the IRT subway emerges from one of its deepest tunnels, under Fort George Hill, onto an elevated structure above Nagle Avenue. You can test your fitness by ascending the hundreds of steps from Broadway to the Cloisters in Fort Tryon Park. One of the stranger corners of upper Manhattan can be found at Tenth Avenue and West 201st Street, where a partially abandoned marina can be found at a small Harlem River inlet known as Sherman's Creek. The marina is slated for restoration; it was an important ferry landing during the colonial period.

SUBWAY: Ⓐ to 190th, Dyckman, or West 207th Street; ① to Dyckman, 207th, 215th, or 225th Street

BUS: Bx7, Bx20, or **M100** on Broadway; **Bx12** on West 207th and Isham Street

♙138 Inwood Primeval
Caves in Inwood Hill Park

Most people think Manhattan is buried under layer upon layer of concrete, with all evidence of its primordial past concealed.

Inwood Hill Park is 196 acres of virgin forest (with the occasional path and rusting lamppost). After the Civil War, prominent families built large mansions here overlooking the Hudson, among them Isidor Straus, who perished in the sinking of the *Titanic* in 1912, and the Lord family of Lord & Taylor. The area officially became a park in 1926.

Enter Inwood Hill Park's northern end at West 216th Street by crossing a short street called Indian Road. The street commemorates the Weekquaeskeek Indians. Remains of their settlements were found in Isham Park, a more formal and landscaped part of Inwood Hill Park, in its northeast corner. (Indian Road is the only road open to traffic in Manhattan actually called "Road.")

Enjoy a short walk along the park path toward the hills, and you'll see a rock with a metal sign on it. Shokoropack Rock is on the exact site where a giant tulip tree once stood; its girth is now marked by a concrete ring around the rock. This is where Dutch governor Peter Minuit supposedly purchased Manhattan Island from the Weekquaeskeeks for the equivalent of 60 Dutch guilders. According to legend, the Native Americans planted it in honor of the transaction and the tree remained on the site until 1933.

MANHATTAN

139 Dyckman Farmhouse

Broadway and West 204th Street

The Dyckman Farmhouse has been here since around 1784 and is Manhattan's last remaining colonial farmhouse. It was built by William Dyckman, grandson of Jan Dyckman, who first arrived in the area from Holland in the 1600s, and wound up owning much of Manhattan Island. During the Revolutionary War, the British held the original Jan Dyckman farmhouse. When they withdrew at the war's end in 1783, they burned it down, perhaps out of spite. The farmhouse was rebuilt the next year, and the front and back porches were added around 1825. The Dyckman family sold the house in the 1870s, and it served a number of purposes, among them roadside lodging. The house was again threatened with demolition in 1915, but it was purchased by Dyckman's descendants and appointed with period objects and heirlooms. It is currently run by the New York City Parks Department and the Historic House Trust as a museum. A replica of one of the occupying British soldiers' log huts, with a log roof, can be found at the back of the house. Call 212 (304-9422) or visit dyckmanfarmhouse.org for details.

140 Seaman Arch

Broadway and West 215th Street

This is the last remnant of the Seaman estate. John and Valentine Seaman obtained 25 acres of land, from Broadway to Spuyten Duyvil Creek and what would be West 214th and 218th Streets in 1851, and set about building a hilltop mansion. The arch, meant to be a gateway to the estate, was first built in 1855. Marble from quarries in the area was used in its construction. Evidence of a large gate, and even a room for a gatekeeper, are still in evidence at the back of the arch.

Between 1905 and 1938, the estate passed to Lawrence Drake, a Seaman nephew, and then to contractor Thomas Dwyer, who built several brick buildings on the site and razed the hilltop estate. Since then, it has served as a relic of the Seamans' once grand domain, but sadly, it has been left to deteriorate. In 2004, it was shored up with a new paint job that is quickly being covered again with graffiti.

141 Marble Hill

West of Broadway and West 225th Street

There's a section of Manhattan sporting winding, quiet streets, country villas, and gently sloping hills that feels like a lifetime away from the traffic-choked grids and honking horns usually characterized with Manhattan. It's not Greenwich Village and it's certainly not Central Park. In fact, it's not on the island of Manhattan at all and still, it's in New York County, otherwise known as Manhattan.

In a little-known quirk of geography, a small piece of the borough of Manhat-

Isham Park in Inwood, just off Broadway and West 207th Street

tan, known as Marble Hill, is on the mainland. It is surrounded on three sides by the Bronx and on the south by the Harlem River. It shares its character with the neighborhoods of Kingsbridge and Kingsbridge Heights on its north and east. It is protected from Spuyten Duyvil, on the west, by a steep hill.

Once it was a part of Manhattan Island, its northern edge defined by the Harlem River and Spuyten Duyvil Creek. In 1895, it was separated from the island by the newly straightened, dredged, and deepened Harlem River Ship Canal, leaving Marble Hill as an island by itself. When the creek was filled around 1917, Marble Hill became a part of the mainland! No one cared much until the El was built through Marble Hill and apartment buildings were constructed in the 1920s, joining the few frame houses that were already there. Marble Hill never changed its designation as part of Manhattan, and so a part of Manhattan it stays, separated from the rest of the borough by the Harlem River.

a. *Congressman and Westchester County judge John Watts (1749–1836) is one of the lucky few to enjoy the distinction of a statue at his gravesite in Trinity Cemetery. George Bissell's rendering of him in his judicial robes was installed in 1890.*

b. *Adolph Weinman's statue of Samuel Rea, president of the Pennsylvania Railroad Company from 1899 to 1925, was salvaged from the original Penn Station when it was destroyed in*

1963. *It can be found in front of 2 Penn Plaza at Seventh Avenue and 32nd Street.*

c. *Alexander Holley (1832–1882), known as the father of the U.S. steel industry, is remembered in Washington Square Park by John Q. Adams Ward's 1890 bust.*

d. *The severe Dutch colonial governor of New Amsterdam from 1653 to 1664, Peter Stuyvesant, is buried on his former property, the courtyard*

f.

g.

h.

of St. Mark's Church on Second Avenue and East 10th Street. Toom Dupuis's bust was sculpted in 1915.

e. O. Grymes's 1939 bust of Daniel Tompkins, governor of New York and vice president under James Monroe, can be found in the courtyard of St. Mark's Church on Second Avenue and East 10th Street.

f. Aida, La Traviata, and Rigoletto composer Giuseppe Verdi is memorialized on Broadway between West 72nd and 73rd Streets by Pasquale Civiletti's 1906 sculpture, flanked by four of his most popular characters: Falstaff, Leonora of La Forza del Destino, Aida, and Otello.

g. Freidrich Beer's bust of literary giant Washington Irving was installed in Bryant Park in 1885, and moved to its present location at Washington Irving High School on Irving Place in 1935.

h. Neil Estern's statue of the Little Flower, Fiorello La Guardia, captures the dynamic NYC mayor in full stride on LaGuardia Place.

Queens

is New York City's largest borough. Until 1898, it was more than double its current size: In that year, residents of its three easternmost towns, Hempstead, North Hempstead, and Oyster Bay, voted to form a separate county, Nassau. Until the early twentieth century (when the gangplank from Manhattan, the Queensboro Bridge, was opened), the borough was a collection of small towns interspersed by farms, marshes, and meadows. These small towns have zealously and miraculously held on to their separate identities through the years. Though they may superficially appear the same at first, if you spend any time in Astoria, Maspeth, or Jackson Heights, which are all relatively close to each other, you will notice a distinct shift in tone and atmosphere from one to the other. Not coincidentally, Queens residents continue to mark addresses on their mail from the immediate neighborhoods where they live: Hollis Heights, Douglaston, and Laurelton natives write those names on their envelopes; Bay Ridge, Bedford-Stuyvesant, or Sheepshead Bay folks simply write "Brooklyn." It's just a matter of tradition and recognition of the separate identity of where Queensites live.

Today, Queens is the most diverse borough in both its physical features and demographics. The land is flat in the north and south, and very hilly in the middle; the Wisconsin Ice Sheet glacier stopped its southern progress in the middle of Long Island, leaving the hilly areas that later became Cypress Hills Cemetery (and many other cemeteries between Glendale and Cypress Hills), Forest Park, Jamaica Estates, and Holliswood. The 7 train, running in Queens between Long Island City and Flushing, has been dubbed the International Express since it runs through so many cultural enclaves, from Irish Woodside, Indian Jackson Heights, Central and South American Corona, and Asian Flushing, with many more nationalities living along its route in Queens.

In general, Queens is divided nearly evenly between the urban and suburban, with the west most closely resembling Brooklyn in appearance with streets lined with apartment buildings and attached homes. Brownstones and row houses are not nearly so prevalent as they are in Brooklyn, though they can be found in Ridgewood as well as on some Long Island City and Astoria blocks. In the east, things are considerably more car-culture with broad, boulevard-like streets punctuated by single-home tracts. Businesses cluster on main streets, so some of Queens' eastern neighborhoods actually resemble small, independent towns.

In the twenty-first century major plans for Queens have centered on the development of coveted waterfront area in Long Island City for both residential and recreational uses. From a Forgotten NY point of view, though, much of old Queens has disappeared in recent years as developers have bought up properties and built bland, blond-bricked multi-family housing. Queens real estate takes many forms, from the fantastically baroque Beaux Arts and Queen Anne style from the late nineteenth century, to the streamlined Art Moderne forms of the early twentieth. What will future generations make of the nondescript buildings of the early twenty-first century?

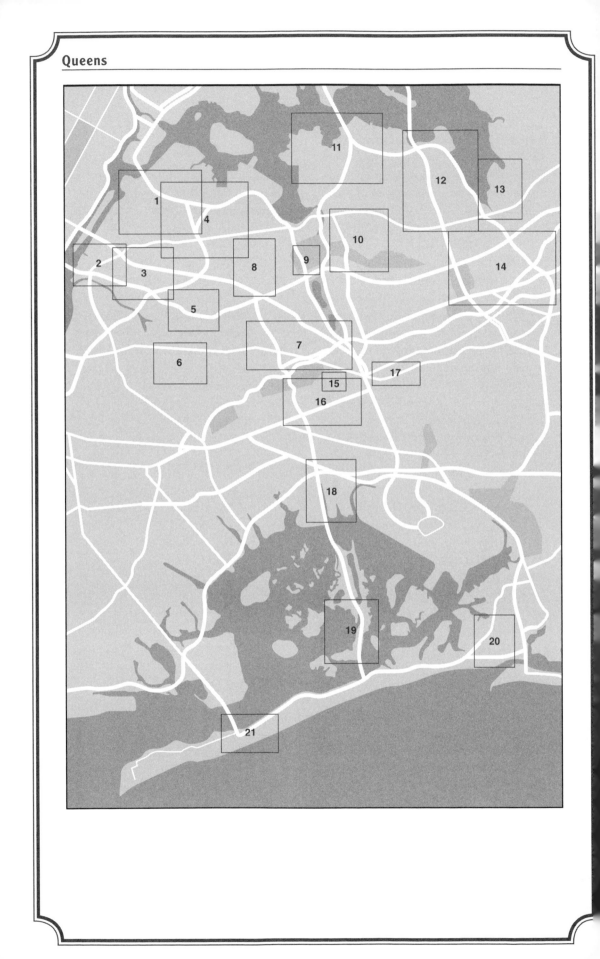

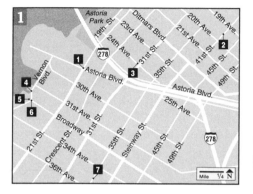

Newcomers will find Astoria extraordi- narily hospitable, with Astoria Park's spectacular views of midtown Manhattan and the Triborough and Hell Gate Bridges. A bustling Greek neighborhood centers along the main shopping drags on 30th Avenue and Broadway.

Astoria dates to the mid-1600s, when William Hallett received a grant from Peter Stuyvesant for the area surrounding what is now Hallett's Cove. The oldest structures in the region date to the mid-1800s, after fur merchant Stephen Ailing Halsey had incorporated the village in 1839. Astoria was named for a man who apparently never set foot in it. A bitter battle for naming the village was finally won by supporters and friends of entrepreneur and real estate tycoon John Jacob Astor (1763–1848). Astor had become the wealthiest man in America by 1840, with a net worth of over $40 million.

SUBWAY: Ⓝ or Ⓦ to Astoria–Ditmars Boulevard, Astoria Boulevard, 30th Avenue, Broadway, or 36th Avenue

BUS: **Q103** on Vernon Boulevard; **Q19A** on 21st Street and Ditmars Boulevard; **B18** on 30th Avenue; **Q104** on Broadway; **Q102** on 31st Street, Queens Plaza, and Vernon Boulevard; **Q66** on 21st Street, 35th Avenue and Northern Boulevard

1 Astoria Village
Astoria Boulevard and 21st Street

Hallett's Cove, the region in Astoria just south of Astoria Park and west of 21st Street, is a mixture of breathtaking houses, ancient churches, and graveyards, as well as utilitarian housing projects and industrial buildings. The area near Astoria Park features views of the Hell Gate (1917) and Triborough (1936) Bridges.

Virtually nothing remains of William Hallett's original settlement along the cove that bears his name today (flags mounted on the neighborhood's streetlamps call this area "Two Coves": Hallett's Cove proper, at Vernon Boulevard and Main Avenue where they meet the East River, and Pot Cove, at the foot of Astoria Park South and Shore Boulevard). It was only after Stephen Ailing Halsey incorporated a village here in 1839 that streets began to radiate east and south from the area. Even if you didn't notice the old-style Victorian buildings found here, its age can be determined by the narrowness of some of its streets as well as the irregularity of its street pattern; 12th Street changes directions three times, and 26th Road slants askew its neighbors.

Astoria Village is centered at 21st Street, Astoria Boulevard, and Newtown Road. West of here, the streets seem more timeless, with old churches, narrow sidewalks, and hidden cemeteries, while east of here, things seem more conventionally Queens-like. Unfortunately, Astoria Village's quality is swiftly disappearing as developers buy up the old mansions, demolish them, and build multi-family brick boxes.

2 Steinway Mansion and Steinway Village

41st Street, between 19th and 20th Avenues

Henry Steinway, a German piano manufacturer, immigrated to New York City from Seesen, Germany, in 1853. Between 1870 and 1873, he purchased 400 acres of land in northern Astoria. Not only did he build the spacious Steinway piano factory, which still cuts an imposing figure, but he also built a small town for factory workers and a public trolley line. From 1877 to 1879, Steinway constructed a group of handsome row houses, rented to workers at the piano factory, on Winthrop Avenue (today's 20th Avenue) and on Albert and Theodore (41st and 42nd) Streets. Even the street names bore witness to the Steinway family: Albert and Theodore were sons of Henry Steinway. William Steinway's mansion on 41st Street still stands on a high hill that has never been leveled, unlike the surrounding area. Today, 41st Street still looks like a country lane.

3 Bohemian Hall

24th Avenue near 31st Street

For many in Astoria, lazy summer evenings mean drinking pitchers of pilsner while sitting on wooden picnic tables in the concrete beer garden of Bohemian Hall. (Any embarrassing behavior can't be viewed past the high brick walls!) The 24th Avenue institution was opened by the Bohemian Citizens' Benevolent Society in 1910, and its garden by 1919, when most of Astoria was still meadow and farmland.

The menu has to be carefully scrutinized, as the large print is in Czech and the small print is in English. The beer garden is one of the last of a once-common New York City breed. Flessel's Tavern in College Point closed its doors in 1997; the Bohemian, thankfully, looks like it will be here for some time yet.

4 Sohmer Piano Factory

Vernon Boulevard, between 31st Avenue and 31st Drive

Ravenswood, a section of Queens just south of Astoria along the East River, is dominated by the massive Con Ed "Big Allis" power plant and the Ravenswood Houses, but a walk through its narrow streets reveals surprising remnants of old-time Queens. In 1887, a Steinway competitor, Sohmer Piano, built what is now the Adirondack Building—a multilevel factory building complete with clock tower. Its original copper roof was replaced with tin and then painted green some years ago. The old factory still has its ancient Hewes and Phillips coal burner.

5 Socrates Sculpture Garden

Vernon Boulevard, between Main Avenue and Broadway

Named in tribute to its proximity to Greek-flavored Astoria, this waterside area along Vernon Boulevard between 31st Avenue and Broadway was a dumpsite until it was "rescued" in 1986 by a coalition of artists/activists headed by Mark di Suvero. It now works both as an outdoor workshop for aspiring artists and as a waterside park.

6 Noguchi Museum

Vernon Boulevard and Broadway

Just south of the Socrates Sculpture Garden on the opposite side of Vernon Boulevard at 31st Drive you will find a museum dedicated to Japanese-American expressionist sculptor Isamu Noguchi (1904–1988).

Though born in Los Angeles, Noguchi spent most of his childhood in Japan before attending Columbia University to study sculpture. Among his more notable works are the bridge in the Peace Park in Hiroshima, a sunken garden for Chase Manhattan Bank Plaza in lower Manhattan, the Billy Rose Sculpture Garden in Jerusalem, and Moerenuma Park in Sapporo, Japan.

More than 250 of Noguchi's works are on permanent display here, including stone, bronze, and wood sculpture; "Akari" paper and bamboo light sculptures; his sets produced for choreographers Martha Graham and George Balanchine; and an outdoor garden. For information and visiting hours, call (718) 204-7088 or go to www.noguchi.org.

7 Museum of the Moving Image

35th Avenue and 36th Street

No visit to Astoria is truly complete without at least a look inside the American Museum of the Moving Image (AMMI), opened to the public in 1988 on the site of Astoria Studio, built by Paramount in 1920. After a few decades, when the U.S. Army used it to produce training films (where Paul Newman and Jack Lemmon made their film debuts), the site was redeveloped for TV and film production in the 1980s, and then as a museum for motion pictures and television. AMMI is the one and only museum in the U.S. devoted to the history, artistry, and technology of motion pictures. For museum hours, call (718) 784-0077 or consult www.ammi.org.

QUEENS

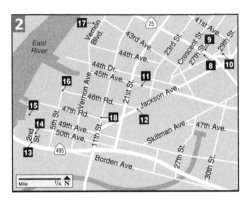

Long Island City originally comprised a collection of several villages settled by the Dutch in the 1600s, including Astoria, Ravenswood, Dutch Kills, and Bowery Bay. The city enjoyed two building booms, one in the mid-1800s, when brothers Charles and Peter Roach dotted the Ravenswood area (now centering around Vernon Blvd. and 34th Avenue) with riverside mansions, and the other after the Queensboro Bridge was built in 1909. Along the East River, Long Island City has traditionally been dedicated to industry over the decades, but the last twenty years have brought an influx of artists from Manhattan seeking cheaper rents.

SUBWAY: ⑦ to Vernon Boulevard–Jackson Avenue, Hunter's Point Avenue, or Queensboro Plaza

BUS: B61 on Jackson Avenue; **Q103** on Vernon Boulevard; **M32** or **Q101** across the Queensboro Bridge, along Queens Plaza and Queens Boulevard; **Q19A** or **Q67** on 21st Street; **Q102** on 31st Street, Queens Plaza and Vernon Boulevard

8 Long Island Star Building
28th Street and 42nd Road

This squat building was home to the *Long Island City Daily Star*, founded in 1865 by

Thomas Todd, memorialized in a plaque on the building's exterior. The newspaper merged with Flushing's *North Shore Journal* in the 1930s and soldiered on until 1968 as the *Long Island Star-Journal*.

9 Brewster Building
Queens Plaza and 27th Street

This six-story 400,000-square-foot Queens Plaza North factory building, built in 1911, once turned out horse-drawn carriages, Rolls Royce automobiles, and World War II fighter planes. Today it's the home of Metropolitan Life Insurance Company, and has been beautifully restored, though its original clock tower has been long absent. The one at the nearby Bank of Manhattan skyscraper a couple of blocks east will have to suffice.

10 Queens Plaza Millstones
Queens Plaza and Northern Blvd

A small traffic triangle in front of the clock-towered Bank of Manhattan, where Northern Boulevard begins its march to the eastern end of Long Island, contains two of the oldest man-made objects in Queens embedded in its concrete.

In 1650, Dutchman Burger Jorissen constructed a gristmill that today would be on Northern Boulevard, between 40th Road and 41st Avenue. The mill existed on the site for about 111 years, until 1861 when it was razed by the Long Island Rail Road. The Payntar family owned the mill property by that time (40th Avenue was called Payntar Avenue until the 1920s) and had placed millstones that had been shipped in by Jorissen around 1657 in front of their house. When Sunnyside Yards, Queens Plaza, and the El were constructed, the millstones were preserved and embedded in the traffic plaza, where nearly no one notices them.

11 Hunter's Point Historic District

45th Avenue between 21st and 23rd Streets

Dominie's Hook, originally the western end of the town of Newtown, was settled by the Dutch in the 1660s. The land was later owned by British sea captain George Hunter. By 1825, it had become known as Hunter's Point. It began the transition from rural farmland in the 1860s when the Long Island Rail Road built a terminal that would be its primary connection with Manhattan until the East River tunnels and Pennsylvania Station were built in 1910.

There's a block in Hunter's Point where, if you can ignore the massive Citibank tower that looms over everything, you would think you're in Park Slope, Sunset Park, Bay Ridge, or so many other Brooklyn neighborhoods featuring attached brownstone buildings on tree-lined blocks. The Italianate houses lining 45th Avenue between 21st and 23rd Streets were built by developers Spencer Root and John Rust in the mid-1870s. Check out the building across the street on the corner under the El on 23rd Street: a sign indicates Ely Avenue, 23rd Street's former name, which is also reflected in the nearby IND subway station.

12 P.S. 1

Jackson Avenue and 46th Street

This Romanesque Revival former public school at 22-25 Jackson Avenue was built in the 1890s when Long Island City was indeed a real city. In the 1970s, it was revived as a contemporary art museum and then began an association with the Museum of Modern Art, housing exhibits that may have been thought too risky or outré for the more stolid MoMA. The museum has cleverly incorporated the old school's interiors as art spaces, down to the bathrooms and boiler rooms. For more information, call (718) 784-2084 or go to www.ps1.org.

13 Miller's Hotel/Waterfront Crabhouse

Borden Avenue and 2nd Street

In the shadow of the old LIRR powerhouse, you will find the Waterfront Crabhouse, located in a two-story brick building with a red awning. Its present blandish exterior reveals no clue of its former role as Tony Miller's Hotel, a social epicenter of Long Island City.

Miller constructed a lavish, three-story hotel here in 1881, described as containing a huge horseshoe-shaped bar formed from a single piece of black walnut, three dining rooms, and thirty bedrooms on the third floor. It attracted a sizable and star-studded clientele. The hotel and restaurant's eminence derived directly from its location across the street from the former Long Island City terminal of the Long Island Rail Road. Prior to 1910, when Penn Station was opened, Long Island City was as far west as the railroad traveled in New York City.

The hotel lost momentum after Miller's death in 1897, and the LIRR Manhattan connection was instituted in 1910. By 1919, Prohibition dealt the final blow and the hotel was shut down, but it made a belated comeback in 1978 when restaurateur Anthony Mazzarella opened the Waterfront Crabhouse.

While the Crabhouse offers a tasty seafood menu and dozens of different brews, its chief attraction for a Forgotten NY enthusiast is its NYC memorabilia collection. "Every nook and cranny of the venerable edifice" (as the late sportscaster Lindsay Nelson used to say about Chicago's Wrigley Field) is packed and jammed with subway signs, board games, advertisements, bottles, framed pictures, and other donated artifacts. One wall is covered in sheet music; another with boxing paraphernalia (Mazzarella is a promoter); another with photographs of what the Crabhouse was like in the golden age of Tony Miller.

14 Pennsylvania Railroad Powerhouse
2nd Street and 51st Avenue

Construction on this big building with its tall arched windows and massive granite base began in 1903. It was designed by McKim, Mead, and White and was completed in 1909, the year before the firm finished Manhattan's classic Pennsylvania Station.

The powerhouse was built when the Long Island Rail Road deemed it necessary to electrify most of the western portion of the railroad in Queens and Nassau counties in preparation for the opening of the East River tunnels leading to the new station. More than 9,500 piles were driven during the plant's construction. When fin-

ished, it supplied 11,000-volt twenty-five-cycle, three-phase alternating current to substations, and 625 volts of direct current are carried on the LIRR's third rails.

While this unheralded masterpiece still stands, its four massive, ebony-colored smokestacks, featured in artwork by Georgia O'Keeffe in the 1930s, were unfortunately torn down in 2005; they were deemed unsafe when the building was being prepared for residential use.

15 Gantry State Park
49th Avenue and the East River

Gantry State Park is located in a new development at water's edge known as Queens West. The developers have cleverly left in the old railroad tracks of an old LIRR freight spur, as well as some of the old railroad ties, as a link from the park of the present to the industrial past. Barge transfer gantries have also been left in place.

16 Pepsi-Cola Neon Sign
46th Road and 5th Street

Pepsi-Cola "turns its back" on Queens in a new riverside park, part of the Queens West project. This massive neon Pepsi sign,

using Pepsi's old script logo and vintage-style bottle, is actually best seen from Dag Hammarskjold Park on East 47th Street and First Avenue in Manhattan, though you can stroll up and almost touch it in its new park setting. Pepsi had been a presence in Hunter's Point for decades, but its riverside bottling plant closed in 1999. The big sign was built in 1936 by Artkraft Signs.

17 Terra Cotta Factory Showroom ⋀

Vernon Boulevard and Queens Plaza South

The New York Architectural Terra Cotta Works was established in 1886 by James Taylor, who was fresh off successes in the Boston firm Lewis and Wood and the Boston Terra Cotta Company. The New York Works would go on to produce terra-cotta for Carnegie Hall and the Ansonia Hotel. While Taylor died in 1898, his NYC terracotta factory would continue to thrive until 1928. Its small office/showroom building, built in 1892, still stands at 42-10 Vernon Boulevard, albeit a bit worse for wear after over 110 years. The little brick building has been landmarked though in 2005, it was uncertain what any future rehabilitation for the building would be.

18 Titanic House

11th Street and 47th Road

The west side of 11th Street as you drive north from the Pulaski Bridge presents a fairly uniform façade of three-story brick buildings. They all look pretty much the same, except for 47-08. It sports an American flag, a couple of green awnings . . . and many photographs and plaques dedicated to R.M.S. *Titanic*.

Collector Joe Colletti assembled the shrine in 1984 after seeing *Raise the Titanic*. A member of the Titanic Memorial Society, he has assembled hundreds of newspaper clippings, movie posters, photographs, and correspondence with survivors both inside his apartment and facing the sidewalk, some of which stops pedestrian and even vehicular traffic outside his brownstone.

QUEENS

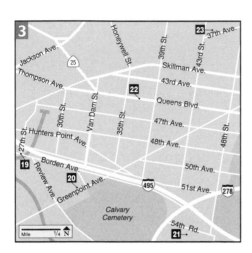

Blissville is the small wedge of Queens positioned between Newtown Creek, Calvary Cemetery, and the Queens-Midtown Expressway. It takes its name from Neziah Bliss, inventor, shipbuilder, and industrialist who owned most of the land in the 1830s and 1840s. Bliss, a protégé of Robert Fulton, was an early steamboat pioneer and owned companies in Philadelphia and Cincinnati. Settling in Manhattan in 1827, his Novelty Iron Works supplied steamboat engines for area vessels. By 1832, he had acquired acreage on both sides of Newtown Creek, in Greenpoint and what would become the southern edge of Long Island City. Bliss laid out streets in Greenpoint to facilitate his riverside shipbuilding concern and built a turnpike connecting it with Astoria; he also instituted ferry service with Manhattan. Though most of Bliss's activities were in Greenpoint, he is remembered chiefly by Blissville and by a stop on the Flushing Line subway (the 7 train) that bears his family name; 46th Street was originally known as Bliss Street.

Laurel Hill today is known as West Maspeth, and, like Blissville, it is a small, isolated little village, with heavy industry dotted with impossibly old little one-family houses. It's hemmed in by Calvary Cemetery and the Brooklyn-Queens Expressway

in the west, the Long Island Rail Road to the south, the Long Island Expressway to the north, and pedal-to-the metal 58th Street (a main truck route) to its east. Its original name, Laurel Hill, is remembered by Laurel Hill Boulevard, which buddies up with the Brooklyn-Queens Expressway for most of its route from the old Penny Bridge Long Island Rail Road stop northeast to Queens Boulevard.

Sunnyside, which extends from the Sunnyside railroad yards along Skillman Avenue in the north to the Queens-Midtown Expressway in the south between 30th and about 58th Streets, was slower to develop than its immediate neighbors to the west, Long Island City and Astoria. Photographs taken in the 1910s show it as mostly undeveloped countryside. The opening of the Queensboro Bridge, and then the IRT Flushing Line along Queens Boulevard, changed Sunnyside into a bustling residential neighborhood. Its crown jewel is undoubtedly Sunnyside Gardens, a 77-acre community of pleasant, low-slung brick apartments with shared backyards, constructed in 1924 in the area between 43rd and 51st Streets and Skillman and 39th Avenues. Sunnyside Gardens' street signs still carry the old names along with their numbers, reflecting the landowners whose farms were turned into the giant Sunnyside yards rail complex in the runup to the completion of Penn Station in 1910.

SUBWAY: None. The closest is Hunter's Point Avenue on the ⑦ line. Sunnyside is accessible from ⑦-train stations along Queens Boulevard.

BUS: Q67 on Borden Avenue and 48th Street; **B24** on Greenpoint Avenue and 48th Street; **M32** or **Q60** on Queens Boulevard; **Q39** on 46th Avenue

19 Borden Avenue Retractile Bridge

Borden Avenue, east of 27th Street

Only four retractile bridges are still in existence in the U.S. Retractile bridges have two sections that roll on wheels set on steel rails and pull away, or retract, from each other, opening the bridge to allow shipping to pass. New York City is fortunate enough to possess two: one at Carroll Street in Cobble Hill, Brooklyn, and this one, opened in May 1908, that spans Borden Avenue across Dutch Kills.

20 City View Best Western

Greenpoint Avenue, between Bradley and Gale Avenues

The aptly named City View Motor Inn, formerly Public School 80, is now one of the most beautiful Best Westerns you're ever likely to glimpse. It was converted to a motel in 1986.

While ogling the City View, take time to admire the cupolas on the 1892 Calvary Cemetery gatehouse, at the cemetery entrance opposite Gale Avenue. Across the Queens-Midtown Expressway, there's the magnificence of St. Raphael's Church at Hunter's Point Avenue built in 1885. Its steeple is visible from all over this low-rise neighborhood.

21 Clifton and Waters: Queens' Former Street Name Bounty

54th Road and 46th Street

An unassuming two-story brick building in West Maspeth with a porch painted red holds a key to Queens' past, before the cartographers decided to number all the streets in the 1920s to make things less (?) confusing.

In the 1920s, many of Queens' towns had their own separate numbering systems, and it was believed that confusion between, say, 2nd Street in Astoria and 2nd Street in Flushing would arise if things were allowed to stay as they were. Hence, a street numbering system roughly based on Philadelphia's plan was drawn up, with lower numbers nearest the river and higher numbers as you go inland. North-south routes would be "Streets," "Places," and "Lanes," while east-west routes would be "Avenues," "Roads," and Drives." Therefore, 1st Street can be found in Astoria near Hell Gate, while 271st Street, the highest numbered street in New York City, is near the Nassau County line. Queens has no First Avenue in the "new" system; Second Avenue comprises a couple of cul-de-sacs in Whitestone, near the Bronx Whitestone Bridge, while 165th Avenue, the highest-numbered Queens avenue, runs for a couple of intermittently paved blocks in Howard Beach.

A couple of well-preserved blue-and-white signs that have survived on the corner of the little red house at 46th Street and 54th Road proclaim it to be the former intersection of Clifton and Waters Avenues.

22 Queens Boulevard Viaduct

Between Van Dam and 48th Streets

The IRT Flushing Line runs on a magnificent concrete viaduct along Queens Boulevard between Van Dam Street and 48th Street. It was built in 1917 under the direction of Squire J. Vickers (1872–1947), an architect and painter who was, in large measure, responsible for the look and feel

QUEENS

of all subway stations built for the IRT, BMT, and IND between the 1910s and 1940s. Vickers' Beaux Arts and Machine Age–style subway signs and station designs survive to this day and many old elements are being rehabilitated and restored.

The Queens Boulevard Viaduct is 4,271 feet in length and contains 20,000 square feet of ornamental, colored tile, most of it arrayed along the top of the viaduct just below the tracks. In the 1990s, its entire track bed was replaced, and new decorative glass murals depicting Queens scenes were installed at the 33rd, 40th, and 46th Street Stations.

23 Knickerbocker Laundry

37th Avenue, between 43rd and 48th Streets

This 88,000-square-foot building was constructed for the Knickerbocker Laundry in 1932 at the height of the Streamline

Moderne movement, and was named "The Most Beautiful Building in Queens" by the Queens Chamber of Commerce in 1936. More examples of Streamline Moderne can be seen in the approaches to the Triborough Bridge, which was built around the same time. It has in the last decade been renovated by the New York Presbyterian Church but if you look closely, a few of its original Streamline Moderne touches can still be spotted.

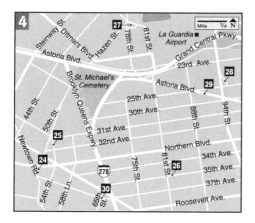

Woodside, a bustling community cen-tered at Roosevelt Avenue and 61st Street, was originally a part of Newtown, a larger colonial village. It was largely a woodsy swamp until the mid-1860s, when developer Benjamin Hitchcock purchased the John Kelly farm and divided it into building lots located along today's Woodside Avenue. Kelly, an early settler, was part owner of a Brooklyn newspaper and sent it dispatches from his home in the "sticks" that he called "Letters from Woodside." Today in Woodside, you are just as likely to exit an Irish bar and enter an Indian restaurant as you are to walk out of a bodega and pass a remnant of the Colonial era.

Today's Jackson Heights is a neighborhood of handsome six-story co-op apartment buildings, many of which surround central gardens. They appeared seemingly out of nowhere beginning in 1913 in the area formerly known as Trains Meadow when the entire area was not much more than grassland. The Queensboro Corporation and developer Edward MacDougall anticipated the impending growth of the area and built now-landmarked housing along today's 82nd Street. The area became known as Jackson Heights after John C. Jackson, who laid Jackson Avenue, now Northern Boulevard, out across the meadow back in 1859. At first,

Jackson Avenue was a toll road, complete with tollhouses and milestones, one of which remained in its original spot until 1987, when it was moved to the Langston Hughes Library in Corona.

SUBWAY: ⑦ to Woodside–61st Street, 69th Street, 74th Street–Broadway, 82nd Street–Jackson Heights, 90th Street–Elmhurst, or Junction Boulevard; Ⓖ, Ⓡ, or Ⓥ to Northern Boulevard, 65th Street, or 74th Street–Broadway

BUS: Q66 on Northern Boulevard; **M32** on Roosevelt Avenue; **Q18** on 58th Street and Woodside Avenue; **Q47** on 73rd and 74th Streets; **Q33** on 82nd and 83rd Streets; **Q19B** on 35th Avenue, 90th Street, and Astoria Boulevard

▲24 Tower Square
Northern Boulevard and Woodside Avenue

William Steinway, the piano manufacturer, electrified his Long Island City streetcar line, the Steinway Railway Company, and hooked up with developer Cord Meyer's Newtown Railway Company, which was extended to Corona in 1894. Two years later, the lines reorganized as the New York and Queens County Railway Company, and a handsome, twin-spired brick depot at Northern Boulevard and Woodside Avenue was constructed for its cars.

Trolley service out of this depot ran from 1894 until September 1937, when

QUEENS

buses took over. The eastern end of the building was torn down in 1930 after a fire. Over the decades, the old, deserted trolley barn was in constant danger of demolition until it was preserved in 1987 as part of the Tower Square Shopping Center. The north tower's clock has been retained, and above the arched entrance you can still find an emblazoned "N.Y. and Queens County Ry. Company" and "Waiting Room."

25 Moore-Jackson Cemetery

54th Street, between 31st and 32nd Avenues

As you walk up 54th Street between 32nd and 31st Avenues, cast a glance toward what looks like an empty lot on your left, and there it is . . . a tombstone, right out in front, reading, "AxM, Dyed the 23rd Nov. 1769." It's a stark reminder that people have been living in Woodside for centuries.

Moore-Jackson Cemetery, on 54th Street near 31st Avenue in Woodside, Queens, was established adjacent to the farmhouse of the Moore family on Bowery Bay Road (today's 51st Street), which was built early in the eighteenth century. The old farmhouse stood until 1901. The burial plot itself dates at least to 1733, which is the date of the earliest recorded stone. The oldest gravestone that is actually legible is that of Augustine Moore, "AxM," who died on the date recorded on the stone, at age seventeen. The marker is likely not in its original spot. In 1937, workers regraded the grounds and placed fallen stones upright, some in different places. The latest

burial took place in 1867. In 1919, a survey counted a total of forty-two gravesites in the small plot.

26 Scrabble

81st Street and 35th Avenue

At the corner of 35th Avenue and 81st Street there's an unusual street sign that has small numbers after each letter: There is a "1" after T, A, E, N, U, and E, and a "4" after the H and V. What's going on?

It's in remembrance of Jackson Heights resident Alfred Butts, who, in the 1940s, created a new word game combining the features of anagrams and crossword puzzles, calling it "Criss Cross Words," later renamed Scrabble. In the game, T, A, E, N, and U carry a one-point value, while H and V are each good for four points.

27 Lent Riker Smith Homestead

19th Road and 78th Street

There's a little parcel of a neighborhood east of Astoria and north of Jackson Heights, east of the bail bonds offices of Hazen Street, north of the whizzing Grand Central Parkway, and west of LaGuardia Airport's expanse, containing a couple of surprising artifacts. Stop for lunch at the chrome-plated Airline Diner, built in 1952, at Astoria Boulevard and 70th Street where a scene from *Goodfellas* was filmed, make your way up Hazen Street, where buses en route to Rikers Island roll past, detour a little down 77th Street, and head east on 19th Road. It will bring you to one of Queens' oldest homes.

It's a colonial farmhouse that was by most accounts built by Abraham Rycken Van Lent in 1729. Some historians date the oldest part of the house to be even older, perhaps dating as far back as 1656, according to an American Historic Buildings Survey. Rycken, whose family later changed its name to Riker, is remembered by most for the offshore island he purchased from New York governor Peter Stuyvesant in 1664, later acquired by NYC's Department of Corrections in 1884. Riker would no doubt have preferred that his well-preserved Queens home be his chief legacy. For more information on this historic home, visit lentrikersmithhomestead.com.

 28 Jackson Tracks

Jackson Mill Road, off 95th Street, between 24th and 25th Avenues

Modern maps show two roads called Jackson Mill Road in Jackson Heights. One runs roughly east-west, from 32nd Avenue and 93rd Street east to 97th Street, and the other, shorter section runs between 24th Avenue and 94th Street in a roughly north-south direction. However, the maps did *not* show the lengthier extension of Jackson Mill Road running south of 24th

Avenue and extending southeast to Astoria Boulevard and 97th Street. According to old maps, the two sections were at one time connected, before the area was built up in the late 1910s.

Two sets of tracks embedded in what little pavement remains can be seen in the short section of the old road south of 25th Avenue. They are the last remnants of a trolley line extension to a long-lost resort area, North Beach, which later became La-Guardia Airport.

29 Fair Theatre ⋀

Astoria Boulevard, between 90th and 91st Streets

A beautifully preserved vintage movie palace exterior, complete with a lightbulb-festooned façade and old-fashioned marquee can be found on Astoria Boulevard between 90th and 91st Streets. The Fair Theatre first opened in 1939 and was designed by Charles Sandblom. It was named for NYC's first World's Fair, which opened nearby in Flushing Meadows Corona Park the same year. These days, the Fair Theatre runs adult films, despite pressure from its next-door neighbor, an evangelical church.

30 Rowan Street IND Sign

At 65th Street IND Station

The walls of the 65th Street IND Station still advertise an exit at Rowan Street, a

former name of 65th Street. Since Queens streets were renamed in the 1920s, the name had been changed by the time the station opened in the 1930s, but old neighborhood names die hard, and IND builders recognized this by including the old name.

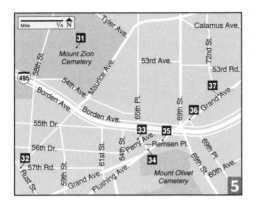

built in the area and a network of saloons and hotels was instituted to serve cemetery visitors.

SUBWAY: Ⓜ to Middle Village–Metropolitan Avenue

BUS: Q58, **Q59** on Grand Avenue; **Q39** or **Q58** on Fresh Pond Road; **Q38** on Eliot Avenue

Maspeth, in a western corner of Queens, seems torn between the grit of Brooklyn and the airy, almost suburban atmosphere enveloping its eastern and southern neighbors, Middle Village and Glendale. Maspeth was settled by Native Americans centuries before Dutch and English colonists arrived in the mid-1600s. It was absorbed by a newer settlement to the east (named, appropriately, Newtown—the present-day Elmhurst), became a part of the borough of Queens, and then became a part of New York City in 1898. "Maspeth" is derived from Delaware Indian terms that have, by different accounts, meant "great brook" or "bad water place"; the latter seems rather appropriate, since Newtown Creek, noxious through most of its recent history, is nearby.

While in Maspeth, pause for the expansive view of the towers of Manhattan from the bridge taking Grand Avenue over the Queens-Midtown Expressway.

Middle Village lies between Maspeth and Forest Hills, but it was named in the 1830s because of its position along Metropolitan Avenue, which was laid out as a toll road between Williamsburg, Brooklyn, and Jamaica in 1816. By the Civil War era, a small scattering of homes, as well as a hotel, sprung up along the road in this area, deemed to be the midpoint between Williamsburg and Jamaica. Cemeteries were

31 The Faces of Mount Zion
54th and Maurice Avenues

Rising real estate costs and an ever-expanding urban frontier led NYC to pass a law in 1852 prohibiting any more burials in Manhattan. Churches and synagogues, which had begun to make a profit running cemeteries, looked east to Queens County. St. Patrick's had opened Calvary Cemetery in Queens in 1848, a couple of years before its big Fifth Avenue cathedral opened.

Mount Zion, a Jewish cemetery, occupies about 80 acres in Maspeth near New Calvary Cemetery and the BQE. It was opened in the early 1890s under the auspices of Chevra Bani Sholom, and was later

managed by the Elmwier Cemetery Association (Elmwier Avenue is a former name of 54th Avenue).

In Mount Zion, the faces of the dead are preserved on some of the tombstones. In a process known as "enameling," photographs of the deceased are burned into porcelain. This was a custom brought to the U.S. by Jewish immigrants from Eastern Europe. Mt. Zion Cemetery is also where many of the victims of the Triangle Shirtwaist Factory fire of 1911 are buried.

32 St. Saviour's Church
Rust Street and 57th Drive

Old St. Saviour's Church, designed by Trinity Church architect Richard Upjohn, has been here since 1847 on property donated by James Maurice, a prominent lawyer, politician, and landowner. It was torched by vandals in 1970 and is considerably different today, having been renamed by a Korean congregation. Maurice's name was affixed to a major Queens thoroughfare running along Mount Zion Cemetery from Maspeth to Woodside. His home still stands on Rust Street and 57th Avenue.

33 Lithuanian Shrine ≺
Perry Avenue near Remsen Place

Outside the A-framed Church of the Transfiguration on Perry Avenue, east of 64th Street, you will find this odd object in the front yard. It is a replica of a traditional Lithuanian roadside shrine. Maspeth has long been home to immigrants from Poland, Lithuania, and other Eastern European countries, as numerous local store signs demonstrate.

34 Queens County Hotel
Grand Avenue and Remsen Place

The Queens County Hotel, built in 1851 on today's Grand Avenue and Remsen Place, served farmers from Long Island who were hauling wagonloads of produce to Brooklyn's Wallabout Market. The hotel was one of many that sprang up on Grand Avenue.

35 Wheelwright
Grand Avenue, west of the Long Island Expressway

On Grand Avenue and Hamilton Place, you will find what used to be Anton Fausner's wheelwright and wagonmaker's shop. The wheelwright's ground floor later housed Maspeth Auto Parts, and several very old signs from that incarnation remain ("Brakes, clutches, pinfitting"). A

house on 58th Avenue, directly behind the wheelwright, has an old wagon wheel in front of it. Coincidence? Unfortunately, the wheelwright's house was razed in 2006, just as this book was going to press.

36 Maspeth Theatre ➤

Grand Avenue and 69th Place

The Maspeth, on Grand Avenue and 69th Place, now a pharmacy, was the largest of the town's three theaters.

37 Maspeth Town Hall

72nd Street, north of Grand Avenue

The "Maspeth Town Hall" was never the actual town hall, though it did serve in a municipal capacity before becoming a police station and, later, a public school. The building went up in 1897, not 1802 as its sign says.

QUEENS

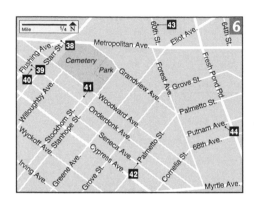

Some infrequent visitors to Ridgewood consider it to be part of Brooklyn, a fact that rankles Ridgewooders to no end; they are proud Queensites to the core. Ridgewood's row upon row of brownstones housed generations of German immigrants in the early twentieth century. Until Prohibition, many worked in the neighborhood's breweries such as Eurich's, Welz, and Zerweck. Today, Ridgewood is a stable middle-class neighborhood centering on its main streets, Myrtle Avenue and Fresh Pond Road (named for a titular body of water that was filled in as development encroached on the area's rurality in the early twentieth century). Among Ridgewood's noteworthy residents were Jimmy Cagney and Phil Rizzuto.

SUBWAY: BMT Ⓜ to Seneca Avenue, Forest Avenue and Fresh Pond Road

BUS: B20 or **Q58** on Fresh Pond Road; **Q39** on Forest Avenue; **B13** on Gates Avenue; **B38** on Seneca Avenue; **Q54** on Metropolitan Avenue; **B54** or **Q55** on Myrtle Avenue

38 The Bohack Smokestack
Flushing and Metropolitan Avenues

Has anyone designed a capital "B" quite like Bohack Supermarkets? You can see plenty of them at the old Bohack warehouse at Flushing and Metropolitan Avenues, where a smokestack is emblazoned with the Bohack name as well. Some NYC guides even list this intersection as "Bohack Square."

Founder H. C. Bohack opened his first store in New York in 1887. By 1940, there were 740 stores in the metropolitan area. The company was sold outside the family in 1965, and by the mid-1970s, the Bohack chain had folded. But every so often, a building façade is renovated, an awning is taken down . . . and that magnificent "B" blazes forth once again.

Long-time Forgotten-NY correspondent Christina Wilkinson at the Vander Ende-Onderdonk House and Arbitration Rock

39 Vander Ende–Onderdonk House
Flushing and Onderdonk Avenues

This house, at Flushing Avenue and Onderdonk Avenue, is one of the oldest houses in Queens. The house is divided into two sections; the dormered part closer to Onderdonk Avenue has been dated to about 1710, with the smaller western section having been added many decades later. It was likely built by Paulus Vander Ende and owned by a succession of heirs until 1831, when it was purchased by Adrian Onderdonk. According to the Ridgewood Historical Society, whose archives and offices are located here, the house has been used as a scrap glass factory, speakeasy, livery stable, greenhouse manufacturer, and, fascinatingly, a factory for spare parts for the Apollo space program.

40 Arbitration Rock ◄
Flushing and Onderdonk Avenues

The Onderdonk House was once a working farm, and now has a big backyard. In the middle of it, you'll find a big, unevenly shaped boulder. It is *claimed* to be the famed "Arbitration Rock" that marked a disputed Brooklyn-Queens boundary. The boulder is supposed to have been located to the west of Flushing Avenue and Onderdonk Avenue until Onderdonk was extended west in the 1930s. The rock was buried beneath the pavement for decades, until a chance excavation in December 2000 revealed it once more, and was subsequently placed in the backyard of the Vander Ende–Onderdonk House. Surveyor Peter Marschalk set the boundary in 1769, originally as the Kings County–Newtown Township line. The rock now rests on the old imaginary Brooklyn-Queens line, before it was altered in the 1920s.

There are two other rocks in the vicinity that may have figured in the Queens-Brooklyn borderline. One is at Varick Avenue and Randolph Street, and the other a half mile southwest at Morgan Avenue and Rock Street.

41 Follow the Yellow Brick Road
Between Onderdonk and Woodward Avenues

Stockholm Street, between Onderdonk and Woodward Avenues, would be an iconic NYC block and would probably be used in countless opening sequences for TV shows and movies set in New York City were it not for its location in relatively remote Ridgewood.

"Follow the yellow brick road" is especially apropos here. The yellow bricks used to build the columned brownstone buildings on this street and to pave the road are exactly the same, coming from the former Kreischer Brick Manufacturing Company in Charleston, Staten Island. Providing a near-perfect aesthetic backdrop are the two 165-foot-tall twin towers of St. Aloysius Church. The street's bricks were recently renovated and new sidewalks have been constructed.

42 Planters Peanuts
Seneca Avenue and Palmetto Street

A view of one of Queens' more spectacular painted ads can be had from the platform of the Seneca Avenue Station of the M train.

But this Planters Peanuts ad has only been here since 1985, when the Seneca Avenue Station appeared in the movie *Brighton Beach Memoirs* and the sign was painted as period scenery. However, other Forgotten Fans have told me that a similar Planters ad was indeed on this site *before* the movie was shot and this ad is a homage. I tend to believe them, as this ad has an aura of authenticity that's hard to fake.

43 Ridgewood Democratic Club
Putnam Avenue and Stier Place

The still-active Ridgewood Democratic Club at Putnam Avenue and Stier Place, just west of Fresh Pond Road, is a building still pretty much in the same condition it was back in the 1930s. Its original stained-glass windows, still marked with an interlocking "RDC," remain in place, al-

though they are cracked and somewhat the worse for wear. It was originally the office of early-twentieth-century local developer Paul Stier. The building was purchased by the Ridgewood Democratic Club (founded 1908) in 1916. It was expanded and renovated to the current configuration and the Club moved in the following year. A large two-story extension with a full basement was added to the rear of the building a little later; the interior floor has a mosaic with the name of the club tiled within.

44 Metropolitan Oval
60th Street, north of 62nd Avenue

Metropolitan Oval has been used continuously for soccer since 1925. Soccer greats Tony Meola, Werner Roth, Tab Ramos, and Edson Nascimento (Pele's son) have all called Met Oval their home field at one time or another. Met Oval had fallen into decrepitude a few years ago (even now, it's practically invisible from the street and you have to walk past a few Dumpsters to reach the entrance) but half a million dollars from the U.S. Soccer Foundation and Nike turned it around, complete with FieldTurf, a state-of-the-art playing surface. It has a pretty nifty view of midtown Manhattan, too.

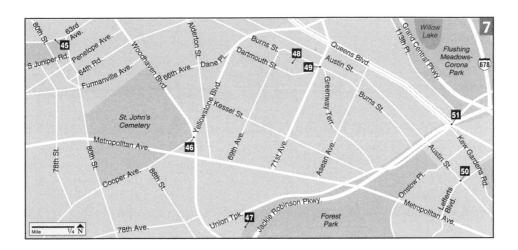

Rego Park was developed by Henry Schloh and Charles Hausmann of the *Real Good* Construction Company in the 1920s. The company's row houses still standing in the area contrast with the modern high-rise apartment buildings along Queens Boulevard.

Its immediate neighbor to the east, Forest Hills Gardens, is one of NYC's most beautiful as well as most insular neighborhoods. In 1909, Cord Meyer, the developer of nearby Elmhurst, sold 100 acres of land south of the Long Island Rail Road to the Russell Sage Foundation, which commenced to piece together a self-contained community from sixteen former truck farms throughout the 1910s and 1920s. It was patterned after a European village by Frederick Law Olmsted Jr., son of the co-developer of Central and Prospect Parks. Winding streets, Tudor brick buildings (many designed by renowned architect Grosvenor Atterbury), short cast-iron streetlamps, and street signs designed specifically for the development make it completely unique in New York City.

The layout of Kew Gardens was inspired by the London suburb that gave it its name. It was conceived and developed in the 1890s by Manhattan lawyer Albon Platt Man and later by his sons, Albon Jr. and Alrick. It fea-

tures block upon block of Spanish Colonial, Italianate, Dutch Colonial, Tudor, and even Japanese-style homes, as well as a cluster of apartment complexes in the vicinity of the Kew Gardens LIRR Station.

SUBWAY: Ⓖ, Ⓡ, or Ⓥ to 63rd Drive–Rego Park, 67th Avenue, Forest Hills–71st Avenue, or 75th Avenue

BUS: Q11 on Woodhaven Boulevard; **Q54** on Metropolitan Avenue; **Q60** on Queens Boulevard; **Q23** on 69th, 71st, and Metropolitan Avenues

45 Pullis Farm Cemetery
Juniper Boulevard North and 81st Street

Though western Queens is well-known for its vast cemeteries, there are also a number of very small ones. A section of Juniper Valley Park is given over to the Pullis Farm Cemetery, once the property of farmer Thomas Pullis, who purchased 32 acres in

QUEENS

the area in 1822. Pullis prohibited the sale of the cemetery in his will, and it continues to be maintained and protected. A memorial marker has replaced the cemetery's old tombstones.

Juniper Valley Park itself dates only to the 1940s, when NYC acquired 100-acre Juniper Valley Swamp to settle a $225,000 claim in back taxes against gangster Arnold Rothstein. The old swamp is now one of Queens' most beautiful parks.

46 Remsen Cemetery
Woodhaven and Yellowstone Boulevards

One more of Queens' tiny cemeteries, the Remsen family plot, can be found in the triangle formed by Woodhaven Boulevard, Trotting Course Lane, and Polo Place.

It's one of a handful of family burial plots that remain scattered around the borough. Among them are two belonging to the Lawrence family in Astoria and Bayside. This cemetery contains eight burials dating from 1790 to 1818. A plaque identifies one of the interred as Colonel Jeromus Remsen (1735–1790), who fought in the Revolutionary War Battle of Long Island.

47 Trotting Course Lane
Margaret Place, off 82nd Avenue

From Woodhaven Boulevard, walk east on 82nd Avenue and then north along Margaret Place. A little dead-end lane issues north from it toward the parking lot that serves a massive high-rise.

This is Trotting Course Lane, which re-ceived its name in the 1800s when horses were the prime mode of transportation. Subway historian Joe Brennan has informed me that Trotting Course Lane was probably named because it led to the Union Course, an important park for trotting races, which was north of Atlantic Avenue between Trotting Course Lane and the "city line" of Brooklyn. In the early twentieth century, the city changed the name of the road to Woodhaven Boulevard, its path was straightened, and it gained additional lanes until it became the freeway it is today, with ten busy lanes of traffic.

An additional relic can be found at the very end of the lane. Turn right, just past the parking lot gate. A path leading into Forest Park runs alongside some ancient, rusted railroad tracks. The tracks belonged to the Rockaway Branch of the Long Island Rail Road; this right-of-way was in operation until 1962.

48 Forest Hills Stadium
Burns Street and 69th Avenue

The Rolling Stones, the Beatles, Jimi Hendrix, Billie Jean King, and Jimmy Connors have all held court at Forest Hills Tennis Stadium at 69th Avenue and Burns Street. The U.S. Open was held here for many decades before it decamped to Louis Armstrong Stadium in 1978, and then to Arthur Ashe Stadium in Flushing Meadows/Corona Park in 1997. The West Side Tennis Club was organized in 1892 and settled here in 1913, with the U.S. Open moving here in the 1920s. The stadium's stone eagles, concrete steps, and wooden benches are still in place. As fewer and fewer events have been held here over the years, the stadium has fallen into gradual disrepair. The West Side Tennis Club hopes to hold more events and restore the stadium to its former glory.

49 Station Square
Continental Avenue and Burns Street

The Forest Hills Long Island Rail Road Station, newly polished and refurbished, looks like no other station in the system, with its distinctive Tudor-style ticket offices with shaped glass and unique luminaires. The station's design dates to 1911 and, as it was built in tandem with Forest Hills Gardens, it was always meant to be the perfect complement to the neighborhood.

50 Kew Gardens Station
Austin Street, Mowbray Drive, and Lefferts Boulevard

At Austin Street and Mowbray Drive you will find the 1909 Kew Gardens station house, a handsome ridge-roofed building, but of even greater interest is the nearby span that takes Lefferts Boulevard over the tracks. It's lined on both sides with commercial buildings. A complicated engineering solution encompasses three separate bridges on Lefferts: one for the

roadway, and two on each side that support the buildings. According to *Kew Gardens: Urban Village in the Big City* author Barry Lewis, the stores' bridges actually run through the building's *roofs*, with the storefronts hung from the bridges like a curtain on a rod. The engineering principle is similar to that of the circa-1565 Ponte Vecchio (Old Bridge) in Florence, Italy.

51 Civic Virtue Statue
Queens Boulevard and Union Turnpike

"Civic Virtue" is probably the most over-the-top classically themed public sculpture in New York City; only the Bailey Fountain at Brooklyn's Grand Army Plaza comes close. In a plaza near Queens Borough Hall at the southeast corner of Queens Boulevard and Union Turnpike, look for a massive statue depicting a nude muscular youth (depicting virtue) with a club slung over his right shoulder. At his feet writhe two mermaids (symbolizing vice). When Frederick MacMonnies created it from a single block of marble in 1919 and placed in Manhattan's City Hall Park, it inspired public outcry from offended feminists and heavy hitters such as Charles Norton, President of Harvard University. Such a sensual depiction would not stand, not in virtuous Manhattan, anyway. Eventually, in 1941, it was packed up, mermaids and all, and shipped to the Queens' Borough Hall Plaza, where, presumably, right-thinking people wouldn't see it.

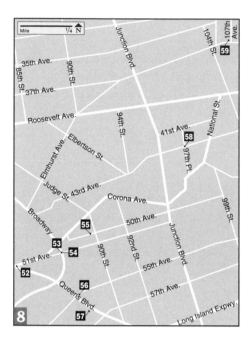

Early British colonists in Maspeth were eventually forced by the local Native Americans to move further east, to about where Queens Boulevard meets Broadway today; the new town was prosaically named Newtown. By the mid-1800s, horsecars and eventually streetcars began to bring in people from all over, and when Cord Meyer developed the area in the 1890s, he lobbied for a classier name: Elmhurst. Strangely, the IND subway, which arrived in 1936, keeps the Newtown name at a station, and Newtown High School retains the old moniker, as do a pair of roads in Astoria that were formerly main thoroughfares leading to the town.

Corona, separated from Elmhurst by Junction Boulevard, was first developed in 1854 when the National Race Course, still remembered by National Street, was built in what was then called West Flushing. In 1867, Benjamin Hitchcock opened a Flushing and Northside Railroad station at National Avenue and, by 1872, residents voted to change the community's name to Corona, Latin for "crown," in an effort to

mark it the king of Queens County towns and to give the area a distinct identity.

Today both areas are bustling neighborhoods with many immigrants from Asia, the Caribbean, and South America.

SUBWAY: ⑦ to 82nd Street–Jackson Heights, 90th Street–Elmhurst Avenue, Junction Boulevard, or 103rd Street–Corona Plaza; Ⓖ, Ⓡ, or Ⓥ to Elmhurst and Grand Avenues

BUS: B58 on Corona and Grand Avenues; **Q60** on Queens Boulevard; **Q72** on Junction Boulevard; **Q23** on 103rd and 104th Streets

52 Elks Lodge
Queens Boulevard and 51st Avenue

The handsome brick building on Queens Boulevard near 51st Avenue was once the largest Elks Lodge on the east coast, with sixty rooms, bowling alleys, billiards, a ladies' lounge, and a 50-foot-long bar. The Ballinger Company designed the granite, limestone, and brick structure dominated by a verdigris-covered elk at the front entrance.

53 St. James Episcopal Church
Broadway and 51st Avenue

One of the first religious buildings in Elmhurst was the old St. James Episcopal Church parish house. It is a relic of colonial rule, having been chartered by George III and erected in 1734. It is Elmhurst's oldest remaining building. It formerly supported a clock tower that a storm blew down in 1882. Last used as a church in 1848, it is now a community center and Sunday school. In recent years, the 260-year-old building has received some much-needed TLC. A "new" St. James, built in 1848, also burned down. Its replacement is an A-frame brick building catercorner to this one.

54 Reformed Dutch Church
Broadway and 51st Avenue

Directly across the street from the old St. James is the Reformed Dutch Church of Newtown, built in 1831 and enlarged in 1851, with stained glass added in 1874. It replaced an older structure built in 1733. On the Corona Avenue side is an ancient graveyard with some tombstones of early Dutch settlers.

55 O'Connell Court
50th Avenue, west of 90th Street

O'Connell Court, on 50th Avenue, between 88th and 90th Streets, is one of those blind alleys in the big city that can reward you with a completely unexpected

surprise. It's an unusual L-shaped dead-end alley. Turn right at the end, and you'll have a surprise view of five-towered Newtown High School, designed in a Baroque style by C. B. J. Snyder and built in 1897. It towers over the little enclave like a medieval castle over a fiefdom. The effect is best in winter, when no greenery interferes with the view.

56 Space-Age Queens Boulevard
Queens Boulevard and 55th Avenue

In the Swingin' Sixties, the Elmhurst stretch of Queens Boulevard became experimental territory for ambitious architectural firms. Inspired, no doubt, by New York's Second World's Fair in Flushing Meadows in 1964 and 1965, they created a group of buildings George Jetson would feel at home zipping past.

Take the angular North Fork Bank building at 55th Avenue. Designed and built for Jamaica Savings Bank in 1968 by William Cann, it sort of looks like a Stealth fighter a couple of decades before the bomber appeared. The building employs thin-shelled concrete that allows it to reach a height of 43 feet without the use of columns in its interior.

57 Elmwood Theatre ➤
Hoffman Drive and 57th Avenue

Elmwood Theatre took its name in 1948 from the two neighborhoods it served: Elmhurst and Woodhaven. It was designed by John Schladitz and built in 1928 as the

Queensboro, in the thick of the era of grand movie palaces, with twinkling stars and floating clouds on the ceiling similar to those at the Loew's Paradise in the Bronx. It showed its last picture in 2002 and is currently a neighborhood church.

58 Tiffany Studios
43rd Avenue and 97th Place

Louis Comfort Tiffany (1848–1933) became the world's foremost purveyor of stained and colored glass in the late 1800s. He is perhaps best known for the beautiful, decorative lamps he assembled using scraps of glass left over from the production of his stained-glass windows. Tiffany was also a premier interior designer; among his clients were Cornelius Vanderbilt and Mark Twain.

In 1893, Tiffany built a two-story brick factory in Corona at what is now 43rd Avenue and 97th Place. Until 1938, it housed the production of lamps, enamelware, jewelry, and thousands of stained-glass windows. Today, the venerable red brick building is a furniture factory.

59 Louis Armstrong House
107th Street, near 37th Avenue

Louis Armstrong, the great jazz trumpeter, purchased a small house at 34-56 107th Street in 1943, and resided there until he died in 1971; his wife, Lucille, remained there until her death in 1983. Since then, the house has been maintained, in turn, by the Louis Armstrong Educational Foundation, the New York City Department of Cultural Affairs, and Queens College. After a million-dollar renovation, the house opened as a museum in 2003. Guided tours are offered: among the highlights are Satchmo's second-floor den, with reels and reels of home recordings and an original oil painting by Astoria native and close friend Tony Bennett. Elsewhere in the residence is a turquoise 1950s-era kitchen and a bathroom with gold-plated fixtures. Louis is buried in Flushing Cemetery along with friend and neighbor Dizzy Gillespie.

The Louis Armstrong House at 34-56 107th Street welcomes visitors. For hours, consult www.satchmo.net or call (718) 478-8274.

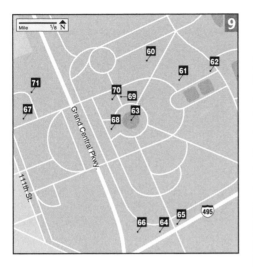

With its World's Fair remnants, some very well maintained, some crumbling, Flushing Meadows Corona Park is unlike any other park in town. It was built by NYC master planner Robert Moses atop a former garbage dump expressly for the 1939 World's Fair.

The 1939 World's Fair may have been more storied and better remembered, but the 1964 Fair had its whiz-bang moments as well. (I was there, eating Belgian waffles and wearing silly hats just like every other eight-year-old in town.) NYC has pretty much lost much of the 1964 World's Fair, other than its more daring, audacious structures. Here and there, you'll see traces of the temporary, yet magnificent, buildings that were supposed to be the portals to the Space Age.

SUBWAY: ⑦ to Willets Point–Shea Stadium. Walk on the bridge crossing over the MTA Corona yards and then down the ramp. Then cross the meadow on your right directly ahead to our first stop, a memorial to George Washington.

60 "George Washington"

Both "George Washington" and the neighboring "Rocket Thrower" are by Boston sculptor Donald De Lue. Strictly speaking, "George Washington" was not created for the World's Fair, but made its first appearance in the park in 1959, and was restored in 1999; appropriately, cherry trees now surround the sculpture.

61 "Rocket Thrower"

"Rocket Thrower" is one of a number of statues created for the World's Fair that had flight or space travel as a theme. (The fair also boasted the Court of Astronauts and a Fountain of the Planets.) This stylized sculpture depicts a giant throwing a rocket (in his right hand) through a network of stars (in his left).

62 Column of Jerash ➤

Thirty-six countries were represented at the 1964 World's Fair, among them Jordan,

QUEENS

63 Unisphere

The 35-ton 140 × 120-foot behemoth, the Unisphere, has become an icon of Queens in the four decades it has been in Flushing Meadows. This surprising and impressive sight rises above the trees and buildings like a second moon.

The Unisphere's three rings represent the orbits of the first American astronaut, the first Russian cosmonaut, and the first communications satellite. It was quite an engineering feat to make the Unisphere stay in place, because the sphere's Pacific Ocean is much lighter than the section showing Africa, Asia, and Europe, and the Unisphere tilts at the same approximate 23.5-degree angle the Earth does as it orbits the sun.

whose young King Hussein presented this approximately 30-ton marble column built by the Romans during their occupation of the Holy Land in 120 A.D. in the city of Jerash. It was originally part of the temple of Artemis, goddess of the hunt. It's likely the second-oldest man-made object in a New York City park (after the Egyptian obelisk known as "Cleopatra's Needle" in Central Park, which is 3,500 years old).

64 New York State Pavilion

Designed by Philip Johnson, the NY State Pavilion was among the most striking buildings at the World's Fair when it opened. It consists of the Tent of Tomorrow, made up of sixteen 100-foot-tall columns supporting a 50,000-square-foot

roof of multicolored panels (which was removed in the 1970s), as well as three towers, measuring 60, 150, and 226 feet tall. Fairgoers could ascend to the top of the towers via Sky Streak capsule elevators.

A second remnant of the New York State Pavilion is Queens Theatre in the Park, which opened as Theaterama, exhibiting Pop Art works by Andy Warhol and Roy Lichtenstein. The theater operated until 1985, when it was closed for renovation, reopening in 1994 as the Queens Theatre in the Park.

65 Exedra

The Vatican Pavilion, located on the northern end of the fairgrounds, was among the World's Fair's most popular attractions. Michelangelo's "Pieta," the moving representation of Mary grieving over the prone body of Christ after His crucifixion, was the main exhibit. The "Pieta" was completed in 1499 and this marked the first time it had been exhibited outside of St. Peter's Basilica in Rome. It was brought and returned on the Italian liner *Cristoforo Colombo* and displayed behind bulletproof Plexiglas.

Today a marble bench, known as the Exedra, marks the location of the Pavilion. It contains an inscription invoking Pope Paul VI's visit to the World Fair in October 1965 near the end of its run.

66 Time Capsule

This little concrete slab, in its own little circular plaza next to the New York State Pavilion, is what remains of the 1939 Westinghouse Pavilion. The electrics giant featured a time capsule at its exhibit, including a slide rule, a woman's hat, synthetic rubber, 10 million words on microfilm taken from books, magazines, and newspapers, and messages to the future from Albert Einstein and others. Westinghouse built a new time capsule in 1964,

incorporating the 1939 contents and adding filtered cigarettes, a Beatles record, irradiated seeds, freeze-dried foods, and a rechargeable flashlight. Do not open till 6964 . . . the time capsule is supposed to last 5,000 years.

67 Hall of Science

The Hall of Science is one of four buildings from the 1964 World's Fair still in active use (the others are Theaterama, now Queens Theatre in the Park; the Port Authority Heliport, now known as Terrace on the Park; and the Singer Bowl, now Louis Armstrong Stadium). The Hall of Science features rolling, undulating sheets of concrete punctuated by squares of stained glass (it's even more impressive from the inside). It was built by Harrison and Abramovitz and expanded in 1999 by the Polshek Partnership. For more information and hours, consult www.nyhallsci.org or call (718) 699-0005.

68 New York City Pavilion

The New York City Pavilion, designed by Aymar Embury II and redesigned in 1994 by Raphael Viñoly, is the only major building remaining from the 1939 World's Fair. It formerly housed a skating rink: one of the signs advertising the long-gone rink was still there in 2005! The pavilion contains one of the 1964 fair's most notable exhibits: the Panorama of New York, a scale model of the entire city with miniatures of every NYC building at the time.

Outside the pavilion is another remnant from the 1939 World's Fair: a memorial plaque dedicated to two of New York's Finest. On July 4, 1940, two detectives, Joseph Lynch and Ferdinand Socha, were sent to inspect a ticking suitcase at the British Pavilion. It turned out to be a bomb that exploded, killing the policemen. The terrorists never identified themselves; it is suspected there may have been a Nazi connection, though the truth may never be known.

69 Freedom of the Human Spirit

The male and female figures of Marshall Frederick's "Freedom of the Human Spirit" are quite unabashedly disrobed. As he explained it, "I realized that great multitudes of people, of all ages, and from all walks of life would see this sculpture. . . . I tried to design the work so that it was as free of the earth, as free in space as possible. . . . The thought that we can free ourselves from earth, from the material forces which try to restrain and hamper us, is a happy, encouraging and inspiring one, and I sincerely hope that my work will convey this message."

The statue originally stood in the 1964 World's Fair's version of the Court of States. In 1996, it was renovated and resurfaced, and moved to its present position in front of the main entrance to the Arthur Ashe Stadium facing the Unisphere.

70 Free Form

José de Rivera's polished, twisting crescent "Free Form," a short walk from "Freedom of the Human Spirit," originally revolved on top of its base (the motor gave out in 1972 and was never restarted). De Rivera (1904–1985) created his statues by forging and hammering with his own hands. Many of his works are steel or bronze bands twisted into three-dimensional shapes.

71 Forms in Transit

Located on an out-of-the-way path between the Hall of Science and the parking lot by the Long Island Rail Road, Polish-born Theodore Roszak's (1907–1981) "Forms in Transit" vaguely resembles the now-retired Concorde jet. A resident of Staten Island since the 1930s, Roszak studied in France, Germany, and Czechoslovakia, and was employed during World War II on the Brewster Aircraft assembly line. The 43-foot-long work is made of aluminum and steel, meant to embody the spirit of flight without depicting a specific airplane. Part of the statue became corroded and was removed in 1970, but the exterior skin has been allowed to remain weathered.

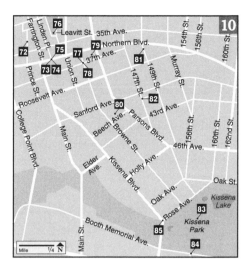

Flushing is among the oldest of Queens' towns, and it pursues an uneasy marriage between its Colonial and modern eras. The land just east of the Flushing River in the center of Queens had been occupied for many centuries by the Matinecock Indians, then by Dutch and English settlers, and later by waves of immigrants, all of whom have put their own particular stamp on the neighborhood.

As recently as the 1950s and 1960s, Flushing was a sleepy town of old-timey Victorian homes protected by shade trees, with a lively downtown centered on Main Street between Northern Boulevard and the Long Island Rail Road Port Washington line. A slow trickle of immigrants from eastern Asia has revitalized the region, but at the cost of its old-fashioned atmosphere as the old Victorian structures were torn down and high-rise apartment buildings and attached homes replaced them. The second NYC World's Fair and Shea Stadium arrived in Flushing Meadows in 1964; the United States Tennis Association moved the U.S. Open to Flushing Meadows Corona Park in 1978. Yet, the Mets and the Open have always seemed to be *in* Flushing, but not *of* it. Junkyards along the Flushing River separate Flushing Meadows

from Flushing, and culturally, Flushing seems a world apart from its neighboring areas. There are proposals to clean up the Flushing River and build a park along it that could possibly make Flushing Meadows more a part of its namesake neighborhood.

Today, Flushing's Colonial relics, some of which are more than 300 years old, sit uneasily in overcrowded streets. The result of Flushing's revival of the past decades is that, paradoxically, a few of its oldest buildings from the seventeenth century are preserved, but most from the eighteenth century and even many from the nineteenth have been wiped out.

SUBWAY: ⑦ to Flushing–Main Street

BUS: Q12 on Roosevelt Avenue, Bowne Street, and Sanford Avenue; **Q13** on 39th Avenue, Union Street, and Northern Boulevard; **Q14, Q20A, Q20B, Q25, Q34, Q44,** or **Q65** on Main Street; **Q17, Q25, Q27,** or **Q34** on Kissena Boulevard

72 Linnean Gardens Remnant
Prince Street, north of 35th Avenue

Flushing has kept many of its old street names. The southern part of the neighborhood features streets in alphabetical order beginning with Ash and ending in Rose. These names are not coincidental: In the Colonial era, Flushing was the home of one of the country's largest plant nurseries.

QUEENS

Planter William Prince established a commercial plant farm, or nursery, in western Flushing in 1737 along Flushing Bay. His son, William Prince Jr., established a new plant business north of Northern Boulevard in 1793; it would later be united with the original gardens and named the "Linnean Gardens" for Swedish scientist Carolus Linneaus, who conceived of the present system of naming, ranking, and classifying organisms.

An odd C-shaped little alley on Prince Street, between 33rd and 35th Avenues, Linneaus Place, hidden among the auto-parts stores and lumberyards that now dominate the area, is the only reminder of the Linnean Gardens.

73 Flushing Horse Trough
Northern Boulevard and Linden Place

In 1909, the car was beginning to make inroads on America's highways. But horse-power was still pretty much the way to get around. That year, Edith Bowdoin presented this concrete horse trough to the American Society for the Prevention of Cruelty to Animals. Incredibly, it is still in place on Northern Boulevard, in the center median at Linden Place; it is now being used as a planter.

74 Friends Meeting House
Northern Boulevard and Linden Place

The Friends Meeting House at Northern Boulevard and Linden Place, built in 1694, has been used for Quaker services

since it was constructed. Not only is the building remarkable for its great age, but at the rear you'll find a quiet churchyard with graves that are hundreds of years old. The Meeting House is quite a rural riposte to bustling Northern Boulevard. The upper floor is used for workshops and community meetings. There you will find original wood timbers supporting the structure, and gaslight fixtures (no longer functional) from the 1800s. The Meeting House is open to the public between noon and 1 PM on Sundays after services. Call (718) 358-9636 for additional information.

75 Flushing Town Hall
Northern Boulevard and Linden Place

Flushing Town Hall was constructed in 1862 by a local carpenter and is an example of Romanesque Revival architecture. The building was magnificently restored in 1995 by the architectural firm Platt Byard Dovell and is currently the seat of the Flushing Council on Culture and the Arts, a vibrant home for local arts programs and jazz concerts. The hall presents a variety of programs, including teacher training workshops, rehearsals, and meetings of cultural and community organizations. For information call (718) 463-7700 or visit www.flushingtownhall.org.

 Lewis Latimer Residence
Leavitt and 137th Streets

Lewis Latimer (1848–1928), inventor and engineer, was born in Massachusetts to parents formerly held in slavery in Virginia. He would assist Alexander Graham Bell, providing the drawings for Bell's patent application for the telephone; he later joined the U.S. Electric Lighting Co., a chief rival of Thomas Edison. There he would produce a long-lasting carbon filament that was a major improvement on Edison's 1878 electric lightbulb. Latimer also developed the first threaded lightbulb socket and assisted in the installation of New York City's first electric streetlamps.

After residing in Brooklyn for a number of years, Latimer moved his family to a small house on Holly Avenue in Flushing, where he corresponded with Frederick Douglass and Booker T. Washington. By 1995, the deteriorating house was declared a landmark and was later restored to its original condition and moved to a new location at 137th and Leavitt Streets, across the street from the Latimer Houses, which were named for the inventor. The house now has limited hours as a museum. For information, call (718) 961-8585.

 John Bowne House
Bowne Street and 37th Avenue

This ancient one-story house was built around 1661 by English settler John Bowne. Peter Stuyvesant, prosecuting a campaign against religious dissenters, had Bowne, a Quaker ally (accounts differ on whether he himself was one), arrested in 1662. He was subsequently exiled to Holland. While he was there, the Dutch West India Company reversed Stuyvesant's policy of intolerance, and Bowne returned home to this house in Flushing in 1664.

Bowne's illustrious descendants included Robert Bowne, who founded financial printers Bowne & Co.; Walter Bowne, NYC mayor from 1829 to 1833; shipping magnate Robert Bowne Minturn; and abolitionist Mary Bowne Parsons, wife of horticulturalist Samuel Parsons, who may have used the Bowne House as an Underground Railroad way station. Unfortunately, it's nearly impossible to enter this historic site these days; funds are lacking to maintain it as a museum, so history fans are missing out on seeing the interior of this 300-year-old house. For more information, call (718) 359-0528 or visit www.bownehouse.org.

 Fox Oaks Marker
Bowne Street and 37th Avenue

A stone marker across the street from John Bowne's house, worn into a rough pyramid by time, reads: "Here stood the Fox

QUEENS

Oaks, beneath whose branches George Fox, founder of the Society of Friends, preached June 7, 1672." Bowne Street is still shaded by oaks.

79 Kingsland Homestead

37th Avenue, west of Parsons Boulevard

The Kingsland Homestead has been located on three sites since its construction. Originally on Northern Boulevard at about 157th Street, it was moved in the 1920s to make way for a proposed but never built Flushing subway; before 1968 it was located at the southeast corner of Roosevelt Avenue and 155th Street, where it was beginning to become rundown. The Queens Historical Society had it moved to its present location in Bowne Park; the institution is housed in the homestead now.

Quaker Joseph Doughty constructed this building about 1790. It is named for his son-in-law, sea captain Joseph King, who bought it in 1802. It was later occupied by the Murray family, who gave their name to Murray Hill and Murray Street in east Flushing. The interior of the homestead has been preserved pretty much as it was in the nineteenth century, and a public exhibit by the Queens Historical Society occupies much of the first floor, including a representation of the Flushing Remonstrance. Kingsland is open from 2:30 to 4:30 PM, Tuesday, Saturday, and Sunday, but you are advised to call ahead for an appointment. For more information, call (718) 939-0647 or visit www.queenshistoricalsociety.org.

80 Waldheim

Ash, Beech, and Cherry Avenues, between Bowne Street and Parsons Boulevard

Waldheim is a Flushing enclave that is beginning to succumb to developers. Shingle, Moorish, Colonial, and Classical Revival homes mix with houses that look like early Frank Lloyd Wright. Enormous, 150-year-old trees overhang the blocks, providing for cool walks in summer, and the homes are set back a good distance from the sidewalks with many displaying well-kept gardens.

In 1903, Franklin R. Wallace sold 10 acres of mostly wooded Flushing property to real estate developers George Appleton and W. B. Richardson. They set to work building luxury housing and cutting through streets, named for plants in homage to Flushing's former plant nurseries. Many of the old woods' huge trees were retained in the street design, and the developers named the tract Waldheim, German for "woods home."

81 Voelker–Orth Museum

38th Avenue and 149th Place

One of Flushing's rare Victorian-era survivors, a small, two-story house at 149-19 38th Avenue, has been restored to its full glory.

Betty Voelker-Orth was born in the house in 1926, and lived there until her death in 1995. In her will, she left the house to the Queens Historical Society, the Queens Botanical Society, and the Audubon Society, with the provision that it be converted into a museum, bird sanctuary, and Victorian garden. She also left a good part of her fortune, which amounted to millions, to the restoration and preservation of the house.

Completed in 2001, the museum stands as a testament to Flushing's old Victorian history and as a small nature retreat. You may contact the museum at (718) 359-6227.

82 Charles Pearl–Matthew Kabriski Mansion

Ash Avenue, east of 147th Street

Ash Avenue moves through Flushing in fits and starts. It goes a block, is interrupted for a block, then runs a block more—and the section between 147th and 149th Streets looks transplanted from another part of town. Its centerpiece is a brilliant white three-story building at 147-38 Ash Avenue, with a complicated set of front porches, including a many-windowed circular corner porch. The house was originally the Charles Pearl mansion. Pearl built the Italianate house on a 5-acre tract facing today's Sanford Avenue and 149th Street. The interior boasts oak and pine floors, marble sinks, and floor-to-ceiling windows.

The Flushing Historic Trust, a preservation group, is attempting to find the funding necessary to maintain the striking building, which is currently endangered, and perhaps turn it into a museum like the one opened in the Voelker-Orth House.

83 Kissena Park

Between Kissena Boulevard, 164th Street, Oak and Rose Avenues, and Booth Memorial Avenue

Kissena Park, a 234-acre tract is one-half "regular" city park with walkways and playgrounds, and half "natural" park with bridle paths and heavily wooded areas. It was developed gradually in the early years of the twentieth century, with NYC slowly acquiring territory from private owners. Kissena Lake was once fed by streams, some of which emanated from the Flushing River, but it was cut off by the Works Progress Administration in 1942 and placed in a concrete container. "Kissena" is thought to be a Chippewa Indian term meaning "it is cold"; though the Chippewa lived in Michigan, nineteenth-century horticulturalist Samuel Parsons, whose tree grove is in the park at Rose Avenue and Parsons Boulevard, probably named it.

QUEENS

84 Velodrome ◅

Booth Memorial Avenue and Parsons Boulevard

One of Kissena Park's most unusual features is its velodrome, NYC's only outdoor bike track, built in 1963 for the Olympic trials held that year. By the 1990s, the Flushing velodrome was in a deteriorated state, and by then was mainly used by kite fliers and toy-car racers. In 2003, the velodrome was completely rehabilitated, repaved, and given a new 400-meter banked asphalt race track. Once again, it is hosting national events.

85 LIRR Creedmoor Branch Marker

Kissena Boulevard and Rose Avenue

Alexander T. Stewart (1803–1876), was the "merchant prince" who opened NYC's first department store on Broadway and Chambers Street in 1848. He also built the Central Railroad of Long Island in 1873, providing passenger service to Bethpage, Long Island, from northern Queens through Stewart's development in Hempstead Plains, Garden City.

The line ran for only six years, until 1879, although a spur to Creedmoor hung on until 1955 when steam engines were retired from LIRR passenger service. Rails from the spur can still be found on the grounds of Creedmoor State Hospital. Tangible remains of the old line are visible more than 100 years later: Kissena Corridor Park follows the route almost exactly.

The city has marked the presence of the Central Railroad at the southeast corner of Rose Avenue and Kissena Boulevard with a small concrete slab and decorative ironwork; blocks of concrete imitating railroad tracks lead off into Kissena Park where steam engines formerly chuffed.

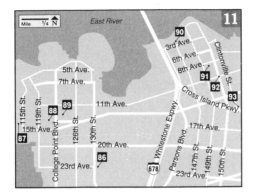

College Point is a neighborhood in northern Queens separated from neighboring Whitestone by the Whitestone Expressway and the Bronx Whitestone Bridge. You can catch a view of this beautiful bridge from Francis Lewis Park at 3rd Avenue and 147th Street, just east of the bridge, and from the Boulevard at Powell's Cove, just to the west.

College Point was originally settled by the Matinecocks, who sold much of it to New Netherland Governor Willem Kieft in 1645. William Lawrence was the first British settler (College Point Boulevard's name until 1969, Lawrence Street, honored the Lawrence family) and by 1838, Augustus Muhlenberg, Rector of St. George's Church on Main Street in Flushing, had founded St. Paul's College in the area. The college foundered within a decade, but College Point and College Place acknowledge its place in the region's history.

Entrepreneur Conrad Poppenhusen (1818–1883) arrived here from Germany in 1854 and converted College Point into a company town. Poppenhusen opened a rubber factory employing hundreds of immigrant workers and native College Pointers. He also built the Flushing and North Side Railroad, now part of the LIRR Port Washington line. Poppenhusen built water and sewage systems, a library, and the Poppenhusen Institute, which included the first free kindergarten in the U.S. He is recalled by the school, an avenue, and an 1884 bust by Henry Baerer at Poppenhusen Triangle at College Place and 12th Avenue.

Whitestone's claim to fame in Colonial days was the patriot Francis Lewis, a member of the U.S. Continental Congress and a signer of the Declaration of Independence. Lewis lived in an estate at today's 7th Avenue and 151st Street; the house was burned by the British in the aftermath of America's declared independence. In 1854, the same year Poppenhusen arrived in College Point, tinware manufacturer John Locke built a stamping mill and brought in workers from Brooklyn.

According to legend, Whitestone takes its name from a large offshore rock where tides from the East River and Long Island Sound meet; other accounts suggest the name is in honor of the White Stone Chapel, erected by early settler Samuel Leggett in 1837. For a time, Whitestone was known as Clintonville, after NYC mayor and New York Governor DeWitt Clinton. Both Leggett and Clintonville are recalled in area street names.

SUBWAY: None. You can make bus connections from the Main Street–Flushing ⑦-train station.

BUS: Q15 on 150th Street; **Q16** on Willets Point Boulevard; **Q25** on Linden Place and 127th Street; **Q20A** on Parsons Boulevard and 20th Avenue; **Q20B** on Parsons Boulevard and 14th Avenue; **Q44** on Parsons Boulevard; **Q65** on College Point Boulevard

QUEENS

86 Flushing Airport
Linden Place and 23rd Avenue

Flushing Airport was opened in 1927 as Speed's Airport (named for former owner Anthony "Speed" Hanzlick). It became the busiest airport in NYC for a time. However, North Beach Airport opened in 1939 and, as LaGuardia Field, it quickly took business away from the older airfield. By the 1970s, it was used mainly by skywriting planes and as a blimp port. A fatal crash into a neighborhood house in 1977 convinced locals that it should be closed, and by 1984 the airport ceased operations.

Upon venturing inside (the best entrance is from 23rd Avenue, east of 130th Street), which can be tricky because the old airport is now very muddy and waterlogged, I found a pair of rusty hangars, an old anchor, and an abandoned fire engine that has since fallen apart, and a sign advertising the Steuben Society of America.

87 Poppenhusen Institute
14th Road and 114th Street

The Poppenhusen Institute was built in

1868. The three-story Second Empire building featured a grand ballroom, savings bank, library, sheriff's office, and courtroom.

Today the institute is used as a community center, and features karate and piano lessons, summertime concerts, a fire department museum and a Native American exhibit. For more information and hours, call (718) 358-0067 or visit www.poppenhuseninstitute.org.

88 Beech Court
121st Street, north of 14th Avenue

The Herman Funke Estate has survived as Beech Court, 14th Avenue, just west of College Point Boulevard, a quiet, secluded cul-de-sac featuring several outstanding homes, including a Queen Anne classic and an Art Moderne, one of two such buildings in the area (the other one is on Malba Drive, a couple of miles to the east).

89 Grand View Hotel
13th Avenue and 123rd Street

The traffic circle at 13th Avenue and 123rd Street is occupied by just one building: the red-bricked, dormer-windowed Grand View Hotel, which was built in 1853 as Herman Schleicher's mansion. Schleicher supported the South in the Civil War and ran guns to the Confederates. The structure later became the Grand View Hotel (its elevation permitted views of the East

River and Flushing Bay) and was divided into apartments in more recent years.

90 Colden-Wesson Mansion
147th Street, north of 3rd Avenue

One of Queens' few remaining eighteenth-century structures is the Colden-Wesson Mansion at 2-11 147th Street, opposite Francis Lewis Park (the historic home stands within the former estate of the Declaration of Independence signer). Built in 1762, it was further enlarged in 1926, and has been owned by the family of Supreme Court Justice Charles Colden and later, by the Wesson family.

91 8th Road
Between 149th and 150th Streets, south of 8th Avenue

You'll have to use a little imagination, but stroll down curving 8th Road, a short alley between 149th and 150th Streets south of 8th Avenue, and Queens' rural past of hay wagons and mooing cows can be visualized in your mind's eye. This little lane may have serviced stables when the area was originally developed in the early 1900s, and it remained unpaved until the mid-1990s.

92 Martin A. Gleason Funeral Home
11th Avenue and 150th Street

The Martin A. Gleason Funeral Home, a converted Victorian-era private house, features a corner double-decked round porch with ionic columns.

93 St. Nicholas Russian Orthodox Church
Clintonville Street, north of the Cross Island Parkway

The beautiful onion dome of St. Nicholas Russian Orthodox Church at 14-65 Clintonville Street is rendered in brilliant Technicolor blue. It has become a neighborhood landmark since its construction in 1968 by architect Sergei Padukow.

QUEENS

QUEENS

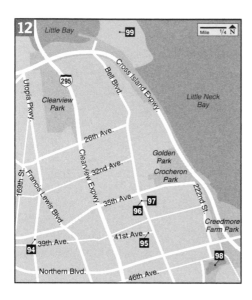

Auburndale and Bayside sprang from a 16,000-acre land grant from New Netherland governor Willem Kieft to English colonists in the 1600s.

Auburndale is a planned development. In 1901, the Thomas Willett farm (probably one of the Willetts remembered by the name Willets Point) was purchased by the New England Development and Improvement Company, and a community was born.

Bayside had been in existence as a community for many years before Auburndale was founded. It was first settled by the British around Alley Creek, the East River inlet now leading to Alley Pond Park, in the early 1700s. It was named Bay Side in 1798, and by the time the one-word spelling appeared in the 1850s, it was a small but potent community giving rise to governmental leaders and statesmen. The neighborhood has always retained a small-town atmosphere centered around Bell Boulevard. The street is named for Abraham Bell, an Irish Quaker who was a partner in a shipping firm and owned a vast farm in the area (the name has nothing at all to do with Alexander Graham Bell). The

city, however, has added to the confusion by naming P.S. 205, at Bell Boulevard and 75th Avenue, the Alexander Graham Bell School, as well as its playground, Bell Park, and later, Telephone Playground, in honor of the inventor.

In the 1910s, Bayside became a film actors' colony with D. W. Griffith, in particular, filming hundreds of productions here until the burgeoning industry decamped to Hollywood. Corbett Road became a favorite spot for stars to make their homes, with W. C. Fields, Norma Talmadge, and John Barrymore all living along the scenic way overlooking Crocheron Park.

SUBWAY: None. Connections with buses can be made from the Flushing–Main Street ⑦-train station.

BUSES: Q13 on Northern and Bell Boulevards; **Q31** on Bell Boulevard; **Q76** on Francis Lewis Boulevard; **Q30** on Horace Harding Expressway; **Q75** or **Q88** on 73rd Avenue

94 Joseph Cornell House
Utopia Parkway, south of Crocheron Avenue

Auburndale produced an unlikely innovator in the art world in the mid-twentieth century: "shadow box" and collage artist Joseph Cornell (1903–1972), who for more than four decades lived in a small house at 37-08 Utopia Parkway, south of Crocheron Avenue. Cornell and his family moved to Bayside from Nyack, New York, after the death of his father in 1917, and after a few years, moved again to Utopia Parkway.

Beginning in the mid-1930s, Cornell took wooden boxes, about one to two feet high, and filled them with found objects: buttons, corks, newspaper clippings, jars, photographs, toys, theatrical poster fragments, and other relics he found in junk shops and flea markets. He would create homages to places he'd never been, to movie stars like Jennifer Jones and Lauren Bacall, and to nineteenth-century ballerinas, which were a favorite subject. Several Cornell pieces are in the permanent collection of the Museum of Modern Art.

"Bayside Story," a collection of bas-reliefs on columns and overhead friezes, features a boxing-glove clad hand raised in victory.

95 Jim Corbett: Bayside's Favorite Son

41st Avenue and 213th Street

Heavyweight boxer Jim Corbett was a Bayside resident. He was a champion from 1892, when he knocked out John L. Sullivan in the first-ever bout using padded leather boxing gloves, to 1897, when he lost to Bob Fitzsimmons. He fought nineteen professional bouts, winning eleven, seven by knockout.

In 1902, Corbett bought a luxurious home on 221st Street, near 36th Avenue, and resided there with his wife, Vera, until his death in 1933. A historic plaque was placed near Corbett's home in 1971. A short road fronting Crocheron Park was named in his honor some time after his death, and Errol Flynn starred in his life story in 1942.

"Gentleman Jim" is also remembered by the newly renovated Bayside Long Island Rail Road Station. Ed McGowin's

96 Lamartine Avenue Signposts

36th Avenue and Bell Boulevard

The southwest and northwest corners of 36th Avenue and Bell Boulevard feature tall signposts apparently built from rocks and pebbles, reminiscent of the cobblestone house found nearby. The odd signposts are notable enough, but their signs hearken back to Bayside's past: They read "Bell Avenue," Bell Boulevard's former name, and "Lamartine Avenue," 36th Avenue's old moniker.

97 Cobblestone House

36th Avenue and Bell Boulevard

At 35-34 Bell Boulevard, just north of the "Lamartine" signpost, stands a magnificent two-story building with an exterior made of cobblestones. There are a number of cobbled-wall houses around town, but this one is the most striking, with its triple-arched front. It was declared a NYC landmark in October 2004. The stones are naturally shaped, i.e. not beveled or cut in any way.

The house was built in 1906, and, according to local legend, housed a speakeasy during Prohibition. Actress Maude Adams (1872–1953), who played Peter Pan in more than 1,500 performances, is thought to have lived in the house during her Broadway days.

98 Oakland Lake

46th Avenue and Cloverdale Boulevard

Oakland Lake is the largest of a number of small "kettle ponds" left over from the passage of a glacier that stopped its southern progress in the middle of Long Island 15,000 years ago. According to the NYC Parks Department, it was once thought to be 600 feet deep, but the lake's depth was found to be just 20 feet in 1969. Similar to what was done with Kissena Lake, Oakland Lake was surrounded with a concrete lining and "citified" in the 1930s.

99 Fort Totten

Bell Boulevard and the Cross Island Parkway

Fort Totten was built in the 1850s in the shape of a rough triangle, with 8-foot-thick solid stone walls. Casements were protected by 2-inch-thick wrought-iron shutters. The arsenal included eight 13-inch-guns. Local

legend says that a tunnel was constructed from the Willets fort across the East River to Fort Schuyler, but no evidence of such a tunnel has been found.

In 2004, reconstruction began on the lengthy tunnel connecting the fort's visitor's center to its historic area, which contains decommissioned mine rooms, torpedo rooms, and gun platforms, all built on 15,000 granite blocks facing the East River. At least some of Fort Totten will become parkland.

Any discussion about Fort Totten would be incomplete without mentioning its longtime historian, Jack Fein, who was stationed at Fort Totten when he first enlisted in the Army in 1936 and has been involved with the fort for now over seventy years. After serving at posts all over the globe in World War II, he became the post adjunct at Totten in 1952, and began to collect and display historical data on the fort. He went on to conduct tours and run the fort's post office. The fort's deactivation and Fein's retirement from active duty both came in 1967, but he was asked to stay on as the fort's historian and tour guide on a volunteer basis. For tour information, call (718) 352-4793, extension 18.

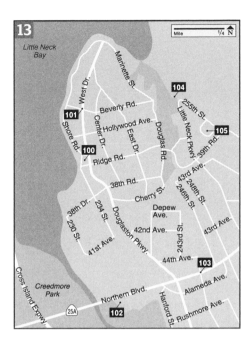

in the area, which has always been among Queens' most affluent. The streets have retained their original names and have ignored the Queens practice of giving every street a number. The Douglas name was appended to the area in 1876, after William Douglas donated a Long Island Rail Road stop.

Little Neck's early days featured a colorful character, the "Bard of Little Neck," Bloodgood Haviland Cutter (1817–1906), potato farmer, poet, and friend of Mark Twain, who immortalized him as the "Poet Lariat" in *The Innocents Abroad*. Twain poked fun at Cutter as a master of doggerel who annoyed fellow passengers on an excursion to the Holy Land in the novel.

SUBWAY: None. Bus connections can be made from the Flushing–Main Street ⑦-train station

BUS: Q12 on Northern Boulevard; **Q30** on Horace Harding Expressway; **Q79** on Little Neck Parkway

100 Van Wyck House
West Drive and Alston Place

This oldest building in Douglaston dates to pre-Revolutionary days. The Cornelius Van Wyck residence was built in 1735, making it one of the few remaining Queens edifices from the eighteenth century. The nearby Greek Revival Allan-Beville House at Center Drive and Forest Road dates to 1848.

101 Douglaston Club
West Drive and Beverly Road

The Wynant Van Zandt residence was built in 1819. It was later William Douglas's residence for many years, as well, so it has been occupied by two of the men most responsible for the settling and development of the

The two most northeastern of Queens' neighborhoods, Douglaston and Little Neck, somehow seem carved out of the rather exclusive, monied precincts of the Nassau County townships immediately to the east, Great Neck and Manhasset. Both neighborhoods are served by a short shopping strip along Northern Boulevard, and the area's hilly topography doesn't lend itself to block upon block of cookie-cutter ranch houses.

Major Thomas Wickes, a patriot originally from Huntington, owned the entire Douglaston peninsula jutting into Little Neck Bay after the Revolutionary War, and subsequently sold it to Wynant Van Zandt in the 1810s. Scotsman George Douglas purchased the peninsula from Van Zandt in 1835. The region was later developed as a suburban resort and exclusive enclave, enjoying pleasant views of Little Neck Bay and Long Island Sound. Streets were laid out in 1906 by the Rickert-Finlay realty company, who had purchased the property from William Douglas, George's son. Eclectic, individualistic homes were built

peninsula. It is now the Douglaston Club, where the young John McEnroe honed his tennis game in the early 1970s.

102 Alley Park Windmill

Northern Boulevard, east of the Cross Island Parkway

No old-fashioned windmills have survived in NYC (a windmill, symbolizing the Dutch colonials, appears on New York City's official seal), but in the Alley Pond Park Environmental Center there's a reasonable facsimile.

The first windmill in the Alley Park–Douglaston area supplied water to a farming community on today's Douglas Manor peninsula, and was built about 1870 on what is now Arleigh Road. Unfortunately, the newly restored windmill burned down shortly after it was installed in Alley Pond Park in 1986. Funds were found to build a new windmill in the old one's image. Today, the Alley Pond Park Environmental Center hosts regular tours and exhibitions at the mill, which is used to pump water from deep underground and is respon-

sible for the constant replenishment of the park's plant life. For information on APEC, call (718) 229-4000 or visit www. alleypond.com.

103 Zion Episcopal Church

Northern Boulevard and 244th Street

Zion Church was completed in 1830 from plans developed by Trinity Church architect Richard Upjohn. Wynant Van Zandt is interred in the family vault beneath the cemetery. In the last century, the church has endured two devastating fires, the worse in 1924.

When the Flushing and Hempstead Turnpike, later known as Broadway and then Northern Boulevard, was being graded and widened, graves of the Matinecock Indians were discovered; they were reinterred in the Zion Episcopal Church cemetery in 1931. A stone marker, designed in two pieces on either side of a tree, is engraved "Here Rest the Last of the Matinecoc."

104 Udall's Cove

Little Neck Parkway and 255th Street

Udall's Cove, accessible from the northern end of Little Neck Parkway at 255th Street, north of the Long Island Rail Road, is a 30-acre park dedicated solely to nature preservation. Udall's contains salt marshes, a forest, a meadow, and a freshwater pond. The remains of Little Neck's clamming past is evidenced by the wood pilings at Virginia Point, the end of Little Neck Parkway, for-

merly known as Old House Landing Road. The cove is named for nineteenth century settler Richard Udall, who owned a mill in the region. The Udall's Cove Preservation Committee, which is responsible for the park's upkeep, was formed in 1969, and the cove was opened to the public in 1972.

105 Long Island Rail Road Grade Crossing

Little Neck Parkway, north of 39th Avenue

One of the busiest remaining grade crossings in NYC is at Little Neck Parkway and 39th Avenue at the LIRR Port Washington branch. Dozens of trains pass by it every day. Admittedly, it is in an outlying area toward Little Neck Parkway's northern end at Little Neck Bay; still, there is some substantial traffic here at times and the potential for mishaps is notable.

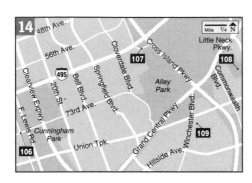

The neighborhoods of Glen Oaks, Bel-lerose, and Floral Park were gradually developed from farmland in the early-to-mid twentieth century, with Glen Oaks remaining the most stubbornly rural until after World War II. Floral Park takes its name from the flower farms so prevalent in that area following the Civil War; Bellerose, from a model community in adjoining Nassau County conceived by Helen Marsh in the early 1900s that a newer development on the Queens side wished to emulate; and Glen Oaks from the Glen Oaks County Club, founded on the former William K. Vanderbilt estate prior to World War II. The country club is now the site of North Shore Towers.

SUBWAY: None. Connections to buses can be made from the ⑦ Flushing–Main Street Station or from the Jamaica–Parsons–Archer terminal of the Ⓔ and Ⓙ trains.

BUSES: Glen Oaks: **Q46** on Union Turnpike; **Q79** on Little Neck Parkway; **Q30** on Horace Harding Expressway. Bellerose and Floral Park: **Q1** on Braddock Avenue; **Q36** on Jamaica Avenue/Jericho Turnpike

106 The Long Island 45
73rd Avenue and 199th Street, south and east to Winchester Boulevard

While making your way through the southeastern part of Auburndale as you get close to Cunningham Park, you may spot the occasional white-painted overpass like the one spanning 73rd Avenue just east of 199th Street. They're not old railroad trestles or park paths . . . instead, they mark one of America's very first parkways designed for automobile traffic.

In 1904, industrialist William Kissam Vanderbilt created a road race that became known as the Vanderbilt Cup Race—it was one of the very first auto races, and it attracted drivers from the world over. The race was run in Nassau County on Jericho Turnpike, Bethpage Turnpike, and Hempstead Turnpike. All are busy highways now, but in those days, they were farm-to-market, unpaved roads.

The race attracted thousands of spectators every year. In 1906, after several spectators broke through a wire fence in Mineola, a race car smashed into the crowd, killing a bystander. Vanderbilt then decided that the race needed a separate course. Construction began in June 1908, and eventually, the first phase of the Motor Parkway was completed in 1910. The parkway pioneered the use of overpasses and bridges to avoid intersections with previously existing roads. It extended about 45 miles east to Lake Ronkonkoma.

A long stretch of the Motor Parkway is still intact and used as a pedestrian and bicycle path between Cunningham Park and Winchester Boulevard just north of Union Turnpike. Some of the parkway's original concrete posts lining the old route can be seen in the underbrush, and other clues, like the "1926" under the overpass at 73rd

Avenue, mark the date of its final western expansion.

In the late 1990s, the Motor Parkway was connected to a lengthy greenway running west along maintained park paths to Kissena Park. The Kissena Park Corridor leads farther west across the Van Wyck Expressway to Flushing Meadows Corona Park, making for a terrific traffic-free bike path.

107 George Washington Plaque
West Alley Road and 233rd Street

At the corner of West Alley Road and 233rd Street, you'll see a small, unobtrusive boulder with a marker on it reading: "George Washington traveled this road on his tour of Long Island, April 24, 1790. Commemorating this event, the Matinecock Chapter, Daughters of the American Revolution, Flushing, New York have set this mark. May 25, 1934."

The president traveled through here to check on soil conditions on Long Island and to personally thank patriots on the island who had risked their lives during the Revolutionary War. In Roslyn, Washington visited the homes of gristmill owner Henrick Onderdonk and Setauket tavern keeper Austin Roe.

Behind the marker on 233rd Street, you'll find an entrance into Alley Pond Park. Indulge your inner Thoreau with a walk along the blazed (marked) paths, some of which go past the park's kettle ponds.

108 Queens Farm Museum
Little Neck Parkway and 74th Avenue

The Queens County Farm Museum occupies 47 acres in the heart of Glen Oaks; its croplands and orchards are used to demonstrate the history of agriculture to students and visitors.

The tract has been farmed for more than 300 years. Earliest records show it being sold by John Harrison to Elbert Adriance in 1697. The farm stayed in the Adriance family until the early 1800s, and Elbert's son, Jacob, constructed the present farmhouse in 1772.

The farmhouse was restored in 1986 to resemble its condition in 1856, when the Cox family, who owned it after the Adriances, last expanded it. Inside, you will find original plank floors, beamed ceilings, and antique glass and hardware. For more information, call (718) 347-3276 or visit www.queensfarm.org.

109 Creedmoor Living Museum ➤
Winchester Boulevard, south of Union Turnpike

Surprisingly enough, Creedmoor Psychiatric Center in Bellerose is home to an art gallery. Founded by a hospital employee, the late artist Bolek Greczynski, and psychologist Dr. Janos Marton in 1984, the museum was conceived as an arts program for hospital residents and is the only museum in the U.S. devoted to the art of the mentally ill. Residents are given materials to create

anything they wish in their own personal styles, giving them a bridge to the outside world. The works are presented as any other art, without a clinical atmosphere. All forms of art, from paintings, collage, to photography and even music are represented in the museum, which is more of a workshop than a formal space. When the Living Museum first opened, horror movie king Vincent Price recorded an opening introductory narration, and the museum was the subject of a 1998 documentary by Academy Award–winning filmmaker Jessica Yu. Visitors are welcome daily at 80-45 Winchester Boulevard, Building 75. Call (718) 264-4000 for an appointment and directions, and Dr. Marton himself will likely pick up the phone; he remains a daily presence at the museum. Parents beware: some of the art is quite frank.

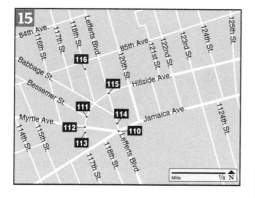

In 1869, developers Albon Platt Man and Edward Richmond laid out a new community just west of Jamaica, with a post office and railroad station, and Richmond named the area for himself (or, perhaps, a London suburb, Richmond upon Thames, a favorite royal stomping ground). Richmond Hill became a self-contained community of Queen Anne architecture west of Van Wyck Boulevard (now known as the Van Wyck Expressway) that remains fairly intact to the present day. Journalist/activist Jacob Riis as well as the Marx Brothers were Richmond Hill residents in the early twentieth century.

SUBWAY: ⓙ to 104th Street, 111th Street, or 121st Street

BUSES: Q55 on Myrtle Avenue; **Q56** on Jamaica Avenue; **Q37** on 111th Street; **Q10** on Lefferts Boulevard

 **110** Triangle Hotel
Jamaica and Myrtle Avenues

Almost as long as there's been a Richmond Hill, the Triangle Hotel (aka Doyle's Hotel) building has marked the plot where Myrtle Avenue meets Jamaica Avenue. It was built by Charles Paulson in 1868 and was originally rented out as a grocery and post office. By 1893, the building, owned by John Kerz and operating as a hotel, included an

eatery named the Wheelman's Restaurant in honor of the new bicycling craze.

Vaudeville-era pianist/composer Ernest Ball (1878–1927) wrote the now-standard "When Irish Eyes Are Smiling" in one of the hotel's guest rooms in 1912. According to the Richmond Hill Historical Society, Babe Ruth (who was a golf enthusiast in nearby St. Albans) and Mae West were patrons of the Triangle Hofbrau, as Wheelman's was later renamed, in the 1920s.

111 Pennsylvania Railroad symbol
Overpass at Hillside Avenue and Bessemer Street

The view of the concrete Richmond Hill trestle from Hillside Avenue lets us see one of the Long Island Rail Road's more intriguing relics: the keystone. The LIRR was run under the auspices of the Pennsylvania Railroad from 1928 to 1966. In those years, the LIRR signage adopted the "Pennsy" keystone symbol for Pennsylvania, the Keystone State. Until 1955, the LIRR's chuffing steam engines all carried

QUEENS

a keystone plate on their noses, when the last steam engine was retired from active service. Steam Engine #39 is exhibited—Pennsy plate included—at the Railroad Museum of Long Island in Riverhead. The nearby Richmond Hill elevated station enjoyed passenger service until 1998.

112 RKO Keith's
Hillside and Myrtle Avenues

Richmond Hill has preserved its very own classic movie palace, and this one has a marquee that has been returned to its look in its halcyon days, with red neon-lit nameplates and a gold border. The theater opened as Keith's Richmond Hill around 1928 at 117-09 Hillside Avenue. The old marquee, which had been hidden under aluminum siding for some years, was restored in 2001 during production for a feature film *The Guru*. Next door is Jahn's, a 1923 ice cream shop, one of a chain initiated in the Bronx in 1897.

113 Bangert's Flowers
117th Street, south of Myrtle Avenue

Bangert's Flowers, at 86-08 117th Street, started out as Fluhr's in 1894, and was sold to the Bangert family in 1927. It boasts what must be its first 1927 marquee, with defunct neon letters and an original FTD sign complete with a wing-footed Mercury and an old FTD slogan: "Flowers by wire . . . the Mercury Way!"

114 Republican Club Building
Lefferts Boulevard, north of Jamaica Avenue

The landmarked Republican Club building pretty much looks the same on the exterior as it did when it was built in a Colonial Revival style by architect Henry Haugaard in 1908. That's the problem with this historic structure—it looks as if it hasn't been touched in decades.

The building has an illustrious history, however. The interior originally boasted oak pews, doors, and paneling, a bowling alley-come-archery range. Signed photographs of Calvin Coolidge, Warren Harding, and Theodore Roosevelt can still be found inside, according to the Richmond Hill Historical Society. The club remained an important gathering place for the Republican Party throughout the twentieth century well into the 1980s. Teddy Roosevelt, Richard Nixon, and Gerald Ford have all given speeches here, and Ronald Reagan appeared here during primary season in 1976 and again during the 1980 campaign.

115 Richmond Hill Public Library
Lefferts Boulevard and Hillside Avenue

The Richmond Hill Public Library was built in 1905 by the architectural firm Tuthill and Higgins, with a grant from philanthropist Andrew Carnegie, on land donated by Albon Platt Man, the developer of Richmond Hill. Stop in and see a large mural painted in 1936 by artist Philip

The Houses of Richmond Hill

Richmond Hill can claim NYC's greatest concentration of Queen Anne–style "painted lady" houses in eclectic configurations painted in every color (tastefully) imaginable.

The Victorian era, from roughly 1865 to 1900, was a period characterized by a booming economy, and architecture responded with an everything-but-the-kitchen-sink attitude. No color or design was written off, and no expense was spared in construction. Yet despite every house on the block being completely different from the others, Victorian neighborhoods retained a unity of spirit that can't be matched in these days of prefabrication. White dominates as the color of choice for many Richmond Hill homes, although color was not a restricting factor and some houses are done in brilliant pinks, yellows, purples, and greens.

Although there was no such thing as zoning in the late 1800s, Richmond Hill founder Albon Platt Man had several methods at his disposal to make sure the community developed according to his specifications. He obtained restrictive covenants that dictated, for example, the absence of front yard fences and uniform setbacks. These stipulations gave Richmond Hill a forest-like atmosphere with plenty of green lawns, a feature that persists to this day.

Most of the houses in Richmond Hill were constructed in the American Queen Anne Shingle–Style, though there are some examples of an earlier style with thin posts and rails called the "Stick Style."

Evergood showing Richmond Hill as a suburban alternative to the hustle and bustle of the big city.

116 Church of the Resurrection
118th Street, near 85th Avenue

Albon Platt Man also donated land for the Church of the Resurrection, Richmond Hill's first church. A small wooden Gothic Revival building built by architect Henry Dudley in 1874, the structure is preserved within the present French Gothic stone building, which was finished in 1904, though further extensions continued until 1926. Social reformer Jacob Riis was a parishioner, and New York Governor Theodore Roosevelt attended Riis' daughter Clara's wedding to Dr. William Fiske here on June 1, 1900.

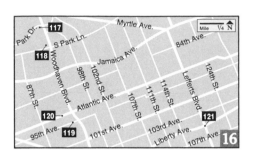

Woodhaven was a racing mecca before it was a town: Union Course, at what is now Jamaica Avenue and Woodhaven Boulevard, was built in the 1820s. The Centerville and Aqueduct Race Tracks would follow. From the 1830s to the 1850s, what is now East New York and Cypress Hills, Brooklyn, as well as Woodville, Queens, were developed by Connecticut businessman John Pitkin. To avoid confusion with an upstate New York State town in the days before zip codes, Woodville residents voted in 1853 to change the village's name to Woodhaven.

SUBWAY: ① to 75th Street, 85th Street–Forest Parkway, Woodhaven Boulevard; Ⓐ to 80th Street, 88th Street, Aqueduct–North Conduit, or Howard Beach–JFK Airport

BUS: Q56 on Jamaica Avenue; **Q24** on Atlantic Avenue; **Q7** on Sutter Avenue; **Q8** on Liberty Avenue; **Q11** on Woodhaven Boulevard

117 Forest Park Carousel

Woodhaven Boulevard, south of Myrtle Avenue

Every year, it seems, sees the closing of more of New York's classic carousels, but Forest Park's ride is still delighting kids big and small as it has since it was moved here from Dracut, Massachusetts, in 1971. This Daniel Muller carousel, built in 1910, contains fifty-four wood horses and other animals; it is one of just two by its designer remaining in the country.

118 FDNY Queens Central Office

Park Lane South and Woodhaven Boulevard

A relic of the days when fire alarms were relayed by telegraph (a practice begun in 1851) can be found at this austere building, dating to the 1920s. Fire alarms from Queens, emanating from streetside fire alarms, phone calls, radio calls from units in the field, and private alarm services go through this building. The alarm is assigned a response of fire units, and the firehouses are notified from this central office.

119 Wyckoff Building ≺
95th Avenue and 93rd Street

The Wyckoff Building's former egg-shaped dome made it a veritable skyscraper. The dome may have been removed, but there's still enough detail on this 110-year-old building to make it one of Woodhaven's treasures; its cornices and eaves have not been lost to development. It was originally the home office for the Woodhaven Bank.

120 Lalance & Grosjean Clock Tower
Atlantic Avenue and 92nd Street

Lalance & Grosjean, the nationally renowned manufacturer that was among the first to make porcelain enamelware, set up business here in 1863. By 1876, they had a large kitchenware factory on Atlantic Avenue between today's 89th and 92nd Streets, and workers' housing on 95th and 97th Avenues between 85th and 86th Streets.

In the 1980s, most of the Lalance & Grosjean red-brick factory buildings were razed in favor of a large Pathmark supermarket, but the clock tower at the corner of Atlantic Avenue and 92nd Street has somehow made it through the years.

The Lalance & Grosjean wood-framed row houses are still there between 85th and 86th Streets, though the ones on 95th Avenue are less modernized than the ones on 97th Avenue, so they are closer in appearance to when the workers occupied them.

121 Liberty Avenue Traffic Lights
Liberty Avenue between about 116th and 123rd Streets

Little olive-green traffic lights with serrated exteriors and fluted bases once were to NYC streets what the passenger pigeon was to the skies. They weren't on every corner but as often as not, two of these, catercornered, were enough to control traffic and allow people to cross the street in peace. Practically none remained by the beginning of the twenty-first century.

In the late 1950s or early 1960s, it was determined to phase the "olives" out and replace them with cylindrical-shafted poles. Some of the new poles carried two lights, but as time went on they all came to include the amber caution light in the middle. After a while, three-color traffic lights became required by law, and this marked the end for most of the remaining "olives," though a handful that were outfitted with three color lights still remain standing.

On Liberty Avenue in Ozone Park, you can still find a stretch of two color traffic lights, both under the El and east of it, on either side of Lefferts Boulevard. The amber function is achieved by flashing both red and green at once at the end of the green cycle.

Jamaica is one of Queens' oldest neigh-borhoods and has a number of remaining Colonial-era buildings. In 1655, Dutch settlers purchased acreage from the Canarsee Indians in the general vicinity of the now-vanished Beaver Pond and set up a small community they named Rustdorp ("peaceful village"). The British took over in 1664 and renamed it Jamaica, an English transliteration of "Jameco," the Indian tribe that lived near what is now called Jamaica Bay. Jamaica originally included all lands south of the present Grand Central Parkway (which explains why Jamaica is so far away from its bay).

Beginning in the 1960s, Jamaica suffered a decline. It was thought that business would improve somewhat when the El originally extending to 169th Street was rerouted underground in 1988, but Jamaica had to wait until crime abated in the 1990s to stage any kind of comeback. Today it is a busy shopping mecca once again, and its Colonial relics are an added attraction to its commercial role.

SUBWAY: 🄴 or **🄹** to Jamaica Center–Parsons–Archer

BUS: Q54 or **Q56** on Jamaica Avenue; **Q6, Q8, Q9, Q30, Q31,** or **Q41** on Jamaica or Archer Avenues; **Q110** on Parsons Boulevard or Jamaica Avenue; **Q4, Q5, Q42, Q83, Q84,** or **Q85** on Archer Avenue; **Q112** or **Q113** on 153rd Street, Parsons Boulevard, Archer Avenue, or Guy Brewer Boulevard; **Q43** on Hillside Avenue; **Q20A, Q20B,** or **Q44** on Sutphin Boulevard and Archer Avenue

122 Red-Brick Pavement

89th Avenue, between Sutphin Boulevard and 144th Street

A short stretch of 89th Avenue between 144th Street and Sutphin Boulevard, just north of Jamaica Avenue, preserves decades-old red-brick pavement. Flat bricks poke out from beneath the asphalt in a few locations around town, from Bennett Court in Bay Ridge to large swaths of the West Village in Manhattan, but this is the longest stretch of red-brick pavement that I've yet found in NYC. Differences in coloration indicate that sections of the bricks have been torn up over the years, but at least there's been an effort made to replace them with bricks of an approximate color.

On 145th Street, where crossing lines would ordinarily be painted, here they're *bricked* in—white bricks replace red ones to form the lines. A Jamaica Avenue street repaving project covered 89th Avenue between Jamaica Avenue and 144th Street with asphalt, but so far, this two-block stretch has been saved.

123 Prospect Cemetery

159th Street, south of Archer Avenue

Prospect Cemetery, entered from 159th Street, south of Archer Avenue and the Long Island Rail Road overpass, is probably the oldest cemetery in Queens, and perhaps the entire city. Records show that it dates to the 1660s. The cemetery boasts fifty-three Revolutionary War veterans, forty-three Civil War veterans, three Spanish–American War veterans, and many interments from prominent Long Island families, such as the Lefferts. The cemetery was designated a city landmark in 1977.

The cemetery's chapel, known as the Chapel of the Sisters, was built in 1856 and

Thomas Wiggins's 1728 stone

commemorates builder Nicholas Ludlum's three daughters, who passed away in their youth. The chapel's interior has been stabilized and is no longer in danger of collapse.

One of the more intriguing of the cemetery's interments is Elias Baylis. A blind churchman from Jamaica, he was held by the British in a prison ship; in 1776 he was released, only to collapse and die in the arms of his daughter while "crossing Brooklyn Ferry." His story is carved on his stone.

For more information, contact the Prospect Cemetery Association at www.prospectcemeteryassociation.org.

124 St. Monica's Steeple
160th Street, south of Archer Avenue

Only the bell tower remains after a succession of fires at St. Monica's Roman Catholic Church on 160th Street, south of the LIRR overpass. It was built in a Romanesque style between 1854 and 1857; the final collapse came in May 1998, leaving it in its present condition. Its cemetery is still intact at Liberty Avenue and Brewer Boulevard. In 2005, York College constructed a child care center here, using the tower as a façade on the 160th Street side.

125 King Mansion
Jamaica Avenue and 153rd Street

The Rufus King Mansion, or King Manor, stands in King Park on Jamaica Avenue between 150th and 153rd Streets. The house was originally built in 1730 along the main route to Brooklyn Ferry at the foot of today's Fulton Street. Rufus King (1755–1827) was a youthful representative at the Continental Congress from 1784 to 1786, a U.S. senator from New York in 1789 and also served from 1813 to 1825, a minister (ambassador) to Great Britain from 1796 to 1803, and ran unsuccessfully for president as a Federalist against James Monroe in 1816.

King Manor became a museum in 1992. It features period furnishings, including objects owned by the King family. Archaeological digs on the grounds have revealed much about life in Jamaica in the early 1800s. Call (718) 206-0545 for hours.

126 Grace Episcopal Church
Jamaica Avenue and Parsons Boulevard

This high-steepled church dates to 1862, replacing an earlier 1822 edifice that burned the year before. The parish itself goes back to 1702, and the surrounding churchyard to 1734. Rufus King and his descendants were enthusiastic parishioners. His son, New York Governor John King, contributed a marble baptismal font to the old church in 1847 and an organ in 1862. Rufus King and his wife, Mary, are buried in the Grace churchyard.

Oddly, an old painted ad for Castro Convertibles faces the churchyard and is not visible from anywhere else. The "first to conquer living space" seems to want to conquer space in the other world, as well.

127 La Casina
160th Street, north of Jamaica Avenue

A marvelous Art Moderne streamlined building front can be seen at 90-33 160th Street. It was built in 1934, when Jamaica was a modest entertainment hub, as La Casina, a nightclub. Its two stepped pyramids flank a marquee-like overhang.

128 First Presbyterian Church
164th Street, north of Jamaica Avenue

Yet another in Jamaica's collection of very old church buildings is the First Presbyterian Church at 89-60 164th Street. Jamaica's Presbyterian congregation, founded in 1663, may be the oldest continuous one in the U.S. The church is housed in three buildings on 164th Street, two of which are very old.

The original congregation's stone church stood from 1699 to 1813 at what is now Jamaica Avenue and Union Hall Street. During the Revolutionary War, the British commandeered it and imprisoned patriots there. In 1813, it was replaced with what is now the church sanctuary in a location at Jamaica Avenue and 163rd Street. It was placed on logs and pulled by mule to its present location in 1920. The First

Presbyterian's manse, or staff living quarters, was erected on Jamaica Avenue in 1834, and was moved to a location just to the north of the sanctuary, well back from the street, that same year. In 1925, the Magill Memorial Building, a combination of church, auditorium, and library, that also included a gym and bowling alleys, was built just north of the manse.

129 Sidewalk Clock
Jamaica Avenue and Union Hall Street

Jamaica's only working sidewalk clock, on the southwest corner of Jamaica Avenue and Union Hall Street, originally stood at 161-11 Jamaica Avenue and was likely built around 1900. It was restored and moved to its present location in 1989, directly across the street from the former site of Gertz, one of Jamaica's largest department stores.

130 Loew's Valencia
Jamaica Avenue and 165th Street

One of the benefits of the Jamaica El being torn down in 1978 is that the Loew's Valencia, at 165-11 Jamaica Avenue, can now

be seen from this very busy stretch of the avenue. The theater, designed by John Eberson in a Baroque Spanish style, opened in 1929. It has an intricately fashioned brick and terra-cotta façade designed to be viewed from up close (the platforms of the Jamaica El were a few feet away). You really have to stop for several minutes to take in all the cherub heads, seashells, and other decorative elements. The Valencia is now a church, the Tabernacle of Prayer, which thankfully has retained most of Eberson's details, inside and out.

Addisleigh Park and St. Albans

Many of the greatest jazz and big band artists were either born, spent a great deal of their lives in, or died in Queens. Southern Queens' ascendance as a mecca for jazz musicians began in 1923 when Clarence Williams, a successful performer and entrepreneur from Plaquemine, Louisiana, purchased a home and eight lots at 171-37 108th Avenue. Anticipating the increasing popularity of jazz in the north, Williams moved to New York with his wife, singer Eva Taylor, in 1923. Desiring open spaces reminiscent of his upbringing in the Louisiana delta, Williams made his home in Queens. He would be the first in a line of jazz musicians to come to southern Queens. The area, named Addisleigh Park, was formally developed in 1926 with several blocks of Tudor-style homes. Addisleigh Park and St. Albans were mostly farmland until the 1890s, when a small commercial community began to take shape around Farmers and Linden Boulevards.

Among St. Albans/Addisleigh Park's galaxy of stars were William "Count" Basie, who arrived in Addisleigh Park in 1946; his home at Adelaide Road and 175th Street still stands. His neighbors were Ella Fitzgerald, who lived on Murdock Avenue between 179th and 180th Streets; Milt Hinton, at 113th Avenue and Marne Place; and Lena Horne, born in Brooklyn, who lived on 178th Street between 112th and Murdock Avenues; John Coltrane; Russell and Illinois Jacquet, and Fats Waller. Many other jazz musicians also called the area home.

The Flushing Council on Culture and the Arts runs informative tours through the neighborhood. For information, call (718) 463-7700.

QUEENS

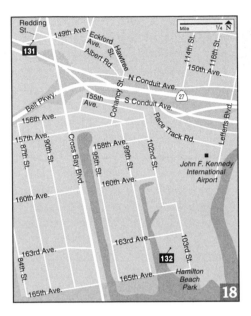

When developers **Benjamin Hitchcock** and Charles Denton built many small houses immediately south of Woodhaven in the 1870s, they chose a name for the area that would be evocative of fresh air and cool breezes far away from congested Manhattan: Ozone Park.

William Howard's resort complex was built on the shores of Jamaica Bay at the turn of the nineteenth century and became a ritzy bathing and boating center—quite a change from its earlier incarnation when the shoreline was bordered by fishing shacks. Howard, a glove manufacturer by trade, built the majestic Hotel Howard in 1899 at the foot of today's 98th Street. A spectacular fire brought it down in 1907, after which the meadows and marshes were landfilled, Hawtree and Shellbank Basins were dug out, and a residential community moved in. Recreational boating is a popular pastime for Howard Beachers today, yet some vestiges of its fishing village past are still around.

SUBWAY: Ⓐ to 80th Street, 88th Street, Aqueduct–North Conduit, or Howard Beach–JFK Airport

BUS: Q11 on Cross Bay Boulevard, Albert Road, or 104th Street; **Q21** on Cross Bay Boulevard; **Q7** on Sutter Avenue; **B15** on South Conduit Avenue

 **131** Southside Burial Ground
Redding Street, Albert Road, and 149th Avenue

Yet another of Queens' many vest-pocket cemeteries can be found in the triangle formed by Redding Street, Albert Road, and 149th Avenue: Southside Burial Ground. It was originally the family plot of the Van Wicklen farming family who settled in Ozone Park in the 1660s and whose descendants lived here well into the twentieth century. The plot contains seventy-nine graves, of which only four tombstones remain: Charles H. Monroe (d. 1872) and his brother Leander (d. 1873) share a stone; George Earney (d. 1909); Jannet, wife of Garret Van Wicklen (d. 1891); and a stone which has toppled to the ground and is unreadable.

132 West Hamilton Beach
102nd Street, south of 160th Avenue

South of the renovated Howard Beach subway-AirTrain station, in a narrow spit of land between the train tracks, Hawtree Basin and Grassy Bay (an arm of Jamaica Bay), you'll find West Hamilton Beach

(earlier called Ramblersville), an isolated neighborhood with a street layout all its own, seemingly independent from NYC. Hawtree Basin was dredged by William Howard soon after his grand hotel and resort burned down in 1907. The area west of Hawtree Basin had a grid network of streets and model homes built on it.

You are never far from the water in this part of town. Small channels and canals meander through the area, and boating is the chief recreation. Shacks, some abandoned, face the channels. On occasion, a boardwalk bridge is necessary to get from one house to another. Tacked-up signs on telephone poles denote local streets like Broadway and Bayview Avenue.

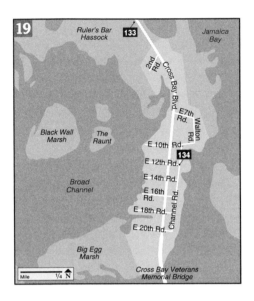

Nestled in the middle of Jamaica Bay is an island known as Broad Channel, named for the waterway through Jamaica Bay which it borders. The Jamaica Bay Wildlife Refuge and a proud, insular neighborhood can be found on this small strip of land. Cross Bay Boulevard is the main artery and carries traffic between Broad Channel and the mainland, as well as to the Rockaway peninsula. Many Broad Channel families have been there for two or three generations.

The 18,000-acre bay was once thought of as NYC's next big commercial port, but those dreams never came to fruition. Instead, it was placed under the jurisdiction of the NYC Parks Department in 1938 by Parks Commissioner Robert Moses, and in 1974, 9,000 acres were transferred to the new Gateway National Urban Recreational Area. Moses had been defeated in an effort to oust all Broad Channelers and make the entire island a wildlife refuge. A smaller refuge was created as part of the deal that brought the subway to Broad Channel.

The town of Broad Channel was largely built by the Broad Channel Corporation, which in the 1910s filled in marshes and rented parcels of land for $116 per year for anyone building a summer home in the area. By this time, however, Jamaica Bay began to be too polluted for any commercial fishing to be feasible.

The Roaring Twenties brought Prohibition and rum-running on the isolated island, which had no vehicular connection to the rest of NYC until Cross Bay Boulevard was built in 1925. When the Broad Channel Corporation went bankrupt in 1939, the city took title to all of the homes on the island (residents did not truly own their own homes until the 1980s, when "tenants" finally purchased the land from the city). Broad Channel did not have sewers until 1988, and it is still protected by a proud volunteer fire department.

SUBWAY: Ⓐ and **Ⓢ** (shuttle from the Rockaway Peninsula) to Broad Channel

BUS: Q21 on Cross Bay Boulevard; **Q53** (express from Woodside)

133 Jamaica Bay Wildlife Refuge
Cross Bay Boulevard, north of 2nd Road

Jamaica Bay Wildlife Refuge is part of the Gateway National Urban Recreational Area, which oversees more than 9,000 acres in northern Broad Channel. The refuge offers one of the very best opportunities to observe migrating wildlife, and its trails offer a wide, flat expanse with views of Coney Island to the west and midtown Manhattan to the northwest. By bus, the best way to get there is to take the 7 train to Woodside–61st Street, get the Q53 bus at 61st and Roosevelt Avenues, and ask the driver to let you know when you arrive at the refuge. The bus runs express all the way to the Rockaways, with stops at the refuge and Broad Channel. The Wildlife Refuge can be contacted at (718) 318-4340.

134 Houses on Stilts

Channel Drive and East 12th Road

Channel Drive is just south of the IND A train subway stop. Seemingly flimsy wooden walkways lead to homes built on stilts over Jamaica Bay. At high tide, water rapidly fills the grassy area below.

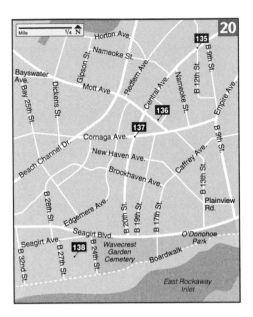

Far Rockaway, the eastern end of the Rockaway peninsula, is a Miss Havisham–esque doyenne whose beauty faded long ago. No border between NYC and any surrounding community could be more stark: this is where the suburban ritziness of Nassau County's Five Towns (Inwood, Hewlett, Lawrence, Woodmere, and Cedarhurst) meets inner-city grit. Tiffany-windowed churches stand near urban housing projects. Far Rockaway, however, is still a thriving neighborhood containing surprising historic elements that make it ripe for urban exploration.

The Canarsee Indians occupied what would become Far Rockaway and the Rockaway peninsula for thousands of years before the arrival of Europeans.

Surprisingly, their ancient name for the place has stuck. "Rekowacky" meant "place of our people."

Far Rockaway was so named for its distance from the older town of Near Rockaway (now called East Rockaway). Both towns were originally in Queens County, but Near Rockaway became a part of the new Nassau County when Queens' three eastern counties decided to secede in 1898, the same year Queens became part of NYC.

SUBWAY: Ⓐ to Mott Avenue

BUS: **Q31** or **Q32** on Central Avenue and Beach 20th Street; **Q22** on Beach 20th Street; **Q22A** on Bayswater and Mott Avenues; **Q113** on Beach 9th Street and Mott Avenue

135 Sage Memorial Church
Central Avenue and Sage Street

Financier and philanthropist Russell Sage (1816–1906) left a considerable fortune to his widow, Margaret Olivia Slocum Sage (1828–1918), who founded Russell Sage College of Troy, New York, and funded the magnificent First Presbyterian Church, aka the Sage Memorial Church on Central Avenue and Sage Street. It was built in 1909 by architects Cram, Goodhue & Ferguson and features stained-glass windows designed by Louis Comfort Tiffany.

136 Beth-El Temple
Mott Avenue and Beach 18th Street

At Mott Avenue and Beach 18th Street you will find a small wooden chapel that has accrued notability by its survival amid the twentieth-century brick architecture

architect Thomas Lamb and contained approximately 1,730 seats. Its principal competitor was the RKO Columbia, which stood about a block away; it's now a parking lot. The Strand later became a movie theater, but has been closed for nearly a quarter century. Only its columned façade remains.

that grew up alongside it. The small, steepled St. John's Episcopal Church's Trinity Chapel, built in 1887, is now the Beth-El Temple.

137 RKO Strand Theatre

Beach 20th Street and Cornaga Avenue

The Strand Theater opened as a vaudeville palace in 1919, and saw Al Jolson and Sophie ("Last of the Red Hot Mamas") Tucker tread its boards. It was designed by theater

138 Remaining Bungalows

Beach 24th to Beach 28th Street, south of Seagirt Boulevard

A touch of Far Rock's seasonal legacy can be seen in this row of bungalows. Small houses like this once lined each and every street from Wavecrest (a planned suburban community built in the late 1800s) all the way to Rockaway Park, about 3 miles west. Bungalows are small houses built for seasonal use, but in some cases, they have come to be occupied year round.

From Beach 24th to Beach 27th Street, south of Seagirt Avenue, a group of well-kept bungalows attempts to hold on. The Beachside Bungalow Preservation Association of Far Rockaway has been set up in an effort to preserve them. For more information, visit www.preserve.org/bungalow.

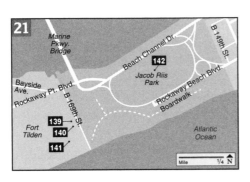

In decades past, New York City has been well protected from foreign attack by two large forts in Queens, one at its southern coast (Fort Tilden) and the other at its northernmost point (Fort Totten). Fort Tilden, near the western edge of the Rockaway peninsula, was conceived as a coastal artillery station with cannons capable of reaching any battleship afloat at the time. It was designed to keep an attacking force far enough out at sea to prevent a bombardment of communication, manufacturing, and shipbuilding facilities, while also training National Guards who would man the guns in times of emergency. The fort became part of the Gateway National Recreation Area in 1974. Call the Fort Tilden Visitor center at (718) 318-4300.

Immediately east of Fort Tilden is the Riis Park recreational area, named for crusading journalist and photographer Jacob Riis (1849–1914) who made his home in Richmond Hill, Queens, in 1886. In 1887, Riis photographed the squalid, inhumane conditions prevalent in NYC's tenements, and his 1890 book *How the Other Half Lives* has been an influential text. His cause was taken up by Police Commissioner Theodore Roosevelt, who encouraged legislation that would help ease the burden on NYC's poorest.

SUBWAY: None

BUS: Q22 on Rockaway Beach Boulevard; **Q35** over Marine Parkway Bridge and on Newport Avenue

139 Nike Missile

A deactivated Nike missile is mounted in front of Fort Totten's Ryan Visitor Center. Such missiles can intercept targets in the stratosphere at twice the speed of sound at a range of 18 to 23 miles.

140 Battery Harris

Fort Tilden's main armament, as first conceived in 1924, was a pair of 16-inch cannon known collectively as Battery Harris I and II. These guns were originally placed out in the open and were able to turn a full 360 degrees to cover a range of 28 miles. This allowed them to reach as far as Long Island Sound, but their primary function was to prevent attack from the east and south.

In 1939, as World War II broke out, it was considered prudent to cover the battery with a casement of thick concrete. This would prevent the battery from being turned on NYC in case a foreign raid on Fort Tilden was successful and would also prevent the guns from being taken out in an air attack. The concrete canopies were completed in 1942. A staircase has been constructed to allow visitors to view a 360-degree panorama of New York Harbor from the top of the Battery Harris I.

141 Magazine Remnants

Magazines were installed at intervals in Fort Tilden. These were ammunition storehouses connected by a standard-gauge railway to a wharf on Rockaway Inlet, at which supplies would be unloaded. The remains of the Fort Tilden railway, as well as a few railroad ties, can be seen faintly in some of the roads. This railroad was not connected in any way to the LIRR Rockaway Branch (later absorbed by the NYC subway in the 1950s).

142 Riis Park

Riis Park was one of NYC's first formal seaside parks after Coney Island became well-established; it was developed by Robert Moses around 1932. Riis Park's 1930s bathhouse and boardwalk clock are both landmarked. The park also features a truly immense parking lot; only the one at Orchard Beach in the Bronx rivals it in size.

a.

b.

c.

d.

a. *Humpback street sign: Willoughby Street, east of Flatbush Avenue Extension, Brooklyn. These signs were common from the 1910s into the 1960s; the cross street was usually shown in the "hump."*

b. *Street sign: Richmondtown, Staten Island. These were once standard issue on every Staten Island street and road, but these are two of less than ten that are left.*

c. *Hudson's Clothing Store ad, Third Avenue and East 11th Street, Manhattan (since painted over).*

d. *Two 1960s-era yellow Staten Island street signs, installed when borough signs were color coded: Manhattan and Staten Island were yellow, Bronx was blue, Brooklyn was black, and Queens was white. By federal mandate, most street signs were changed to green in the 1980s.*

e. *Metal signs coated in porcelain with the street name in bas-relief were common in Brooklyn from the 1940s into the 1960s. This one can still be found on Corso Court in Gravesend, Brooklyn.*

e.

g.

f.

f. *Charles H. Fletcher's Castoria, a mild stomach remedy, was featured in hundreds of painted ads in NYC and other cities in the early years of the twentieth century. This one can be seen clearly on Archer Avenue, just east of Sutphin Boulevard in Jamaica, Queens.*

g. *Illuminated Eagle Clothes sign, Third Avenue and 6th Street in Brooklyn. Tall signs like this were erected near the elevated IND line that runs nearby.*

h. *Ads for Avignone Pharmacy and Hygrade's Beef Hot Dogs on Bleecker and Downing Streets in Manhattan.*

h.

Staten Island

was first occupied by Europeans in Dutch settlements during the 1640s and 1650s. Those early homesteads were scuttled during the Dutch-Indian War under Directors-General Willem Kieft and Peter Stuyvesant. Permanent settlement in Staten Eylandt (or "State Island,") began in the 1660s in the area now occupied by Fort Wadsworth and South Beach.

The Island became a staging area for British troops during the Revolutionary War's Battle of Long Island in 1776. Redcoats departed from the island and landed at Denyse Ferry in Brooklyn, and the island was occupied until the war's end in 1783. Though many British sympathizers lived on Staten Island, they were forced to house and supply British troops, who largely depleted the island of its forests.

In the nineteenth century, Staten Island became a fishing and industrial mecca with businesses as diverse as oyster cultivation, brewing, and, later, linoleum production. The island was also home to a number of lavish resorts in New Brighton and Port Richmond in the 1830s, and Sailors' Snug Harbor was moved to New Brighton from its original home in Greenwich Village in 1831.

After the Civil War, the Staten Island Ferry and Railroad arrived when the first railroad bridge to New Jersey was built by 1889. The sparsely populated island began to thrive after consolidation, as immigrants from eastern Europe more than doubled its numbers in the early years of the twentieth century. Proctor & Gamble constructed a massive manufacturing center at the north shore in 1907 that became known as Port Ivory, for the company's Ivory Soap. Miller

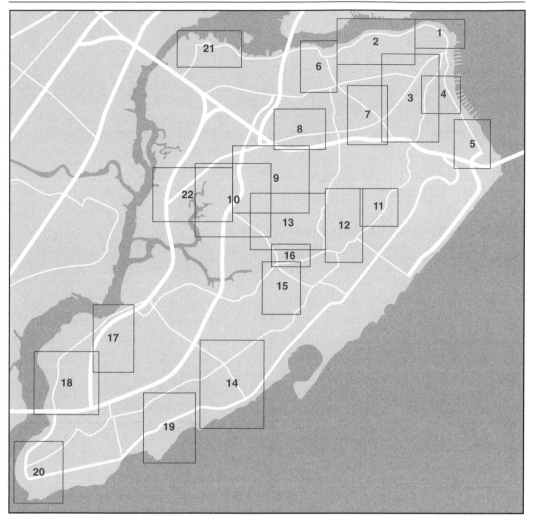

Field in New Dorp became an air defense station and training ground. Staten Island maintained its rural persona with dairy and vegetable farms well into the 1970s.

Despite the construction of two major bridges in 1928, the Outerbridge (named for its engineer, not its position) and the Goethals, both connecting Staten Island to New Jersey, the island has never quite been able to shake the perception that even though it is a part of NYC, it is a separate entity, quite removed from the clamor of the other four boroughs. Even after the completion of the Verrazano-Narrows Bridge in 1964, which gave Staten Island an automobile connection with the rest

of New York City, the island stubbornly retained a small-town, rural feeling. Large swaths of land on the south shore remained woodland. Streets existed on maps only as placeholders for future development. But by the late 1980s, housing construction began to boom and its old undeveloped areas have largely been filled in.

Despite all that, though, Staten Island still maintains large tracts of "wilderness" areas that are carefully maintained by the NYC Parks Department. Discussions are under way for a large public park—possibly to include a golf course—to be built atop the Fresh Kills Landfill in Travis, formerly the world's biggest dump.

ST. GEORGE

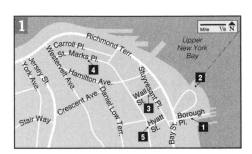

Many New Yorkers, if they have any im-pression of Staten Island at all, know it primarily from the small area of St. George that can be glimpsed when the ferry gets close to the island. St. George is a neighborhood of winding streets (Staten Island, in its flatter areas, follows a rough grid plan, but in hilly areas, streets wind to and fro), San Francisco–style hills, mom-and-pop shops, exquisite Victorian-era architecture, and a few Art Deco masterpieces as well. It's a beehive of activity weekdays, since courts and most governmental administrative buildings are located where Bay Street meets Richmond Terrace, including the imposing Borough Hall with its elegant clock tower, designed by Carrere and Hastings and completed in 1906. Its main hall displays twelve murals depicting early Staten Island life painted by F. C. Stahr. On weekends, St. George is a sleepy place; Bay Street, except for its busy car traffic, seems almost deserted.

St. George was named for land baron George Law, who had acquired waterfront rights at bargain prices. He agreed to relinquish some of the property for a ferry terminal—provided it be named for him! Prominent residents of St. George have been New York Governor Daniel Tompkins and subway bankroller August Belmont.

Since the summer of 2001, when the Richmond County Bank Ballpark opened, St. George has become a baseball hotbed with the arrival of the Class-A Staten Island Yankees. The Manhattan skyline can be seen directly behind the centerfield fence.

BUS, SIR: St. George is the island's bus and Staten Island Railway terminal; many of the island's bus routes begin and end here at the ferry.

1 Ferry Terminal
Bay Street and Richmond Terrace

Until 2005, when a multimillion dollar restoration project was completed, the Staten Island Ferry Terminal Building had remained pretty much unchanged from when it was first built in 1951 (replacing an earlier terminal that had burned down in 1946). It is NYC's only true waterfront railroad-ferry terminal; a railroad has run passenger service from St. George since the 1880s.

Staten Island Railway, formerly known as Staten Island Rapid Transit, extends from the Terminal to Tottenville. There are two defunct branches along the north and south shores of Staten Island; the North Shore branch, which made its last passenger runs in 1953, still has a number of extant remnants. The South Shore branch, which ran to Wadsworth Avenue in South Beach (a tiny, wooden platform that could only accommodate one or two cars) has been almost completely covered by new construction. In Rosebank and South Beach, a surprising artifact can still be ferreted out here and there.

Until 2006, the St. George Terminal featured a couple of very old objects hiding in plain sight: a track indicator with an incandescent green bulb, and an illuminated 1970s-era Hagstrom map that still pretty much gets the job done for the main streets and major routes. The St. George Terminal is the only station in the entire system where payment is required, via MetroCard. Since the majority of the railroad's patrons use it to get to and from the ferry, they must pass through the card-controlled turnstiles here.

🦪 2 Staten Island Lighthouse Museum Site

Borough Place, near Bay Street

Lighthouses surround Staten Island, some of them readily visible with the naked eye. One, the Robbin's Reef Lighthouse, is in Upper New York Bay and is closely passed by the Staten Island Ferry each day. In the early twentieth century, it was maintained by a woman named Kate Walker, who for thirty years rowed out to the light and back. The 60-foot-tall Great Beds Lighthouse can be spotted by sharp-eyed observers off Wards Point, the southernmost point in New York state. Thirty-five-foot-tall Old Orchard Lighthouse can be seen

from the end of Crooke's Point in the Great Kills Park National Recreation Area. In addition, there are four lighthouses located on Staten Island proper.

A walk to the end of Borough Place, a dead end off Bay Street along the bus ramps of the Staten Island Ferry Terminal, will reveal a walkway lined with six very old buildings that played important roles in nineteenth-century shipping as part of the United States Lighthouse Service Depot. Four of them, in fact, are on the National Register of Historic Places. The 30-acre site was selected as the location for the National Lighthouse Museum in 1998.

A four-story brick building, known as the Barracks, dates to 1864 and is the oldest building still standing here. It was used by the Lighthouse Service as a depot and was converted to a barracks in the 1940s. The Second French Empire Administration Building was constructed in 1869. It housed the offices of the Superintendent and Engineer of the Depot. The four-story lamp shop, built in 1868, housed the lamp and lens works. Lighthouse lenses can frequently run as large as 18 feet high and weigh hundreds of pounds; therefore, the floors of this building are reinforced with

steel beams and columns. A newer lamp shop, a brick building dating to 1907, is nearby. The Dutch-roofed machine shop (1912) housed the construction of lightship anchors, chain, and buoys. It is currently being refitted to house the first formal Museum exhibits. For more information, visit www.lighthousemuseum.org.

3 Staten Island Museum

75 Stuyvesant Place at Wall Street

Founded in 1881 as the Natural Science Association of Staten Island, and opened to the public in 1907, the organization formally known as the Staten Island Museum of the Staten Island Institute of Arts & Sciences has been located in its own four-story building atop one of the borough's steeper hills since 1918.

The Staten Island Museum's permanent collection consists of "Above the Molding," a collection of paintings of New York Harbor and the Staten Island Ferry; specimens from the museum's vast insect collection (entomologist William T. Davis was a co-founder of the institute); and an exhibition centering on Staten Island's first human inhabitants, the Lenape Indians, whose artifacts date back over 12,000 years.

The institute also has a vast collection of: 55,000 photographs, 6,600 postcards, 3,100 maps, and 15,000 books—the largest collection of Staten Island–related materials anywhere in the world.

The Staten Island Museum is open every day from Tuesday to Sunday, and on Monday by appointment. Its archives can be viewed on Tuesday, Wednesday, and Thursday. For hours, call (718) 727-1135 or go to www.statenislandmuseum.org.

4 St. George Houses

Between Hamilton and Westervelt Avenues

St. Mark's Place may be Staten Island's most beautiful street, at least the stretch between Nicholas Street and Westervelt Avenue. Nearly a score of old-style mansions and buildings constructed in the late 1890s line the quiet byway.

At 103, 115, 119, and 125 St. Mark's Place, you will find four eclectic and finely detailed Shingle-style dwellings designed by Edward Alfred Sargent (1842–1914), perhaps the greatest architect who worked extensively in Staten Island. At the corner of St. Mark's Place is another Sargent creation, a peaked and gabled mansion commissioned in 1885 by the president of the Richmond County Medical Society: 33 Westervelt Avenue. Between Nicholas Street and St. Peter's Place are, for the moment, four Victorian-era homes at 202, 204, 208, and 216 Richmond Terrace; the Pavilion on the Terrace catering hall, a Greek Revival building at 404 Richmond Terrace, is the oldest building in the area, dating to 1835. It is the last remaining of four such doric-columned buildings.

Phelps Place is a tiny cul-de-sac on Hamilton Avenue a little east of its junction with Westervelt Avenue. The mansion at its rear is notable not only as an example of Shingle-style architecture, but it was also part of the estate of millionaire banker Anson Phelps Stokes I. His son, Isaac Newton Phelps Stokes, became perhaps the borough of Manhattan's greatest historian. Stokes's six-volume *Iconography of Manhattan Island*, published between 1915 and 1928, presents hundreds of thoroughly annotated maps and prints that delineate Manhattan's progress from before the Colonial era to the twentieth century.

5 St. George Theatre

Hyatt Street and St. Mark's Place

With so many of NYC's grandest theaters either under renovation or being considered for renovation, it's heartwarming to see one such magnificent silver-screen palace fully restored and ready to make magic once again.

The exterior of the St. George Theater at 35 Hyatt Street, designed by Eugene DeRosa and opened in 1929, is relatively unimpressive. Only upon entering the theater does its grandeur evoke any awe. Its interior, based on Spanish Baroque architecture, has been given tender loving care by a dedicated band of workers led by owner Rosemary Cappozalo, and will now serve as a performing arts center and luxury banquet hall.

STATEN ISLAND

The New Brighton neighborhood was originally conceived in 1834 by a group of wealthy businessmen. Its street pattern, curving around the high hills fronting Staten Island's waterfront, survives to the present; the organization's name, the New Brighton Association (named in honor of Brighton, a British resort town), became the name of the entire region, which stretches from St. George on the east to Hamilton Park on the west.

BUS: S40 on Richmond Terrace; **S44** on Richmond Terrace, Lafayette Avenue, and Henderson Avenues

Hamilton Park Cottage

🐾6 Hamilton Park Houses

105 Franklin Avenue, 66 Harvard Avenue, and 1 and 22 Pendleton Place

This neighborhood, one of Staten Island's most impressively concentrated areas of beautiful architecture, was begun by developer Charles Kennedy Hamilton in 1853.

In 1859, he built what is now known as the Hamilton Park Cottage at 105 Franklin Avenue with the assistance of German architect Carl Pfeiffer. Its triple-arched entrance, known as a loggia, begs to be photographed.

The oldest country home in the area, 66 Harvard Avenue, was built between 1845 and 1853 for the Pritchard family.

On Pendleton Place, which curves off from Franklin Avenue four blocks south of Richmond Terrace, are two residences built for William S. Pendleton, an engraver, lithographer, realtor, and owner of a ferryboat company: 22 Pendleton Place (a Gothic Revival villa built in 1855) and 1 Pendleton Place, which dates from 1860 (a larger Stick-style mansion across the street), were both designed by British architect Charles Duggin.

The tower at 1 Pendleton is of special note. It is square for the first three stories, then becomes an octagonal tower with a conical, bracket-supported roof.

7 Tysen-Neville House

Richmond Terrace and Tysen Street

The Tysen-Neville House (or the Neville-Tysen House) at 806 Richmond Terrace, near Tysen Street, was built around 1800. It acquired its porches and hexagonal cupola around 1910.

In the 1800s, retired seamen from nearby Sailors' Snug Harbor frequented a tavern located in this building called the

Old Stone Jug. It was saved from demolition in 1991 by a coalition including the NYC Landmarks Preservation Commission, which provided a loan of $91,000 for repairs. The house is currently privately owned.

Snug Harbor staff building

8 Sailors' Snug Harbor

Richmond Terrace, between Tysen Street and Snug Harbor Road

Sailors' Snug Harbor, an 83-acre national historic landmark district, was founded in the Washington Square area of Manhattan by Robert Richard Randall when he specified that his fortune be left to the care of retired seamen who had no other means of support. Randall was the bachelor son of a privateer and knew well the toll a life at sea can take on the body and psyche. After Randall's death in 1801, more than twenty years was spent in adjudicating claims to Randall's fortune, and by 1821, lower Manhattan had grown considerably and land for the sort of retreat Randall had had in mind was unavailable. But there was a solution in Staten Island: Snug Harbor trustees purchased Isaac Housman's farm in then-rural Richmond County in the 1830s, and architect Minard Lefever was commissioned to build Snug Harbor's magnificent Greek Revival edifices, only some of which remain today.

At its peak, Snug Harbor was home to more than 1,000 seamen, but by 1976, operations had relocated to North Carolina. The buildings were allowed to deteriorate

for a while, and some were demolished, but seven have been landmarked and Snug Harbor, open to the public in 1976, has become a NYC cultural center. The institute includes the Staten Island Botanical Garden and Children's Museum.

Looking through north gate (through a fence that has been in place since 1842) on Richmond Terrace, your gaze immediately falls on the classically arched Main Hall, built in 1833 and designed by Minard Lefever, originally the administration building. Under the Obelisk in front of the Main Hall are the remains of Snug Harbor founder Randall; he is also memorialized in a sculpture near the Institute of Arts and Sciences.

The Newhouse Center for Contemporary Art, accessible from the rear of the Main Hall, exhibits modern paintings, sculpture, and mixed media installations, and presents performance art, photography, and crafts.

Next to the Main Hall is the Noble Maritime Museum, in a building dating to 1844, which houses a permanent collection tracing the history of Snug Harbor.

Built in 1892, the Music Hall is the second-oldest concert hall in New York City. Only Carnegie Hall is older—by a year. It has been restored by noted architect Rafael Viñoly and is now used year-round for performing arts, concerts, and musicals.

Along Cottage Road you will find the main attractions of Staten Island Botanical Garden which features: the Chinese Scholars' Garden, the Butterfly and Sensor Gardens, and the Connie Gretz Secret Garden ("secret" because it is walled in by hedges). There are also five charming 1880s-era buildings originally home to Snug Harbor staff. Near the west gate at the Snug Harbor Road entrance is the Governor's House, which was originally the Snug Harbor bookkeeper's office. The Chinese Scholars' Garden, accessible for a separate admission, is notable for its collection of intricately carved teakwood bridges.

Snug Harbor is open year-round. Call (718) 448-2500 or consult www.snug-harbor.org for hours.

🐚9 Allison Pond

Prospect and Brentwood Avenues

Allison Pond is a small glacial leftover that once provided water to nearby Sailors' Snug Harbor. The pond and its surrounding park, once the property of engineer George William Allison (1888–1939), were bequeathed to the city in 1943. The pond is stocked with fish for recreational angling.

🔫10 Cruser House

1262 Richmond Terrace at Pelton Avenue

One of Staten Island's oldest homes is the Cornelius Cruser House. Like many of NYC's oldest Colonial-era homes, it was originally a very small dwelling that was added to by successive owners over the years. The oldest part of the Cruser House is a stone cottage built in 1722 by the Dutch immigrant Cornelius Van Santvoord; Cruser added the central section in 1770, while Daniel Pelton built the two-story brick section in the 1830s.

The house was occupied by General Courtlandt Skinner of the American Tories, and he, in turn, put up one Prince William Henry, who later became King William IV of England, Queen Victoria's predecessor. Legend has it that infamous spy Major John André also stayed here.

11 Staten Island Cemetery

Richmond Terrace and Alaska Street

More than any other borough, Staten Island has many small cemeteries, some well-kept and cared for, others in a complete state of abandonment with broken and vandalized headstones. Staten Island Cemetery falls somewhere in the middle. It's accessible from 1642 Richmond Terrace by what looks like a driveway up a hill alongside an auto body shop at Alaska Street, but expands into a fairly large, 1.5-acre plot. The first interments here in the 1820s were relatives of Joseph Ryers, a freed slave who had purchased the property next to the Trinity Chapel of St. Andrews here in 1812. Nearby Trinity Place was named for the church.

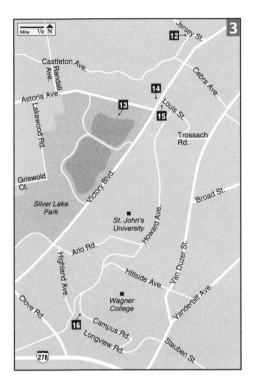

Grymes Hill is easily seen from the Sta- pleton Staten Island Railway Station, looming over Staten Island's north-shore communities. Grymes, along with Ward, Emerson, Todt, and other mid-island hills, are the legacies of a glacier that reached its southernmost limit and provides NYC with its only mountainous areas. From their summits can be glimpsed both the towers of Manhattan and the Watchung Mountains in northwest New Jersey. Vistas are precious and few, though; much of these hills are occupied by private estates. Grymes Hill itself is named for the widow of the first governor of Louisiana, Suzette Grymes, whose mansion, Capo di Monte, was one of the first in the area. It was built by Major George Howard between 1830 and 1836. The region was home to prominent families: shipping scion Edward Cunard's mansion is now a part of the Wagner College campus and boasts a magnificent view of Manhattan from Howard Avenue;

and the ever-present Vanderbilts, who also owned estates on the hill. St. John's University is also represented here with a campus on Howard Avenue, formerly called Serpentine Road, not for its snaking route but for the native rock.

BUS: **S48**, **S61**, **S62**, **S66**, or **S67** on Victory Boulevard

🚋 12 S. R. Smith Infirmary
Castleton Avenue and Jersey Street

The Samuel R. Smith Infirmary (aka The Frost Building), at 101 Castleton Avenue, was built in 1889 by architect Alfred Barlow; it has housed Staten Island Hospital and a training school for nurses during its long history. Herman Melville's sister-in-law (her husband was director of Snug Harbor in the 1890s) was a secretary here. The hospital moved out in 1979; for a time the building was marketed as condominiums, which would at least have kept it in decent condition, but the building has been left to the ravages of the elements for more than two decades. Nevertheless, it continues to make a distinct impression with its four conical towers.

13 Silver Lake Park ➤
Victory Boulevard and Forest Avenue

Silver Lake was made part of New York's Catskill water supply system as a reser-

voir from 1913 to 1971. The reservoir today is part of the drainage system for underground storage tanks. The 209 acres stretching between Victory Boulevard, Forest Avenue, and Lakewood Road, exist today due to the efforts of Staten Island writer John DeMorgan, who pressed the State Assembly Committee on Cities to appropriate funds to establish Silver Lake Park in February 1900.

Silver Lake Park provides the best public vista in the Grymes Hill area, especially from about 630 Victory Boulevard, in front of Notre Dame Academy. Clear days here provide breathtaking views of New Jersey's Watchung Mountains as well as Newark Airport and Newark itself.

14 Spectacular Views
Victory Boulevard and Louis Street

From Victory Boulevard at about Louis Street, midtown Manhattan seems to float on air directly in front of you. Walk up Louis Street and, from its intersection at Sunrise Terrace (the street lives up to its name in the AM), there's another priceless view of the city.

15 Hero Park
Louis Street and Howard Avenue

On steep Louis Street, where it meets Howard Avenue, is Hero Park. Opened in 1920,

it was dedicated to 144 Staten Island soldiers who perished in World War I. The small, picturesque park is on land donated by Dr. Louis Dreyfus, a wealthy chewing gum manufacturer.

In the middle of the park is a large, irregularly shaped granite boulder. The rock, according to a sign removed decades ago, had been known as Sugarloaf Rock; tablets placed on the rock once identified the 144 veterans, but it has been lost to vandalism. The NYC Parks Department wound up removing them rather than continue to combat the miscreants.

16 Augustinian Retreat House
Campus Road, near Howard Avenue

This ravaged building, now hidden under a thick canopy of weeds, ailanthus, and ivy, was the home of the Augustinian Academy, a Roman Catholic institution incorporated in 1870. The society purchased this property from Erickson N. Nichols in 1922 and built a prep school here; classes were held until 1969, when it was converted to a retreat house. The Augustinians sold the property in 1985, and it has passed through many hands since, with Wagner College owning it now. The academy's Celtic cross–shaped fountain and bell tower are still discernible.

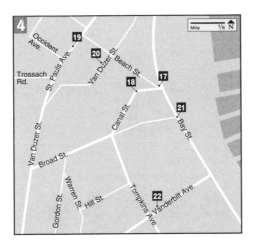

Stapleton and Clifton are two adjacent neighborhoods on Staten Island's northeast coast along Upper New York Bay. The Vanderbilt family held much land here in the early nineteenth century. In 1836, Minthorne Tompkins (the son of Vice President Daniel Tompkins) and merchant William Staples established a ferry to Manhattan and founded the village at Bay and Water Streets. German immigrants built numerous breweries in the area in the 1800s, including Bachmann, Bechtel, and Piels, whose brewery was in business on Staten Island until 1963.

Among the most notable and strangest aspects of Stapleton's history was the presence of the National Football League, which fielded a team known as the Staten Island Stapletons here from 1929 through 1932. The "Stapes" were a semipro team founded by restaurateur Dan Blaine in 1915, who played halfback for the team until 1924. The Stapes started out playing exhibition games against pro teams from the NFL and the 1920s version of the American Football League. In 1929, the Stapes joined the NFL, playing in tiny Thompson's Stadium on Tompkins Avenue, a site now occupied by Stapleton Housing. Led by halfback Ken Strong, a New York University graduate, the Stapletons compiled

a 14–22–9 record against NFL competition in four years. The Stapes then played an exhibition schedule in 1933, with some games against NFL teams, before Blaine folded the team and Strong joined the New York Giants.

BUS: S51, **S74**, or **S76** on Bay Street; **S78** on Van Duzer Street and St. Paul's Avenue

SIR: Stapleton and Clifton Stations

17 Paramount Theater
Bay and Water Streets

Paramount, at 560 Bay Street near Prospect Street, is now likely Staten Island's premier "ghost theater" now that the St. George has been reactivated. It was designed by architects Rapp and Rapp, with a contrasting orange brick façade. It opened in 1935, with a capacity of 2,500 seats and two pipe organs—an extravagant feature during the Depression. In its later days, it became an adult-movie house and then a rock club. The interior has been gutted, but its beautiful outsides are still in view.

STATEN ISLAND

18 Edgewater Village Hall

Canal and Wright Streets

This red-brick Romanesque Revival build-ing designed by Stapleton resident Paul Kuhne in 1889 is Staten Island's only re-maining village hall. Nearby is a band shell, where you can visualize oompah bands and barbershop quartets performing as they must have in the area in the 1800s. Across the park, at the triangle formed by Beach and Water Streets, note the classi-cally domed Staten Island Savings Bank with its twin-columned entrance.

19 St. Paul's Avenue

Between Cebra and Occident Avenues

St. Paul's Avenue runs along Ward and Grymes Hills on Stapleton's western edge. The twisting road, known as Mud Lane in the nineteenth century before the use of macadam was widespread, is the location of several spectacular Victorian-era houses. St. Paul's, along with St. Mark's Place in St. George, is under consideration as a historic district.

Development of the area, known as Sta-

387 St. Paul's Avenue

pleton Heights, was initiated in the 1850s. In the ensuing decades, a variety of wildly ornamental buildings were constructed, including 387 St. Paul's Avenue, opposite Occident Avenue, a Queen Anne built by architect George Kafka for brewer George Bechtel in 1887—likely Staten Island's most beautiful private dwelling. Along St. Paul's Avenue you can also find its name-sake Episcopal church at 225 and Shingle-style buildings at 139 and 231.

20 Van Duzer's Houses ➤

364 and 390 Van Duzer Street

On twisting Van Duzer Street, skirting Ward and Grymes Hills, and parallel to St. Paul's Avenue, there's a group of very old homes. Two feature striking two-story porches with four doric columns apiece: 364 and 390 Van Duzer Street, both built in 1835. The one at 364 was the home of Suzanne Tompkins Smith, daughter of New York Governor and Vice President Daniel Tompkins, and her hus-band, Richard.

364 Van Duzer Street

🚌21 Edgewater Hall
691 Bay Street

Not to be confused with the Edgewater Village Hall in Tappen Park, this three-story red-brick building is one of Stapleton's most distinctive commercial buildings. When built in 1876, the hall was the first home of the Staten Island Savings Bank; the bank's brick arches and vault can still be found in the interior. In the 1970s, the hall was home to a rock club and is now a restaurant.

22 Vanderbilt Avenue Cottages
Vanderbilt Avenue, between Tompkins Avenue and Talbot Place

Clifton has always been associated with the Vanderbilt family; its scion Cornelius operated a ferry to Manhattan here in 1810. In 1900, the firm of Carrere and Hastings built eight houses along the family's namesake street: 110 to 144 Vanderbilt Avenue.

STATEN ISLAND

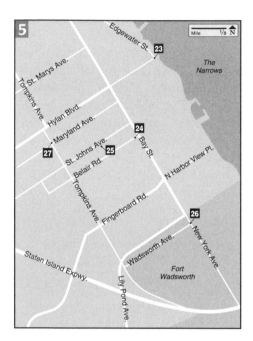

Rosebank is a pleasant village in southeast Staten Island with tree-lined streets and old homes that are gradually giving way to new construction. Beautiful views of the Narrows, the Verrazano-Narrows Bridge, and Bay Ridge, Brooklyn, can be glimpsed from Alice Austen and Arthur Von Briesen Parks. Rosebank is anchored by the campanile of St. Mary's Roman Catholic Church, built in 1857 at 1101 Bay Street at St. Mary's Avenue, and the slim spire of St. John's Episcopal Church built in 1871 at 1331 Bay Street, opposite Belair Road. Rosebank, primarily an Italian neighborhood in the early twenty-first century, has been home to pioneering photographer Alice Austen and Italian unifier Giuseppe Garibaldi.

BUS: S51 on Bay Street; **S52** on Tompkins Avenue

SIR: Clifton Station

23 Alice Austen House
Hylan Boulevard and Edgewater Road

Alice Austen (1866–1952) was born to a prosperous family in what was then a part of Clifton and is now Rosebank. Her father, Edward Munn, disappeared before her birth; her mother, Alice Cornell Austen, moved with her daughter to her parents' house, Clear Comfort, at 2 Hylan Boulevard. Parts of the house date all the way back to 1691.

Alice was introduced to photography by her uncle, Oswald Müller, in 1876, when she was ten. Aside from Müller's original demonstrations, her photographic skills and techniques were entirely self-taught. Her subjects ranged from her family and friends on Staten Island engaging in lawn tennis, bicycling, beach outings, and costume parties. While in Manhattan, she captured images of pushcart vendors, bootblacks, organ grinders, and rag pickers. Austen loved to capture the constant parade of ships that passed in the Narrows, just beyond her front lawn. Her work was intimate, personal, and sensitive toward its subjects.

Austen never thought about selling any of her work, since her family was wealthy and prominent. However, the 1929 stock market crash took her life savings at age sixty-three. After getting by for a number of years by running a tea room, in 1945 she was forced to sell her possessions and move out of the house that had been home to her family for more than 100 years.

At that time, she called on an old friend, Loring McMillen of the Staten Island Historical Society, for assistance. McMillen was able to rescue some of the cardboard boxes in the basement containing 3,500 glass-plate negatives: these comprise the collection of Alice's photographs we have today. Oliver Jensen published several of the pictures in *Life* and *Holiday* in 1951, and the proceeds from the sale allowed Austen to move into a comfortable nursing home, where she remained until her death in 1952.

In 1985 Clear Comfort was refurbished to the way it appeared in Alice's day as a museum. Hundreds of her pictures are on display. The house is open from Thursday to Sunday in spring, summer and fall. Call (718) 816-4506 or go to www.aliceausten. org.

24 Woodland Cottage

33 Belair Road, near Bay Street

On Belair Road, between Bay and Wingham Streets, you'll find the remnants of suburban development that began here in the 1830s, most notably Woodland Cottage at 33–37 Belair Road. The Gothic Revival cottage was built in 1845 and served as the rectory of St. John's Episcopal Church between 1858 and 1869. Of special note are the second-floor casement windows with diamond-shaped panes.

25 Staten Island Rapid Transit Remnant

St. John's Avenue and Clayton Street

At St. John's Avenue and Clifton Street you will find a ten-foot-high concrete slab stamped with the date 1935. This part of Rosebank is burgeoning with development—new houses are going up by the dozens. New residents, no doubt, wonder

what this Ozymandias-like slab signifies. It's a former pylon for Staten Island Rapid Transit, whose South Beach branch crossed St. John's Avenue here until 1953. The line was elevated in 1935, and the concrete supports were identified with that date.

26 Fort Wadsworth

Bay Street at Wadsworth Avenue

The southeastern tip of Staten Island, its closest approach to Long Island, has been protected by fortifications since 1663, when a Dutch blockhouse was established here. The area known as Signal Hill was a crucial site from which to spy approaching British vessels.

Battery Weed (originally called Fort Richmond, but renamed in 1863 for General Stephen Weed after his death at age twenty-nine at Gettysburg), was designed by the U.S. army's chief engineer, General Joseph G. Totten, and was built between 1845 and 1861, while Fort Tompkins was built between 1858 and 1876. Fort Tompkins was renamed Fort Wadsworth for General James S. Wadsworth, who was killed at the Civil War's Battle of the Wilderness in 1864. Staten Island's and Manhattan's Wadsworth Avenues also bear his name.

In September 1995, the fort became part of the National Park System and is open to the public, though part of it is still used by the Coast Guard. You can roam its heights for premium views of the Verrazano-Narrows Bridge along a designated 1.5-mile trail that winds past Battery Weed and other fortifications. Call (718) 354-4500 for general information and hours.

27 Garibaldi-Meucci Museum
Tompkins and Maryland Avenues

From 1851 to 1853, Italian nationalist Giuseppe Garibaldi resided in Rosebank at the home of his friend, Antonio Meucci, now recognized by many as the inventor of the telephone. (He was unable to afford a pat-

ent for his telephone, and Alexander Graham Bell was subsequently recognized as the inventor.) Garibaldi, during his time on Staten Island, worked as a candlemaker in Meucci's factory and fished in the island's many lakes.

In 1907, the house was moved to its present location at 420 Tompkins Avenue. It was surrounded by a pantheon with classical pediments and columns (since removed) erected by the Garibaldi Society proclaiming the house as the Garibaldi Memorial. That seemed to be the modest Meucci's fate: stymied by Bell in life, and overshadowed by Garibaldi in death. Meucci's elaborate monument in the front yard, with depictions of classic Roman mythological tales, was erected in 1923.

Since 1956, the Order of the Sons of Italy has maintained the house as a museum containing many letters and photographs documenting the lives of the inventor and the revolutionary, including examples of Meucci's handmade furniture and a library of rare and out-of-print books. Garibaldi's revolver, which had been with a private collector for many years, was donated to the museum in 2005.

Contact the museum at (718) 442-1608 or visit www.garibaldimeuccimuseum.org.

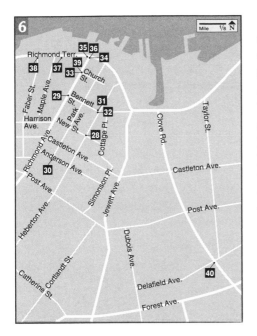

Port Richmond dates back to the 1690s and early 1700s when Dutch and French colonists settled here. After the landowning Haughwout family laid out the town's street grid system in the 1830s, the town became a commercial and industrial hub, and many of the buildings from Port Richmond's "golden age" can still be found here. The Bayonne Bridge to New Jersey, the longest steel-arch bridge in the world when it was completed, has provided a beautiful backdrop here since 1931.

BUS: S53 on Port Richmond Avenue; **S40** on Richmond Terrace

No Staten Island neighborhood seems to preserve as much of its past as Port Richmond. Much of that preservation, though, like much of the rest of New York City's artifacts, has been by pure indifference and neglect.

28 Northfield Township District School/P.S. 20

160 Heberton Avenue at New Street

This Romanesque Revival building with its distinctive clock tower was built in 1891. It "may be considered the most elaborately ornamented school ever constructed on Staten Island," according to the Preserva-

tion League of Staten Island. Look for the clock tower and carved cherub heads on keystones above the windows.

29 Ritz Theatre
Port Richmond Avenue at Anderson Street

The Ritz was constructed in 1924 with more than 2,100 seats. In the early 1970s, it became a prime rock venue, but since 1985 it has been a showroom for a tile company.

30 Catholic Youth Organization
120 Anderson Avenue at Park Avenue

This massive building with its six ionic columns was a Masonic temple; it is now headquarters for the local Catholic Youth Organization.

31 Carnegie Library
75 Bennett Street at Heberton Avenue

Rather similar in style to the Carnegie Library in Tottenville, this building at 75 Bennett Street, facing Veterans Park (the first planned open space on the island) has a marvelously shaded setting. It was designed by Staten Island resident John Carrere with Thomas Hastings and was completed in 1904.

32 Heberton Cottage
121 Heberton Avenue

Abolitionist Captain John Houseman, an oysterman, was the first owner of this pic-

turesque cottage featuring rich detailing and a wide porch. Stroll along Heberton Avenue, between Bennett Street and Post Avenue, for more Victorian-era buildings in Second Empire, Italianate, and Colonial Revival styles.

33 Dutch Reformed Church
Port Richmond Avenue at Church Street

This church was erected in 1845, replacing two earlier structures, but its parish is much older: It is the oldest religious congregation on the island, with roots going back to the 1660s. The churchyard commands the most attention, since it contains dozens of stones dating back to the early 1700s that have weathered well, unlike the ones from the 1800s cut from marble.

34 Griffith Block
Port Richmond Avenue, between Richmond Terrace and Church Street

This lengthy brick building was built in 1874 for Charles Griffith, a boot and shoe dealer. Directly abutting it on Richmond Terrace until 1945 was an eighteenth-century private residence known to be the

last home of Aaron Burr, the third vice president of the U.S.

35 Port Richmond National Bank
26 Port Richmond Avenue

Evidence of the former role of this 1870s slate-mansard roof building across the street from the Griffith Block can still be glimpsed where there are still shadows of a removed sign: "Chase Bank." It was originally Port Richmond National Bank.

36 Bayonne Ferry
Richmond Terrace at Port Richmond Avenue

There's a very old, rusted, arrow-shaped sign pointing toward New Jersey on Richmond Terrace just east of Port Richmond Avenue, and if you look carefully you can just make out the words "To Bayonne" on

each side. This is one of the last remnants of the Port Richmond to Bergen Point (later Bayonne) Ferry, which ran off and on from 1701 to 1931.

37 Empire Theater
Richmond Terrace, between Port Richmond Avenue and Maple Avenue

Port Richmond's Empire Theater, with its two castle spires, was built in 1916 and closed for good in 1978, following a run as a porno palace. It was designed by Port Richmond resident James Whitford. The building is now the headquarters of Farrell Lumber.

38 Faber Park
Richmond Terrace and Faber Street

Jenny Faber, a member of the Faber pencil manufacturing family, lived in Port Richmond, and in 1869, she was granted rights to the land along the Kill Van Kull in Port Richmond on the condition that she build a dock "for commerce or enjoyment." Part of it would eventually become Faber Park and Pool. Under Parks Department jurisdiction, architect Frederick H. Zurmuhlen Jr. built a seawall, a playground, and a pool—the largest in Staten Island when it was completed in 1932. Faber Park has enjoyed spectacular views of the nearby Bayonne Bridge since 1932.

39 Staten Island Rapid Transit Remnants
Port Richmond Avenue and Church Street

By 1953, ridership of Staten Island Rapid Transit had dropped to such a degree (due to reduced bus fares) that its parent, the Baltimore & Ohio Railroad, threatened to terminate all of its passenger service. NYC agreed to subsidize service on the Tottenville line and terminate service on the North Shore and South Beach branches. The B&O ended its involvement with Staten Island Rapid Transit in 1971, selling it to NYC for $3.5 million. Quaint B&O passenger coaches that had operated on the line since 1925 were replaced by modern R-44 subway cars. Finally, the MTA changed the name of the SIRT in 1994, renaming it the Staten Island Railway.

In Port Richmond and along the island's north shore, traces of the old line still remain, including intact elevated stations at Port Richmond (Port Richmond Avenue) and Tower Hill (Sharpe Avenue and Grove Street).

40 Scott-Edwards House
752 Delafield Avenue at Clove Road

This one-story brownstone, about a ten-minute walk from Port Richmond proper, was built around 1730 at what is now 752 Delafield Avenue. It was originally owned by Captain Nicholas Manning, and later by New York Supreme Court Justice Ogden Edwards, who added the Greek portico in the 1840s.

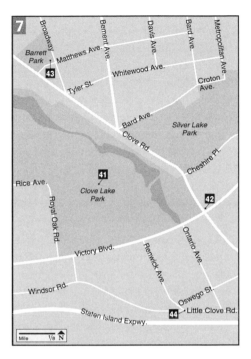

🖰 41 Clove Lakes Park

Clove Road and Victory Boulevard

This 198-acre park's name, and that of the road that borders it, has nothing to do with clover; instead, it is derived from the Dutch term for "cleft," and to gain perspective on why, observe how the nearby Staten Island Expressway separates Grymes Hill to its north and Emerson Hill to its south. The expressway describes Clove Road's former route "cleaving" the hills.

Of all of Staten Island's green spaces this, along with Silver Lake Park to the east, is the most developed and it most closely resembles landscaped Central and Prospect Parks; it's dotted with bridges, walkways, and brooks.

At the northern edge of the park, a little south of Forest Avenue, there is a 107-foot-tall, 300-year-old tulip tree that, according to Bruce Kershner of *Secret Places of Staten Island*, is the largest living thing in Staten Island. At the park's southern edge, a little north of Victory Boulevard and Renwick Avenue, you will find a three-foot-diameter Bartram's Oak, planted by naturalist William T. Davis in 1888.

Sunnyside, wedged between Victory Boulevard and the Staten Island Expressway west of Clove Road, is a small section of the island with a rich history. Sunnyside (the name comes from a nineteenth-century boarding house at Clove Road and Victory Boulevard) was a fox hunting grounds. The Richmond County Country Club was formed here in 1888. From the start, the area was associated with the Vanderbilt family, who owned elaborate houses and spacious property in the area, with street names like Labau Avenue named for Vanderbilt in-laws. Since the early 1920s, Sunnyside has been the home of the borough's premier green space: Clove Lakes Park. The area has a distinct, though definitely non-intrusive funkiness. At 1174 Victory Boulevard, you'll find Clove Lakes Book Store, one of the island's best independent bookstores.

BUS: S61, S62, or **S66** on Victory Boulevard; **S53** on Clove Road

42 John King Vanderbilt House

1197 Clove Road, near Victory Boulevard

This house at 1197 Clove Road dates to 1836. It was originally a country farmhouse in a Greek Revival design owned by a cousin of Cornelius Vanderbilt, and was subsequently owned and restored by Dorothy Valentine Smith, who helped found the Historic Richmond Town collection.

43 Staten Island Zoo
Broadway, north of Clove Road

The Staten Island Zoo at 614 Broadway opened in 1936 and remains New York City's premier facility for reptile research, with its rattlesnake collection being one of the country's biggest. Its African Savannah collection features antelopes, leopards, and mandrills. There's an aquarium and red panda and emu exhibits. For Staten Island Zoo hours, call (718) 442-3100 or visit www.statenislandzoo.org.

44 Moses' Folly
Little Clove Road and Northern Boulevard

At Little Clove Road and Northern Boulevard look for a break in the fence and a blue blaze on a tree, and ascend a very steep hill to the concrete ramps bridging the expressway. Richmond Parkway (now called the Korean War Veterans Parkway) was going to extend through La Tourette and High Rock Parks to meet the expressway here, until environmentalists and neighborhood activists got the plan terminated as part of a twenty-five-year battle. In 1964, ramps were installed here, but now they take hikers across the road as part of the Blue Trail. The ramps are now known as "Moses' Folly" for Triborough Bridge and Tunnel Authority president Robert Moses, who was thwarted in this case.

After crossing the expressway, you can observe steep 70-foot cliffs via a pathway leading to the right. If you stay on the Blue Trail you will reach Todt Hill Road and Ocean Terrace, the highest point on the eastern seaboard south of Maine.

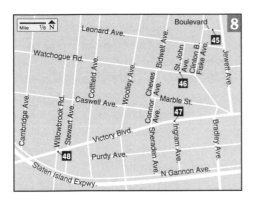

Westerleigh was developed in 1887 by Christopher S. Williams and William H. Boole, and was originally known as Prohibition Park. It is lined with narrow, brick streets and one-family houses, some of them in ornate Victorian style. Most of the streets in Westerleigh are named for candidates of the Prohibition Party, such as Neal Dow (1880), John St. John (1884), Clinton B. Fiske (1888), John Bidwell (1892), and John Woolley (1900). "Dry" states such as Maine, Ohio, and Virginia are also featured on the Westerleigh map. The neighborhood takes its present name from the Westerleigh Collegiate Institute. Formed in 1895, the institute was the first in Staten Island to provide an education from kindergarten to the collegiate level.

BUS: S61 or **S62** on Victory Boulevard; **S66** on Jewett Avenue

45 Westerleigh's Homes ➤
The Boulevard, between Jewett and Clinton B. Fiske Avenues

Westerleigh is full of vintage homes built in the 1880s and 1890s. While all the avenues and side streets provide prime viewing, the most elaborate and beautiful are along The Boulevard between Jewett and Willard Avenues.

46 Peter Housman House
Watchogue Road and St. John Avenue

One house in Westerleigh predates even the Prohibitionists. It was built between 1730 and 1760 on the vast Thomas Dongan estate. The oldest part of the house is the small, stone unit closest to St. John Avenue. Millwright Peter Housman acquired it around 1760 and added the rest.

47 Modern Architecture ➤
Victory Boulevard and Ingram Avenue

In a neighborhood known for its original Victorian-era houses, you will find two examples of more modern architecture at the northeast and northwest corner of Ingram Avenue and Victory Boulevard.

The Society of St. Paul Seminary at 2187 Victory Boulevard was designed by Silverman & Cika and opened in 1969. "Striking" doesn't do it justice: it's a rough

Society of St. Paul Seminary

rhomboid shape, flanging outward at the bottom. The middle section is a solid slab, but the wings are windowed from top to bottom, with staircases jutting out at odd angles from the top of the building and then down the back.

Across Ingram Avenue is 2177 Victory Boulevard, an Art Moderne one-story white slab trimmed in red, with circular and half-moon windows, hosting a group of ophthalmologists.

48 Willowbrook Tablet

Victory Boulevard and Willowbrook Road

At the triangle formed by the busy intersection of Victory Boulevard and Willowbrook Road where they meet Wyona Avenue, there's a short marble slab with a bronze tablet that reads: "To mark the crossing of the blazed trail and Willow Brook Trail, 1793. Erected by the Staten Island chapter of the Daughters of the American Revolution, 1921."

The inscription provides a glimpse into the antiquity of some of the dirt paths that eventually became tremendously busy roads. The "blazed trail" was, at one time, a walkway meandering through woods delineated by markings on trees and stones. It was gradually widened and straightened, and by the early 1700s, it was the chief road to the ferry at the Arthur Kill. It went by a variety of names, eventually becoming Richmond Turnpike. After 1918, to commemorate America's involvement in World War I, it was renamed Victory Boulevard.

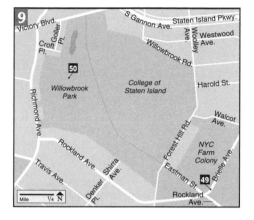

Mention "Willowbrook" to anyone over forty and the groundbreaking reports aired by Geraldo Rivera in 1972 uncovering the brutal conditions at Willowbrook State School will instantly come to mind. The facility was shut down in 1987, and its campus was taken over in 1993 by the College of Staten Island.

There are also the ghosts of other former institutions here such as the abandoned Staten Island Farm Colony, the borough's former poorhouse, and large sections of Seaview Hospital, some containing incred- ible terra-cotta artwork that has been left to the elements for decades.

BUS: S54 or **S57** on Brielle Avenue; **S62** on Victory Boulevard

49 Staten Island Farm Colony
Brielle Avenue, north of Rockland Avenue

"Poor farms" were established around the turn of the twentieth century as a means of rehabilitation for the mentally ill and im- poverished; many of them included farms and gardens tended by the residents and patients (the Queens Farm on Little Neck Parkway employed patients from nearby Creedmoor Hospital).

The New York Farm Colony was estab- lished in 1902 when the Richmond County Poor Farm was reorganized on Brielle Av- enue, across the street from Seaview Hos- pital. Its present gambrel-roofed Dutch Colonial brick-and-fieldstone buildings, some of which were designed by Renwick, Aspinwall & Owen, were built between 1904 and 1916.

After the last residents of the Farm Colony were moved out in 1975, the buildings languished in abandonment and decay. In 1984, 22 acres of the property were made part of the Staten Island Greenbelt, making them more difficult to demolish. The Farm Colony is beautiful in its desolation and magnificent in its decrepitude.

50 Homestead Remnants and Willowbrook Park

Willowbrook Park, south of Victory Boulevard

Willowbrook Park stretches between Victory Boulevard in Bulls Head and Forest Hill Road in Heartland Village. It features gigantic tulip trees, a swamp where American troops hid from the British in the 1770s, and a surprising ruin.

Enter the park at Victory Boulevard and Morani Street, and follow the well-marked White Trail south past Willowbrook Lake, strike left at the picnic area, and turn right at the athletic fields. The trail enters the wilderness at the fence at the end of the paved road. After a brisk walk of about ten minutes along the trail, in the center of Willowbrook Park is a tall, stone chimney and hearth, standing all alone. Like the Heyerdahl House remnants to the southwest, where the White Trail also leads, this

is the last remnant of a nineteenth-century dweller. Bruce Kershner, author of *Secret Places of Staten Island*, says the chimney is made of non-native rock that was carried 50 to 100 miles north by an Ice Age glacier.

Farther along on the trail are more signs of ancient habitation: wildly overgrown hedges. The trail leads to Forest Hill Road, though you may elect to continue past the road along the White Trail, as it travels south past Heyerdahl Hill into Egbertville and Lighthouse Hill.

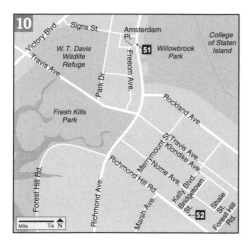

New Springville is in central Staten Island, bordered by Willowbrook Park, the William T. Davis Wildlife Refuge, Bulls Head, and Heartland Village. The Staten Island Mall, the island's largest shopping area, was built nearby in 1973. Heartland is a quiet neighborhood of one- and two-family dwellings built along streets named for 1960s astronauts and, oddly enough, Alaskan themes (Klondike, Yukon, and Platinum—which is mined in Alaska). Bulls Head was named for a sign depicting a ferocious bull that hung outside an eighteenth-century tavern on today's Victory Boulevard.

BUS: S44 on Richmond Avenue; **S61** on Travis Avenue or Merry Mount Street

51 Ichabod Crane's Grave

Richmond Avenue and Amsterdam Place

This Ichabod Crane is buried in a corner of New Springville Cemetery. He isn't the Ichabod Crane of fantasy and fiction, but rather, an army colonel who lived in the early and mid-nineteenth century. He acquired 5 acres and built a small one-and-a-half-story farmhouse at what is now 3525 Victory Boulevard in Travis. The house was demolished in 1989, but several of his personal items were retained by the Preservation League of Staten Island and can be found in exhibits at a collection in Richmond Town Restoration.

You can find his grave easily by going into the cemetery through the entrance on Richmond Avenue, just south of Son-Rise Charismatic Interfaith Church (*it* was built in 1848). Walk directly ahead until you see a white shaft on your left.

Crane and Washington Irving apparently met during the War of 1812 while both were serving in the U.S. Army. Irving used his name, without permission, in *The Legend of Sleepy Hollow*. Reportedly, Crane was horrified. Perhaps not coincidentally, a nearby street was named Sleepy Hollow Road when it was built in the 1970s.

52 Decker Farmhouse

435 Richmond Hill Road, near Bridgetown Street

The Decker family has roots in Staten Island that go back to the beginnings of Dutch

STATEN ISLAND

colonization in the 1600s, and Deckers can be found in many Staten Island cemeteries. One of the Decker farms in what is now Heartland Village, at 435 Richmond Hill Road, is one of NYC's two farm museums (the other being the Queens Farm Museum in Glen Oaks). On Decker's 20 acres, immigrant farmers are trained to grow native crops as part of the New Farmer Development Program.

The farmhouse, owned and operated by the Staten Island Preservation Society, was built by Japhet and Sarah Alston in 1809; the property was sold to Lorenzo Decker in 1841, and the Decker family farmed and lived here until 1955, when Alberta Decker donated the property to the Staten Island Historical Society.

The Decker Farm is open to the public and visitors can learn about farm life with hands-on activities such as rug beating, hay raking, and apple and pumpkin picking in the fall. For hours, call Historic Richmondtown at (718) 351-1611, extension 280.

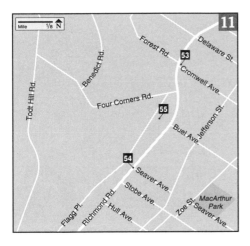

Irish Catholic Thomas Dongan (1634–
1715) was appointed governor of New York
by the Duke of York in 1682, and remained
at that post until 1689. Dongan convened
the first-ever representative assembly in
New York history. He became the second
Earl of Limerick in 1698. As part of his appointment, he was granted 5,100 acres in
what is now Dongan Hills, which he later
expanded to 25,000 acres. His legacy is remembered here, along with three streets
on the island named for him.

BUS: S74 on Richmond Road; **S51** on
Bay Street, Father Capodanno Boulevard,
and Midland Avenue

SIR: Dongan Hills Station

53 Billiou-Stillwell-Perine House
1476 Richmond Road at Cromwell Avenue

This house on 1476 Richmond Road predates Thomas Dongan's gubernatorial
era. Pierre Billiou (1625–1708), a French
Huguenot judicial officer and delegate
to the New York general assembly, built a
simple stone structure here in 1662 when
the region was known as Oude Dorp

("Old Town"). Billiou's daughter married
Thomas Stillwell, and the Stillwells occupied the dwelling until 1764, gradually
adding to the structure; members of the
Perine family then lived here until 1919.

54 Victory Diner ➤
Richmond Road at Seaver Avenue

The Victory, Staten Island's only chrome-
plated railroad-car-style diner, was built on
Victory Boulevard in 1932 and was moved
to 1781 Richmond Road in 1964. Before its
move from Castleton Corners in 1961, the
building served as a temporary branch of
the Staten Island Savings Bank.

55 Flagg Place
*Between Four Corners and Todt Hill Roads,
above Richmond Road*

Among Staten Island's most picturesque
roads is Flagg Place, along the steep es-
carpment above Richmond Road between
Four Corners and Todt Hill Roads. Some
of Staten Island's largest and most elaborate mansions have been constructed here
to take advantage of the view of Raritan
Bay.

The street is named for eminent architect Ernest Flagg (1857–1947), whose

STATEN ISLAND

landmarked thirty-three-room mansion at 209 Flagg Place is now a mission center for the Society of St. Charles Borromeo (known as the Scalabrinian Fathers).

From Flagg Place you have an exhilarating view of the Verrazano-Narrows Bridge, facing the bridge towers head-on with the Brooklyn-side tower in the rear.

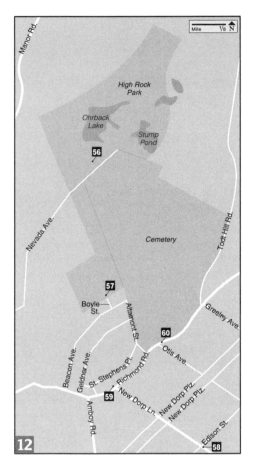

New Dorp is a transliteration of the Dutch "*Nieuw Dorp*," or "New Town," so called because it was settled in 1670, ten years after nearby "*Oude Dorp*," a name remembered in the street name Old Town Road. The town grew around the junction of Richmond and Amboy Roads, where there were taverns serving stagecoaches. The Vanderbilt family was prominent in the area and owned several racing and trotting tracks in the area. The family helped found the New Dorp Moravian Church and Cemetery along Richmond and Todt Hill Roads; the Vanderbilt Mausoleum, designed by Richard Morris Hunt, can be found at the cemetery's rear section.

BUS: S74 on Richmond Road; **S78** on Hylan Boulevard

SIR: New Dorp Station

56 High Rock Park
Nevada Avenue, east of Rockland Avenue

Accessible from the end of Nevada Avenue at the park's western end, or Altamont or Boyle Streets at the park's eastern end, is High Rock Park—one of NYC's most tranquil areas, and also one of its newest large parks, opening in 1965 after decades in private ownership.

The park contains marked trails and many other unmarked ones that wind past kettle ponds deposited by glaciers in the park's southern region and small creeks and streams. Persimmon groves (rare in the northeast), red maples, blueberries, and skunk cabbage can be found along the trails. You may also happen upon the visitor's center deep in the park, a stone structure built in 1921.

57 New Dorp Lighthouse
Boyle Street, north of Beacon Avenue

The New Dorp Lighthouse is now part of a private dwelling on Boyle Street, very close to High Rock Park. Its 40-foot tower, rising 192 feet above sea level, aided shipping between 1856 and 1964. It acted in concert with the Elm Tree Lighthouse at the end of New Dorp Lane at Miller Field.

58 Lane Theater ➤
168 New Dorp Lane, near 9th Street

The Art Deco Lane Theater opened in 1937 at 168 New Dorp Lane near 9th Street. It was developed by the Moses brothers, Charles, Elias, and Lewis, and designed by renowned architect John Eberson. Until 2001, it had been recast as a nightclub that

has since closed. The distinctive red and blue façade is still visible. Its Art Moderne foyer and corridors remain intact, though they are inaccessible at present.

60 Lakeman-Cortelyou House
2286 Richmond Road

59 Mayer House
2475 Richmond Road, near Odin Street

The beautiful Italianate mansion with the cupola set way back was built in 1855 and was the home of Gustave A. Mayer, inventor of the Nabisco Sugar Wafer.

This Dutch farmhouse built by Abraham Lakeman in 1678 is the second-oldest building in Staten Island (only Britton Cottage in Richmond Town Restoration is older). It is now owned and beautifully maintained by Moravian Florist.

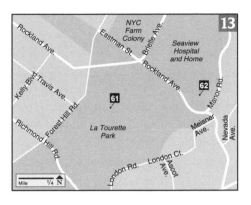

La Tourette Park is a vast expanse: 511 acres of parkland in the heart of Staten Island, stretching from Seaview Hospital in Willowbrook southwest to Richmond Avenue near the Staten Island Mall, originally belonging to the farming La Tourette family who sold their property to NYC in 1928. The 1870 La Tourette mansion on Richmond Hill Road, north of Richmond Town, is now the clubhouse of the La Tourette Golf Course.

BUS: S74 on Richmond Road

SIR: New Dorp Station

61 Heyerdahl Hill

In La Tourette Park, west of Rockland Avenue and Manor Road

Bucks Hollow and Heyerdahl Hill are the most isolated and remote regions of Staten Island. On a high hill with nothing but tangled weeds and snarled vines lies the remains of one man's dreams to bring cash crops to Staten Island.

Reaching Heyerdahl Hill requires a trek on the White Trail, discernible from white blazes painted on trees. Begin at Rockland and Meisner Avenues and follow the trail through Egbertville Ravine. A wood bridge takes the White Trail over Richmond Creek. The traffic noise falls away; at this point the Yellow, Red, and White Trails all converge. Stay with the White Trail.

At length, Buttonbush Swamp will appear to your left. You are entering Bucks Hollow; parts of the hollow were used by Revolutionary spies as escape routes from Richmondtown to reach a ferry at Kill Van Kull which took them to Continental army units in New Jersey.

After passing Buttonbush Swamp, notice the trail gradually getting narrower. That is your cue to keep an eye out on the right for another narrow, unmarked trail that leads off to your right. Take it. You will be climbing for about half a mile up a very steep incline; the sides of the trail are lined with bayberry. Follow the trail to the left after it reaches the top of the steep hill. It winds around a little, but soon you will arrive at a clearing of sorts. You are now in one of the most isolated regions of New York City; and you have arrived at the only structure within about a mile from here.

In the early 1800s, M. Heyerdahl built this now-ruined stone house in Bucks Hollow, a long distance from the nearest large settlement in Richmondtown. It was his hope to establish wine vineyards and orchards, but Staten Island's rocky soil was an impediment, and he had to move out in the early twentieth century. Nature has

STATEN ISLAND

been taking over ever since. The trails we used to arrive here were likely carriage and cart paths used by the family and their employees.

62 Moses Mountain

East of Rockland Avenue and Manor Road

To reach Moses Mountain, take the Yellow Trail from the junction of Rockland Avenue and Manor Road and follow it as it winds around an artificial 240-foot hill created by 50,000 tons of rock blasted to create the Staten Island Expressway in the early 1960s. At its peak, you can see all of Staten Island's highest hills in a magical panorama: Todt Hill, Lighthouse Hill, and Heyerdahl Hill. In spring and fall migration seasons, Moses Mountain provides a prime hawk- and osprey-watching vista.

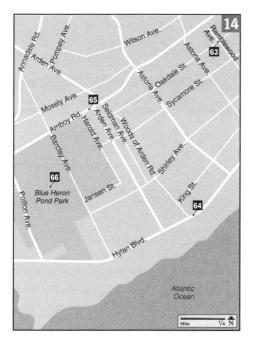

Annadale, which takes its charming name from Anna Seguine, a member of a prominent local family in the nineteenth century, and Eltingville, named for the farming Eltinge family, grew up as immigrant communities along Staten Island Rapid Transit stops. Well into the twentieth century, Annadale had few telephones, no dentists, a single general health-care practitioner, and no public school; children attended schools in the next town, Huguenot. However, milk, bread, and ice were delivered directly to area homes. As with other rural Staten Island communities, the opening of the Verrazano-Narrows Bridge changed everything, and soon streets and subdivisions were laid out. You can still glimpse a bit of the old days at the local train stations that still retain some of the atmosphere they used to have.

BUS: **S78** on Hylan Boulevard; **S55** on Annadale Road

SIR: to Great Kills, Eltingville, or Annadale Stations

63 Wood Duck Pond
Oakdale Street and Ramblewood Avenue

Down the southeast coast of Staten Island, retreating glaciers left a number of small ponds that serve as way stations for migrating shorebirds. While they are recognized by the Parks Department, they don't turn up on many maps. One such pond in Eltingville attracts the brilliantly plumaged wood duck.

Enter the Wood Duck Pond area from Ramblewood Avenue, up the block from Oakdale Street. Ramblewood Avenue is a dead end, but a park path has been clearly marked by the Parks Department. It's best visited in the fall when hundreds of migrating wood ducks congregate here to feed.

64 Olmsted House
4515 Hylan Boulevard, near Woods of Arden Road

You have to walk up a lengthy driveway marked "Private Property" to see 4515

STATEN ISLAND

Hylan Boulevard, just east of Woods of Arden Road, but area residents know the historic home, so you shouldn't expect much trouble. It was built in 1720 and was owned by Jacques Poillon (his family owned a lot of property in Eltingville during the Colonial era) and from 1846 to 1853 by Frederick Law Olmsted, the co-designer of Central Park, who remodeled the house and planted two cedars of Lebanon on the grounds that still stand. It is heavily shrouded by vegetation, so it's hard to see even in winter.

65 Brougham Cottage
4746 Amboy Road, west of Arden Avenue

This small oak-beamed farmhouse on 4746 Amboy Road, just west of Arden Avenue at the edge of Blue Heron Pond Park, was built around 1732. Known as the Brougham Cottage or the Little Woods of Arden House, it has been maintained in excellent condition. In 1925, a 1732 English penny inside a clay ball embedded in the hearth was found, indicating the building's likely construction date. A two-story section was added in the early 1800s.

Spring Pond in the Blue Heron Pond Park Reserve

66 Blue Heron Pond Park Reserve
Poillon Avenue, south of Amboy Road

From Annadale Station, take a short walk down Poillon (pronounced "pooyon") and you're at the gate of the Blue Heron Park Reserve, marked with colorful pink and orange cornflowers.

Blue Heron Park, in Staten Island's southwest corner, is only one in a series of reserves known as the Bluebelt. Others include Long Pond, Lemon Creek, Jack's Pond, Kingfisher Pond, and Wood Duck Pond.

Set off along the trail next to the Blue Heron Pond Visitors Center. You will soon find yourself alongside Spring Pond—the largest pond in the park, and a favorite blue heron haunt. Then cross Poillon Avenue to the main path. Just before the tall forest drops away, a thin path leads away to Blue Heron Pond, where you just may glimpse one.

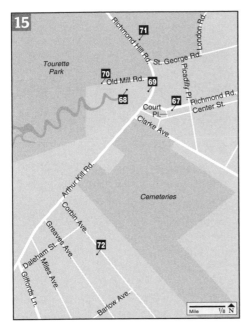

the oysters found in Richmond Creek and other area streams. The town gradually gained in importance and became the county seat. The town was called Richmond and later, Richmond Town evolved.

BUS: S54 or **S74** on Richmond Road

67 Richmond Town Restoration

Richmond Road, Center Street, Court Place, and Arthur Kill Road

HISTORIC RICHMOND TOWN, CENTER STREET:

a. *Richmond County Courthouse*
This columned Greek Revival building stands at Historic Richmond Town's core at Center Street and Court Place. It was Richmond's main courthouse between 1837 and 1919, and today hosts the visitor center and museum store.

b. *Richmond Town Museum*
Just across the street from the visitor center is the Staten Island Historical Society Museum, opened in 1838 as the Richmond County Clerk's and Surrogates' Office. Today it hosts three floors of changing and permanent exhibits, including some very old and valuable maps.

c. *Tinsmith Shop*
Built in Woodrow around 1840, it func-

So many of Staten Island's Colonial-era dwellings have been lost to ruin, neglect, and overzealous development. That's why Historic Richmond Town is such a miracle since it depicts the island's small-town past.

Historic Richmond Town was established in 1958 by the Staten Island Historical Society and the City of New York at the area surrounding the junction of Richmond, Richmond Hill, and Arthur Kill Roads. Colonial-era homes from all over the island have been moved to this 25-acre site over the years. Besides the houses, keep an eye peeled for a roadside milestone, a family cemetery, a transplanted Staten Island Rapid Transit railroad station house (from New Dorp), and an original hitching post along Center Street. To contact Historic Richmond Town, call (718) 351-1611, or go to www.historicrichmondtown.org. This section will cover many of Historic Richmond Town's highlights.

As far back as 1685, the area was an important crossroads, and a town called Cocclestown was established, named for

tioned as a grocery store run by the Colon family. After its relocation here, it was refitted as a metalwork shop, where demonstrations are given during tour hours.

COURT PLACE:

d. *Stephens-Black House/General Store*
In this 1840 building native to Richmond Town and owned by Stephen D. Stephens, and later by Joseph Black until 1926, an old-time general store, complete with potbelly stove, has been reconstructed (the building was partially demolished in 1944). It serves as Historic Richmond Town's post office.

e. *Print Shop*
This was originally a one-room grocery, the Eusabia Johnson store, built in Eltingville in 1860. It has been recast as an old-fashioned print shop, when "leading" meant an actual slug of lead inserted between lines of type to increase spacing.

f. *Carpenter Shop*
One of Historic Richmond Town's "new" buildings, this was constructed from the remains of an 1835 farmhouse.

g. *John H. Bennett House*
To see it now, you'd never imagine shipping merchant John Bennett's mansion, built in 1839, was cast as a bus terminal and lunch counter in the 1950s. It has been revived as a showcase for dolls and toys used by Richmond Town children in the Colonial era.

RICHMOND ROAD (NORTH SIDE):

h. *Crocheron House*
At St. Patrick's Place is this Federal-style mansion built in Greenridge, west of Richmond Town, by merchant Jacob Crocheron in 1819; it was moved here in the 1960s.

i. *Guyon-Lake-Tysen House*
The Dutch Colonial dwelling was built in New Dorp by Joseph Guyon in around 1740. (You can find his name inscribed in one of the walls.) This was once the seat of a 112-acre estate that included granaries and cider houses; it passed through the Lake and Tysen families, and was then donated to Historic Richmond Town and moved here in 1969.

j. *Britton Cottage*
Like the Guyon-Lake-Tysen House, this house was originally built in New Dorp (at the foot of New Dorp Lane at Raritan Bay) in 1670, making it Historic Richmond Town's oldest dwelling. It was gradually added to over the centuries and was owned by botanist Nathaniel Britton from 1895 to 1915.

Behind Britton Cottage, along Richmond Creek, are three additional buildings:

k. *Basketmaker's House*

The Basketmaker's House, originally known as Morgan Cottage, was built around 1815 as a farmer's house. It was originally located in New Springville to the northwest.

l. *Kruser-Finley House*

This farmhouse was built in 1790 in Egbertville, a half mile east of Historic Richmond Town, with additions in 1820 and 1850. It has been also been used as a cooper's (barrelmaker) shop.

m. *Dunn's Mill*

A reconstruction of a nineteenth-century mill built at Richmond Creek by John Dunn.

RICHMOND ROAD (SOUTH SIDE):

n. *Guyon Store*

Built by James Guyon Jr. as a general store in 1819, it later became a private residence and is now furnished as a tavern of the mid-nineteenth century.

o. *Edwards-Barton House*

One of Historic Richmond Town's two Victorian-era buildings, The Edwards-Barton House was built at Richmond Road and Court Place in 1869 in a Gothic Revival style by county executive Webley Edwards, whose daughter Ella and husband Willis Barton resided here until the mid-twentieth century.

ARTHUR KILL ROAD:

p. *Treasure House*

Treasure House, where three of Staten Island's major roads meet, was built here in 1700, and was enlarged between 1740 and 1860. During the Revolution, British troops hid away a cache of gold sovereigns worth about $7,000; the money was found here by painters in 1854.

q. *Christopher House*

Set way back from the road, this fieldstone farmhouse owned by Joseph Christopher dates to 1720 and was moved here from Willowbrook.

r. *Boehm House*

Built in Greenridge around 1750, a mile west of Historic Richmond Town, this was the home of educator Henry Boehm for many years in the mid-nineteenth century.

s. *Voorlezer House*

This house was built around 1695 by the Reformed Dutch Church, and functioned as a church, school, and home for the lay minister/teacher until 1701 (*"voorlezer"* means approximately "to read in front of" in Dutch). The ensuing centuries found it being used as a private residence, a storefront, and a lunch counter until 1939, when it was restored by the Staten Island Historical Society. It is now a national historic landmark and is recognized as the United States' oldest schoolhouse.

t. *Parsonage*

Set on a hill at Arthur Kill Road and Clarke Avenue is Historic Richmond Town's other Victorian building, also a

Gothic Revival. It was the official residence of the minister of the Reformed Dutch Church from its opening in 1855 to 1875. It has also been the home of Staten Island historian Henry Steinmeyer; today it is the restoration's restaurant.

68 Stone Bridge

Richmond Hill Road, crossing over
Richmond Creek

Staten Island's oldest stone bridge carries narrow, yet busy, Richmond Hill Road over Richmond Creek. This simple structure was built by the Rev. David Moore, rector of nearby St. Andrew's Church in 1845. The bridge is best seen from the St. Andrew's churchyard.

69 St. Andrew's Church and Churchyard

Old Mill Road, near Richmond Hill Road

The Episcopal Church of St. Andrew was granted a charter by British Queen Anne in 1712. The church barracked British troops during the Revolutionary War, and traces of their fortifications can be detected on Fort Hill to the rear of the church. The present church is a Romanesque structure built in 1872. The churchyard contains dozens of headstones dating back to the early 1700s, recognizable by the winged angel carvings at their tops. Family members of Mother Elizabeth Bayley Seton, America's first canonized saint (in 1975) are interred here.

70 Old Mill Road

La Tourette Park

Just north of the St. Andrew's churchyard entrance on Richmond Hill Road, you'll see a road called Old Mill Road trailing off into the distance. It looks like a dead end with a gate at the end of the road at the

St. Andrew's Church rectory. It *is* a dead end—but to cars only. For hikers and pedestrians, it's a gateway to the wilderness.

Once you're through the gate, Old Mill Road becomes the stagecoach and cart path it used to be. It was once the main route between Richmond Town and New Springville, on the other side of Staten Island.

After about fifteen minutes of hiking, you'll come to a clearing and you'll find a fork in Old Mill Road. At this point once stood a fruit orchard and two gristmills. The ruins of these mills can still be found in the marshland off to the left. Continue along the road on the right and then forward for about half a mile. You'll come upon the end of Old Mill Road at a wider path where you have the option to go right or left. This is the original path of Forest Hill Road, which was redirected some decades ago and is now a major feeder road into the Staten Island Mall complex.

Continue to your right along the old Forest Hill Road path. You will eventually reach La Tourette Brook, lined by ancient stone walls. At this point, reverse course and follow Forest Hill Road down to its intersection with Old Mill Road. If you continue forward you will reach the busy intersection of Forest Hill and Richmond Hill Roads.

Once back on Old Mill Road and walking back toward Historic Richmond Town, check carefully on your left for the Blue Trail, marked with blue blazes, which leads you past the unmarked site of Fort Hill, a

British fort during the Revolution. You will eventually come across a clear spot with the La Tourette Park Golf Course on your left, and a gorgeous vista on your right. In this view from the crest of the cliffs overlooking Old Mill Road and the rest of La Tourette Park, the twisting, turning Richmond Creek is plainly visible. Beyond that is the neighborhood of Eltingville; look off to your left for the steeples of Historic Richmond Town.

71 La Tourette House
Richmond Hill Road, north of Old Mill Road

Take the Blue Trail ahead to busy Richmond Hill Road. Cross the road very carefully, and enter the golf course parking lot. The grand three-story building here with the shady porch is the La Tourette family mansion, built in 1836 (the porch was added about a century later). The mansion is now the clubhouse of the La Tourette Park Golf Course.

72 Kingfisher Pond
West of Corbin Avenue, between Daleham Street and Barlow Avenue

A short walk west from Historic Richmond Town along Arthur Kill Road, past the United Hebrew Cemetery, leads to the towns of Great Kills and Eltingville. Southern Staten Island is studded with protected wilderness areas; one of these is Kingfisher Pond, located at Miles Avenue and Fairfield Street (look for the big Parks Department leaf sign, and hike a short distance through the brush).

Staten Island's Kingfisher Pond Park is the newest addition to Staten Island's Bluebelt project. It provides flood protection and water-pollution control, as well as a respite from suburban monotony. It also preserves some ancient architectural aspects of the region.

Centuries ago, Native Americans and, later, Dutch farmers, made this region their home. Hiking through Kingfisher Pond Park, you will come upon what appear to be randomly strewn rocks, but they are actually the remnants of stone walls built by Colonial settlers in the 1700s.

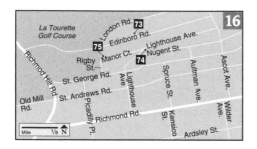

Staten Island, by far New York City's most mountainous borough, supports a few inland lighthouses. The most spectacular one is located on this 220-foot hill that looms above Egbertville Ravine. It's an area of great wealth, but in some ways, it's still emerging from its rural past. In this casual setting, though, are some architectural marvels crucial to New York City's status as a place where if you turn a corner . . . anything can happen.

BUS: S54 or **S74** on Richmond Road

73 Staten Island Lighthouse ➤
Edinboro Road, east of Rigby Street

The Ambrose Channel Range Light was built here in 1912, and the Coast Guard still uses it. It's more commonly known as the Staten Island Lighthouse, the largest of the borough's lighthouses. Even though it's far inland, its light can be seen far out to sea.

The 90-foot-tall octagonal structure, made with light brown bricks, can be seen from the bottom of the hill at Lighthouse Avenue and Richmond Road. To get closer to the lighthouse, climb steep Lighthouse Avenue, follow it all the way to Terrace Court, double back on Edinboro Road, and walk west; it will appear on your left just before you reach Rigby Street.

74 Museum of Tibetan Art
338 Lighthouse Avenue, near Manor Court

Who would ever think that Staten Island would be the world's capital of artwork collected from Tibet? It's all because of Edna Coblentz (1887–1948) who became an art dealer in Manhattan after her acting career stalled. As a child, Edna had discovered thirteen Tibetan figurines in an attic trunk; her grandfather had brought them to the U.S. from a trip to the far east, and she subsequently became fascinated with Tibetan artwork. She had moved to Lighthouse Hill with her husband, Harry Kaluber, in 1921. After some years exhibiting her collection in midtown Manhattan, Edna, who adopted the nom de plume Jacques Marchais, financed the construction of the Museum of Tibetan Art, built to resemble a Buddhist temple, with meditation gardens and a lotus and fish pond which also contains a

large turtle or two. The primary collection is Buddhist art from Tibet, Mongolia, and northern China, from the fifteenth to early twentieth centuries, including paintings, ritual artifacts, figurines, musical instruments, and photographs. In June 1991, the Dalai Lama was an honored guest at the museum.

After Jacques and her husband passed away in the late 1940s, their friend, Helen Watkins, took over the museum, which has been maintained privately since then with the aid of government grants and admission fees. For information, call (718) 987-3500 or go to www.tibetanmuseum.org.

75 Crimson Beech

Manor Court, east of Rigby Street

A beautiful hillside setting at Manor Court near the eastern edge of La Tourette Park is the home of the only private dwelling designed by Frank Lloyd Wright in New York City. The house is named for a copper beech tree that originally graced the property. A

1967 hurricane felled the original tree, but a new one was planted in its place.

The lengthy red-and-tan building is at the edge of Lighthouse Hill, 200 feet above sea level, and takes full advantage of the spectacular hillside and ocean views. It is in the mold of Wright's famed "prairie" design ranch houses, and was built in 1959. The house was commissioned and built for William Cass and his wife, Catherine, who occupied it for forty years. According to the New York City Landmarks Preservation Commission, prefabricated units were shipped from Madison, Wisconsin, and assembled here by Wright's associate, Morton Delson.

STATEN ISLAND

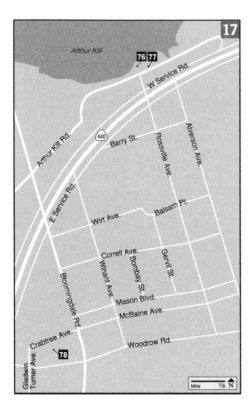

Named for local wealthy eighteenth-cen-tury landowner William Ross, this small town in southwestern Staten Island now called Rossville was known before the Revolutionary War by a picturesque term, named after an area tavern: Blazing Star. The Old Blazing Star Ferry and steamships whose wrecks are still sinking in the Arthur Kill connected Rossville with New Jersey. The West Shore Expressway, built in the 1970s, spurred development south of the highway. North of the expressway are auto repair shops, huge abandoned gas tanks, pipe factories, abandoned cemeteries, and assorted detritus that has been there for decades and may remain for decades more.

BUS: S74 on Arthur Kill Road, Rossville Avenue, and Bloomingdale Road

76 The Rossville Boatyard

Arthur Kill Road and Rossville Avenue

Walk from Arthur Kill Road and Rossville Avenue in the weeds toward the Arthur Kill, and a strangely beautiful yet disconcerting tableau appears before your eyes: a vast assemblage of sinking ships, known officially as the Witte Marine Equipment Company, where their spare parts are salvaged. Vessels from all decades of the twentieth century lie in a state of decomposition and rust at this far redoubt. Most are fireboats, tugs, or cargo ships. The former piers have collapsed and are for the most part impassable, which makes them a magnet for daredevil urban explorers.

The boatyard contains at least one derelict that is associated with a tragic event in New York City history, the *Abram S. Hewitt*. The fireboat, named for NYC mayor Abram Stevens Hewitt (1822–1903) was built by New York Shipbuilding in Camden, New Jersey, and launched the year the mayor died; she served in the NYC fireboat fleet until 1958. It was the last coal-burning fireboat in operation. The *Hewitt* is one of the last physical links to the *General Slocum* tragedy of June 15, 2004, when a fire onboard the pleasure boat resulted in the deaths of more than 1,000. The *Hewitt* tried unsuccessfully to reach the burning craft as it steamed toward North Brother Island.

77 Blazing Star Cemetery

Arthur Kill Road and Rossville Avenue

The boatyard can be clearly seen through the trees at Rossville (Blazing Star) Cemetery, one of a few cemeteries scattered along twisting Arthur Kill Road, a 300-year-old route which winds for miles between Richmondtown and Tottenville. This is the

burial ground of the Sleight family, and you can find several stones here going back to the 1820s.

 **78 Sandy Ground**

Crabtree Avenue, west of Bloomingdale Road

Walk down Crabtree Avenue from Bloomingdale Road: At first it looks like the rest of its brother streets lined with new, homogeneous housing. Continue down the road and you come upon a cemetery associated with the nearby Rossville African Methodist Episcopal Zion Church. Soon, Crabtree Avenue begins to look like a rural country lane.

The intersection of Crabtree Avenue and Woodrow Road was once the center of a small settlement named Sandy Ground. Before the Civil War, the community was founded by New York City's first community of free blacks, oystermen who moved north from the Maryland shore to work then-burgeoning oyster beds along the Staten Island shore. After the water became too polluted in the 1910s, the oyster beds were condemned, and many residents moved away. Yet, the community's unique identity was able to persist until the 1960s.

The Sandy Ground Historical Society at 1538 Woodrow Road exhibits letters, photographs, film, art, quilts, and rare books, all collected from area homes over the past few decades. Call (718) 317-5796 for visiting hours.

In 1854, Balthazar Kreischer constructed a small company town in this remote corner of Staten Island that centered around Arthur Kill Road and Kreischer and Androvette Streets. His brickworks employed almost 150 and produced 20,000 bricks per day. Kreischerville, as the town was known, was entirely self-contained, with a hotel (still standing at Androvette and Kreischer Streets, now a Knights of Columbus), church, and grocery store. The factory closed in 1927. In the aftermath of World War I, many German-sounding names were purged from New York City directories, and so Kreischerville became known as "Charleston."

BUS: S74 on Arthur Kill Road

79 P.S. 4 and West Baptist Cemetery

Arthur Kill Road, north of Sharrotts Road

Public School 4 is used by special education students. It is probably the building with the highest concentration of Kreischer brick in the area. Immediately across the street is the West Baptist Cemetery, with many interred members of the Storer family; the name also shows up on Storer Avenue. The cemetery was associated with the long-gone West Baptist Church that was established in 1847, but has disappeared long ago. Some of the stones have inscriptions in German.

80 Killmeyer's Old Bavaria Inn

Arthur Kill and Sharrotts Roads

This vintage German-style beer garden at 4254 Arthur Kill Road was built by Nicholas Killmeyer as a roadhouse: Killmeyer's Union Hotel in the mid-1800s. Now known as Killmeyer's Old Bavaria Inn, it boasts its original pressed-tin ceiling, a menu full of sauerbraten, braunschweiger, and other treats, and dozens of brands of German beer. Oompah bands play on Sunday afternoons and rock bands play the beer garden in the back on summer evenings. The gorgeous, intricately woodworked bar, built in 1890, is reason enough to visit.

white, with picket fences. The houses were built around 1890 and leased to workers in the brick factory. Note the distinctive Kreischer yellow-bricked sidewalks.

83 Kreischer Mansion
Arthur Kill Road, near Kreischer Street

Balthazar Kreischer's son Charles constructed this grand Stick-style mansion at 4500 Arthur Kill Road, just south of Englewood Avenue, in 1885; his brother Edward's identical building was on the adjoining plot. In the early 2000s, the house was completely renovated.

81 Free Hungarian Reformed Church
Winant Place, west of Arthur Kill Road

This church at 25 Winant Place was originally constructed by the Kreischers in 1883 for a Lutheran congregation. At present, it is the Free Magyar (Hungarian) Reformed Church. A piece of paper with an apparent handwritten signature of Balthazar Kreischer himself was recently uncovered in the church. The gateposts are Kreischer brick.

84 Clay Pit Ponds Park
Carlin Street, north of Sharrots Road

Clay Pit Ponds State Park Preserve is a 260-acre natural area near the southwest shore of Staten Island, north and east of Kreischerville. Once the site of a clay-mining operation, the park preserve today contains a mixture of wetlands, sandy barrens, and woodlands. The preserve is accessible from the end of Carlin Street, off Sharrots Road. Call (718) 967-1976 for park hours.

82 Kreischer Worker's Homes
Kreischer Street, between Arthur Kill Road and Winant Place

Lining Kreischer Street is a series of modest, two-story dwellings, painted green and

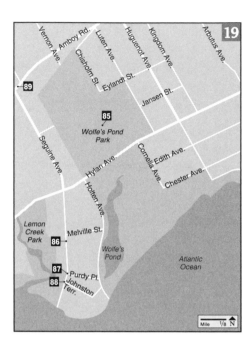

This small neighborhood in southeast-ern Staten Island, according to tradition, is so-called because before the Revolutionary War, the Duke of Nassau (a British prince who later became King William III) once anchored a vessel in the bay at the foot of today's Seguine Avenue. The French Huguenot Seguine family were early settlers in the area: Seguine Avenue, Prince's Bay's major north-south thoroughfare south of Hylan Boulevard, is lined with craggy osage orange trees, planted by the Seguines at the encouragement of family friend Frederick Law Olmsted, the co-creator of Central and Prospect Parks, who lived nearby in Eltingville.

BUS: S78 on Hylan Boulevard; **S55** on Seguine Avenue and Hylan Boulevard

SIR: Prince's Bay Station

85 Wolfe's Pond Park
Hylan Boulevard, west of Cornelia Avenue

Named for a freshwater pond situated only a few yards from salty Raritan Bay, Wolfe's Pond Park is named for original landowner Joel Wolfe, who farmed the land here until 1857. It became a public park in 1929. A walk on the path along Wolfe's Pond enables you to get "lost" in the jumble of galleries and paths in the forest. One of the paths takes you to a giant black oak tree whose trunk boasts a five-foot diameter.

86 Seguine Mansion
Seguine Avenue and Hank Place

Joseph H. Seguine's grand Greek Revival mansion, built in 1840 at 440 Seguine Avenue, is reminiscent of Southern plantation houses. Joseph Seguine was a prosperous oyster trader, entrepreneur, farmer, and the first president of the Staten Island Railroad, which still has a Prince's Bay stop.

The house's most attractive feature, the porch with two-story pillars, is best seen by the public from Lemon Creek Park at the foot of Seguine Avenue in winter.

87 Manee-Seguine Homestead
Seguine Avenue and Purdy Place

This boarded-up, abandoned farmhouse awaiting renovation or demolition at 509 Seguine Avenue may be one of Staten

Island's oldest dwellings. It has passed through the Seguine and Manee families; the Manees likely added to an original one-room residence built in the late 1690s with a two-story fieldstone section early in the eighteenth century. The Manee family sold the house and lands to the Seguines in 1786, and Joseph H. Seguine spent his boyhood here. By the 1870s, the house had been sold to Stephen Purdy, who operated it as a resort hotel for a few decades. The old house is best seen today from Purdy Place in winter; a closer view can be had if you brave the weeds and thorns and walk right up to it from there.

of the Woodrow and Prince's Bay neighborhoods until reaching the bay in Lemon Creek Park, a 105-acre preserve containing Staten Island's largest salt marsh. Purple martins, rare in the New York City area, can be found here.

88 Lemon Creek 𐤠
Seguine Avenue and Johnston Terrace

This brook babbles from Woodrow and Foster Roads, occasionally underground, but mostly along the streets and backyards

89 Abraham Wood House
5910 Amboy Road, near Seguine Avenue

This Greek Revival building was constructed by farmer and oysterman Abraham J. Wood in 1840.

STATEN ISLAND

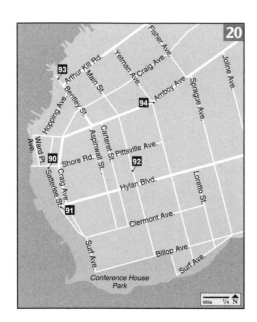

Tottenville is the southernmost tip of Staten Island and the southernmost point in New York state. British naval officer captain Christopher Billopp was its first European settler in 1678. He built a stone mansion at the foot of today's Hylan Boulevard that would figure prominently in American history as the Conference House. The Billopps remained Tories, loyal to the British, throughout the Revolution and so had their lands confiscated at the end of the war. The story goes that Staten Island is a part of New York state, not New Jersey, because Captain Billopp won a bet that he could circumnavigate Staten Island in one day.

The Totten family owned a large amount of property in the area in the eighteenth century, and after a series of names like Unionville, Bentley Dock, and others, the village settled on a name reflecting its major property holders.

Tottenville has been the terminus of the South Shore line of the Staten Island Railway since the 1860s, and three of the island's major roads, Arthur Kill Road, Amboy Road, and Hylan Boulevard, also lead here. Tottenville is home to two Staten Island Railway stations: one at the line's terminus and another called Atlantic, after the now-defunct Atlantic Terra Cotta Company, once one of Staten Island's largest employers, which made decorative materials used on skyscrapers and fire-resistant cladding.

BUS: S74 on Arthur Kill Road; **S78** on Hylan Boulevard

SIR: Tottenville Station

90 Biddle Mansion
Satterlee Street, near Shore Road

Captain Henry Biddle's grand mansion at 70 Satterlee Street was built on the water's edge in 1840 in a Dutch Colonial style with unusual two-story porticoes.

91 Conference House
Satterlee Street and Hylan Boulevard

The brick mansion built by Christopher Billopp around 1680 at the end of Hylan Boulevard was almost a century old on September 11, 1776, when Benjamin Franklin, John Adams, and Edward Rutledge met here with Admiral Lord Richard Howe in an attempt to stave off any future hostilities with Britain. While Howe proffered a proposal from George III to grant the patriots more rights than other British colonies enjoyed if they ended their fight for liberty, Franklin and the others stood firm and insisted upon American independence.

In the 1920s, the Conference House Association was formed, and remaining features from the building's past were restored to what they looked like when Howe met the patriots' delegation. In front of the house, a vast lawn descends to the Arthur Kill, where you can walk the beach and new park paths to Ward's Point, a quiet, mostly deserted area beneath high bluffs. The Conference House welcomes visitors: call (718) 984-0415 or go to www.theconferencehouse.org.

92 Main Street

From Arthur Kill Road to Hylan Boulevard

Tottenville is home to one of New York City's five Main Streets; there is one in each borough. Here, it's more or less a classic "Main," with mom-and-pop shops and the hulks of former banks. The grand Masonic Temple at 236 Main Street was formerly a post office; its terra-cotta ornamentation comes courtesy of the old Atlantic works. Across the street at 207 Main Street is the old Stadium Theater; its name can be faintly seen on the marquee. Elsewhere on Main Street, some very old ads remain: an old neon sign for Norge Appliances and a 1940s-era decal for "O'Sullivan's heels and soles—excellent work."

93 Perth Amboy Ferry

Arthur Kill Road and Bentley Street

A line of wooden pilings marks the remains of the ferry that ran from Tottenville to Perth Amboy, New Jersey, from the Tottenville Staten Island Railway Station on Bentley Street. The ferry began operations in 1867 and ran continuously until 1963; its boats were comparable in size to the South Ferry–St. George ferry until 1948, when a smaller fleet was in operation.

94 Tottenville Library

Amboy Road and Yetman Avenue

In 1904, Tottenville got its very own world-class Classical Revival library building designed by Carrere and Hastings, thanks to millionaire philanthropist Andrew Carnegie.

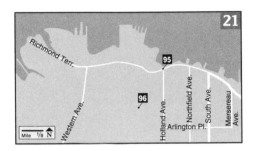

Mariners Harbor, Arlington, and How-land Hook are neighborhoods in northwestern Staten Island that stretch along the Kill Van Kull (separating Staten Island from New Jersey), between the Bayonne Bridge and the Arthur Kill. The huge Bayonne Bridge looms in the east, and Shooter's Island, now a wildlife preserve but formerly home to an oil refinery plant and shipyard, can be viewed from the shore. In an unusual arrangement, about a quarter of the island is in New Jersey, with three-quarters in New York; the birds don't mind.

BUS: S40 on Richmond Terrace; **S48** on Forest Avenue and South Avenue

95 Mariners Marsh

Richmond Terrace, near Holland Avenue

Mariners Marsh is a nature preserve in the far western corner of the island. It had a former life as an iron foundry and Downey Shipyard from 1907 to 1931. Concrete hulks of the old foundries are still found deep within the marsh. There are also rusted railroad tracks, a legacy of the lost shipbuilding businesses at Howland Hook. The tracks connected the waterfront with the now-dormant Arlington Yards.

North of the Arlington Yards in the western section of the marsh can be seen what remains of the old Procter & Gamble factory along Western Avenue. Beginning in 1907, P&G manufactured dozens of products, employing thousands over the years; Howland Hook became so identified with the factory that it became known as "Port Ivory" for P&G's Ivory Soap. At its height in the 1920s, the site employed 1,500. Port Ivory closed down in 1991, and while its old buildings remained intact until about 2000, the factory is now 99 and $^{44}/_{100}$ percent gone.

96 Arlington Yards

Accessible from Mariners Marsh Park

These railroad yards south of Mariners Marsh were formerly storage yards for the old SIRT passenger line, whose branch along Staten Island's north shore ceased operations in 1953, but whose rails and trestles are still remarkably intact; there is talk about reactivating the line for freight. The nearby Arthur Kill Bridge remains the only connection from Staten Island to New Jersey by rail.

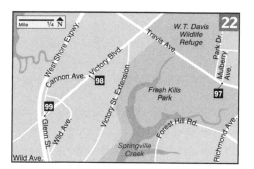

Travis is a lonely outpost even by Staten Island standards. A small village of about 2,000 at the western end of Victory Boulevard, it was an important crossing point (via the New Blazing Star Ferry) over the Arthur Kill to Carteret, New Jersey, in the colonial period. Just as Procter & Gamble made Mariners Harbor a company town for many years, so did the American Linoleum Company in Travis between 1873 and 1931. The industry became so identified with the region that the town became known as Linoleumville during that time. After the company moved to Philadelphia, residents voted to rename the town for early settler Captain Jacob Travis. The neighborhood is close to the old Fresh Kills Landfill, the largest waste disposal facility in the world covering more than 2,000 acres.

Travis maintains a small-town atmosphere; you can find barns complete with clucking chickens to the rear of some houses. It maintains its own volunteer fire department, Oceanic Hook and Ladder. Travis' annual Fourth of July parade, said to be the country's oldest, perennially attracts the NYC mayor and other politicians.

BUS: **S62** on Victory Boulevard

97 William T. Davis Wildlife Refuge
Travis and Mulberry Avenues

The 814-acre Davis Wildlife Refuge, named for the great Staten Island naturalist and entomologist, was NYC's first such sanctuary, and was established by Davis in 1933 during the heart of the Depression. The park is about equal in size to Central Park and contains a salt marsh featuring more than 100 species of birds. The refuge is best seen by canoeing in the broad Main and Springville Creeks.

98 The Cannon on Cannon Avenue
Cannon Avenue and Victory Boulevard

At the intersection of Victory Boulevard and Cannon Avenue, named for a promi-

STATEN ISLAND

nent local French Huguenot family, is a war memorial consisting of a small cannon and a stone marker depicting a gun-toting doughboy. The cannon was found decades ago and likely dates to the Revolutionary War, when British soldiers were housed in the area.

99 Sylvan Cemetery
Victory Boulevard and Glen Street

Located at the "V" formed by Victory Boulevard and Glen Street along the West Shore Expressway is one of NYC's spookiest locales: Sylvan, or Grove, Cemetery. Many of its stones are tipped over or have been vandalized or graffitied. What memorials remain remember the Prices and Cannons, for which Travis streets are named, as well as the Deckers, who are buried in many Staten Island cemeteries. In recent years, Friends of Abandoned Cemeteries, which has cleaned up other burial grounds in the borough, has been effective in stabilizing its condition and making it easier to walk through.

Sources

Bronx

MOTT HAVEN, THE HUB, MELROSE, AND CONCOURSE VILLAGE

Berman, Avis. "Beaux-Arts Battle in the Bronx." *New York Times*, 2 October 2005.

Gardner, Amanda. "Ruins with Tales to Tell." *New York Daily News*, 6 May 2000.

Hermalyn, Gary, and Robert Kornfeld. *Landmarks of the Bronx*. New York: Bronx County Historical Society, 1990.

"Jake Ruppert." BaseballLibrary.com. www. baseballlibrary.com/baseballlibrary/ ballplayers/R/Ruppert_Jake.stm.

McNamara, John. *History in Asphalt*. New York: Bronx County Historical Society, 1991.

————. *McNamara's Old Bronx*. New York: Bronx County Historical Society, 1989.

Reier, Sharon. *The Bridges of New York*. New York: Dover, 2000.

White, Norval, and Elliot Willensky. *AIA Guide to New York City*. New York: Three Rivers Press, 2000.

HIGH BRIDGE AND MORRIS HEIGHTS

Crowley, Jim. *Lighthouses of New York*. Saugerties: Hope Farm Press, 2000.

Lederer, Joseph. *All Around the Town: A Walking Guide to Outdoor Sculptures in New York City*. New York: Scribner, 1975.

McNamara, John. *McNamara's Old Bronx*. New York: Bronx County Historical Society, 1989.

Sullivan, C. J. "Bronx Stroll: Grand Concourse Solitaire." *New York Press*, 15–21 November, 2000.

White, Norval, and Elliot Willensky. *AIA Guide to New York City*. New York: Three Rivers Press, 2000.

HUNTS POINT AND LONGWOOD

Hermalyn, Gary, and Robert Kornfeld. *Landmarks of the Bronx*. New York: Bronx County Historical Society, 1990.

Kraybill, Charles. Charlie's Photo Guide to Old Bronx Movie Houses. "East Morrisania and Longwood." kraybill.home. mindspring.com/41/41theatres.html.

Kuntzman, Gersh. "Family History Shows Bronx as Rural Paradise." *New York Post*, 28 August 2000.

McNamara, John. *McNamara's Old Bronx*. New York: Bronx County Historical Society, 1989.

Upham, Ben. "The Timetable of Age Overtakes Stations." *New York Times*, 12 November 2000.

MOUNT HOPE, MOUNT EDEN, AND CROTONA PARK

Hermalyn, Gary, and Robert Kornfeld. *Landmarks of the Bronx*. New York: Bronx County Historical Society, 1990.

McNamara, John. *History in Asphalt*. New York: Bronx County Historical Society, 1991.

———. *McNamara's Old Bronx*. New York: Bronx County Historical Society, 1989.

UNIVERSITY HEIGHTS, TREMONT, AND FORDHAM

Berger, Joseph. "In Nearly All Its Grandeur, Paradise Reopens in Bronx." *New York Times*, 23 October 2005.

Friends of the Old Croton Aqueduct. *The Old Croton Aqueduct in New York City*. Dobbs Ferry: Friends of the Old Croton Aqueduct, Inc. 2004.

Graves, Neil. "Fame Is a Bust for Honorees in Bronx Hall." *New York Post*, 19 November 1999.

Kugel, Seth. "For an Opulent Movie Palace, New Hope for a Revival." *New York Times*, 3 August 2003.

McNamara, John. *History in Asphalt*. New York: Bronx County Historical Society, 1991.

———. *McNamara's Old Bronx*. New York: Bronx County Historical Society, 1989.

Samtur, Stephen, and Martin Jackson. *The Bronx: Lost, Found and Remembered, 1935–1975*. New York: Back in the Bronx, 1999.

Siegal, Nina. "Plugging a Hole in the Reservoir of Memory." *New York Times*, 7 May 2000.

Sullivan, C. J. "Bronx Stroll: The Big Clock." *New York Press*, 29 December 2000.

BELMONT, BRONX PARK SOUTH, AND WEST FARMS

Brennan, Joseph. "Bronx Railroad Stations." *Abandoned Stations*. 2001, 2002. www.columbia.edu/~brennan/abandoned/bronx.html.

Bryk, William. "The Road of Hubris." *New York Press*, 19 February 2002.

Hermalyn, Gary, and Robert Kornfeld. *Landmarks of the Bronx*. New York: Bronx County Historical Society, 1990.

Mittelbach, Margaret, and Michael Crewdson. *Wild New York*. New York: Three Rivers Press, 1997.

BEDFORD PARK AND NORWOOD

Hermalyn, Gary, and Robert Kornfeld. *Landmarks of the Bronx*. New York: Bronx County Historical Society, 1990.

McNamara, John. *History in Asphalt*. New York: Bronx County Historical Society, 1991.

———. *McNamara's Old Bronx*. New York: Bronx County Historical Society, 1989.

White, Norval, and Elliot Willensky. *AIA Guide to New York City*. New York: Three Rivers Press, 2000.

Twomey, Bill. Personal correspondence with the historian: Spring 2005.

KINGSBRIDGE AND KINGSBRIDGE HEIGHTS

White, Norval, and Elliot Willensky. *AIA Guide to New York City*. New York: Three Rivers Press, 2000.

SPUYTEN DUYVIL

McNamara, John. *McNamara's Old Bronx*. New York: Bronx County Historical Society, 1989.

Twomey, Bill. *The Bronx in Bits and Pieces*. Lincoln: iUniverse, 2004.

RIVERDALE AND VAN CORTLANDT PARK

McNamara, John. *History in Asphalt*. New York: Bronx County Historical Society, 1991.

———. *McNamara's Old Bronx*. New York: Bronx County Historical Society, 1989.

Dolkart, Andrew S., and Matthew A. Postal. *Guide to NYC Landmarks*. 3rd Ed. Hoboken: John Wiley, 2004

Levin, Sondra. "Landmarks Give Bronx

Revival Status and Beauty." *Bronx Times*, 8 February 2001.

PARKCHESTER, UNIONPORT, AND WESTCHESTER SQUARE

McNamara, John. *McNamara's Old Bronx*. New York: Bronx County Historical Society, 1989.

Tunick, Susan. *Terra-Cotta Skyline*. New York: Princeton Architectural Press, 1997.

Twomey, Bill. *The Bronx in Bits and Pieces*. Lincoln: iUniverse, 2004.

White, Norval, and Elliot Willensky. *AIA Guide to New York City*. New York: Three Rivers Press, 2000.

MORRIS PARK, PELHAM PARKWAY, AND BRONXDALE

Arcara, Roger. *Westchester's Forgotten Railway: An Account of the New York, Westchester, and Boston Railway Company*. New Rochelle: I & T Publishing, 1972.

Samtur, Stephen, and Martin Jackson. *The Bronx: Lost, Found and Remembered, 1935–1975*. New York: Back in the Bronx, 1999.

EASTCHESTER AND CO-OP CITY

Friedman, Rob. "Welcome to Freedomland, USA." ourworld.compuserve.com/homepages/robfriedman.

Hermalyn, Gary, and Robert Kornfeld. *Landmarks of the Bronx*. New York: Bronx County Historical Society, 1990.

Twomey, Bill. *The Bronx in Bits and Pieces*. Lincoln: iUniverse, 2004.

WAKEFIELD, WOODLAWN, AND WOODLAWN HEIGHTS

Critchell, David. "Big City Country Roads: Short on Charm, Long on Potholes." *New York Times*, 27 February 2000.

"From Abandoned to Abundant: 2002 Garden Crusader Winner: Grand Prize." Gardeners' Supply Company. www.gardeners.com/gardening/content.asp?copy_id=5154.

McNamara, John. *History in Asphalt*. New York: Bronx County Historical Society, 1991.

PELHAM BAY PARK

Hermalyn, Gary, and Robert Kornfeld. *Landmarks of the Bronx*. New York: Bronx County Historical Society, 1990.

McNamara, John. *History in Asphalt*. New York: Bronx County Historical Society, 1991.

CITY ISLAND

Crowley, Jim. *Lighthouses of New York*. Saugerties: Hope Farm Press, 2000.

Hermalyn, Gary, and Robert Kornfeld. *Landmarks of the Bronx*. New York: Bronx County Historical Society, 1990.

Seitz, Sharon, and Stuart Miller. *The Other Islands of New York City*. Woodstock: Countryman Press, 1996.

Twomey, Bill. *The Bronx in Bits and Pieces*. Lincoln: iUniverse, 2004.

SCHUYLERVILLE AND THROGS NECK

McNamara, John. *History in Asphalt*. New York: Bronx County Historical Society, 1991.

Twomey, Bill. *The Bronx in Bits and Pieces*. Lincoln: iUniverse, 2004.

Brooklyn

DUMBO AND VINEGAR HILL

Russell, Bill. "The Jay Street Connecting RR (JSC)." Penny Bridge, www2pb.ipsoft.net/railinfo/car-floats/jay-street-connecting.html.

White, Norval, and Elliot Willensky. *AIA Guide to New York City*. New York: Three Rivers Press, 2000.

Yuban Coffee. "The Yuban Story." www.yuban.com.

BROOKLYN HEIGHTS

Cooke, Hope. *Seeing New York*. Philadelphia: Temple University Press, 1995.

Grutchfield, Walter. "Mason Mints sign." www.waltergrutchfield.net/peaks.htm.

Joshi, S. T. *H. P. Lovecraft: A Life*. West Warwick: Necronomicon Press, 1996.

Lancaster, Clay. *Old Brooklyn Heights*. New York: Dover Books, 1979.

Wolfe, Gerard R. *New York: 15 Walking Tours, An Architectural Guide to the Metropolis*. New York: McGraw-Hill, 2003.

DOWNTOWN

Friedman, Joe. *Inside New York*. London: Phaidon 1992.

Lanigan-Schmidt, Therese. *Ghosts of New York City*. Atglen: Schiffer, 2003.

Morrone, Francis. *An Architectural Guidebook to Brooklyn*. Layton: Gibbs-Smith, 2001.

Williams, Ellen, and Steve Radlauer. *Historic Shops and Restaurants of New York*. New York: Little Bookroom, 2002.

FORT GREENE AND CLINTON HILL

Didik, Frank. "Didik Long Ranger." www.didik.com/didik_ct.htm.

Fort Greene Park Conservancy. "The History of Fort Greene Park." www.fortgreenepark.org/pages/history1.htm.

Leahy, Jack. "A Seminary Prep School to Be Closed." *New York Daily News*, 12 April 1985.

Manbeck, John B., ed. *The Neighborhoods of Brooklyn*. New Haven: Yale University Press, 1998.

Morrone, Francis. *An Architectural Guidebook to Brooklyn*. Layton: Gibbs-Smith, 2001.

White, Norval, and Elliot Willensky. *AIA Guide to New York City*. New York: Three Rivers Press, 2000.

Wolfe, Gerard R. *New York: 15 Walking Tours, An Architectural Guide to the Metropolis*. New York: McGraw-Hill, 2003.

PROSPECT HEIGHTS AND CROWN HEIGHTS

"Crow Hill and Some of Its Suggestions." *Brooklyn Eagle*, 9 December 1888. www.bklyn-genealogy-info.com.

Cudahy, Brian. *The Malbone Street Wreck*. New York: Fordham University Press, 1999.

Curtis, Lisa. "New Toy Box." www.gobrooklyn.com/html/issues/_vol25/25_49/bcmdesign.html.

Diamond, Douglas. "The New Franklin Shuttle." The Third Rail. www.thethirdrail.net/0003/bf_dd1.htm.

Lederer, Joseph. *All Around the Town: A Walking Guide to Outdoor Sculptures in New York City*. New York: Scribner, 1975.

White, Norval, and Elliot Willensky. *AIA Guide to New York City*. New York: Three Rivers Press, 2000.

GOWANUS AND COBBLE HILL

Jacobsen, Mark. "Signs of the Times." *New York* magazine, 19 February 2001.

Morrone, Francis. *An Architectural Guidebook to Brooklyn*. Layton: Gibbs-Smith, 2001.

Reier, Sharon. *The Bridges of New York*. New York: Dover, 2000.

Trancho-Robie, Corie. "Pippin on Third." www.callalillie.com, 14 June 2004.

RED HOOK

Brooklyn Historical Society. *Red Hook & Gowanus, Neighborhood History Guide*. New York: Brooklyn Historical Society, 2000.

Landmarks Preservation Commission, 18 December 2001 Designation List 332.

Jamieson, Wendell. "Long Voyage to the Bottom of the Harbor." *New York Times*, 18 August 2003.

———. "Sunny's Wonderful Saloon." *New York Times*, 27 October 2002.

Schlesinger, Toni. "On the Waterfront." *Village Voice*, 6 February 2002.

"Waterfront Museum and Showboat Barge." www.waterfrontmuseum.org/barge.htm.

WILLIAMSBURG

Federal Writers' Project Guide to 1930s New York, *The WPA Guide to New York City*. New York: Pantheon, 1982.

Hudes, Karen. "Love Among the Ruins." *Time Out New York*, 27 November 2003.

White, Norval, and Elliot Willensky. *AIA Guide to New York City*. New York: Three Rivers Press, 2000.

GREENPOINT

Historical Signs. New York City Department of Parks and Recreation, www.nycgovparks.org/sub_your_park/historical_signs.html.

Morrone, Francis. *An Architectural Guidebook to Brooklyn*. Layton: Gibbs-Smith, 2001.

Reiss, Marcia. *Brooklyn, Then and Now*. San Diego: Thunder Bay, 2002.

BUSHWICK

"Dr. Frederick A. Cook, the Man Who Inspired Enron." Peary & Henson Foundation. www.pearyhenson.org/dr_frederick_cook/index.html.

"Who Was Frederick A. Cook?" Frederick A. Cook Society, The. www.cookpolar.org.

"RKO Bushwick Theatre." Cinema Treasures. www.cinematreasures.org/theater/1322.

White, Norval, and Elliot Willensky. *AIA Guide to New York City*. New York: Three Rivers Press, 2000.

PARK SLOPE

Ansonia Clock Co. www.ansonia.com.

"Battle of Long Island." U.S. History.com. www.u-s-history.com/pages/h1279.html.

Hamill, Denis. "Factory Holds Memories, $800G Condos." *New York Daily News*, 20 July 2004.

Lederer, Joseph. *All Around the Town: A Walking Guide to Outdoor Sculptures in New York City*. New York: Scribner, 1975.

Maust, Don, ed. *Early American Clocks*. Uniontown: Warman, 1971

Morrone, Francis. *An Architectural Guidebook to Brooklyn*. Layton: Gibbs-Smith, 2001.

White, Norval, and Elliot Willensky. *AIA Guide to New York City*. New York: Three Rivers Press, 2000.

PROSPECT PARK

DeMause, Neil, and Richard Berenson. *Prospect Park and Brooklyn Botanic Garden*. New York: Silver Lining, 2001.

Lancaster, Clay. *Prospect Park Handbook*. New York: Walton H. Rawls, 1967.

GREEN-WOOD CEMETERY

Collins, Glenn. "Stories of the Civil War, Carved on Headstones." *New York Times*, 4 July 2003.

Richman, Jeffrey. *Brooklyn's Green-Wood Cemetery: New York's Buried Treasure*. Lunenberg: Stinehour, 1998.

Ziel, Ron, and George Foster. *Steel Rails to the Sunrise*. New York: Hawthorn, 1965.

SUNSET PARK

Kirkeby, Marc. "The King in Kings County."

Robbins, Michael W. and Wendy Palitz, eds. *Brooklyn: A State of Mind*. New York: Workman, 2001.

White, Norval, and Elliot Willensky. *AIA Guide to New York City*. New York: Three Rivers Press, 2000.

BAY RIDGE

Hoffman, Jerome. *Bay Ridge Chronicles 1524–1976*. New York: Bay Ridge Bicentennial Committee, 1976.

Merlis, Brian, and Lee Rosenzweig. *Bay Ridge and Fort Hamilton: A Photographic Journey*. New York: Israelowitz, 2000.

FLATBUSH, KENSINGTON, AND MIDWOOD

Abel, Allen. *Flatbush Odyssey*. Toronto: McClelland & Stewart, 1995.

Allbray, Nedda. *Flatbush, the Heart of Brooklyn*. Charleston: Arcadia, 2004.

Cullen, Eileen, and Gloria Fischer, Mary Kay Gallagher, and Margery Nathanson. *Prospect Park South: A History*. New York: Prospect Park South Association, 1997.

"Farragut Theater." Cinema Treasures. www.cinematreasures.org/theater/6266.

"Kenmore Theatre." Cinema Treasures. www.cinematreasures.org/theater/1749.

"Loew's Kings Theatre." Cinema Treasures. www.cinematreasures.org/theater/1360.

White, Norval, and Elliot Willensky. *AIA Guide to New York City*. New York: Three Rivers Press, 2000.

MIDWOOD AND SOUTH GREENFIELD

Gopnik, Adam. "New York Journal." *The New Yorker*, 5 February 2001.

Linder, Marc, and Lawrence S. Zacharias. *Of Cabbages and Kings County: Agriculture and the Formation of Modern Brooklyn*. Iowa City: University of Iowa Press 1999.

Matus, Paul. "The Little Station in the Woods." The Third Rail. www.thethirdrail.net/9912/index.htm.

Merlis, Brian. *Welcome Back to Brooklyn*. New York: Israelowitz, 1993.

Rawson, Elizabeth Reich. "Midwood." *The Encyclopedia of New York City*. Kenneth T. Jackson, ed. New Haven: Yale University Press, 1995.

Wright, Carol von Pressentin, Sharon Seitz, and Stuart Miller. *City Guide: New York*. London: A & C Black, 2002.

EAST FLATBUSH AND FLATLANDS

Dillard, Maud Esther. *Old Dutch Houses of Brooklyn*, New York: Richard R. Smith, 1945.

"Interactive Dig, Brooklyn." Archaeology.org, Archaeological Institute of America. www.archaeology.org/online/features/lott/index.html.

Williams, Joe, and Bill Hutchinson. "Old Slave Shelter Found in Brooklyn." *New York Daily News*, 2000.

Wright, Carol von Pressentin, Sharon Seitz, and Stuart Miller. *City Guide: New York*. London: A & C Black, 2002.

CANARSIE

Federal Writers' Project Guide to 1930s New York, *The WPA Guide to New York City*. New York: Pantheon, 1982.

Kluger, Ira. M. "The Pieter Clasen Wyckoff House from Farm Dwelling to Museum: A Chronology." The Wyckoff Association. www.wyckoffassociation.org/association/history_cronology.html.

Potter, Gene. "The Lott Family in Brooklyn." www.lottsinbklyn.homestead.com.

Whitehorne, Wayne. "BMT 14th Street—Canarsie Line." NYCsubway.org.www.nycsubway.org/lines/canarsie.html.

FLOYD BENNETT FIELD AND MARINE PARK

"Floyd Bennett Field." Deep Creek Yacht Club. deepcreekyachtclub.com/WebPage/FloydBennettField.html.

Jackson, Kenneth T., ed. *The Neighborhoods of Brooklyn*. New Haven: Yale University Press, 1998.

BATH BEACH AND GRAVESEND

Hamill, Denis. "Boro's Past Comes Alive on Grounds of Church." *New York Daily News*, 13 June 2000.

Hoffman, Jerome. *Bay Ridge Chronicles 1524–1976*. New York: Bay Ridge Bicentennial Committee, 1976.

Ierardi, Eric J. *Guide Map to Historical Sites in Gravesend, Brooklyn*. New York: Gravesend Historical Society, 1996.

Israelowitz, Oscar. *Flatbush Guide*. New York: Israelowitz, 1990.

White, Norval, and Elliot Willensky. *AIA Guide to New York City*. New York: Three Rivers Press, 2000.

CONEY ISLAND

Denson, Charles. *Coney Island Walking Tour*. Berkeley: Dreamland Press, 1998.

———, *Coney Island Lost and Found*. Berkeley: Ten Speed Press, 2002.

SHEEPSHEAD BAY

Merlis, Brian, Lee Rosenzweig, and I. Stephen Miller. *Brooklyn's Gold Coast: The Sheepshead Bay Communities*. New York: Sheepshead Bay Historical Society, 1997.

BEDFORD-STUYVESANT AND CROWN HEIGHTS

White, Norval, and Elliot Willensky. *AIA Guide to New York City*. New York: Three Rivers Press, 2000.

BROWNSVILLE AND EAST NEW YORK

Fortunoff's: Our History. www.fortunoffs.com/history.asp.

"Loew's Pitkin Theatre." Cinema Treasures. www.cinematreasures.org/theater/3887.

White, Norval, and Elliot Willensky. *AIA Guide to New York City*. New York: Three Rivers Press, 2000.

HIGHLAND PARK AND CYPRESS HILLS

Cypress Hills National Cemetery. Historical Information. www.cem.va.gov/nchp/cypresshills.htm.

Kennedy, Randy. "He Was Custer's Bugler. Then, the Subway Called." *New York Times*, 29 July 2003.

New York City Department of Parks and Recreation. "Mayor Michael Bloomberg Announces Ridgewood Reservoir to Become Parkland." www.nycgovparks.org/sub_newsroom/press_releases/press_releases.php?id=19083.

Manhattan

THE BATTERY, WALL STREET, AND CITY HALL

Berger, Meyer. *Meyer Berger's New York*. New York: Random House, 1960.

Bryk, William. "Big Bang on Wall Street." *New York Press*, 1 March 2001.

Chandler, Harry A. "Trinity Church and Burial Ground." *Valentine's Manual of Old New York, Vol. 6*. Henry Collins Brown, ed. New York: Henry Collins Brown, 1921.

Columbia Electronic Encyclopedia, 6th Ed. "Ohio Company of Associates." New York: Columbia University Press, 2005.

Diamonstein, Barbaralee. *The Landmarks of New York City*. New York: Harry N. Abrams, 1998.

"Ohio Company of Associates." www.infoplease.com/ce6/history/A0836450.html.

Pirmann, David. "City Hall (IRT East Side Line)." NYCSubway.org.www.nycsubway.org/perl/stations?5:979.

Stookey, Lee. *Subway Ceramics*. Brattleboro: Lee Stookey, 1994.

SOUTH STREET SEAPORT

Collins, Glenn. "A Distant Past Is Just a Local Stop." *New York Times*, 28 April 2003.

Crowley, Jim. *Lighthouses of New York*. Saugerties: Hope Farm Press, 2000.

Gayle, Margot, and Edmund V. Gillon, Jr. *Cast-Iron Architecture in New York*. New Hyde Park: Dover 1974.

Moscow, Henry. *The Street Book*. New York: Hagstrom, 1978.

White, Norval, and Elliot Willensky. *AIA Guide to New York City*. New York: Three Rivers Press, 2000.

TRIBECA AND SOHO

Allen, Oliver E. *Tales of Old Tribeca*. New York: Tribeca Trib, 1999.

"Down Under: The Subway Celebrates Its Centenary." The Economist Cities Guide. www.economist.com/cities/displayObject.cfm?obj_id=3285030&city_id=NY.

Fierstein, Sanna. *Naming New York*. New York: New York University Press, 2001.

Rogers, Josh. "Ferry Owner Says Bye to Tribeca." *Downtown Express*, 17 November 2003.

"The African Burial Ground: Return to the Past to Build the Future." www.africanburialground.gov/ABG_Main.htm.

White, Norval, and Elliot Willensky. *AIA Guide to New York City*. New York: Three Rivers Press, 2000.

LOWER EAST SIDE

Kahn, Robert, ed. *City Secrets, New York City*. New York: Little Bookroom 2002.

Kamil, Seth, and Eric Wakin. *The Big Onion Guide to New York City*. New York: New York University Press, 2002.

Manhattan. Hagstrom Maps. New York: Hagstrom, 1945.

Pollack, Michael. FYI Column. *New York Times*, 5 December 2004.

White, Norval, and Elliot Willensky. *AIA Guide to New York City*. New York: Three Rivers Press, 2000.

GREENWICH VILLAGE

Dunlap, David. *On Broadway: A Journey Uptown Over Time*. New York: Rizzoli, 1990.

Gussow, Mel. "The House on West 11th Street." *New York Times*, 5 March 2000.

Hyman, Martin D. "A Comfortable Little Hotel." *Seaport* Magazine, Summer 1991.

Janvier, Thomas. *In Old New York*. New York: St. Martin's Press, 2000.

Lambe, Clare. "What's Up with That." *Time Out New York*, 15 April 2004.

Miller, Terry. *Greenwich Village and How It Got That Way*. New York: Crown, 1990.

EAST VILLAGE

Dunshee, Kenneth. *As You Pass By*. New York: Hastings House, 1952.

Hemp, William. *New York Enclaves*. New York: Clarkson Potter, 2003.

Miller, Eric. "Festive Art in a Festive Neighborhood: Street Mosaics in New York City's East Village." University of Pennsylvania, 2000. www.ccat.sas.upenn.edu/~emiller/mosaics_paper.html.

Miller, Terry. *Greenwich Village and How It Got That Way*. New York: Crown, 1990.

CHELSEA

Grutchfield, Walter. "Stern Brothers." *14 to 42*. www.14to42.net/sternbros.htm.

Kannapell, Andrea, and Jesse McKinley, Daniel B. Schneider, Kathryn Shattuck, and Jennifer Steinhauer. *The Curious New Yorker*. New York: Times Books, 1999.

Miller, Terry. *Greenwich Village and How It Got That Way*. New York: Crown, 1990.

White, Norval, and Elliot Willensky. *AIA Guide to New York City*. New York: Three Rivers Press, 2000.

MADISON SQUARE PARK AND GRAMERCY PARK

Lederer, Joseph. *All Around the Town: A Walking Guide to Outdoor Sculptures in New York City*. New York: Scribner, 1975.

White, Norval, and Elliot Willensky. *AIA Guide to New York City*. New York: Three Rivers Press, 2000.

PENN STATION AREA

Diehl, Lorraine B. *The Late, Great Pennsylvania Station*. New York: Four Walls Eight Windows, 1996.

Naureckas, Jim. New York Songlines. www.nysonglines.com.

Ziel, Ron, and George Foster. *Steel Rails to the Sunrise*. New York: Hawthorn, 1965.

GRAND CENTRAL, MURRAY HILL, AND TURTLE BAY

Berger, Meyer. *Meyer Berger's New York*. New York: Random House, 1960.

Naureckas, Jim. New York Songlines. www.

home.nyc.rr.com/jkn/nysonglines/36st. htm.

"The Wall: Where Is It Now?" Time.com. www.time.com/time/daily/special/ photo/berlin2/4.html.

Weber, Rennie C. "Sale of Amster Yard: Remembering Jimmy." Turtle Bay Organization. www.turtlebay-nyc.org/articles/sale081799.html.

White, Norval, and Elliot Willensky. *AIA Guide to New York City*. New York: Three Rivers Press, 2000.

TIMES SQUARE

Dunlap, David. "Crossroads of the Whirl." *New York Times*, 28 March 2004.

Lederer, Joseph. *All Around the Town: A Walking Guide to Outdoor Sculptures in New York City*. New York: Scribner, 1975.

Risen, Clay. "The Knickerbocker." *Morning News*, 9 September 2003. www.themorningnews.org/archives/new_york_new_york/the_knickerbocker.phpthemorningnews.org.

HELL'S KITCHEN

Berger, Meyer. *Meyer Berger's New York*. New York: Random House, 1960.

CENTRAL PARK

Berenson, Richard, and Carroll Raymond. *Barnes & Noble Complete Illustrated Map and Guidebook to Central Park*. New York: Silver Lining, 1999.

Bryk, William. "Central Park Still Awaits the British." *New York Press*, 5 February 2002.

Gayle, Margot, and Michele Cohen. *Art Commission and the Municipal Art Society Guide to Manhattan's Outdoor Sculpture*. New York: Prentice Hall Press, 1988.

Silver, Nathan. *Lost New York*. New York: Houghton Mifflin, 2000.

UPPER EAST SIDE, YORKVILLE, AND CARNEGIE HILL

Dunlap, David. "Bell Tolls for Reminder of Trolleys Past." *New York Times*, 11 July 2003.

Fierstein, Sanna. *Naming New York*. New York: New York University Press, 2001.

Gray, Christopher. *New York Streetscapes*. New York: Harry N. Abrams, 2002.

Hunting, Mary Anne. "Seventh Regiment Armory." *Antiques* Magazine, January 1999.

Kahn, Robert, ed. *City Secrets, New York City*. New York: Little Bookroom, 2002.

Lippincott, E. E. "A Historic Lamp Is Lost: Fingers Are Pointed Everywhere." *New York Times*, 8 July, 2001.

Trancho-Robie, Corie. "The Shively Sanitary Tenements." www.callalillie.com, 2 February 2004.

White, Norval, and Elliot Willensky. *AIA Guide to New York City*. New York: Three Rivers Press, 2000.

ROOSEVELT ISLAND

Seitz, Sharon, and Stuart Miller. *The Other Islands of New York City*. Woodstock: Countryman Press, 1996.

"The Tram." Roosevelt Island Operating Corporation. www.rioc.com/transportation.html#tramway.

White, Norval, and Elliot Willensky. *AIA Guide to New York City*. New York: Three Rivers Press, 2000.

UPPER WEST SIDE

Gayle, Margot, and Michele Cohen. *Art Commission and the Municipal Art Society Guide to Manhattan's Outdoor Sculpture*. New York: Prentice Hall Press, 1988.

Gray, Christopher. "A Tiny Street Where Interim Became Permanent." *New York Times*, 16 January 2000.

Prager, J. Simon. "Eleven Horsemen of the Metropolis." *New York* magazine. 6 March 1978.

White, Norval, and Elliot Willensky. *AIA Guide to New York City*. New York: Three Rivers Press, 2000.

MORNINGSIDE HEIGHTS AND MANHATTANVILLE

Brennan, Joseph. "Tracks on Broadway." www.nycsubway.org/nyc/tracks.

Bryk, William. "I Fights Mit Sigel." *New York Press*, 21 June 2000.

Gayle, Margot, and Michele Cohen. *Art Commission and the Municipal Art Society Guide to Manhattan's Outdoor Sculpture*. New York: Prentice Hall Press, 1988.

Moscow, Henry. *The Street Book*. New York: Hagstrom, 1978.

Washington, Eric K. *Manhattanville: Old Heart of West Harlem*. Charleston: Arcadia, 2002.

HARLEM AND HAMILTON HEIGHTS

Dorkin, Andrew, and Gretchen Sorkin. *Touring Historic Harlem*. New York: New York Landmarks Conservancy, 1997.

Dunshee, Kenneth. *As You Pass By*. New York: Hastings House, 1952.

White, Norval, and Elliot Willensky. *AIA Guide to New York City*. New York: Three Rivers Press, 2000.

WASHINGTON HEIGHTS

Gray, Christopher. "An Elevated 1893 Roadway with a Lacy Elegance." *New York Times*, 9 July 2000.

"Hooper Fountain." New York City Department of Parks and Recreation. www.nycgovparks.org/sub_your_park/historical_signs/hs_historical_sign.php?id=8726.

"John T. Brush." Baseball Library.com. www.baseballlibrary.com/baseballlibrary/ballplayers/B/Brush_John_T.stm.

Ullmann, Albert. *Landmark History of New York*. New York: D. Appleton, 1903.

White, Norval, and Elliot Willensky. *AIA Guide to New York City*. New York: Three Rivers Press, 2000.

New York Times, eds. FYI Column. *Only in New York*. New York: St. Martin's Griffin, 2004.

INWOOD AND MARBLE HILL

Burrows, Edwin, and Mike Wallace. *Gotham*. New York: Oxford University Press, 1995.

Mittelbach, Margaret, and Michael Crewdson. *Wild New York*. New York: Three Rivers Press, 1997.

White, Norval, and Elliot Willensky. *AIA Guide to New York City*. New York: Three Rivers Press, 2000.

Yeadon, David. *New York's Nooks and Crannies*. New York: Scribner, 1979.

Queens

ASTORIA

"About the Museum." Museum of the Moving Image. www.ammi.org/site/about/index.html.

"Captain James Lawrence." Burlington City, New Jersey. www.08016.com/lawrence.html.

"Chronology of the Life of Isamu Noguchi." Noguchi Museum. www.noguchi.org/chrono.html.

Seyfried, Vincent. "Astoria." *The Encyclopedia of New York City*. Kenneth T. Jackson, ed. New Haven: Yale University Press, 1995.

"Socrates History." Socrates Sculpture Park. www.socratessculpturepark.org/History/History.htm.

"Steinway History." Steinway & Sons. www.steinway.com/factory/steinway_history.shtml.

White, Norval, and Elliot Willensky. *AIA Guide to New York City*. New York: Three Rivers Press, 2000.

LONG ISLAND CITY AND HUNTER'S POINT

Brill, Louis M. "The Pepsi-Cola Generation." Signweb. www.signweb.com/neon/cont/pepsigen.html.

"Dutch Kills." Greater Astoria Historical Society. www.astorialic.org/neighborhoods/dutchkills.shtm.

Gerber, Joanne. "History and the Waterfront Crabhouse." *Queens Ledger*, 29 October 1981.

Greater Astoria Historical Society. *Long Island City*. Charleston: Arcadia, 2004.

"Hunters Point." Greater Astoria Historical Society. www.astorialic.org/neighborhoods/hunterspoint.shtm.

Kelsey, J. S. "History of the Long Island Star 1865–1896." Greater Astoria Historical Society. www.astorialic.org/starjournal/1800s/star_1896.shtm.

"Queens Man Turns His Home Into a Shrine to the RMS *Titanic*." *Newsday*, 25 August 2005.

Reifschneider, Felix. "History of the Long Island Rail Road." Third Rail, ed. Paul Matus. www.thethirdrail.net/0103/reif1.html.

Seyfried, Vincent. "300 Years of Long Island City." Garden City: Edgian Press, 1984.

Tunick, Susan. *Terra-Cotta Skyline*. New York: Princeton Architectural Press, 1997.

White, Norval, and Elliot Willensky. *AIA Guide to New York City*. New York: Three Rivers Press, 2000.

BLISSVILLE, WEST MASPETH, AND SUNNYSIDE

Kroessler, Jeffrey, and Nina Rappaport. *Historic Preservation in Queens*. New York: Queensborough Preservation League, 1990.

New York Transit Museum. *Subway Style: 100 Years of Architecture & Design in the New York City Subway*. New York: Stewart, Tabori & Chang, 2004.

"Map of the Northerly Part of the Borough of Queens, New York." Ritter-Swenson Queens Real Estate, 1938.

Reier, Sharon. *The Bridges of New York*. New York: Dover, 2000.

Ritter, Lawrence S. *East Side, West Side:*

Tales of New York Sporting Life, 1910–1960. New York: Total Sports, 1998.

WOODSIDE AND JACKSON HEIGHTS

"Fair Theatre." Cinema Treasures. www.cinematreasures.org/theater/4030.

Gregory, Catherine. *Woodside: A Historical Perspective 1652–1994*. New York: Woodside on the Move, 1994.

"Map of the Northerly Part of the Borough of Queens, New York." Ritter-Swenson Queens Real Estate, 1938.

"Scrabble History." Ideafinder. www.ideafinder.com/history/inventions/story059.htm.

Seyfried, Vincent. *Brooklyn Rapid Transit Trolley Lines in Queens*. East Norwich: N.J. International, 1998.

MASPETH AND MIDDLE VILLAGE

Stankowski, Barbara. *Maspeth, Our Town*. New York: Maspeth Savings & Loan Association, 1977.

Yang, John. *Mount Zion: Sepulchral Portraits*. New York: D.A.P., 2001.

RIDGEWOOD

"The Bohack Family." *Newsday*: Long Island, Our Story. www.newsday.com/community/guide/lihistory/ny-history-famboha,0,106322.story.

Kroessler, Jeffrey, and Nina Rappaport. *Historic Preservation in Queens*. New York: Queensborough Preservation League, 1990.

Lewis, Michael. "Historic Field Sees 21st Century Future." *Artificial Turf News*. www.artificialturf.org/display.cfm?newsID=200.

White, Norval, and Elliot Willensky. *AIA Guide to New York City*. New York: Three Rivers Press, 2000.

REGO PARK, FOREST HILLS, AND KEW GARDENS

"The History of the Pullis Farm Cemetery Landmark." Juniper Park Civic

Association. www.junipercivic.com/berry/0703/pullis.html.

Kershaw, Sarah. "Protector of the Long Departed." *New York Times*, 29 December 2000.

Kilgannon, Corey. "Nostalgia, Anyone? Hope Rises at Forest Hills." *New York Times*, 12 September 2004.

Lederer, Joseph. *All Around the Town: A Walking Guide to Outdoor Sculptures in New York City*. New York: Scribner, 1975.

Lewis, Barry. *Kew Gardens: Urban Village in the Big City*. New York: Kew Gardens Council for Recreation and the Arts, 1999.

"Our History." The West Side Tennis Club at Forest Hills. www.foresthillstennis.com/wstcnew/about%20wstc/wstchistory.htm.

ELMHURST AND CORONA

Alpern, Andrew, and Seymour Durst. *New York's Architectural Holdouts*, New York: Dover, 1984.

Kroessler, Jeffrey, and Nina Rappaport. *Historic Preservation in Queens*. New York: Queensborough Preservation League, 1990.

Seyfried, Vincent. *The Story of Corona*. New York: Edgian Press, 1986.

White, Norval, and Elliot Willensky. *AIA Guide to New York City*. New York: Three Rivers Press, 2000.

FLUSHING MEADOWS PARK AND 1939 AND 1964 WORLD'S FAIR REMNANTS

"Flushing Meadows–Corona Park Today." nywf64.com/fmcp03.shtml.

"Flushing Meadows Corona Park Virtual Tour." New York City Department of Parks and Recreation. www.nycgov-parks.org/sub_your_park/vt_flushing_meadows/vt_flushing_meadows_park.html.

Lederer, Joseph. *All Around the Town: A Walking Guide to Outdoor Sculptures in New York City*. New York: Scribner, 1975.

FLUSHING

Berliner III, Sam. "Central Railroad of Long Island." home.att.net/~Berliner-Ultrasonics/lirr-crr.html.

Bertrand, Donald. "Mansion Rescue Mission." *New York Daily News*, 27 May 2001.

DeWan, George. "The Blooming of Flushing." *Long Island: Our Story*. New York: Newsday, 1998

Graziano, Paul. "A Brief History of Waldheim." www.votegraziano.com/plans_waldheim.html.

Grumet, Robert Steven. *Native American Place Names in New York City*. New York: Museum of the City of New York, 1981.

"The House: History." Bowne House Historical Society. www.bownehouse.org/photo/history.shtm.

Kroessler, Jeffrey, and Nina Rappaport. *Historic Preservation in Queens*. New York: Queensborough Preservation League, 1990.

Rhoades, Liz. "City to Spend $192,000 on Velodrome in Kissena Park." *Queens Chronicle*, 3 October 2002.

Sherman, Dick. "Flushing Museum Takes Root." *New York Daily News*, 18 July 2000.

Zaremba, Peter. "My Corona." *Time Out Book of New York Walks*. London: Penguin, 2000.

COLLEGE POINT AND WHITESTONE

Freeman, Paul. Abandoned & Little-Known Airfields. www.airfields-freeman.com.

Kroessler, Jeffrey, and Nina Rappaport. *Historic Preservation in Queens*. New York: Queensborough Preservation League, 1990.

AUBURNDALE AND BAYSIDE

Alperstein, David. *Fort Totten at Willets Point*. New York: EPVA, 1979. *Art En Route*. MTA guide to art in the MTA Network, 2002.

Chang, Sophia. "Emblematic Bell Blvd. Home Earns Landmark Status." *Bayside Times*, 11 November 2004.

FitzGerald, Claire. "Volunteer Guards Fort Totten for Queens to Enjoy." *Bayside Times*, 24 April 1997.

Judd, Walter. "Jim Corbett." *Bayside Times*, 2 June 1984.

Kroessler, Jeffrey, and Nina Rappaport. *Historic Preservation in Queens*. New York: Queensborough Preservation League, 1990.

"Oakland Lake." New York City Department of Parks and Recreation. www.nycgovparks.org/sub_your_park/historical_signs/hs_historical_sign.php?id=12634.

Solomon, Deborah. *Utopia Parkway: The Life and Work of Joseph Cornell*. New York: Farrar Straus & Giroux, 1997.

White, Norval, and Elliot Willensky. *AIA Guide to New York City*. New York: Three Rivers Press, 2000.

DOUGLASTON AND LITTLE NECK

Feinstein, John. *Hard Courts*. New York: Villard Books, 1991.

Kroessler, Jeffrey, and Nina Rappaport. *Historic Preservation in Queens*. New York: Queensborough Preservation League, 1990.

"The Story of the Douglaston Estate Windmill." Alley Pond Environmental Center, 1995.

"Udalls Park Preserve." New York City Department of Parks and Recreation. www.nycgovparks.org/sub_your_park/historical_signs/hs_historical_sign.php?id=11331.

GLEN OAKS, BELLEROSE, AND FLORAL PARK

Berliner III, Sam. "Long Island Motor Parkway." www.home.att.net/~berliner-ultrasonics/limtrpwy.html.

DeWan, George. "A Long Island Victory Tour." *Long Island: Our Story*. New York: *Newsday*, 1998.

Goode, Erica. "A Protected Space, Where Art Comes Calling." *New York Times*, 30 July 2002.

Mittelbach, Margaret, and Michael Crewdson. *Wild New York*. New York: Three Rivers Press, 1997.

Seyfried, Vincent, and William Asedorian. *Old Queens: New York in Early Photographs*. New York: Dover, 1991.

RICHMOND HILL

Ballenas, Carl, and Nancy Cataldi. *Richmond Hill*. Charleston: Arcadia, 2002.

"Historical Places of Interest in Richmond Hill, NY." Richmond Hill Historical Society. www.richmondhillhistory.org/rh-places.html.

Lewis, Barry. *Kew Gardens: Urban Village in the Big City*. New York: Kew Gardens Council for Recreation and the Arts, 1999.

"RKO Bushwick Theatre." Cinema Treasures. www.cinematreasures.org/theater/3972.

WOODHAVEN

White, Norval, and Elliot Willensky. *AIA Guide to New York City*. New York: Three Rivers Press, 2000.

JAMAICA

"History of the First Presbyterian Church in Jamaica, New York City." First Presbyterian Church in Jamaica. www.firstchurchjamaica.org/church_history.htm.

Kahn, Jonathan. "King Manor." *The Encyclopedia of New York City*. Kenneth T. Jackson, ed. New Haven: Yale University Press, 1995.

Kroessler, Jeffrey, and Nina Rappaport. *Historic Preservation in Queens*. New York: Queensborough Preservation League, 1990.

Millionaire, Tony, and Marc H. Miller. *Queens Jazz Trail*. New York: Ephemera Press, 2000.

Simunek, Chris. "Summer Dead Tour." *New York Press*, 14 September 2004.

White, Norval, and Elliot Willensky. *AIA Guide to New York City*. New York: Three Rivers Press, 2000.

OZONE PARK AND HOWARD BEACH

"Howard Beach History." Howard Beach. com. www.howardbeach.com/history/ default.htm.

BROAD CHANNEL

Seitz, Sharon, and Stuart Miller. *The Other Islands of New York City*. Woodstock: Countryman Press, 1996.

Yeadon, David. *New York's Nooks and Crannies*. New York: Scribner, 1979.

FAR ROCKAWAY

"RKO Strand Theatre." Cinema Treasures. www.cinematreasures.org/theater/3973.

Seyfried, Vincent, and William Asedorian. *Old Rockaway: New York in Early Photographs*. New York: Dover, 2000.

FORT TILDEN AND RIIS PARK

"The History of Fort Tilden, New York." www.geocities.com/fort_tilden.

Staten Island

ST. GEORGE

Crowley, Jim. *Lighthouses of New York*. Saugerties: Hope Farm Press, 2000.

Eisenstein, Hank, and Peggy Darlington. "SIRT: Staten Island Rapid Transit." NYCSubway. www.nycsubway.org/nyc/ sirt.

Morrone, Francis. "The Ghost of Monsieur Stokes." *City Journal*, Autumn 1997.

Robinson, Gail. "One Family Restores a Non-Landmark Theater." *Gotham Gazette*, 15 August 2005. www.gothamgazette.com/article/fea/20050815/ 202/1513.

NEW BRIGHTON

Dickenson, Richard, ed. *Holden's Staten Island*. New York: Center for Migration Studies, 2002.

White, Norval, and Elliot Willensky. *AIA Guide to New York City*. New York: Three Rivers Press, 2000.

Yeadon, David. *New York's Nooks and Crannies*. New York: Scribner, 1979.

GRYMES HILL AND SILVER LAKE

Dickenson, Richard, ed. *Holden's Staten Island*. New York: Center for Migration Studies, 2002.

STAPLETON AND CLIFTON

Hogrogian, John. "The Staten Island Stapletons." Professional Football Researchers Organization. www.footballresearch. com/articles/frpage.cfm?topic=stapes/.

"Paramount Theater." Cinema Treasures. www.cinematreasures.org/theater/1864.

White, Norval, and Elliot Willensky. *AIA Guide to New York City*. New York: Three Rivers Press, 2000.

Zavin, Shirley, and Elsa Gilbertson. *Staten Island Walking Tours*. New York: Preservation League of Staten Island, 1986.

ROSEBANK

Dickenson, Richard, ed. *Holden's Staten Island*. New York: Center for Migration Studies, 2002.

Garibaldi-Meucci Museum. www.garibaldimeuccimuseum.org/.

Novotny, Ann. *Alice's World*. Old Greenwich: Chatham Press, 1976.

PORT RICHMOND

Eisenstein, Hank, and Peggy Darlington. "SIRT: Staten Island Rapid Transit." NYCSubway. www.nycsubway.org/nyc/ sirt/.

White, Norval, and Elliot Willensky. *AIA Guide to New York City*. New York: Three Rivers Press, 2000.

Zavin, Shirley, and Elsa Gilbertson. *Staten Island Walking Tours*. New York: Preservation League of Staten Island, 1986.

SUNNYSIDE

Dickenson, Richard, ed. *Holden's Staten Island*. New York: Center for Migration Studies, 2002.

Kershner, Bruce. *Secret Places of Staten Island*. Dubuque: Kendall-Hunt, 1998.

WESTERLEIGH

Dickenson, Richard, ed. *Holden's Staten Island*. New York: Center for Migration Studies, 2002.

"Westerleigh Park." New York City Department of Parks and Recreation. nycgovparks.org/sub_your_park/historical_signs/hs_historical_sign.php?id=12295/.

White, Norval, and Elliot Willensky. *AIA Guide to New York City*. New York: Three Rivers Press, 2000.

WILLOWBROOK

Dickenson, Richard, ed. *Holden's Staten Island*. New York: Center for Migration Studies, 2002.

Kershner, Bruce. *Secret Places of Staten Island*. Dubuque: Kendall-Hunt, 1998.

Preservation League of Staten Island. "The Future of the Farm Colony Historic District." www.preservesi.org/fall02/fall02.htm#darmcolony/.

NEW SPRINGVILLE AND HEARTLAND VILLAGE

Preservation League of Staten Island. "Colonel Ichabod B. Crane House: Artifacts Find a Permanent Home." www.preservesi.org/dec97.htm#crane/.

Trust for Public Land, The. "NYC's Last Working Farm Protected." www.tpl.org/tier3_print.cfm?folder_id=631&content_item_id=14025&mod_type=1/.

DONGAN HILLS

Dickenson, Richard, ed. *Holden's Staten Island*. New York: Center for Migration Studies, 2002.

Mondello, Thomas. Orchard Inn Reunion. orchardinnreunion.homestead.com/orchard_memory_10.html/.

White, Norval, and Elliot Willensky. *AIA Guide to New York City*. New York: Three Rivers Press, 2000.

NEW DORP

Crowley, Jim. *Lighthouses of New York*. Saugerties: Hope Farm Press, 2000.

Dickenson, Richard, ed. *Holden's Staten Island*. New York: Center for Migration Studies, 2002.

Kershner, Bruce. *Secret Places of Staten Island*. Dubuque: Kendall-Hunt, 1998.

"Lane Theater." Cinema Treasures. www.cinematreasures.org/theater/3414/.

LA TOURETTE PARK

Kershner, Bruce. *Secret Places of Staten Island*. Dubuque: Kendall-Hunt, 1998.

ANNADALE AND ELTINGVILLE

Dickenson, Richard, ed. *Holden's Staten Island*. New York: Center for Migration Studies, 2002.

Egish, Gertrude. *Next Stop: Annadale*. 2nd Ed. New York: Staten Island Historical Society, 1997.

Kershner, Bruce. *Secret Places of Staten Island*. Dubuque: Kendall Hunt, 1998.

Preservation League of Staten Island. "The Little Woods of Arden House." www.preservesi.org/sept97news.htm#woods/.

RICHMONDTOWN AND GREAT KILLS

Dickenson, Richard, ed. *Holden's Staten Island*. New York: Center for Migration Studies, 2002.

Kershner, Bruce. *Secret Places of Staten Island*. Dubuque: Kendall-Hunt, 1998.

LIGHTHOUSE HILL

Crowley, Jim. *Lighthouses of New York*. Saugerties: Hope Farm Press, 2000.

Ferrer, Margaret. *Richmond Town and Lighthouse Hill*. Charleston: Arcadia, 1996.

Jacques Marchais Museum of Tibetan Art. www.tibetanmuseum.org/.

ROSSVILLE AND WOODROW

Dickenson, Richard, ed. *Holden's Staten Island*. New York: Center for Migration Studies, 2002.

KREISCHERVILLE

Dickenson, Richard, ed. *Holden's Staten Island*. New York: Center for Migration Studies, 2002.

White, Norval, and Elliot Willensky. *AIA Guide to New York City*. New York: Three Rivers Press, 2000.

Zavin, Shirley, and Elsa Gilbertson. *Staten Island Walking Tours*. New York: Preservation League of Staten Island, 1986.

PRINCE'S BAY

Dickenson, Richard, ed. *Holden's Staten Island*. New York: Center for Migration Studies, 2002.

Kershner, Bruce. *Secret Places of Staten Island*. Dubuque: Kendall-Hunt, 1998.

Preservation League of Staten Island. "The Abraham Manee House—Another S.I. Landmark at Risk." www.preservesi.org/dec97.htm#manee/.

TOTTENVILLE

Dickenson, Richard, ed. *Holden's Staten Island*. New York: Center for Migration Studies, 2002.

White, Norval, and Elliot Willensky. *AIA Guide to New York City*. New York: Three Rivers Press, 2000.

NORTHWEST STATEN ISLAND

Dickenson, Richard, ed. *Holden's Staten Island*. New York: Center for Migration Studies, 2002.

Kershner, Bruce. *Secret Places of Staten Island*. Dubuque: Kendall-Hunt, 1998.

Seitz, Sharon, and Stuart Miller. *The Other Islands of New York City*. Woodstock: Countryman Press, 1996.

TRAVIS

Kershner, Bruce. *Secret Places of Staten Island*. Dubuque: Kendall-Hunt, 1998.

Acknowledgments

Forgotten-ny.com, the website, wouldn't have happened had I not stumbled on three influential websites in 1997: Jeff Saltzman's Streetlite Nuts (http://streetlights.tripod.com/), a compendium of pictures and descriptions of New York City streetlamps; Steve Anderson's nycroads.com, an indispensable collection of pictures, descriptions, and histories of the highways of New York and environs; and Frank Jump's Faded Ads (www.frankjump.com), presenting a plethora of decades-old NYC advertising from another age with evocative descriptions. I was inspired to create Forgotten-ny.com by these sites. All three web innovators were on my initial ForgottenTour in June 1999, which amounted to a mini–all star NYC urban exploration voyage down Broadway—the one in Brooklyn.

Forgotten-ny.com would also not be the website it is today without the assistance, aid, and, most important, friendship of Maspeth's Christina Wilkinson, the Queen of Queens; she has a passion for urban exploration and preservation that rivals and occasionally surpasses my own, and her contributions as a Forgotten NY correspondent have been recognized by City Councilman Dennis Gallagher and State Senator Serphin Maltese, who have awarded her, respectively, with a Legislative Proclamation and a Certificate of Appreciation and Recognition for her site contributions.

The talents of Gary Fonville and Mike Olshan, who have contributed much editorial material and photography, must also be recognized, as well as the friendship of Vinny Losinno, who often has provided transportation for your auto-free webmaster.

My best friend, Mary Beth Henry, has been with me on many of my Forgotten voyages and has seen most of my ever-changing moods, most of them surly ones, and she has persevered with me nonetheless; and Brian Black, Gary Jucha, and Gerry Sankner, who have been with me for thirty years, have supported me through their occasional mystification at what I have been trying to accomplish with my admiration for rusty lampposts and abandoned railroad tracks.

In early 2003 I received an email from Matthew Benjamin, an editor at Harper-Collins, inquiring whether I would like to write a book based on Forgotten-ny.com. After thinking about it for . . . two seconds, I assented to submit a chapter or two and a table of contents, and a few months later, I was offered a contract to write this book. I am thankful to Matthew for guiding the book from start to finish, excising my excesses, and putting me back on track when I wandered off. Special thanks must also go to Keelin, who produced the maps you see throughout the book, Emily Taff, who created the wonderful design, and Jessica Peskay, who carried the book through production and made sure the photos looked as good as they did in my head, and all other personnel from the venerable publisher who made a boyhood dream come true.

Forgotten-ny.com would not have gotten anywhere without the friendship and support of Forgotten Fans worldwide, most notably:

Paul Matus of software-arts.com, my webhost, who has made things as cheap as reasonably possible over the years; and Julia Solis of www.darkpassage.com and Sharon Seitz and Stuart Miller of *Other Islands of New York City*, who have inspired me to keep exploring. In the 1990s, I was awed by Dawn Eden and Paul Lukas in the *New York Press*. I'm still awed, but now they're my friends. Amy Langfield of www.newyorkology.com has provided long-term help and assistance. Jen Chung and Jake Dobkin of www.gothamist.com give Forgotten-ny.com a needed plugaroo now and then, as does Jon Brownstoner (he doesn't want you to know his real name) of www.brownstoner.com. Hundreds of sites have linked to mine; I thank them all. Former Zappa bandmate Nigey Lennon and Eric Weaver have been banishers of discouragement over the years. And, of course, we can't leave out our beautiful Forgotten-ny.com T-shirt model, Linda Mena. Buy yours today!

Have I left anyone out? The *New York Times* has been a Forgotten ally over the years. There's David Kirby, who profiled Forgotten-ny.com in the *Times* just a couple of weeks after it debuted in March 1999, sending it on its way; Robert F. Worth, who covered ForgottenTour 15 in Jamaica; and David Dunlap and Christopher Gray, who have slipped mentions of FNY into their architecture columns. Clay Risen of www.

themorningnews.org wrote an informative and, most important, flattering piece about me early on, as well as Joe Cunningham, who profiled your webmaster in the *New York Post,* and Mae Anderson, who did it for the *New York Daily News.* I'm grateful for all my press mentions.

My family has been indispensable in their support, especially my aunt and uncle, Mary and James King; my cousin Michel and her husband, Tom; my cousin Eileen and her husband, Tom; my cousin Jim and his wife, Kathleen; as well as others throughout the USA and Canada.

And, of course, there's the friendship and aid of Jami Bernard, Melissa Cahill, Neil deMause (www.fieldofschemes.com), Joe DiMarco, Doug Douglass, Bernie Ente, Mike Epstein (www.satanslaundromat. com), Steve Garza, Don Gilligan, Gerri Guadagno (the official Forgotten-ny.com mermaid in the Coney Island Mermaid Parade), Andy Hoffer, Barbara Jacksier and Ev Chasen, Caren Lissner, Cate Ludlam of Prospect Cemetery, Steve Molaro (who gave me a copy of Adobe Pagemaker on which the first Forgottenpage was written), Francis Morrone, Bob Mulero, Rachel Neilson (Australia's biggest Forgotten Fan), Mary Ondrejka, Rochelle Rabin (who aided with the contracts), Larry Rogak, Janet Rosen, Peter Sefton, Jeannie Siegel, Bob Singleton of the Greater Astoria Historical Society, Larry Steller, Paul Stingo, Yvonne Temann, Mike Walker, Leo Yau, Lucy Yau, and Isaac Newton Phelps Stokes. I've never read his multivolume *Iconography of New York City.* But I will someday.

And, everyone I haven't mentioned, who will let me know about it as soon as they see this!

Index

The Special Interest Icons appearing next to many of the entries are as follows:

🕊Quiet Places, 🪖Truly Forgotten, 🐍History Happened Here, 🔔What Is This Thing?, and 🎭 Forgotten People. In addition, the place entries are further identified by the borough they are in: BX—The Bronx, BKN—Brooklyn, MAN—Manhattan, QNS—Queens, SI—Staten Island. A separate list of the maps appears after this Index.

A

A&S, 60
Abraham, Abraham, 60
Abraham Wood House, SI, 333
Abram S. Hewitt (fireboat), 328
Acanthus Columns, Bartel-Pritchard Square, BKN, 91
Adams, John, 208, 334
Adams, Maude, 258
Adams, Thomas, 88
Addisleigh Park, QNS, 273
Adee family, 49
Admiral Farragut Bas-relief, BX, 11
Adriance, Elbert, 263
Adriance, Jacob, 263
advertising/street signs, 282–83
Aerens, Hugh, 113
African Burial Ground, MAN 🪦, 148
Albemarle and Kenmore Terraces, BKN, 107
Alexander, William (Lord Stirling), 89
Alexander Avenue, BX, 5–6
Alice and Agate Courts, BKN, 128
Alice Austen House, SI 🕊, 298–99
Allen, Oliver E., 147
Allen, Woody, 123, 184
Alley Pond Park Windmill, QNS, 260
Alleys of Sheepshead Bay, BKN, 126
Allison, George William, 292
Allison Pond, SI 🕊, 292
Allmendinger, Louis, 82
Almirall, Raymond, 88
Alston, Japhet and Sarah, 312

Alvord, Dean, 106
Ambrose (LV87) lightship, 142–43
American Bank Note Factory, BX 🪖, 14–15
American Express Co., 147
American Linoleum Company, 337
Amster Yard, MAN 🕊, 173
Ancient Poster Art, MAN, 151
André, John, 292
Andrew Freedman Home, BX 🪖, 11
Ansonia Clock Factory, BKN, 89
Appleton, George, 250
Apthorp, Charles, 191
Aqueduct Walk, BX, 19
Arbitration Rock, QNS 🔔, 235
Arbuckle Brothers Coffee Company, 55, 56
Arion Mannerchor, BKN, 83
Arlington Yards, SI, 336
Armstrong, Louis, 242
Art Deco Sears, BKN, 109
Arthur, Chester Alan, 166
Artkraft Signs, 223
Astor, John Jacob, 149, 217
Astor, William, 201
Astoria Village, QNS 🕊, 217–18
Astor Row: Porches in Manhattan, MAN, 201
Astral Apartments, BKN, 80
Astral Oil Works, 80
Atlantic Avenue Tunnel, BKN 🪖, 62–63
Atlantic Terra Cotta Company, 334, 335
Atterbury, Grosvenor, 237
Au, Ernest Von, 58
Audubon, John James, 206
Audubon Ballroom and Loew's 175th Street Theatre, MAN, 207
Audubon Terrace, MAN, 206–7
Augustinian Retreat House, SI 🪖, 294
Austen, Alice, 298–99
Avenue A, MAN, 186–87
Avenue H Station, BKN, 110

B

Babb, Cook & Willard, 6
Bacon, Henry, 179
Baerer, Henry, 87, 253

Bailey Avenue and West 231st Street, BX, 27
Bailey Fountain, 86–87
Ball, Ernest, 265
Ballinger Company, 240
Balzano, Sunny and John, 74
Bangert's Flowers, QNS, 266
Barkaloo, Harmans and Jacques, 103
Barkaloo, William Harmans, 102–3
Barlow, Alfred, 293
Barnard, Edward Sibley, 94
Barrymore, Ethel, 175
Barrymore, John, 256
Bartel, Emil, 91
Bartel-Pritchard Square, 91
Barton, Ella and Willis, 323
Bartow-Pell Mansion, BX, 44
Basie, William ("Count"), 273
Batterson, James, 167
Battery Harris, QNS, 280–81
Battery Park Control House, MAN, 138–39
Battle of Brooklyn Remnants, BKN, 92
Baum, Dwight James, 30, 31, 33
Baylis, Elias, 271
Bayonne Ferry, SI, 303
Beard, William, 74–75
Beard Street Warehouse Pier, BKN, 74–75
Bechtel, George, 296
Beech Court, QNS 🏛, 254
Beecher, Henry Ward, 58, 96
Beer, Freidrich, 213
Bell, Abraham, 256
Bell, Alexander Graham, 19, 249, 256, 300
Bell Tower, BX 🚋, 30
Belmont, August, 286
Bennett, Floyd, 117
Bennett, John, 322
Bennett, Joseph S., 103
Bennett, Tony, 242
Bennett Avenue, MAN, 208
Berlin Wall, MAN 🗿, 173
Bertine, Edward, 5
Bertine Block, BX, 5
Beth-El Temple, QNS, 278–79
Biddle, Henry, 334
Biddle Mansion, SI, 334
Bidwell, John, 307
Billings, Cornelius, 204
Billiou, Pierre, 313
Billiou-Stillwell-Perine House, SI, 313
Billopp, Christopher, 334
Bissel Gardens, BX, 41–42
Bissell, George, 166, 212
Bitter, Karl, 29, 196
Black, Joseph, 322
Blackwell, Mary and Robert, 189
Blackwell Farmhouse, MAN, 189
Blaeser, Gustaf, 183
Blaine, Dan, 295
Blazing Star Cemetery, SI, 328–29

Bliss, Eliphalet, 102
Bliss, George, 190
Bliss, Neziah, 224
Block, Adrian, 35
Blockhouse, The, MAN 🔫, 180–81
Blondell, Joan, 160
Blue Heron Pond Park, SI 🏛, 320
Bluemner, Oscar, 8
Blumstein, Louis, 201
Blumstein's, MAN 🔫, 200–201
Bly, Nellie (Elizabeth Cochrane), 190
Boehm, Henry, 323
Boehm House, 323
Bogardus, James, 144, 200
Bohack, H. C., 234
Bohack Smokestack, The, QNS, 234
Bohemian Citizens' Benevolent Society, 218
Bohemian Hall, QNS, 218
Boller, Alfred, 205
Bombs of Wall Street, The, MAN 🔫, 140
Bomelstein's Clock, BKN, 81
Boole, William H., 307
Booth, Edwin, 165
Borden Avenue Retractile Bridge, QNS 🚋, 225
Boudin, Katherine, 158
Bowdoin, Edith, 248
Bowling Green, MAN 🔫, 139
Bowling Green subway station, 138–39
Bowne, John, 249
Boys' High, BKN, 127–28
Brennan, Joe, 238
Brevoort, Henry, 158
Brewster Building, QNS, 220
Bridge Café, 142
Briggs, Josiah A., 16
Britton, Nathaniel, 322
Britton Cottage, 322–23
Broad Channel Corporation, 276
Broadway Alley, MAN, 167
Broadway Junction, BKN, 131
Broadway's Sidewalk Clock, MAN, 141
Broken Angel, BKN 🗿, 127
Bronck, Jonas, 20
Bronx Borough Courthouse, BX, 8
Bronx Terminal Market, BX, 7
Bronx Victory Memorial, BX 🚋, 43
Brooklyn Children's Museum, BKN, 69–70
Brooklyn Clay Retort and Fire Brick Works,
    BKN, 75–76
Brooklyn Fire Headquarters, BKN, 61–62
Brooklyn Heights Mews, BKN, 58–59
Brooklyn Improvement Company, 72
Brooklyn Lyceum, BKN, 88
Brooklyn Navy Yard, BKN, 64–65
Brooklyn Working Artists Coalition, 75
Brougham Cottage, SI, 320
Brown, Charles S., 129
Brown, H. K., 95
Brownstone Haven, BKN 🗿, 82

BRPR and the East Gun Hill Road Bridge, BX 🚗, 25
Brush, John Tomlinson, 206
Buek, Charles, 201
Bulfinch, Charles, 54
Bungalows, BKN 🚗, 124
Bunny, John, 203
Bunny Theatre, MAN 🎭, 203
Burgee, John, 188
Burr, Aaron, 107, 149, 303
Bush, Irving T., 101
Bush Terminal, BKN, 101
Butler, John, 22
Butts, Alfred, 228
Byrd, Richard, 117
Byrne, John J., 89

C
Cable-stayed bridge, MAN, 177
Cadman, Samuel Parkes, 61
Cadman Plaza, BKN, 61
Calder, Alexander Stirling, 175
Calhoun School, MAN, 193
Cameo Theatre, MAN 🚗, 176
Camperdown Elm and Cleft Ridge Span, BKN, 94
Canarsie Pier and the Belt Parkway Bike Path, BKN, 116
Canarsie's Log Cabin, BKN, 116
Canda, Charles, 97
Canda, Charlotte, 97–98
Candy Men, The, BKN 🚗, 58
Cann, William, 241
Cannon Avenue, SI, 337–38
Cappozalo, Rosemary, 289
Carlisle, Kitty, 160
Carmel, Charles, 95
Carnegie, Andrew, 184, 266, 335
Carnegie Library, SI, 302
Caroline Pratt Ladd House, BKN, 67
Carrere and Hastings, 286, 297, 335
Carrere, John, 302
Carroll Street Bridge, BKN, 72
Cartwright, Alexander, 165
Case, George, 113
Cass, William and Catherine, 327
Cassatt, Alexander, 168
Cathedral Preparatory Seminary, BKN, 67
Catholic Youth Organization, SI, 302
Chair in the Square, BX, 36
Chambellan, René, 172
Chanin Building, MAN, 172–73
Chapel of the Good Shepherd, MAN, 190
Charles Lane and Sing Sing, MAN 🚗, 155
Charles Pearl–Matthew Kabriski Mansion, QNS, 251
Charles Ryder, Ryder–Van Cleef, and Samuel Hubbard Homes, BKN, 119–20
Charlton-King-Vandam Street houses, MAN, 149

Chelsea Hotel, 162
Chelsea Market, MAN, 163
Cherokee, The, MAN, 186
Chevra Bani Sholom, 231–32
Childs Restaurant, MAN, 169
Childs Restaurant chain, 124, 169
Christopher, Joseph, 323
Christopher House, 323
Church, Benjamin, 27
Churcher, Richard, 140
Churchill, Randolph Spencer, 71
Church of the Generals, BKN 🚗, 105
Church of the Pilgrims, BKN 🚗, 58
Church of the Resurrection, QNS, 267
City Hall Subway Station, MAN, 141
City Island Bridge, BX, 45–46
City Island Museum, BX, 46–47
City Reliquary, The, BKN 🚗, 77–78
City View Best Western, QNS, 225
Civic Virtue Statue, QNS, 239
Civiletti, Pasquale, 213
Clarke, Thomas, 162
Clay Pit Ponds Park, SI, 331
Clift, Montgomery, 92
Clifton and Waters Avenues, QNS 🚗, 225
Clinton, Charles, 185
Clinton, DeWitt, 96, 253
Clinton, George, 176
Clinton, Henry, 92
Clinton Court, MAN 🚗, 176
Clock Tower, 52nd Precinct Station House, BX, 24
Clove Lakes Park, SI 🐾, 305
Cobblestone House, QNS, 257–58
Coblentz, Edna (Jacques Marchais), 326–27
Cocks, Samuel, 155
Colden, Charles, 255
Colden-Wesson Mansion, QNS, 255
Colgate, Robert, 34
Colletti, Joe, 223
Colon family, 322
Colonnade Row, MAN, 160
Coltrane, John, 273
Columbia Presbyterian Medical Center, 207
Column of Jerash, QNS, 243–44
Concert Grove, BKN, 94–95
Conference House, SI 🚗, 334–35
Conkling, Roscoe, 166
Consumers Park Brewery, 69
Cook, Frederick A., 83–84
Cooper, Peter, 96
Corbett, Jim, 257
Corbin, Austin, 125
Cornell, Joseph, 256–57
"Corner, The", MAN 🚗, 164
Cornwallis, Charles, 89
Cortelyou, Isaac, 88
Cortelyou, Jacques, 88
Cox family, 263

Cram, Goodhue & Ferguson, 278
Crane, Ichabod, 311
Crawford, Joan, 160
Creedmoor Living Museum, QNS, 263–64
Crimson Beech, SI, 327
Crocheron, Jacob, 322
Crocheron House, 322
Cromwell, William, 34
Crowley, Jim, 143
Cruser, Cornelius, 292
Cruser House, SI 🐾, 292
Culyer, John Y., 108
Cunard, Edward, 293
Cunard Lines, 163
Cunningham, Robert and James, 173
Currier, Nathaniel, 96
Cutter, Bloodgood Haviland, 259
Cypress Hills National Cemetery, 131–32

D

Dalai Lama, 327
Daus, Rudolph L., 62, 88
Davis, Alexander Jackson, 72, 92
Davis, Miles, 42
Davis, William T., 288, 305, 337
Decker, Alberta, 312
Decker, Lorenzo, 312
Decker family, 311, 338
Decker Farmhouse, SI 🏠, 311–12
Deegan, William, 6–7
Delafield, Edward, 31
Delafield, Joseph, 31, 33
Delamarre, Jacques, 172
De Lancey, James, 150
DeLemos and Cordes, 144
Delson, Morton, 327
De Lue, Donald, 243
Deluise, Dom, 160
DeMorgan, John, 294
Dennison, Ethan, 124
Densely, Robert, 126
Denson, Charles, 123
Denton, Charles, 274
Denyse, Denyse, 104–5
Denyse Ferry Wharf, BKN 🐾, 104–5
de Rivera, José, 246
DeRosa, Eugene, 289
Desolation of West Street, The, BKN 🏠, 81
Devoe family, 42
Diamond, Bob, 63
Dickens, Charles, 190
Dickerson, Warren C., 14
Dickson, Walter, 189
Didik, Frank, 64
Dietzel, Oscar and Maggie, 98
Dietzels' Train, The, BKN, 98
di Suvero, Mark, 219
Dodge, William, Jr., 34
Dodge Mansion, BX 🏠, 34

Dolan, Owen, 36
Dollar Savings Bank, BX, 20
Domino Sugar Plant, BKN, 78
Dongan, Thomas, 307, 313
doorways, 50–51
Doubleday, Lloyd, 116
Doughty, Joseph, 250
Douglas, George, 259
Douglas, William, 259
Douglass, David Bates, 96
Douglaston Club, QNS, 259–60
Dow, Neal, 307
Drake, Joseph Rodman, 15
Drake, Lawrence, 210
Drake Cemetery, BX 🍴, 15
Dreyfus, Louis, 294
Duane Park, MAN, 146–47
Dudley, Henry, 267
Duffield and Concord Streets, BKN 🍴, 64
Duffy, Francis, 175
Duggin, Charles, 290
Dunn, John, 323
Dunn's Mill, 323
Dupuis, Toom, 213
Dutch Reformed Church, SI, 302
Dwyer, Thomas, 210
Dyckman, Jacob, 26
Dyckman, Jan, 210
Dyckman, William, 210
Dyckman Farmhouse, MAN 🐾, 210

E

Eagle Avenue Bridge, BX, 8
Eakins, Thomas, 86
Earney, George, 274
East 53rd Street Houses, MAN, 173
East 92nd Street Houses, MAN, 187
Eastern Parkway, BKN, 70
Eberhard Faber Pencils, BKN, 81
Eberson, John, 19, 273, 315
Ebinger, Arthur, 108
Ebinger's Bakery, BKN, 108–9
Eden, Rachel, 16
Edgehill Church, BX, 29
Edgewater Hall, SI 🍴, 297
Edgewater Village Hall, SI, 296
Edsall, Thomas, 29
Edsall Avenue, BX 🏠, 28–29
Edwards, Ogden, 304
Edwards, Webley, 323
Edwards-Barton House, 323
Ehrlich Brothers Emporium, 164
Ehrlich Brothers "K," MAN 🐾, 164
Eidlitz, Cyrus, 36
Eidlitz, Leopold, 36
1890s Meet the 1970s, The, MAN, 145
8th Road, QNS, 255
Eldridge Street Synagogue, MAN, 150–51
Elks Lodge, QNS, 240

Ellington, Duke, 42
Elmwier Cemetery Association, 232
Elmwood Theatre, QNS, 241–42
Elowitz, Alex, 123
Eltinge family, 319
Elvis Presley and the Long Island Rail Road, BKN, 101
Embury, Aymar, III, 245
Emmons Avenue Mansion, BKN, 126
Empire Stores, BKN, 56
Empire Theater, SI, 303
Episcopal Church of the Holy Spirit, MAN, 190
Episcopal Church of the Transfiguration, 167
Eppig, Leonard, 84
Erasmus Hall Academy, BKN, 107–8
Ericsson, John, 82
Eskimo Pie/Thomson Meter Building, BKN 🚋, 54–55
Esplanade's Rail Stations, The, BX, 38
Estern, Neil, 213
Eternal Light Memorial Flagpole, 167
Evarts, William Maxwell, 161
Evergood, Philip, 266–67
Excelsior Power Company, MAN, 143–44
Execution Rock Lighthouse, BX 🚋, 17
Exedra, QNS, 245

F

Faber, Eberhard, 81
Faber, Jenny, 303
Faber Park, SI, 303–4
Faces of Mount Zion, The, QNS, 231–32
Fair Theatre, QNS, 229–30
Farragut, David, 11, 42, 166
Farragut Theater, 108
Farrell, James, 103
Farrell House, BKN, 103
Father Duffy, MAN 🗽, 175
Fausner, Anton, 232
FDNY Queens Central Office, QNS, 268
Featherbed Lane, BX, 16
Fedde, Elizabeth, 99
Federal Hall and the Map of Ohio, MAN 🐎, 140
Federal Seaboard Terra Cotta Corporation, 36
Fein, Jack, 258
Ferrer, Fernando, 41
Ferris Cemetery, BX, 36
Ferris family, 36
Ferry Terminal, SI, 286–87
Fields, W. C., 256
Filippo, Antonio de, 82
Finnish Co-op, BKN 🚋, 100
Finnish Home Building Association, 100
Firemen and Fire Horse Memorials, MAN 🐴, 195–96
First Presbyterian Church, QNS, 272
Fish, Preserved, 161

Fish Building, BX, 11–12
Fiske, Clinton B., 307
Fitzgerald, Ella, 273
Flagg, Ernest, 313
Flagg Place, SI, 313–14
Flanagan, Adam, 187
Flatbush at the Movies, BKN, 108
Flatbush Dutch Reformed Church, BKN 🐎, 106–7
Flatbush Toll House, BKN 🐴, 95
Flatbush Town Hall, BKN, 108
Flatlands Dutch Reformed Church, BKN, 114
Fletcher, Ellen, 142
Floriendo, Antonio, 75
Floyd Bennett Field, BKN 🗽, 117
Flushing Airport, QNS 🚋, 254
Flushing Horse Trough, QNS 🐴, 248
Flushing Town Hall, QNS, 248–49
Follow the Yellow Brick Road, QNS, 235
Fontanne, Lynn, 187
Forest Hills Stadium, QNS, 238–39
Forest Park Carousel, QNS, 268
Former Gage & Tollner, BKN, 62
Forms in Transit, QNS, 246
Fort Greene Park, BKN 🗽, 65
Fort Hamilton, 104, 105
Fort Schuyler, BX, 49
Fort Totten, QNS, 258
Fortunoff, Max and Clara, 130
Fortunoff's Sign, BKN, 130
Fort Wadsworth, SI, 299–300
14th Regiment Armory, 89
Fox, George, 249–50
Fox Oaks Marker, QNS 🐴, 249–50
Franklin, Benjamin, 144, 334–35
Franklin Shuttle, BKN, 68–69
Franz Sigel, MAN 🗽, 196
Frazee, John, 98
Frederick, Marshall, 246
Frederick Loeser & Company, 61
Freedlander, Joseph, 8
Freedman, Andrew, 11
Freedom of the Human Spirit, QNS, 246
Free Form, QNS, 246
Free Hungarian Reformed Church, SI, 331
Freeman, Frank, 61
Friends Meeting House, QNS 🐎, 248
Frisch, Frankie, 24
Fulton, Robert, 19, 65, 155
Fulton Fish Market, 142
Fulton Street's Old Department Stores, BKN 🚋, 60–61

G

Gage, Charles, 62
Gage & Tollner, 62
Gair, Robert, 54
Gallagher, Jimmy, 148
Gantry State Park, QNS, 222

INDEX

Garden Place, BX, 42
Garibaldi, Giuseppe, 183, 298, 300
Garibaldi-Meucci Museum, SI 🐾, 300
Geer, Seth, 160
Gehrig, Lou, 9
General Theological Seminary, MAN, 162–63
General Worth, MAN ⚓, 166–67
George III, King (Britain), 139, 240–41
George Washington, QNS, 243
George Washington Plaque, QNS, 263
Giants' Last Stand, The, MAN, 205–6
Gilbert, Cass, 13
Gilbert, C. P. H., 88
Gilbert, William, 15
Gillespie, Dizzy, 242
Gingerbread House, BKN, 103
Glover, John, 44
Glover's Rock, BX 🐾, 43–44
Goethe, Johann Wolfgang von, 182
Golden Swan Park, MAN 🚐, 156
Grace Episcopal Church, QNS, 271–72
Grain Elevator Terminal, BKN 🐴, 76
Grand Army Plaza, BKN, 86–87
Grand Boulevard and Concourse, BX, 8–9
Grand Concourse Overpass, BX, 16
Grand View Hotel, QNS, 254–55
Granite Helmar Construction, 122
Grant, Ulysses S., 69, 86, 197
Grashorn, Henry, 123
Grashorn Building, BKN 🚐, 123
Graveyards of Gravesend, BKN, 119
Gray, Christopher, 187
Graybar Building Rats, MAN 🐴, 172
Grecynski, Bolek, 263
Greeley, Horace, 96
Green, Andrew H., 180
Greene, Nathaniel, 65
Greenpoint Terminal Warehouse, 81
Green's Private Bench, MAN, 180
Griffith, Charles, 302
Griffith, D. W., 256
Griffith, Jane and Charles, 98
Griffith Block, SI 🐾, 302–3
Griffou, Marie, 156
Grinnell, William, 144
Grove Court, MAN, 155
Gruppe, Karl, 29
Grutchfield, Walter, 58
Grymes, O., 213
Grymes, Suzette, 293
Guardhouses, BKN 🐴, 125–26
Guyon, James, Jr., 323
Guyon, Joseph, 322
Guyon-Lake-Tysen House, 322
Guyon Store, 323

H

Hadley, George and William, 33
Hadley House, BX 🐾, 33

Haffen, Louis, 16
Haight, George Coolidge, 162
Half Cemetery, The, MAN, 157–58
Half Moon Overlook, BX 🐴, 29
Halleck, Fitz-Greene, MAN ⚓, 182
Hallett, William, 217
Hall of Fame for Great Americans, BX 🐴, 18–19
Hall of Science, QNS, 245
Halsey, McCormack and Helmer, 20
Halsey, Stephen Ailing, 217
Hamilton, Alexander, 107, 182, 202, 208
Hamilton, Charles Kennedy, 290
Hamilton, Robert Ray, 193
Hamilton Park Houses, SI 🐴, 290
Hamilton's House, MAN 🐾, 202
Handy, W. C., 202
Hanzlick, Anthony ("Speed"), 254
Hardy, Hugh, 158
Harlem's Fire Tower, MAN 🐴, 200
Harrison, John, 263
Harrison and Abramovitz, 245
Harsen, Jacob, 191
Hartford Faience Company, 164
Hart Island, BX, 46
Hastings, Thomas, 167, 302
Hatfield, Robert Griffith, 186
Haugaard, Henry, 266
Haughwout family, 301
Hausel, Max, 8
Hausmann, Charles, 237
Haussmann, Baron, 8, 70
Healy, Thomas, 194
Heath, William, 25
Heber, Carl, 82
Heberton Cottage, SI, 302
Heine, Heinrich, 9
Heins, George C., 21, 139, 141
Helmle and Huberty, 79, 82
Helmle, Huberty, & Hudswell, 91, 94
Henderson, Fletcher, 202
Henderson, Fred, 122
Henderson, John, 187
Henderson Place, MAN 🐴, 187
Henderson's Dance Hall, BKN, 122
Hendrick I. Lott House, BKN, 113–14
Hendricks, Harmon, 155
Henry and Abraham Wyckoff House, BKN 🐾, 113
Henry Hudson Park, BX, 29–30
Henry Street Settlement, MAN, 151–52
Herman, Dave, 77–78
Herman Funke Estate, 254
Herman Ridder Junior High School, BX, 17
Hernshead, MAN 🐴, 179
Hero Park, SI, 294
Herter, Ernst, 9
Herter Brothers, 150
Hess, David, 153–54

Hess Estate Triangle, MAN 🐎, 153–54

Hewitt, Abram Stevens, 328

Heyerdahl, M., 317

Heyerdahl Hill, SI, 317–18

Hicks, John and Jacob, 57

Hicks, Mabel Middagh, 57

Higgins, Charles, 90, 97

Higginson, William, 101

High Bridge, BX, 12

High Island, BX, 46

Highland Boulevard, BKN, 133

High Line to Nowhere, MAN, 163–64

High Rock Park, SI, 315

Hinton, Milt, 273

Hirons, Frederic, 124

Hitchcock, Benjamin, 227, 240, 274

Hoe, Peter, 15

Hoe, Richard, 15

Hoffman, Dustin, 158

Hoffman, Malvina, 172

Holland, George, 167

Holley, Alexander, 212

Holy Trinity Russian Orthodox Church, BKN, 129

Homestead Remnants and Willowbrook Park, SI, 310

Hooker, William, 57

Hooper, John, 206

Hooper Fountain, MAN 🐎, 206

Horgan, Arthur, 27

Hornaday, William, 21

Horne, Lena, 273

Hotel Griffou, MAN 🚋, 156–57

Houghton, George, 167

Houseman, John, 302

Houses on Stilts, QNS, 277

Housman, Isaac, 291

Housman, Peter, 307

Howard, George, 293

Howard, William, 274, 275

Howe, Richard, 334–35

Howe, William, 105

Howells, William Dean, 156

Howland Hook, 336

Hudson, Henry, 29–30

Hudson Street Compass, MAN 🐎, 147

Hudson Waterfront Museum, BKN, 74

Humboldt, Alexander von, MAN 🗿, 183

Hunt, Robert Morris, 315

Hunt, Thomas, 13

Hunter, George, 221

Hunter family, 46

Hunter's Point Historic District, QNS 🏠, 221

Hunt family, 15

Huntington, Anna, 194, 207

Huntington, Archer, 207

Huntington Free Library, BX, 37

Huss, George Martin, 206

Hussein, King (Jordan), 244

Huston, Tillinghast, 9

Hutchinson, Anne, 44

Hylan, John, 84

I

Ichabod Crane's Grave, SI 🔭, 311

I. Miller Building, 175

Independence Plaza, 146

Indian Field, BX 🔭, 42

Indian Lake, BX, 17

Indian Pond, BX, 33

Inwood, MAN 🏠, 209

Irving, Washington, 160, 213, 311

Isaacs-Hendricks House, MAN, 155

Israelowitz, Oscar, 120

Ives, James, 96

J

Jackson, John (Vinegar Hill), 54

Jackson, John C. (Jackson Heights), 227

Jackson, Thomas J. ("Stonewall"), 105

Jackson Mill Road trolley tracks, QNS 🐎, 229

Jacquet, Russell and Illinois, 273

Jagiello, Ladislaus, MAN 🗿, 182–83

Jallade, Louis, 54

Jamaica Bay Wildlife Refuge, QNS, 276

Jamaica Savings Bank, 241

James Amster Associates, 173

James Leeson's Grave, MAN 🚋, 139–40

Jane Griffith, BKN, 98

Janvier, Thomas A., 156–57

Jarmulowsky, Sender, 150

Jarmulowsky's Bank, MAN, 150

Jarrett de la Marie, Charles Albert, 98

Jay Street Connecting Railroad, BKN, 55

Jefferson, Joseph, 167

Jennie Jerome, BKN 🗿, 71

Jensen, Oliver, 299

Jerome, Jennie, 71

Jerome, Leonard, 71

Jerome Park Reservoir, BX, 27

Jervis, John, 12

Jim Corbett: Bayside's Favorite Son, QNS 🗿, 257

J.L. Kesner Company, 164

Joan of Arc, MAN, 194

John Bowne House, QNS 🔭, 249

John H. Bennett House, 322

John King Vanderbilt House, SI, 305–6

John Milner Associates, 115

John Paul Jones Park, 104

Johnson, Eusabia, 322

Johnson, George, 14

Johnson, Isaac Gale, 29

Johnson, Jerry, 71

Johnson, Philip, 188, 244

Johnson family, 120

Jones, Allan, 160

Jones, Howard E. and Jessie, 103

Jorissen, Burger, 220–21
Joseph Cornell House, QNS 🐿, 256–57
Joseph K. Brick Company, 75–76
Joseph Rose House, 142
J.P. Morgan Inc., 140
Jumel, Stephen and Eliza, 208
Juniper Valley Park, 237–38

K

Kafka, George, 296
Kalman, Maria, 34
Kalmbacher, George, 94
Kaluber, Harry, 326
K & E, MAN, 144–45
Keeler, Ruby, 160
Kelly, John, 227
Kenmore, The (movie theater), 108
Kennedy, John F., 31
Kennedy, J. Sarsfield, 103
Kershner, Bruce, 305, 310
Kerz, John, 265
Keuffel & Esser Building, 144–45
Kew Gardens Station, QNS, 239
Kieft, William, 118, 253, 256, 284
Killmeyer, Nicholas, 330
Killmeyer's Old Bavaria Inn, SI, 330
Kimball, Francis, 29, 87
King, David, Jr., 202
King, John, 271
King, Joseph, 250
King, Rufus and Mary, 271
Kingfisher Pond, SI 🏞, 325
King Mansion, QNS 🛞, 271
King Model Homes, 202
Kingsbridge Armory, BX, 26–27
Kingsbridge Terrace Community Center, BX, 27
Kings County Savings Bank, 78–79
Kingsland Homestead, QNS, 250
Kinney, Belle, 43
Kiselewski, Joseph, 36
Kissena Park, QNS 🏞, 251
Knickerbocker Hotel, 174
Knickerbocker Laundry, QNS, 226
Koster & Bial's vaudeville theater, 164
Kreischer, Balthazar, 330, 331
Kreischer, Charles, 331
Kreischer, Edward, 331
Kreischer Brick Manufacturing Company, 235, 331
Kreischer Mansion, SI, 331
Kreischer Worker's Homes, SI, 331
Kroehl, Julius, 200
Kruser-Finley House, 323
Kuhne, Paul, 296

L

La Casina, QNS, 272
Ladies' Pavilion, MAN 🏞, 180

Lady Moody House, BKN, 119
LaFarge, Christopher, 21, 139, 141
La Grange Terrace, 160
La Guardia, Fiorello, 31, 81, 148, 213
Lakeman, Abraham, 316
Lakeman-Cortelyou House, SI, 316
Lalance & Grosjean Clock Tower, QNS, 269
Lamartine Avenue Signposts, QNS, 257
Lamb, Thomas, 14, 129, 207, 279
Lamb & Rich, 187
lampposts, 134–35
Lampposts: Harlem Nocturne, MAN, 204–5
Lane Theater, SI, 315–16
Latimer, Lewis, 249
La Tourette family, 317, 318
La Tourette House, SI, 325
Launitz, Robert, 98
Law, George, 286
Lawrence, William, 253
Lawrence family, 238
Leading Ladies, MAN, 175
LeCount, Teresa, 41
Lee, Robert E., 105
Leeson, James, 139–40
Lefever, Minard, 291
Lefferts, James, 68
Lefferts, John, 95
Lefferts, Peter, 95
Lefferts family, 68, 95, 270
Lefferts Homestead, BKN, 95
Leggett, Samuel, 253
Leggett family, 15
Lemon Creek, SI, 333
Lent Riker Smith Homestead, QNS, 228–29
Leone, Sebastian, 52
Lescaze, William, 77
Lewis, Barry, 239
Lewis, Francis, 253
Lewis Lattimer Residence, QNS 🐿, 249
Liberty Avenue Traffic Lights, QNS, 269
Lichtenstein, Roy, 245
Lighthouse Park, MAN, 190
Lighting the Way, MAN, 179
Lightship, MAN, 142–43
Lightship *84*, BKN 🚢, 75
Lincoln, Abraham, 19, 86, 95, 159
Lincoln on Horseback and Other Grand Army Plaza Sights, BKN, 86–87
Lindemann, Charles, 84
Linnean Gardens Remnant, QNS, 247–48
LIRR Creedmor Branch Marker, QNS 🚃, 252
LIRR in Gravesend, The, BKN, 120
Litchfield, Edwin, 72, 89, 92
Litchfield Villa, BKN, 92
Lithuanian Shrine, QNS 🕯, 232
Little Church Around the Corner, MAN, 167
Little Red Schoolhouse, BX, 40
Locke, Alexander, 84
Locke, John, 253

Loeser's, 61
Loew's Kings, 108
Loew's 175th Street Theatre, MAN, 207
Loew's Paradise Theatre, BX, 19
Loew's Pitkin Theatre, BKN, 129
Loew's/Shore Theater, BKN, 123
Loew's Valencia, QNS, 272–73
Lombard Lamp, MAN, 178–79
Long Island Motor Parkway, The, QNS, 262–63
Long Island Rail Road Grade Crossing, QNS, 261
Long Island Safe Deposit Company, BKN, 56
Long Island Star Building, QNS 🚃, 220
Longwood Historic District, BX, 14
Lookout Hill and the Maryland Monument, BKN 🐚, 92
Lord family, 209
Lorelei Fountain, BX, 9
Lorillard, Jacob, 21
Lorillard family, 21, 24
Lorillard Snuff Mill, BX 🚃, 24
Lott, Hendrick I., 113–14
Lott, Jeremiah, 57
Lott, Johannes, 113
Louis Armstrong House, QNS, 242
Louis Valentino, Jr., Pier, BKN, 73
Lovecraft, Howard Phillips (H. P.), 59
Loy, Myrna, 160
Ludlum, Nicholas, 271
Lunt, Alfred, 187
Lynch, Joseph, 245

M

MacCracken, Henry Mitchell, 18
MacDonald, James W. A., 182
MacDougall, Edward, 227
Machlouzarides, Costas, 193
MacKenzie-Childs, Richard and Victoria, 148
MacMonnies, Frederick, 86, 87, 239
Macomb, Robert, 205
Macy, Rowland Hussey, 203
Macy's, 60, 202–3
Macy's Uptown, MAN 🚃, 202 3
Madison Square Park Statues, MAN 🐚, 165–66
Magazine Remnants, QNS, 281
Magnanti, Angelo, 20
Magonigle, H. Van Buren, 195
Main Street, SI, 335
Major Deegan Monument, BX 🐚, 6–7
Malbone, Ralph, 70
Malboneville, BKN 🚃, 70
Malcolm X, 207
Man, Albon Platt, 237, 265, 266, 267
Man, Alrick and Albon, Jr., 237
Manee family, 333
Manee-Seguine Homestead, SI, 332–33
Manhattan Beach, 125–26
Manhattan Bridge Vista, BKN, 55

Manning, Jack, 189
Manning, Nicholas, 304
Marble Hill, MAN, 210–11
Marcus Garvey (Mount Morris) Park, 200, 207–8
Marie, Romany, 154
Marie's Crisis, 154
Marine Park, BKN, 117
Mariner's Marsh, SI 🚃, 336
Marschalk, Peter, 235
Marsh, Helen, 262
Marshall, Thurgood, 199
Martin, John (Giovanni Martini), 132
Martin, Walter C., 17
Martin A. Gleason Funeral Home, QNS, 255
Marton, Janos, 263, 264
Maryland Monument, 92
Mason, Au & Magenheimer Candy Company, 58
Mason, Joseph, 58
Maspeth Theatre, QNS, 233
Maspeth Town Hall, QNS, 233
Maurice, James, 232
Maxey, Thomas, 190
Maxwell, Henry, 87
Mayer, Gustave A., 316
Mayer House, SI, 316
Mazzarella, Anthony, 222
Mazzini, Giuseppe, MAN 🐚, 183
McCann, Joseph, 188
McCarren, Patrick, 81
McCarren Park Pool, BKN, 81–82
McCarthy, John, 190
McElfatrick, William, 85
McEnroe, John, 260
McGolrick, Edward, 82
McGowin, Ed, 257
McGown, Catherine, 181
McGown's Pass, MAN 🐚, 181
McGraw, John, 206
McKim, Charles, 195
McKim, Mead, and White, 66, 168, 222
McMillen, Loring, 299
McNamara, John, 16, 36, 37
Melville, Herman, 42, 167
Metropolitan Hospital, 190
Metropolitan Life Insurance Company, 35, 220
Metropolitan Oval, QNS, 236
Meucci, Antonio, 300
Meyer, Cord, 227, 237, 240
Millay, Edna St. Vincent, 155
Miller Highway, MAN 🚃, 146
Miller, Israel, 175
Miller, Marilyn, 175
Miller, Tony, 221–22
Miller's Hotel/Waterfront Crabhouse, QNS 🚃, 221–22
Milliard, Larry, 123

Milligan, Samuel, 157
Minerva, BKN, 97
Minuit, Peter, 138, 209
Mitchel, John Purroy, MAN 🐦, 182
Mitchell, Alfred, 131
Modern Architecture, SI, 307–8
Monroe, Charles H. and Leander, 274
Monroe, James, 161
Monsignor McGolrick Park, BKN, 82
Montauk Club, BKN, 87
Montgomery Place, BKN 🐾, 88
Moody, Deborah, 118, 119
Moody, Henry, 118, 119
Mooncurser Records, BX, 47
Moore, Augustine, 228
Moore, Clement Clarke, 162–63, 206
Moore, David, 324
Moore, Marianne, 94
Moore-Jackson Cemetery, QNS, 228
Moran, Fred, 123
Morris, Gouverneur, 4, 6
Morris, Roger, 207–8
Morris, William Lewis, 34
Morris family, 6, 10
Morris-Jumel Mansion and Sylvan Terrace,
    MAN 🐦, 207–8
Morrone, Francis, 79
Morse, Samuel, 19, 96
Moses, Charles, Elias, and Lewis, 315
Moses, Robert, 25, 57, 93, 146, 191, 243, 276,
    281, 306
Moses' Folly, SI, 306
Moses Mountain, SI, 318
Mosholu Parkway, BX, 24–25
Motor Parkway, 262–63
Mott, Jordan, 4
Mott Avenue Sign, BX 🏛, 7
Mould, Jacob Wrey, 180
Mount Tom, MAN 🐾, 193
Mount Vernon Hotel Museum, MAN, 185
Mount Zion Cemetery, 231–32
Muhlenberg, Augustus, 253
Muller, Daniel, 268
Müller, Oswald, 298
Mundell, William, 56, 89
Munson, Thurman, 9
Murdock, Harvey, 88
Murray, Robert, 171
Murray family, 250
Museum of the Moving Image, QNS 🐦, 219
Museum of Tibetan Art, SI, 326–27
Music Pagoda, Binnenwater, and Boathouse,
    BKN, 93–94

N
Namm, Adolph I., 60
Nassau, Duke of, 332
Nast, Thomas, 163
National Biscuit Company, 163

National Cemetery, BKN, 131–32
Naughton, James, 127
Navy Commandant's House, BKN, 54
NBC Studios, BKN 🐾, 111
Netanyahu, Jonathan, 38
Neville & Bagge, 17
New Dorp Lighthouse, SI 🐾, 315
New England Development and Improvement
    Company, 256
Newgate State Prison, 155
New Lots Reformed Church, BKN, 130
Newtown High School, 240, 241
New Utrecht Reformed Church, 118
New York and New Jersey Telephone Com-
    pany Building, BKN, 62
New York Architectural Terra Cotta Works,
    223
New York Botanical Garden, BX, 23
New York City Pavilion, QNS, 245–46
New York Giants (baseball team), 205–6
New York Marble Cemeteries, The, MAN,
    160–61
New York, New Haven, and Hartford Railroad
    Stations, BX 🏛, 13–14
New York State Pavilion, QNS, 244–45
New York Times, 174
New York, Westchester, and Boston Railroad,
    BX, 22
New York Zoological Park (Bronx Zoo), 21
Nichols, Erickson N., 294
Nicolls, Richard, 127
Nike Missile, QNS, 280
Nimham, Abraham, 42
Noble, William Clark, 32
Noguchi, Isamu, 219
Noguchi Museum, QNS, 219
Northern Dispensary, MAN, 156
Northfield Township District School/P.S. 20,
    SI, 301–2
Norton, Charles, 239

O
Oakland Lake, QNS, 258
Ocean Avenue Bridge, 125
Ocean Parkway Milestones, BKN 🐾, 111–12
O'Connell Court, QNS 🐾, 241
Octagon, MAN 🐦, 190
Odd Townhouse, The, MAN 🐦, 158
O'Donovan, William, 86
Ohio Company of Associates, 140
O'Keeffe, Georgia, 222
Old Broadway, MAN, 198
Old Grapevine, 158
Old Gravesend Cemetery, 119
Old Mill Road, SI 🐾, 324–25
"Old Put, The," BX 🏛, 32–33
Old Stone House, The, BKN 🐦, 88–89
Olmsted, Frederick Law, 24, 38, 65, 68, 70, 91,
    94, 111, 178, 180, 191, 320, 332

Olmsted, Frederick Law, Jr., 237
Olmsted House, SI, 319–20
Omega Oil, 176–77, 202
Omega Oil and the Missing El, MAN, 176–77
Onassis, Jacqueline Kennedy, 171
Onderdonk, Adrian, 234
Onderdonk, Henrick, 263
125th Street Streetcars, MAN 🚃, 197–98
145th Street Bridge, BX, 7
155th Street Viaduct, MAN, 205
O'Neill, Eugene, 156
1005 Jerome Avenue, BX, 10
Organization of American States, 148
Oriental Pavilion, BKN, 94
Original "21," The, MAN 🚃, 156
Ostrowski, S. K., 183
Otway, Howard, 160
Owl's Head Park, BKN, 102

P

Padukow, Sergei, 255
Paine, Thomas, 154
Palmer, Benjamin, 26, 45
Paramount Theater, SI, 295
Parfitt Brothers, 84
Park of Edgewater, BX 🪨, 49
Parkchester, sculptures of, BX, 35–36
Parrots of Brooklyn College, BKN, 110–11
Parsons, Samuel, 249, 251
Partridge, William, 69, 196
Patchin Place, MAN, 157
Paterno, Charles, 204
Paulson, Charles, 265
Paul VI, Pope, 245
Pavement, unusual, BKN, 73
Payntar family, 221
Peace Fountain, MAN 🐾, 196–97
Pearl, Charles, 251
Pelham Cemetery, BX 🪨, 46
Pell, Thomas, 44
Pell family, 44, 45
Pelton, Daniel, 292
Pendleton, William S., 290
Penn Station Remnants, MAN, 169–70
Pennsylvania Railroad Powerhouse, QNS, 222
Pennsylvania Railroad Symbol, QNS 🚃,
    265–66
Pepsi-Cola Neon Sign, QNS, 222–23
Perine family, 313
Perkins, George Walbridge, 34
Perkins, Joseph, 14
Perry, Robert, 83–84
Perth Amboy Ferry, SI, 335
Peter Housman House, SI, 307
Peter Minuit Plaza, MAN, 138
Petit, John, 106
Pfeiffer, Carl, 290
Philbin, Regis, 38–39
Philipse, Frederick, 26, 32

Philipse, Mary, 207
Piano Row, BX, 5
Piatti, Patrizio, 98
Piccirilli, Attilio, 196
Piccirilli Brothers Monument Sculptors, 5
Pickford, Mary, 175
Pier 41, BKN, 73
Pierrepont, Henry, 96
Pieter Claesen Wyckoff House, BKN 🐿, 115
Pilcher and Tachau, 26–27
Pineapple, Orange, and Cranberry, BKN 🚃, 57
Pitkin, John R., 129, 268
Planters Peanuts, QNS, 235–36
Platt Byard Dovell, 248
Poe, Edgar Allan, 20, 191, 193
Poe Park, BX 🐿, 20
Poillon, Jacques, 320
Pollock, St. Clair, 197
Polo Grounds, 205
Polshek Partnership, 245
Pomander Walk, MAN, 194
Ponselle, Rosa, 175
Poppenhusen, Conrad, 253
Poppenhusen Institute, QNS, 254
Popper, Herman, 122
Popper Building, BKN, 122
Porter, Josiah, 32
Port Richmond National Bank, SI, 303
Post, George, 79
Power, Jim, 159–60
Powers, Christie, 154
Pratt, Charles, 67, 80
Prentiss, Clifton and William, 96–97
Prentiss Brothers, The, BKN, 96–97
Presley, Elvis, 101
Price, Vincent, 264
Price family, 338
Prince, William, 248
Prince, William, Jr., 248
Prison Ship Martyrs Monument, BKN, 65–66
Pritchard, William, 91
Pritchard family, 290
Procter & Gamble, 284, 336
Prospect Cemetery, QNS 🚃, 270–71
Prospect Park South, BKN, 106
P.S. 1, QNS, 221
P.S. 4 and West Baptist Cemetery, SI, 330
Pullis, Thomas, 237–38
Pullis Farm Cemetery, QNS, 237–38
Purdy, Stephen, 333
Pynchon, Thomas, 155

Q

Quaker Cemetery, BKN, 92
Queensboro Bridge, 185
Queensboro Corporation, 227
Queens Boulevard Viaduct, QNS, 225–26
Queens Boulevard, space-age architecture,
    QNS, 241

Queens County Hotel, QNS, 232
Queens Farm Museum, QNS 🏛, 263
Queens Plaza Millstones, QNS, 220–21
Quimby, Susan, 207

R
Randall, Robert Richard, 291
Randel, John, Jr., 137
Rapp and Rapp, 295
Rattlesnake Brook in Seton Falls Park, BX 🏛, 40
Ravine, BKN, 93
Rea, Samuel, 212
Real Good Construction Company, 237
Red-Brick Pavement, QNS, 270
Red Hook/Van Brunt Stores, BKN, 75
Reformed Church and Liberty Pole, BKN 🔫, 118–19
Reformed Dutch Church, QNS, 241
Regis Philbin Avenue, BX, 38–39
Relics of the Queensboro, MAN 🏛, 185
Remaining Bungalows, QNS 🏛, 279
Remsen, Jeromus, 238
Remsen Cemetery, QNS, 238
Renaissance Ballroom, MAN, 201
Rennert, Catherine, 187
Renwick, Aspinwall & Owen, 309
Renwick, James, Jr., 34, 189, 190
Republican Club Building, QNS, 266
Reservoir Oval and Keeper's House, BX 🏛, 25
Revere Sugar Refinery, BKN 🏛, 75
Revolutionary Cemetery, BKN, 102–3
Rhind, J. Massey, 87
Rice, Isaac Leopold, 48
Richards, Daniel, 73
Richardson, W. B., 250
Richman, Jeffrey, 96
Richmond, Edward, 265
Richmond, Eric, 88
Richmond Hill (QNS) Victorian-era houses, 267
Richmond Hill Public Library, QNS, 266–67
Richmond Town Restoration, SI 🔫, 321–24
    Arthur Kill Road, 323–24
    Court Place, 322
    Historic Richmond Town, Center Street, 321–22
    Richmond Road (North Side), 322–23
    Richmond Road (South Side), 323
Richter, C. L., 182
Rickert-Finlay realty company, 259
Ridgewood Democratic Club, QNS, 236
Ridgewood Reservoir, BKN, 132–33
Riis, Jacob, 265, 267, 280
Riis Park, QNS, 280, 281
Risse, Louis, 8, 16
Ritz Theatre, SI, 302
Rivera, Geraldo, 309
Riverside Drive Horse Trough, MAN 🏛, 192–93
Riverside Swastikas, MAN 🏛, 194

RKO Bushwick, BKN, 84–85
RKO Keith's, QNS, 266
RKO Strand Theatre, QNS 🏛, 279
Roach, Charles and Peter, 220
Robeson, Paul, 208
Robinson, Jeremiah and George, 74
Roche, William, 201
Rockefeller, John D., 174, 204
Rocket Thrower, QNS, 243
Rodman, Thomas Jefferson, 104
Rodman Gun at John Paul Jones Park, BKN, 104
Roe, Austin, 263
Rogers, Randolph, 166
Roosevelt, Eleanor, 109
Roosevelt, Theodore, 165, 266, 267, 280
Root, Spencer, 221
Ross, William, 328
Rossville Boatyard, The, SI 🔫, 328
Roszak, Theodore, 246
Rothstein, Arnold, 238
Rouse & Goldstone, 150
Rowan Street IND Sign, QNS, 230
Ruckstall, Frederic Wellington, 97
Ruggles, Samuel, 165
Ruppert, Jacob, 9
Ruppert Place, BX, 9
Ruskin, John, 108
Russell, Lillian, 104
Russell Sage Foundation, 237
Russian Orthodox Cathedral of the Transfiguration, 82
Rust, John, 221
Rutgers, Henry, 150
Ruth, Babe, 9, 265
Rutledge, Edward, 334
Ryder, Charles, 119
Ryder, Lawrence, 119
Ryers, Joseph, 292
Ryn, Jan Jansen ver, 119

S
Sage, Margaret Olivia Slocum, 278
Sage, Russell, 278
Sage Memorial Church, QNS, 278
Sailors' Snug Harbor, SI 🔫, 291–92
St. Albans, QNS, 273
St. Andrew's Church and Churchyard, SI 🔫, 324
St. Ann's Episcopal Church, BX, 6
St. Barbara's, BKN, 84
Saint-Gaudens, Augustus, 87, 166
St. George Houses, SI, 288
St. George Theatre, SI, 289
St. James Episcopal Church, QNS, 240–41
St. John, John, 307
St. John's Episcopal Church, 105
St. Mark's Place Mosaics, MAN, 159–60
St. Monica's Steeple, QNS, 271

St. Nicholas Russian Orthodox Church, QNS, 255
St. Paul's Avenue, SI, 296
St. Peter's, BX, 36
St. Saviour's Church, QNS, 232
Samuel Tilden, MAN, 196
Sandblom, Charles, 230
Sands brothers, 54
Sandy Ground, SI, 329
Santa Anna, Antonio López de, 88
Sargent, Edward Alfred, 288
Saunders, Dave, 36
Savage, Eugene, 86
Scammel, Alexander, 152
Schein, Francoise, 148
Schermerhorn, Peter, Jr., 143
Schermerhorn Row, MAN, 143
Schickel, William, 164
Schiff, Jacob, 151, 152
Schiller, Johann von, MAN, 182
Schladitz, John, 241
Schleicher, Herman, 254
Schloh, Henry, 237
Scholz, Leopold, 43
Schuyler, Philip, 49
Scott, Winfield, 30
Scott-Edwards House, SI, 304
Scrabble, QNS, 228
Sculptures of Parkchester, The, BX, 35–36
Seaman, John and Valentine, 210
Seaman Arch, MAN, 210
Sears Roebuck and Co., 109
"Seat, The" (Saunders sculpture), 36
Second Empire Music School, The, BKN, 90
Seguine, Anna, 319
Seguine, Joseph H., 332, 333
Seguine Mansion, SI, 332
"Senate, The," MAN, 161
Seneca Village, 191
Seton, Elizabeth Bayley, 324
Seton Falls Park, 40
7th Regiment Armory, MAN, 185–86
Seward, William Henry, 166
Sharps, David, 74
Shearith Israel Cemetery, 157
Shell Mansion/Fontbonne Hall, BKN, 103–4
Sheridan, John, 43
Sheriff Street, MAN, 152
Sherman, William Tecumseh, 86
Shively, Henry, 186
Shively Sanitary Tenements, 186
Shrady, Henry, 79
Shreve, Richmond, 77
Shuttleworth, Edwin, 17
Shuttleworth House, BX, 17
Sibirsky, Charles, 90
Sidewalk Clock, QNS, 272
Sidewalk Subway Map, The, MAN, 148
Sidney, J. C., 42

Sigel, Franz, 196
Silver Beach, BX, 48–49
Silver Lake Park, SI, 293–94
Silverman & Cika, 307
Simcoe, Colonel, 42
Sisters of Charity, 181
Sixth Avenue Medallions, MAN, 148–49
Skene, Alexander, 87
Skinner, Courtlandt, 292
Slattery, Vincent, 27
Sleight family, 329
Sloan and Robertson, 172
Slocum, Henry, 87
Smallpox Hospital, MAN, 189
Smith, Dorothy Valentine, 306
Smith, Henry Atterbury, 186
Smith, Suzanne Tompkins and Richard, 296
Smith, William Stephen and Abigail, 185
Sniffen, John, 172
Sniffen Court, MAN, 172
Snyder, C. B. J., 241
Socha, Ferdinand, 245
Society of St. Paul Seminary, 307–8
Socrates Sculpture Garden, QNS, 219
Sohmer Piano Factory, QNS, 218
Soldiers and Sailors Monument (Grand Army Plaza), 86
Soldiers and Sailors Monument, MAN, 193–94
Southern Boulevard Cinemas, BX, 14
Southside Burial Ground, QNS, 274
Spanish Bricks, BKN, 100
Spectacular Views, SI, 294
Spencer, William, 48
Split Rock, BX, 44
S. R. Smith Infirmary, SI, 293
Stahr, F. C., 286
Staple and Collister, MAN, 147
Staples, William, 295
Star of Hope, 167
Stars of Madison Square Park, The, MAN, 167
Staten Island Cemetery, SI, 292
Staten Island Farm Colony, SI, 309–10
Staten Island Lighthouse, SI, 326
Staten Island Lighthouse Museum Site, SI, 287–88
Staten Island Museum, SI, 288
Staten Island Rapid Transit Remnant, SI, 299
Staten Island Rapid Transit Remnants, SI, 304
Staten Island Stapletons, 295
Staten Island Zoo, SI, 306
Station Square, QNS, 239
statues, 212–13
Steinmeyer, Henry, 324
Steinway, Henry, 218
Steinway, William, 218, 227
Steinway Mansion and Steinway Village, QNS, 218

Stephens, Stephen D., 322
Stephens-Black House, 322
Stepped Streets, BX, 28
Stewart, Alexander T., 252
Stier, Paul, 236
Stillwell, Thomas, 313
Stillwell Avenue station, BKN, 122
Stokes, Anson Phelps, I, 288
Stokes, Isaac Newton Phelps, 288
Stone Bridge, SI, 324
Stoneham, Horace, 205
Stonehurst house, BX, 34
Storer family, 330
Stoughton, Charles, 25
Stoughton and Stoughton, 193
Stranahan, James, 87
Straus, Isidor, 209
Straus family, 60
Strecker Laboratory, MAN, 189
streetcars, 197–98
street signs/advertising, 66–67, 282–83
Striver's Row, MAN, 201–2
Strong, Ken, 295
Studebaker Showroom, BKN, 69
Stuyvesant, Peter, 107, 114, 115, 212–13, 217,
    229, 249, 284
Stuyvesant family, 165
Subway Doors to Nowhere, MAN, 174–75
"Subway Map Floating on a New York Side-
    walk" (Schein artwork), 148
Sunny's Bar, BKN, 74
Sunnyslope Mansion, BX 🐘, 15
Sunset Park, BKN, 100
Sunset Park Stables, BKN, 101
Sutton Square and Riverview Terrace, MAN, 184
Suydam, Ella, 114
Swanson, Gloria, 160
Swedish Cottage, MAN, 179
Sylvan Cemetery, SI 🐘, 338
Sylvan Terrace, MAN, 208

T
Taggia, Martini di Arma di, 174
Talmadge, Norma, 256
Tandy, Vertner, 202
Taylor, Eva, 273
Taylor, James, 223
Taylor & Levi, 164
Tenement Museum, MAN, 151
Tennis House, BKN, 91
Terminal Hotel, BKN, 122
Terra Cotta Factory Showroom, QNS 🐘, 223
That Thing at Ocean Parkway and Avenue U,
    BKN 🐾, 120
Thayer, Barbara, 177
Theatre 80, 160
Theodore Roosevelt's Birthplace, MAN, 165
Third and Third: Litchfield's Improvement,
    BKN, 72

Thomas Adams House, BKN, 88
Thomas Paine and Greenwich Village, MAN,
    154
Thompson, Samuel C., 16
Thomson Meter, 54–55
Thorvaldsen, Albert, MAN 🐾, 183
Throckmorton, John, 48
Thunderbolt and Playland, BKN 🐘, 123–24
Tiffany, Charles Lewis, 96
Tiffany, Louis Comfort, 29, 96, 107, 186, 242,
    278
Tiffany Studios, QNS, 19, 242
Tilden, Samuel, 196
Time Capsule, QNS, 245
Times Tower, 175
Timpano, May, 123
Tin Pan Alley, MAN, 168–69
Titanic House, QNS, 223
Titanic Memorial, MAN, 143
Todd, Thomas, 220
Todd Shipyards, BKN, 76
To Let: Flats, painted sign, BKN, 58
Tollner, Eugene, 62
Tompkins, Daniel, 213, 286
Tompkins, Minthorne, 295
Tooker and Marsh, 69
Totten, Joseph G., 299
Totten family, 334
Tottenville Library, SI, 335
Tower Square, QNS 🐾, 227–28
Tramway, MAN, 184–85
Travis, Jacob, 337
Treasure House, 323
Treffurth's, MAN 🐘, 157
Triangle Hotel, QNS 🐘, 265
Trinity Cemetery (Broadway and Wall St.),
    139–40
Trinity Cemetery (Broadway and West 155th St.),
    MAN, 206
Trinity Church, 140, 147
Trolley Remnants, BKN, 115–16
Trotting Course Lane, QNS 🐘, 238
Tulfan Terrace, BX, 30
Tully and Fanning, 30
Turini, Giovanni, 183
Tuthill and Higgins, 266
Twain, Mark, 157, 162, 242, 259
Tweed, William Marcy ("Boss"), 96
21 Club, 156
Twomey, Bill, 25
Tysen-Neville House, SI, 290–91

U
Udall, Richard, 261
Udall's Cove, QNS 🐾, 260–61
Ulmer, William, 84
Unisphere, QNS, 244
Upjohn, Richard, 58, 96, 260
U.S. Grant, BKN, 69

V

Valentine, Isaac, 25
Valentine-Varian House, BX, 25
Valentino, Louis, Jr., 73
Van Cleef, John, 119
Van Cortlandt, Augustus, 33
Van Cortlandt, Frederick, 32
Van Cortlandt, Jacobus, 31–32
Van Cortlandt Mansion, BX 🐾, 32
Van Cortlandt Park, BX, 31–32
Vanderbilt, Cornelius, 171, 242, 297
Vanderbilt, John King, 305–6
Vanderbilt, Mrs. William K., 186
Vanderbilt, William Kissam, 262
Vanderbilt Avenue Cottages, SI, 297
Vanderbilt family, 160, 293, 295, 297, 305, 315
Vander Ende, Paulus, 234
Vander Ende–Onderdonk House, QNS, 234
Van Duzer's Houses, SI, 296
Van Lent, Abraham Rycken, 229
Van Nuyse, Johannes, 113
Van Nuyse–Magaw House, BKN, 113
Van Santvoord, Cornelius, 292
Van Sicklen, John and Abraham, 119
Van Sicklen Cemetery, 119
Van Twiller, Wouter, 153
Van Wicklen, Jannet, 274
Van Wicklen family, 274
Van Wyck, Cornelius, 259
Van Wyck House, QNS, 259
Van Zandt, Wynant, 259, 260
Varian family, 23
Vault Hill, BX 📷, 33
Vaux, Calvert, 15, 38, 65, 68, 70, 91, 94, 111, 178, 180, 191
Vecht, Klaes Arents, 88
Vecht-Cortelyou House, 88–89
Velodrome, QNS, 252
Verdi, Giuseppe, 213
Vickers, Squire J., 225–26
Victory Diner, SI, 313
Village Cigars, 153–54
Village Volcano, The, MAN 🐾, 154–55
Vinegar Hill, BKN 🐾, 54
Viñoly, Rafael, 70, 245, 291
Vitagraph Smokestack, BKN, 111
Vitagraph Studios, 111
Voelker-Orth, Betty, 250
Voelker-Orth Museum, QNS 🐾, 250–51
Vonroll of Switzerland, 185
Voorhies, Luther, 106
Voorlezer House, 323

W

Wadsworth, James S., 299–300
Wald, Lillian, 151, 152
Waldheim, QNS, 250
Walker, Kate, 287
Wallace, Franklin R., 250

Wallenberg, Raoul, 30
Wallenberg Forest, BX 🐾, 30
Waller, Fats, 273
Walsh, Harold V., 47
Ward, John Quincy Adams, 140, 166, 212
Warhol, Andy, 245
Warner Brothers, 111
Warren, Gouverneur, 87
Warren and Wetmore, 193
Washington, George, 26, 27, 32, 33, 41, 44, 79, 89, 119, 140, 144, 150, 208, 243, 263
Washington Mews, MAN 🐾, 156
Watkins, Helen, 327
Watts, John, 212
Wave Hill, BX 🐾, 34
Wechsler, Joseph, 60
Weed, Stephen, 299
Weinman, Adolph A., 169, 182, 212
Weir, James, 100
Weir Florist, BKN, 99–100
Well House, BKN, 93
Wesson family, 255
West, Mae, 80, 265
West Baptist Cemetery, 330
Westerleigh's Homes, SI, 307
West Farms Soldiers' Cemetery, BX, 21–22
West Hamilton Beach, QNS 🚐, 274–75
Westinghouse, 245
West Side Railroad Remnants, MAN 🐾, 192
West Side Tennis Club, 238–39
Wheeler, John, 20
Wheelwright, QNS, 232–33
White, Alfred Tredway, 72
White, S. B., 13
White, Stanford, 18, 91, 92, 165, 186
White Elephant, The, BX 🚐, 37
White Star Lines, 163
Whitford, James, 303
Whitman, Walt, 59, 65, 97
Who Is Buried at Grant's Tomb?, MAN 🐾, 197
Wickes, Thomas, 259
Wilkerson, Cathlyn, 158
Willett, Thomas, 256
William IV, King (Britain), 292
William Barthman Jewelers, 141
Williams, Christopher S., 307
Williams, Clarence, 273
Williams, Percy, 85
Williams, Simon, 40
Williamsburg Art and Historical Center, BKN, 78–79
Williamsburg Associated Architects, 77
Williamsburg Houses, BKN, 77
Williamsburg Savings Bank Dome, BKN, 79
Williamsburg Trust Company, BKN, 79
William T. Davis Wildlife Refuge, SI, 337
Willowbrook Park, 310
Willowbrook Tablet, SI 🐾, 308
Wills, Harry, 202

Wilson, H.W., Lighthouse, BX 🐘, 10–11
Wilson, Robert, 122
Withers, Frederick Clarke, 37, 189, 190
Witte Marine Equipment Company, 328
Wolfe, Joel, 332
Wolfe's Pond Park, SI, 332
Wood, Abraham J., 333
Wood, Arthur, 127
Wood Bridge, BKN, 125
Wood Duck Pond, SI 🐚, 319
Wood Shelters, MAN, 179
Woodland Cottage, SI, 299
Woodlawn Cemetery, BX, 42
Woolley, John, 307
Workingmen's Cottages, BKN 🏚, 72
Worth, William Jenkins, 166–67
Wondrous Vista, MAN, 152
Wright, Frank Lloyd, 327
Wyatt, Greg, 196
Wyckoff, Henry and Abraham, 113
Wyckoff, Pieter Claesen, 115
Wyckoff Building, QNS, 268–69

Y

Yankee Ferry, MAN, 147–48
York, Alvin, 184, 187
York, Duke of, 115, 147, 313
You Can See All the Stars on St. Mark's Place,
    MAN 🐘, 160
Yu, Jessica, 264

Z

Zion Episcopal Church, QNS, 260
Zurmuhlen, Frederick H., Jr., 304

Map Index

Each borough is broken out into smaller regions that are within walking distance of each other. The numbers on the left hand side of each region entry are keyed to overall borough maps that open the sections.

BRONX, 3

1. Mott Haven, The Hub, Melrose, and Concourse Village, 4
2. High Bridge and Morris Heights, 10
3. Longwood and Hunts Point, 13
4. Mount Hope, Mount Eden, and Crotona Park, 16
5. University Heights, Tremont, and Fordham, 18
6. Belmont, Bronx Park South, and West Farms, 21
7. Bedford Park and Norwood, 23
8. Kingsbridge and Kingsbridge Heights, 26
9. Spuyten Duyvil, 28
10. Riverdale and Van Cortlandt Park, 31
11. Parkchester, Unionport, and Westchester Square, 35
12. Morris Park, Pelham Parkway, and Bronxdale, 38
13. Eastchester and Co-op City, 40
14. Wakefield, Woodlawn, and Woodlawn Heights, 41
15. Pelham Bay Park, 43
16. City Island, 45
17. Schuylerville and Throgs Neck, 48

BROOKLYN, 53

1. DUMBO and Vinegar Hill, 54
2. Brooklyn Heights, 57
3. Downtown, 60
4. Fort Greene and Clinton Hill, 64
5. Prospect Heights and Crown Heights, 68
6. Gowanus and Cobble Hill, 71
7. Red Hook, 73
8. Williamsburg, 77
9. Greenpoint, 80
10. Bushwick, 83
11. Park Slope, 86
12. Prospect Park, 91
13. Green-Wood Cemetery, 96
14. Sunset Park, 99
15. Bay Ridge, 102
16. Flatbush and Kensington, 106
17. Midwood and South Greenfield, 110
18. East Flatbush and Flatlands, 113
19. Canarsie, 115
20. Floyd Bennett Field and Marine Park, 117
21. Bath Beach and Gravesend, 118

22. Coney Island, 121
23. Sheepshead Bay, 125
24. Bedford-Stuyvesant, 127
25. Brownsville and East New York, 129
26. Highland Park and Cypress Hills, 131

MANHATTAN, 137
1. The Battery, Wall Street, and City Hall, 138
2. South Street Seaport, 142
3. Tribeca and Soho, 146
4. Lower East Side, 150
5. Greenwich Village, 153
6. East Village, 159
7. Chelsea, 162
8. Madison Square Park and Gramercy Park, 165
9. Penn Station Area, 168
10. Grand Central, Murray Hill, and Turtle Bay, 171
11. Times Square, 174
12. Hell's Kitchen, 176
13. Central Park, 178
14. Upper East Side, Yorkville, and Carnegie Hill, 184
15. Roosevelt Island, 188
16. Upper West Side, 191
17. Morningside Heights and Manhattanville, 195
18. Harlem and Hamilton Heights, 199
19. Washington Heights, 204
20. Inwood and Marble Hill, 209

QUEENS, 216
1. Astoria, 217
2. Long Island City and Hunter's Point, 220
3. Blissville, West Maspeth, and Sunnyside, 224
4. Woodside and Jackson Heights, 227
5. Maspeth and Middle Village, 231
6. Ridgewood, 234
7. Rego Park, Forest Hills, and Kew Gardens, 237
8. Elmhurst and Corona, 240
9. Flushing Meadows Park and 1939 and 1964 World's Fair Remnants, 243
10. Flushing, 247
11. College Point and Whitestone, 253
12. Auburndale and Bayside, 256
13. Douglaston and Little Neck, 259
14. Glen Oaks, Bellerose, and Floral Park, 262
15. Richmond Hill, 265
16. Woodhaven, 268
17. Jamaica, 270
18. Ozone Park and Howard Beach, 274
19. Broad Channel, 276
20. Far Rockaway, 278
21. Fort Tilden and Riis Park, 280

STATEN ISLAND, 285
1. St. George, 286
2. New Brighton, 290
3. Grymes Hill and Silver Lake, 293
4. Stapleton and Clifton, 295
5. Rosebank, 298
6. Port Richmond, 301
7. Sunnyside, 305
8. Westerleigh, 307
9. Willowbrook, 309
10. New Springville and Heartland Village, 311
11. Dongan Hills, 313
12. New Dorp, 315
13. La Tourette Park, 317
14. Annadale and Eltingville, 319
15. Richmondtown and Great Kills, 321
16. Lighthouse Hill, 326
17. Rossville and Woodrow, 328
18. Kreischerville, 330
19. Prince's Bay, 332
20. Tottenville, 334
21. Northwest Staten Island, 336
22. Travis, 337

MAP INDEX

KEVIN WALSH is an urban explorer extraordinaire and the creator of www. forgotten-ny.com, a website dedicated to uncovering the lost history of the city. He hosts sold-out Forgotten New York Tours throughout the boroughs and is a much sought-after expert on little-known facts about NYC. He grew up in Bay Ridge, Brooklyn, watching the Verrazano-Narrows Bridge being built, and presently lives in Flushing, Queens. In the photo above, he is relating the story of the B&B Carousell in Coney Island on a recent Forgotten New York tour.